T0314019

THE PEOPLE'S POST OFFICE

The History and Politics of the Japanese Postal System, 1871–2010

Harvard East Asian Monographs 338

THE PEOPLE'S POST OFFICE

The History and Politics of the Japanese Postal System, 1871–2010

Patricia L. Maclachlan

Published by the Harvard University Asia Center
and distributed by Harvard University Press
Cambridge (Massachusetts) and London, 2011

Printed in the United States of America

The Harvard University Asia Center publishes a monograph series and, in coordination with the Fairbank Center for Chinese Studies, the Korea Institute, the Reischauer Institute of Japanese Studies, and other faculties and institutes, administers research projects designed to further scholarly understanding of China, Japan, Vietnam, Korea, and other Asian countries. The Center also sponsors projects addressing multidisciplinary and regional issues in Asia.

Library of Congress Cataloging-in-Publication Data

Maclachlan, Patricia L.
    The people's post office : the history and politics of the Japanese postal system, 1871–2010 / Patricia L. Maclachlan.
        p. cm. -- (Harvard East Asian monographs ; 338)
    ISBN 978-0-674-06245-0 (hardcover : alk. paper) 1. Postal service--Japan--History--19th century. 2. Postal service--Japan--History--20th century. 3. Postal service--Japan--History--21st century. 4. Japan--Politics and government. I. Title.
    HE7275.M233 2011
    383'.49520904--dc23

2011044758

Index by the author

∞ Printed on acid-free paper

Last figure below indicates year of this printing

21 20 19 18 17 16 15 14 13 12 11

For Zoltan and Catherine Barany

Acknowledgments

I am very grateful to a number of individuals and institutions that helped me bring this project to completion. First, I thank the Abe Fellows Program of the Japan Foundation's Center for Global Partnership for awarding me a generous grant to conduct much of my fieldwork. My thanks also to Rikkyō University, whose financial support helped me launch this project in 2002, and to the Nissan Institute of Japanese Studies, which offered me an academic home in 2003. I would also like to underscore my continuing gratitude to Houston-based Mitsubishi Caterpillar Forklift America, Inc., whose endowment to the University of Texas at Austin financed many short-term research trips to Japan over the years.

My thanks also to the following institutions for inviting me to give lectures on portions of my research: the Tokyo offices of the Abe Fellowship Program; the Center for Japanese Studies at the University of California, Berkeley; the Center for Japanese Studies at the University of California, Los Angeles; the College Women's Association of Japan; the Department of Political Science at the University of Florida; the Reischauer Institute of Japanese Studies at Harvard University; the Faculty of Economics at Keiō University; the University of Pennsylvania Law School; the Department of East Asian Studies at Princeton University; the John Goodwin Tower Center for Political Studies at Southern Methodist University; the Stanford Project on Japanese Entrepreneurship and the Public Policy Program at Stanford University; the Department of Political Science at Villanova University; the Japan Studies Program of the Jackson School of International Studies at the University of Washington; and the Woodrow Wilson International Center for Scholars. Preparing these lectures helped me to hone my ideas, and audience feedback prevented me from straying down the wrong path.

Professor Igarashi Akio of Rikkyō University gave me invaluable advice during my residency at the university, and introduced me to several individuals who proved essential to my research. Chief among those contacts was Hirabayashi Takeo of the *Mainichi shinbun*, a good friend who put me in touch with journalists and politicians who had close connections to the postal system. Professor Yoshino Naoyuki of Keiō University was an important mentor, meeting with me on numerous occasions to share his scholarly insights into the postal services and his experiences as a participant in Prime Minister Koizumi's reform process. Inoue Keikō, of the Communications Museum, introduced me to the museum's extensive archives in 2002 and generously spent the better part of a day in summer 2010 helping me to gather photographs and other illustrations for the book.

Others offered me advice and kernels of wisdom that helped me fine-tune my argument and build my confidence in the overall project. Carol Gluck, of Columbia University, gave me a great pep talk in 2009 that inspired me to resolve some irksome challenges that had arisen during a round of revisions. The University of Vermont's Matthew Carlson, who has also explored the political significance of the postal sector, shared with me his data on the postmasters. Ellis Krauss (University of California, San Diego) and Ethan Scheiner (University of California, Davis) helped me grasp some of the finer points of the Japanese electoral system. And special thanks to William Hammell, the director of the publications program of the Harvard University Asia Center. Will's encouragement and fine editorial skills made the publishing process far less stressful than I know it can sometimes be.

I am also grateful to several friends and colleagues who commented on various drafts or portions of this book. Ulrike Schaede, of the University of California, San Diego, was the first to read the manuscript in its entirety and gave me very useful advice on how to tackle the comparative dimensions of this project. Four University of Texas colleagues— Kirsten Cather, Mark Metzler, David Sena, and Nancy Stalker—made excellent suggestions for the revision of Chapter 1. Sheldon Garon of

Princeton University served as a patient sounding board for many of my ideas, introduced me to the Communications Museum, and shared many of his own findings from his research on postal savings systems. I am especially grateful to Steven Erickson (Dartmouth College) and Leonard Schoppa (University of Virginia), who "anonymously" reviewed my manuscript for the Harvard University Asia Center and offered superb advice for revisions. I was very pleased when these two scholars later revealed their identities to me because it gave me the chance to thank them by name.

I would also like to thank the many individuals whom I have interviewed over the years on various aspects of this project—the politicians, bureaucrats, journalists, postal workers and union officials, and commissioned postmasters. These men and women—many of whom asked to remain anonymous—told fascinating stories that made researching this book so enjoyable. Needless to say, while my interviewees, friends, and reviewers contributed much to this book's development, I alone am responsible for its shortcomings.

To conclude, heartfelt thanks to my husband, Zoltan Barany, and our daughter, Catherine, for tolerating my many research trips and long stints in front of the computer as I (yes, slowly) stitched this book together. This project was an opportunity for us to spend several months in Japan as a family, and aside from our first hot-and-harried day in Tokyo in 2002, the experience was a terrific one for us all: Zoltan developed a deep fondness for Tokyo; Catherine lived it up at the delightful Kodomo no ie nursery school in Nishi-Ikebukuro; and we all enjoyed the sights, sounds, and tastes of neighborhood Tokyo. I would like to dedicate this book to Zoltan and Catherine, and to the memory of our time in Japan.

Austin, Texas
October 2011

Contents

Tables and Figures

Tables

Figures

Preface

On a summer afternoon in 2002, I arrived in Tokyo with my family to begin the first leg of my research project on Japanese postal politics. Our visit did not begin well. Tired, hot, and hungry after a long day of travel, we felt our moods take a nosedive as we entered our empty apartment and realized that we had nothing to eat—or to eat with. Since I was the only Japanese speaker in our little group, I left the apartment in search of provisions.

After fifteen minutes or so of wandering through a maze of deserted side streets, I found a small grocer and stocked up on food and supplies. Jetlag then got the better of me. For what seemed like an hour, I meandered aimlessly through that neighborhood, my grocery bags growing heavier and heavier with each passing block. One of my milk cartons burst through its bag and exploded onto the pavement, drenching my shoes. I would have gladly asked someone for directions, but there was no one in sight.

Just as my irritability threatened to get the better of me, I heard the sound of a moped in the distance. It was a mail carrier on his rounds. He put-putted up to one house and then another, depositing his small bundles into each mailbox and then dropping the squeaky lids with a clang. When he was within a few feet of me, I stepped into his path and forced him to stop. "Please tell me how to get to the university guest house," I pleaded. "I'm lost."

Straddling his red moped, the mail carrier took a moment to look me over. He then reached for two of my bags, put them into the now empty box behind his seat, and motioned for me to follow him.

I marched dutifully behind my mail carrier as he wove his way toward my building. When we arrived, he silently handed me my bags, acknowledged my thanks with a nod of his head, and puttered off. I was impressed. "The Japanese post office is a fine institution," I thought to myself as I trudged up the stairs to our apartment. "Maybe Koizumi should just leave it alone."

In early 2002, despite Prime Minister Koizumi Juni'chirō's resolve to carry out "structural reform with no sanctuaries" (*seiiki naki kōzō kaikaku*), it appeared that the government would have no choice but to leave the post office alone. Local postmasters and their employees were lobbying hard against Koizumi's proposed changes, while friends of the post office in the ruling Liberal Democratic Party (LDP) heaped abuse on their leader for tampering with a near sacred institution. The media recounted stories of elderly Japanese in the countryside who depended on the local post office for their financial and shopping needs, and scores of books appeared extolling the postal system's contributions to Japan's economic, social, and cultural development. Meanwhile, foreigners like myself marveled at the high quality of service at the local post office, quick to compare it to the long queues and surly employees in facilities back home. Japanese citizens like—even love—their local post office, including many of those who support its transformation for financial or political reasons.

I had good reason to believe, in short, that mine would be a project on the politicization of the postal services and the failure of reform. Subsequent events threw me for a loop. After the 2002 passage of a modest set of bills to open the mail sector to limited participation by private firms and lay the institutional groundwork of Japan Post, a public corporation that began operations in 2003, Koizumi launched an all-out campaign to privatize the services (mail, savings, and insurance). Much to everyone's surprise, Koizumi not only fulfilled many of his postal privatization objectives but also appeared to transform the very foundations of policymaking and electoral politics in Japan. So what began as a study of the politicization and resilience of the state-run postal services soon expanded to include questions of institutional and political transformation. How did the postwar Japanese postal system become so heavily politicized and resistant to reform, only to succumb to comprehensive change under one man's watch?

My objective in this book is to make sense of these seemingly contradictory trends of institutional "stickiness" and sudden change within the postal system by analyzing the interplay among the institutions, interests, and leaders involved in the system's evolution from the early Meiji period until 2010, three years after postal privatization officially began. To that end, I explore how the institutional relationship between the postal system and the Japanese state positioned the former to play a leading role in the country's political and economic development; how conservative politicians, the commissioned postmasters (*tokutei yūbin-kyokuchō*), and other interests built on the system's historical institutional legacy to politicize the services after World War II; and how entrepreneurial bureaucrats and politicians took advantage of political and institutional changes at critical junctures in Japan's modern history to introduce unanticipated changes to the postal services. Along the way, I identify the postal system's remarkable range of economic, social, and cultural functions—functions that transformed the local post office into a near-sacred embodiment of tradition as Japan grappled with the challenges of globalization and its underlying free-market principles. In the concluding chapter, I look into the future of the postal system, assess the resilience of Koizumi's reforms, and explore the significance of lingering opposition to the privatization of one of Japan's most enduring social and political sanctuaries.

A Note on Theory, Methods, and Sources

In this book, I trace the history of Japanese postal politics as a case study of the timing of institutional change within the postal sector in relation to developments in broader institutional and political contexts. More specifically, while my analysis emphasizes institutional factors, both within and outside of the postal services, and their capacity to shape the broad parameters of change, I also recognize the ability of entrepreneurial leaders to put the postal services on surprising new paths— and of vested interests to prevent change from occurring at all. I pursue these and related points in greater detail in the Introduction.

Although this is primarily a book about Japan, no study of the Japanese postal system would be complete without references to the British system on which it was modeled. Thus, Chapter 1, which traces the evolution of the Japanese services from premodern times until World War II, highlights some of the similarities and differences between the two systems. The primary purpose of this comparison is to pinpoint the historical institutional foundations of the Japanese system's postwar politicization—a phenomenon that was not duplicated in the postwar British case. But the comparison stops there. Since the modern Japanese and British postal systems embarked on vastly different political trajectories after their initial establishment, the remaining chapters focus on the institutional, interest group, and leadership variables that influenced the Japanese case.

Empirically—and in keeping with this book's historical as well as political science focus—I have drawn from an eclectic array of primary and secondary sources. I conducted much of my historical research on Japan at Rikkyō University and the National Diet Library in Tokyo, and at the Nissan Institute of Japanese Studies at the University of Oxford. I also logged many hours at the government-run archives of the Communications Museum (Teishin sōgō hakubutsukan) in the Ōtemachi district of Tokyo, where I had unlimited access to government and other documents relating to the Japanese postal services. References in Chapter 1 to the nineteenth-century British case are the result of research that I conducted at the library systems of University of Oxford and the University of Edinburgh, and at the British Postal Museum and Archive in London.

Newspaper articles were very useful to me as I pieced together a chronology of postal events, as were the memoirs of several key figures in Japanese postal history. I also benefited from the many books on the postal system published during the 1990s and 2000s. Written primarily for a general audience, these volumes offer a revealing glimpse into the values and ideas that emerged from the services and that helped transform debates about postal reform into a veritable "culture war."

Personal interviews were an important component of my research, although the results of these interviews were mixed. Given how politically explosive the notion of postal reform had become by the early 2000s, it was perhaps not surprising that bureaucrats and politicians were guarded in their assessments of the functions and politics of the postal system, although a few provided me with frank commentary. I benefited particularly from my conversations with scholars who had researched and/or contributed to the administration or privatization of the postal services, and with journalists who had covered the "postal beat." These men and women had fascinating stories to tell about the postmasters' representative organizations, the policymaking process, Koizumi's privatization plans, and the values and ideals that had come to be embodied in modern Japan's state-run postal services.

I also relied heavily on conversations with active and retired commissioned postmasters. My first contact with the postmasters occurred quite by accident while sitting in the tiny, windowless reading room of the Communications Museum during that first summer in Tokyo. From the start, it was hard for me not to notice that virtually all of the Japanese assembled around me were elderly men. Two or three of them showed up every day, others once a week or every two weeks. All of them seemed to know one another. In time, I learned to distinguish the philatelists from the postal history buffs, and the Meiji from the postwar history specialists. I soon thought of them all as *yūsei otaku*— obsessive fans of the postal system.

After one the regulars broke the ice and asked me why I was spending so much time at the archive, I learned that most of my neighbors were retired postmasters. A few of them seemed a little suspicious of me when I explained what I was doing, but most went out of their way to help me. One of the amateur historians in the group, whose writings were filed away on the archival shelves, directed me to some very useful sources. Another, an octogenarian, offered me an impassioned account of the history of the commissioned post office system, describing the government's alleged failure to properly compensate the prewar and wartime postmasters for their sacrifices on behalf of the "emperor's post office." Still another, a devotee of Maejima Hisoka (1835–1919; the Meiji founder of the modern Japanese postal system) and the leader of a regional chapter of Taiju zenkoku kaigi, the association of retired postmasters, invited me to his home in Kamakura and gave me a tour of his post office, now run by a former (female) employee. My visit, one of the highlights of my fieldwork, is briefly recounted at the beginning of Chapter 3.

To more fully understand the post office's functions in less populated areas, I made two visits to the outskirts of Kitakyūshū City on the southernmost island of Kyushu. In August 2002, I toured several post offices and met with a group of postmasters who were active in the regional branch of Zentoku (Zenkoku tokutei yūbinkyokuchō kai; the National Association of Commissioned Postmasters). Annoyed by the postal privatization movement, my hosts seemed confident that Koizumi was a passing phenomenon and that the political situation would "soon return to normal." When I returned four years later, the postmasters were reeling from the changes wrought by Koizumi's victories in 2005 and bracing themselves for the possible demise of the commissioned post office system. On both occasions, my hosts taught me about their profession and their politics, gave me access to some of their organization's internal literature, and introduced me to their employees.

My personal interactions with the commissioned postmasters also led to some invaluable insights into the postal system's cultural importance. While the postwar media uncovered instances of corruption among the postmasters and Koizumi focused his attention on the system's financial and political ramifications, many postmasters around the country continued to uphold the values of Maejima's innovations: financial stability, government paternalism, self-sacrifice on behalf of the common good, respect for local community, and many other values that we now tend to associate with a bygone era in Japan. Granted, we have good reason to suspect that many of these values had been reinvented or mythologized as the postmasters and other interest groups connected to the state-run services struggled to survive changing political and economic times. Nevertheless, these values resonated with ordinary Japanese over the generations as they struggled to adapt to the transformative pressures of political modernization, rapid economic growth, urbanization, unemployment, demographic change, and economic globalization.

Put simply, the local post office has become all but synonymous with a more "traditional" Japan. Thus, this book seeks not only to explain the political functions and institutional trajectory of the postal services, but also to highlight the post office's role in helping ordinary Japanese navigate the winding roads of modernity.

THE PEOPLE'S POST OFFICE

The History and Politics of the
Japanese Postal System, 1871–2010

INTRODUCTION

The Japanese Post Office
in Theoretical and Comparative Perspective

The post office is properly a mercantile project. The government advances the expense of establishing the different offices, and of buying or hiring the necessary horses or carriages, and is repaid with a large profit by the duties upon what is carried. It is perhaps the only mercantile project which has been successfully managed by, I believe, every sort of government. The capital to be advanced is not very considerable. There is no mystery in the business. The returns are not only certain, but immediate.

—Adam Smith, *The Wealth of Nations*

The post office may very well be the most taken-for-granted of public institutions. With remarkable predictability, mail carriers the world over deliver letters at uniform rates to the remotest of communities and in all kinds of weather, acquiring a reputation for reliability and perseverance.[1] Before the introduction of the telephone, the telegraph, and the steam engine, the "post" was often the sole means of communication

---

EPIGRAPH: Adam Smith, *An Inquiry into the Nature and Causes of the Wealth of Nations*, Book V, Chapter II, Part I (1776).

1. This reputation is most famously embodied in the inscription above the entrance to the James A. Farley Post Office in New York City: "Neither snow nor rain nor heat nor gloom of night stays these couriers from the swift completion of their appointed rounds." Numerous other countries, including Japan, have similarly praised their postal employees.

and transportation. During the mid- to late nineteenth century, many postal systems launched financial services that hastened the expansion of commerce and trade and introduced ordinary citizens to the world of modern finance. All the while, the post office functioned as a focal point of community life, helping local populations adapt to the standardized rhythms of modernity. Put simply, the post office is a fundamental component of modern society, but it tends to receive attention only when it falls short of its responsibilities or is targeted for reform.

When we examine those instances in which postal systems are stumbling or in flux, we find that Adam Smith was only partly right. Although it is true that every sort of government has had a hand in the management of postal systems and that the business of establishing mail services should be fairly simple, Smith did not anticipate the expansion and administrative sophistication of postal services in modern societies and the economic pressures these developments consequently imposed both on nation-states and ordinary people. Nor did he foresee the diversification of some postal systems' political, security, and social functions and the vested interests that developed around them—interests that often had negative repercussions for the efficiency and effectiveness of political and economic institutions. The postal system is *not* a straightforward mercantile enterprise, and by examining how and why this is the case, we open a window onto the complexities and pathologies of modern political economies.

The Japanese Postal System

In perhaps no other country has the postal system had more influence on the economy, politics, and society than in Japan. Based on the British model, the post-1868 Japanese post office served as a vehicle for political and economic modernization and the dissemination of nationalist values among local residents. The postal savings and insurance systems produced massive amounts of capital for industrial and military development and, after World War II, Japan's meteoric economic rise. Locally, the post office occupied a pivotal position in towns and villages, dispensing letters, essential financial services, and, more recently, welfare benefits for Japan's most vulnerable citizens. In so doing, the post office came to epitomize convenience, financial security, state paternalism, and a host of other values that helped define modern Japan for its people.

As generations of Japanese took advantage of the postal system's diverse services, few dwelled on one of its most distinctive features: its unprecedented degree of politicization.[2] From the establishment of individual post offices to the state's investment of capital drawn from the postal savings and insurance systems, postal functions became enmeshed in a web of vested interests whose influence reverberated throughout the financial and political spheres. The commissioned postmasters (*tokutei yūbinkyokuchō*) stood out in this regard. From the mid-1950s, local commissioned postmasters and their spouses and retired colleagues constituted one of the country's best organized, secretive, and influential interest groups. Politically, they participated in the electoral machine of the Liberal Democratic Party (LDP) by systematically gathering the vote behind individual politicians and recruiting new members for both the party and individual candidate support organizations (*kōenkai*). As they reached the pinnacle of their power during the early 1980s, the postmasters associations purportedly represented 1 million votes at election time. Meanwhile, the postmasters cooperated with their LDP allies to defeat or weaken reformers' efforts to adapt state-run postal institutions to a changing economy, thereby placing Japan well behind Europe on the road to postal reform.[3] In sum, the commissioned post office system stood at the center of Japan's conservative political-economic establishment, contributing not only to its long-term survival but also to its complexities and inefficiencies.

Although postwar Japan produced plenty of critics of the modern postal system, it was not until the turn of the twenty-first century that postal reform gained significant political traction, thanks largely to the actions of one man: Koizumi Jun'ichirō (1942–). To Koizumi and his political and academic allies, postal institutions symbolized much of what ailed contemporary Japan: the inefficient allocation of financial resources, "excessive" government interference in domestic markets, the

---

2. I use the term "politicization" in this study to refer to the performance of political functions by actors in the postal system. As Chapter 1 will illustrate, this can include spying, censorship, and other national security functions, as well as participation in electoral campaigns.

3. Starting in the early 1990s, Britain, Germany, several other continental European countries, Australia, and New Zealand corporatized or privatized all or part of their postal systems.

government's indebtedness to self-seeking interest groups, and Japan's seeming inability to adapt swiftly to global economic change. Upon assuming the prime ministership in 2001, Koizumi defied the wishes of his conservative LDP colleagues by embarking on a four-year crusade to privatize the postal services and sever the ties that bound the LDP to the commissioned postmasters and other vested interests. While many hailed the plan as a necessary component of structural reform within the political economy, others bemoaned the potential loss of traditional institutions and the conservative values they represented. Few, however, expected the plan to succeed, given the staunch opposition of the postmasters, the postal workers, politicians from across the political spectrum, and many postal bureaucrats. But succeed it did. By late 2005, it appeared that Koizumi had transformed not only the post office but also the very institutional and ideological foundations of Japanese finance and politics. By many accounts, it was one of the most astonishing political achievements in postwar Japanese history.

The story of the Japanese state-run postal system and Koizumi's campaign to radically reform it raise a number of intriguing questions. Why did the system become so deeply politicized and resistant to change? And how did Koizumi, of all people—an iconoclastic politician from outside the LDP mainstream—succeed in privatizing it? To what extent, finally, will Koizumi's postal privatization plan actually change the institutions and politics of the postal system? These and related questions are the focus of this book.

The Argument in Brief

To explain the politicization and privatization of the Japanese postal system, this book traces the origins and subsequent evolution of the system from a historical institutionalist perspective.[4] In so doing, I ex-

---

4. In keeping with the general trends of this literature, I define institutions as the rules and norms that structure relationships within and among groups of actors in a polity. I have been particularly inspired by the following sources: John Campbell, *Institutional Change and Globalization*; Hall, *Governing the Economy*; Hall and Soskice, eds., *Varieties of Capitalism*; Pierson, *Politics in Time*; Pierson and Skocpol, "Historical Institutionalism in Contemporary Political Science"; Steinmo, Thelen, and Longstreth, eds., *Structuring Politics*; and Thelen, *How Institutions Evolve*.

plore the shifting relationship between the postal services and the state and explain how that relationship both reflected and contributed to political and economic development in modern Japan. As such, this book serves as a case study not only of how postal systems can acquire functions beyond the realm of communications, but also of how important public institutions can evolve in a symbiotic fashion with their broader environments.

I also examine the interest groups that developed around postal institutions, paying particular attention to the commissioned postmasters. Although by no means the sole ingredient in the postal system's politicization, the postmasters played a pivotal role in the Japanese post office saga by virtue of their distinctive position at the intersection of Japan's bureaucratic and electoral worlds. As I explore the history of that position, I explain the postmasters' electoral significance for conservative politicians as well as their impact on policymaking in the postal sphere. The postmasters' story also serves as a stand-alone study of Japan's postwar interest group environment and the circumstances in which specific interest groups gain (and lose) electoral significance.

Finally, this book assesses the impact of individual leaders on the Japanese postal system. Although several individuals—including members of the post–World War II American occupying forces—helped shape the postal system since 1868, three had *critical* influence on the system's economic and political trajectory: Maejima Hisoka, the mid-level bureaucrat who laid the institutional foundations of the postal system during the formative years of the early Meiji period; Tanaka Kakuei (1918–1993), the foremost political broker of early postwar Japan and the architect of the electoral alliance between the postmasters and the LDP; and Koizumi Jun'ichirō, the political maverick who sidelined the proponents of the state-run system and imposed market-oriented rules on the post office.[5] To varying degrees, each of these men demonstrated

---

5. This book also acknowledges the contributions of Hashimoto Ryūtarō (1937–2006), who as prime minister between 1996 and 1998 managed to accelerate the political and bureaucratic momentum toward postal privatization. But while I argue that Koizumi's accomplishments on postal reform would have been far less extensive had Hashimoto not laid some of the groundwork for him, I stop short of categorizing Hashimoto's role as "critical." As Chapter 5 illustrates, this is because Hashimoto's accomplishments in the postal sphere were in many ways attributable to Koizumi, who put intense pressure

a remarkable ability to shape their political and institutional environments in accordance with their beliefs and policy preferences. But they
were also the products of historical and institutional circumstance. As
a result of developments beyond their control, each had access to resources that gave them unprecedented leverage over their environments,
while simultaneously facing significant institutional constraints to the
fulfillment of their goals. These men made history, in other words, but
it was history and institutions that gave them—or deprived them of—
the tools to do so.

Although my primary objectives are to explain the causes and implications of the postal system's politicization and recent privatization,
I also look at the system's social and cultural significance. Throughout
the book, I illustrate how the postal services assumed an array of social
and cultural functions that enhanced the post office's legitimacy in the
eyes of ordinary Japanese. This is not to suggest that these factors had
a direct, causal impact on policymaking outcomes within the postal
sphere; these outcomes, I believe, are more effectively explained by the
interplay among institutions, interests, and leadership. I will show, however, how they influenced the *language* of postal politics as different actors manipulated the post office's social and cultural values for political
gain, thus elevating the debate over postal privatization to a level of rhetorical intensity that is rare in Japanese politics. I will also illustrate how
the multifaceted significance of the postal system transformed the local
post office—that nineteenth-century harbinger of modernity—into a
potent symbol of tradition and of popular ambivalence about the country's embrace of neoliberal economic reform.

EXPLAINING THE POSTMASTERS' POLITICIZATION

The extent to which the Japanese postmasters became involved in electoral affairs may be internationally unprecedented. From the mid-1950s,
the postmasters cultivated an exchange relationship with the LDP in

---

on the reform process via his position as Minister of Health and Welfare. In a similar
vein, I portray the contributions of Takenaka Heizō (1951–) to the postal privatization
process as important but not critical: although he gave concrete expression to many of
Koizumi's proposals, Takenaka's effectiveness was ultimately contingent on Koizumi's
leadership.

which they systematically gathered party and *kōenkai* members, votes, and financial contributions for the party in return for protective government policies.[6] This is particularly striking when compared to the British postal system, which served as a model for Japanese postal institutions but produced no cohort of significantly politicized postmasters.

How can we explain this discrepancy? Arguments that focus on electoral systems give us few clues. We might expect the postwar Japanese postmasters to have been most influential in Lower House elections, where the organized vote was indispensable to individual LDP candidates operating within the pre-1994 multi-member district system. The postmasters were, after all, among the country's best organized interest groups. But the postmasters were in fact far more active in Upper House elections, in which multi-member districts are combined with a nationwide proportional representation (PR) district.[7] The postmasters' importance in Lower House elections did increase following the 1994 transition to an electoral system consisting of PR and single-member districts (SMD); consider, for example, their mass mobilization in SMD behind the so-called postal rebels during the 2005 election and their extensive support for the Democratic Party of Japan (DPJ) in 2009. But if the switch to this new electoral system was indeed responsible for the postmasters' mass mobilization during recent Lower House elections, why have postmasters not rallied en masse behind politicians in Britain's SMD electoral system? Clearly, while electoral rules help shape the scope and effectiveness of postmaster participation in election campaigns, they

------

6. Although postmasters in other Western countries have performed certain electoral functions in the past, the closest approximation to the Japanese case may have been the postmasters of the United States during the nineteenth and early twentieth centuries. But while American postmasters were often important determinants of the electoral fortunes of individual members of Congress, they split their allegiance between the two main political parties and did not achieve the level of organization and systematic electoral participation that characterized their postwar Japanese counterparts. For more on the political functions of the American postmasters, see relevant sections of Cullinan, *The United States Postal Service*; Fowler, *The Cabinet Politician*; Fuller, *The American Mail*; John, *Spreading the News*; Priest, "The History of the Postal Monopoly in the United States"; and Tierney, *The U.S. Postal Service*.

7. The postmasters' preferred candidates—most of them retired postal officials themselves—normally ran in the Upper House's national PR district.

are poor predictors of how and why postmasters get involved in those campaigns in the first place.

A more persuasive explanation emphasizes the role of innovative leadership during periods of political and institutional uncertainty. In early Meiji Japan, Maejima Hisoka was largely responsible for introducing modern postal institutions, including the commissioned post office system, while in the postwar period Tanaka Kakuei arranged the electoral marriage between local postmasters and the LDP. As Minister of Posts and Telecommunications in the late 1950s, Tanaka recruited the postmasters to help gather the vote behind the LDP at a time when the newly unified party faced severe electoral challenges from the radical Japan Socialist Party (JSP). Tanaka's efforts to expand the party's base of support among organized interest groups also helped pave the way for long-term one-party dominance, which in turn strengthened the postmasters' loyalty to the LDP.

There were no such instances of political entrepreneurship during the last 150 years or so of British postal history.[8] Roland Hill, the primary architect of modern postal institutions and a leading bureaucrat in the post-1840 postal system, was an innovative leader *par excellence*, but one of his main objectives was to construct an efficient postal administration that was *insulated* from politics. Hill was motivated by several centuries of deeply politicized patronage appointments to the position of postmaster general and the gross financial and administrative inefficiencies that subsequently ensued. To the best of my knowledge, there were no noteworthy examples of politicians after Hill's time who looked to the postmasters as a vehicle for gathering the vote in national elections.

Although entrepreneurship (or the lack thereof) during periods of political and institutional flux is an important determinant of the electoral marriage between postmasters and political parties in Japan, this explanation begs a question: why do innovative political leaders in some countries recruit postmasters for electoral purposes, but not in others? The answer, I believe, has to do with the nature of the postmasters

---

8. I use the term "political entrepreneurship" in this study to refer to the capacity of risk-taking actors to develop or recombine political/institutional resources in ways that advance specific political, bureaucratic, or economic objectives.

themselves, which in turn reflects the evolving historical relationship between postal institutions and the state.

In order for any group to effectively gather the vote without resorting to coercive measures, it needs persuasive powers and access to networks of voters. In theory, postmasters in any country with a state-run postal system are inherently well poised to acquire both sets of resources given their status as civil servants and—for those who administer smaller post offices, at least—close association with local residents. In Britain, modern postmasters have been weak on both counts. For generations, the vast majority of postmasters have been "sub-postmasters," mostly small retailers who administer postal services to supplement their primary income. Historically, the government found these positions difficult to fill, let alone control,[9] a fact that is symptomatic of the position's relative lack of prestige. The sub-postmasters also lack discrete professional organizations that might strengthen their electoral allure. Although the sub-postmasters established a national association in 1894,[10] relatively late in the history of the post-1840 centralized postal system, the organization lost its clout as the sole representative of the postmasters after it merged with postal unions in 1972. Lacking strong, independent organizations, the sub-postmasters have been poorly situated to coordinate vote mobilization campaigns across individual electoral districts. Small wonder, then, that members of Parliament neglected the sub-postmasters as potential electoral allies.[11]

The British postmasters' relative political insignificance can be explained at least partly by the nature of the postal system's haphazard development in relation to the expansion of state authority. Since late Elizabethan times, the postal network developed in fits and starts in response to the communications and military needs of the Crown. Fearing by the late seventeenth century that its enemies were mobilizing mail carriers—both licensed postmasters and unlicensed couriers—for seditious purposes, the Crown gradually moved to impose monopoly control

---

9. Daunton, *Royal Mail*, 279–81.

10. Clinton, *Post Office Workers*, 38.

11. There is also little evidence to suggest that Britain's small number of more prestigious "head postmasters" were attractive candidates for electoral mobilization. Although their hiring was occasionally influenced by local MPs, this practice all but disappeared by the turn of the twentieth century (Daunton, *Royal Mail*, 276–77).

over the country's mail services. But the Crown's efforts to rein in the services were only partially successful, thanks largely to its fixation on revenue extraction. Until the early nineteenth century, the state would farm out sections of the postal network to the highest and/or most distinguished bidder, but only rarely were the "farmers" selfless and far-sighted enough to cover the costs of expanding and improving the quality of postal services. Many local postmasters, meanwhile, were being hired in slapdash fashion and acquiring notoriety for neglecting their duties and bilking public funds; not a few complained about their poor pay and onerous financial obligations to the Crown. By the time the system was overhauled in 1840, the postmasters had developed into a socially diverse, decentralized, and unorganized network of public servants.

Historically, Japanese political authorities were much more successful in harnessing postal networks to state goals. During the Tokugawa era (1600–1867), the military government based in Edo (present-day Tokyo) established a national communications network that would have been the envy of the British Crown in terms of the relatively high qualifications of its stationmasters and the degree of central government control over the system. Shortly after the Meiji Restoration in 1868, the state reformed and expanded the postal system with astonishing speed, building on both Tokugawa precedents and British practices. By 1880, post offices were in place throughout the country, serving as effective local vehicles for both the dissemination of state information and the population's identification with the modern nation-state.

The Japanese postal network's historically close relationship with the state had profound implications for the political functions of the postmasters. In addition to fulfilling residential and financial requirements that were customary in most countries, Meiji postmasters were recruited almost exclusively from among low-ranking local notables in the expectation that they would become trusted intermediaries between the state and local residents. Japanese postmasters also had to perform their postal duties with virtually no financial compensation, unlike their British counterparts. Their reward for services rendered: the prestige of serving as local representatives of the Meiji state—a perquisite that many postmasters used to secure supplementary positions in business and local elected government. In time, many postmasters acquired reputations as committed local officials who placed service to the emperor above their own pecuniary needs. During the early postwar period, the postmasters' social status made them attractive to conservative politicians as electoral partners.

The Japanese postmasters were also advantaged by their participation in dense organizational networks that could be mobilized for electoral purposes. These networks were the handiwork of the prewar state. In contrast to the British case, Japanese postmasters were forcibly mobilized by Meiji bureaucrats into a tightly knit federation of organizations that stretched from the national level to the local neighborhood. Designed to enable the state to communicate quickly and effectively with the postmasters and to control their every move—from their initial hiring to setting the schedules and agendas of their professional meetings—these organizations helped shape a remarkably homogeneous and socially cohesive network of postmasters that covered all corners of the country. For postwar conservative politicians looking for intermediaries between themselves and potential voters, these networks proved invaluable.

The political implications of the postal system's relationship to the state underscore Paul Pierson's observations about the importance of *timing* in the establishment and evolution of public institutions, as well as the complementarity between those institutions and their broader institutional and political environments.[12] To summarize, the key to explaining why Japanese postmasters acquired the persuasive powers and organizational networks to participate in electoral politics lies in their relationship with the state. In Britain, the postmasters as an occupational group evolved in a decentralized and often haphazard fashion over the course of many centuries, receiving few opportunities—from the state or elsewhere—to enhance their social standing or build strong organizations. Consequently, modern Britain experienced no mass mobilization of postmasters behind political parties. In Japan, many generations of strong bureaucratic control over the recruitment and organization of local postmasters produced a socially homogeneous group that acquired both the prestige and the dense organizational networks necessary for systematic participation in electoral politics. I illustrate these points in

---

12. Pierson, *Politics in Time*, 11–13. Hall makes similar observations in *Governing the Economy*.

greater detail in Chapter 1, which sets the historical stage for the rest
of the book. In Chapter 2, I explore the development of Japan's postal
system after World War II and the emergence of the postmaster-LDP
alliance. Chapter 3 looks inside the professional activities and associations of the postmasters, focusing on both their strengths and weaknesses within the electoral and policy processes.

THE JAPANESE POSTAL REGIME

Although the exchange relationship between the commissioned postmasters and the LDP lay at the heart of post-World War II postal politics, bureaucrats were also important. Long accustomed to microman-
aging the postmasters, officials in the postwar Ministry of Posts and
Telecommunications (Yūseishō; MPT) established close ties with the
postmasters and the ruling party. The result was an iron triangle that
exercised tight control over postal policymaking and contributed to the
longevity of the so-called 1955 system of LDP dominance. As Chapter 4
illustrates, other interests also fell in line behind the postal services, producing a veritable regime with distinctive institutions and power relationships, rules of engagement, and policy preferences.[13] The economic
glue that held the regime together was the Fiscal Investment and Loan
Program (FILP; *zaisei tōyūshi* or *zaitō*). Funded mainly by postal savings
deposits and insurance premiums, the FILP supplied the government
with funds for investment in industrial development, public works, and a
variety of other projects that helped solidify the support of the electorate
and the political parties—both conservative and leftist—for the state-
run postal services.

The postal regime persisted alongside the state-run postal services
until the turn of the twenty-first century, giving concrete expression to
the institutionalist notion of "path dependence"; the more regime members invested their time, money, votes, and occupational futures into the
postal system, the more committed to those investments they became.
The regime had, to a degree, become "locked in" to its particular political
trajectory, finding it increasingly difficult—and costly—to change. As

---

13. As Chapter 4 explains, my analysis of the notion of "regime" is drawn from
Pempel, *Regime Shift*.

Chapter 3 shows, this was especially apparent in the case of the post-masters, whose leaders went to extraordinary lengths to force compliance with occupational norms.

The postal regime also functioned as a formidable stumbling block to the mounting movement for postal reform. From the 1950s, when postal reform first appeared on the government agenda, through Koizumi's attempt to liberalize the mail service in 2002, the regime mobilized its vast networks of interest groups and politicians to halt or drastically minimize change. This does not mean that postal institutions completely escaped reform; as Chapters 4 through 6 show, the postal system was subjected to a number of small but significant changes over the years. But as a result of their organizational strength and political tenacity, anti-reform interests like the postmasters and their bureaucratic and LDP allies managed to keep radical reform at bay for decades.

Although the postal system and its underlying political regime managed to defeat the forces of radical exogenous change, internally, the postal services proved to be fairly dynamic. As Kathleen Thelen explains, the long-term survival of institutions depends on their periodic rejuvenation as they seek to strengthen their broader relevance.[14] The political history of the Japanese postal regime bears this out, as several chapters in this book illustrate. That the state-run postal system and postal regime survived for so many years—and despite the institutional rigidities within the commissioned post office system that I describe in Chapter 3—is testament in part to their ability to adapt to changing times. During the latter half of the twentieth century, the postal system introduced a spate of new mail, savings, and insurance services to its customers. Postal workers assumed volunteer functions in their communities as they tried to transform their facilities into post offices that the "people could love." Threatened by the rise of the postal reform movement, post offices in sparsely populated areas networked with local governments and retail shops to carry out social services for the elderly (*himawari* services). More recently, many post offices assumed government functions in the wake of local government amalgamations and the gradual decentralization of state power. And there may be no more "adaptable" postal service than the postal savings system, which sup-

---

14. Thelen, *How Institutions Evolve*, 8.

plied the state with a vast reservoir of funds for investment in a shifting array of state projects. To be sure, these and other instances of institutional adaptation and innovation were at least partly motivated by the drive for institutional preservation in a rapidly changing society and political economy. But for many ordinary Japanese, institutional dynamism within the confines of state control helped preserve the postal system's legitimacy, transforming the services into what many praised as a quintessentially Japanese set of institutions and values.

THE POST OFFICE'S SOCIAL AND CULTURAL DIMENSIONS

Institutions have a symbiotic relationship with the values and ideas that help define them. And so it was with the Japanese postal system. Almost from the start, the post office embodied many of the values and preferences that we now associate with Japan's more "traditional" political economy: state activism and paternalism, the valorization of public service over profit, a belief in government or public enterprise as the only valid caretaker of the public interest, a penchant for economic security and stability, economic nationalism, "financial socialism"[15]—and the list goes on. As I illustrate in the second half of this book, proponents of the state-run postal system frequently evoked these values as they fended off criticisms from the advocates of postal privatization, reminding their audiences that the postal services were in the business of serving the people rather than "making money." But there were also instances in which members of the postal regime invented new values—or repackaged old ones—in their efforts to achieve their foremost objective: institutional survival. This is illustrated most effectively by the post office's embrace of social welfare values amidst mounting calls during the 1980s for radical postal reform.

Whether innate to the postal system or "invented" by its politically savvy defenders,[16] these traditional values fueled the postal regime's rhetorical backlash against Koizumi and his reformist allies during the early 2000s. Those who championed postal reform in the name of free markets, competition, and globalization were branded un-Japanese hand-

---

15. The term "financial socialism" is usually used in a derogatory sense to refer to governmental policies that serve costly social—as well as financial—objectives.

16. Hobsbawm and Ranger, *The Invention of Tradition.*

maidens of impersonal economic forces—cultural apostates willing to sell Japan's distinctive traditions and national identity to the lowest bidder. Not to be outdone, Koizumi risked the very future of his government to "storm the castle" of the "feudal" postal regime and subject the postal services to market forces. The ensuing battle, some onlookers concluded, was tantamount to a modern-day "Sekigahara."[17]

The cultural dimensions of Japanese postal politics by no means determined the winners and losers in the battle over postal reform, but they most certainly influenced the language of that battle. On a deeper level, they reflected the post office's multifaceted significance for ordinary Japanese. As this book explains, it was in part through the postal network that ordinary Japanese acquired a sense of local community and nationhood during the Meiji period. Their patriotism deepened as the postal savings system taught them how to save for the sake of industrial development and empire building, and as they purchased commemorative postage stamps celebrating the virtues of the emperor system and Japan's military accomplishments. The expansion of the postal network facilitated communications among ordinary Japanese and the widely popular custom of exchanging postcards (*nengajō*) at New Year's. Children around the country took school trips to their local post offices to learn the history of communications in Japan and proper letter-writing etiquette. Local postmasters emerged as community leaders, volunteering as coaches for children's sports teams, participating in parent-teacher associations, and heading local neighborhood associations. Meanwhile, the postmasters and their employees tended to the elderly in ways that softened the negative side effects of depopulation in remote communities. The post office may have been taken for granted by most ordinary Japanese, but it in fact represented the very warp and woof of modern society. Changing the post office meant changing Japan.

EXPLAINING KOIZUMI'S VICTORY

Although Koizumi was well aware that postal privatization stood to transform Japanese politics and finance, he seemed less concerned about

---

17. The bloody Battle of Sekigahara, fought in 1600, ushered in the Tokugawa period. Today, the term is sometimes used in Japan as a metaphor for turning points in political conflicts.

the social and cultural significance of the post office as he embarked on his crusade. He thus sparked what may very well have been the most divisive political conflict since the 1960 Security Treaty Crisis. Given the intensity of opposition to postal privatization, how can we explain Koizumi's victory in October 2005?

The easy explanation is that this was an instance of "punctuated equilibrium" in which an innovative leader created an unforeseen opportunity for radical institutional change.[18] Koizumi sidelined the anti-privatization camp during the legislative process by defying decision-making norms and then defeated the last strongholds of resistance by calling a snap election. Although this explanation effectively highlights Koizumi's innovative leadership skills, it does not explain why *Koizumi* accomplished what he did, and not, say Nakasone Yasuhiro (1918–) or Hashimoto Ryūtarō, both of whom had hoped for some degree of postal privatization during their tenures as prime minister.

Scholars who attribute policy outcomes primarily to the balance of power among interest groups might explain the timing of Koizumi's success as a function of the postal regime's declining political influence relative to that of the liberal economic reform movement. As Chapter 3 explains, there is plenty of evidence to support this view. Thanks to inherent vulnerabilities within the postmasters associations, generational changes among both the postmasters and the LDP, fissures among postal bureaucrats as a result of the corporatization of the postal services in 2003, and heightened media attention to scandal within the postal services, the postal regime was losing some of its leverage over the proponents of reform. But while the relative decline of the postal regime undoubtedly contributed to Koizumi's successes, this explanation neglects the fact that the regime was still far better organized than the pro-privatization camp. More importantly, it also overlooks the novel institutional opportunities that enabled Koizumi to put the regime on the political defensive.

Although there would have been no postal privatization during the 2000s without Koizumi Jun'ichirō, his crusade ultimately succeeded because of institutional changes introduced well before he had assumed power. As described in Chapter 5, Hashimoto Ryūtarō's government

18. See Pierson, *Politics in Time*, 134–35.

(1996–1998) introduced a series of reforms that strengthened the policymaking power of the prime minister relative to that of the bureaucracy and LDP politicians. Of particular note was the establishment of the Council on Economic and Fiscal Policy (CEFP). A supra-ministerial advisory committee headed by the prime minister and consisting of key economic ministers and private sector representatives, the council's mission was to formulate broad government policy on the economic and financial fronts. As such, the CEFP transcended many of the traditional constraints of the policymaking system, including bureaucratic localism and inter-ministerial turf battles. It was the CEFP and important supporting institutions, Chapter 6 argues, that enabled Koizumi to sideline normal interest group alignments in the postal services and to hammer together a blueprint for postal privatization.

Unfortunately for Koizumi, these new policymaking institutions proved powerless in the Upper House, which defeated his privatization legislation in August 2005. Koizumi then proceeded to call a snap Lower House election, casting it strictly in policy terms and withholding the LDP's endorsement of Lower House incumbents who had voted against privatization in July. As Chapter 6 further explains, Koizumi's landslide victory in the election was attributable to new electoral rules that enabled him to secure the support of Japan's rapidly expanding cohort of floating voters. Had Koizumi been in power while the old multi-member district system was still in effect, the election would have been lost to local voters and special interests clamoring for particularistic favors—precisely the sorts of favors that were financed through the FILP by the postal savings and insurance systems. In sum, Koizumi was able to draw up a comprehensive blueprint for postal privatization, win the 2005 election, and then pass his postal legislation because of new institutional opportunities to change policymaking and electoral customs to his advantage.

Institutions provide spaces for the exercise of innovative leadership, and innovative leaders learn how to adapt to those institutions and shape their future trajectories. Maejima Hisoka was the first such innovator in the history of the state-run postal services, introducing a host of new services and institutions and then grafting onto them some of the economic and social missions of the Meiji state. Tanaka Kakuei was the second, inheriting an array of well-entrenched postal institutions and then harnessing them to the electoral objectives of the LDP. Koizumi broke rank with his predecessors by transforming the postal institutions themselves and hence the interests that supported them. It appeared, in short, that Koizumi had destroyed much of Maejima's and Tanaka's handiwork, leaving behind a postal system that promised to transform Japanese finance and politics.

THE FUTURE OF JAPANESE POST OFFICE POLITICS

As the Conclusion explains, on October 1, 2007, the postal services were divided into four private companies under a government-owned holding company—one each for the mail, postal savings, and postal insurance services, and a fourth for the country's network of post offices. The 2005 legislation stipulates that the holding company must sell its shares between 2011 and 2017. As the services are increasingly exposed to market forces, post office clients should have access to a broader range of products and services. The privatization process should also reduce the size of the postal savings and insurance services, shrink the FILP, and thus invigorate private financial markets. All told, these changes should accelerate Japan's long-term economic growth rates.

Administratively and politically, Koizumi and his team of reformers took advantage of new institutional opportunities to create a top-down system of executive leadership centered in the cabinet office—a system that weakened the control of the LDP and the bureaucracy over the policy process. Koizumi also reduced the powers of the Ministry of Internal Affairs and Communications (Sōmushō) by transferring the postal financial services under its jurisdiction to the private sector. Meanwhile, the September 11, 2005 election severed the electoral partnership between the LDP and the postmasters associations, pushed the postmasters toward the People's New Party (PNP) and the DPJ, and forced anti-postal privatization LDP Diet members to throw their lot behind the reformers. It appeared, in short, that the postal regime had been eviscerated and that the "1955 system" was finally dead.

Does this mean that Japan was now on the threshold of a new era—of a "2005 system," as one observer predicted?[19] Not quite. Koizumi

19. Yamawaki, *Yūsei kōbō*, 5.

may have laid the foundations for remarkable change, but not all of those changes are living up to their potential. The postal savings service will remain a formidable competitor in Japanese financial markets over the short to medium term, given its sheer size and other protective measures that were conceded by the Koizumi government during the policy formulation process. Although the official linkages between the postal savings system and the FILP were cut several years ago, administrators of the postal savings system will continue to voluntarily invest in the FILP for as long as private sector interest rates remain low and the global financial outlook is uncertain. This means that for the time being, at least, the FILP will occupy a reduced but nevertheless important position in the government's arsenal of policy instruments. And for as long as the FILP survives, interest groups will be tempted to pressure the ruling party for a piece of the fund's pie.

Koizumi's efforts to destroy the postal regime also suffered some setbacks. Plans to streamline the national network of post offices were diluted by a government commitment to retain one post office for every town and village in Japan. Efforts to destroy the organizational foundations of the commissioned postmasters were scuttled by the chief executive officer of the new government holding company. Koizumi's expulsion from the LDP of Diet members who had voted against his privatization legislation in the summer of 2005 was partially reversed in 2006, when Prime Minister Abe Shinzō (1954–) readmitted eleven of those rebels into the party in a bid to shore up the LDP's fortunes in the 2007 Upper House election. One of those rebels went on to occupy two successive cabinet positions.[20] Asō Tarō (1940–), who as Minister of Internal Affairs and Communications had staunchly opposed certain details of Koizumi's privatization plan, became prime minister in September 2008. And on August 30, 2009, the DPJ, led by Hatoyama Yukio (1947–), won a landslide victory in the Lower House election, promising to undo some of Koizumi's structural reforms. As of this writing, the remobilized postmasters are pressuring the powers-that-be to amend Koizumi's postal privatization blueprint after unabashedly throwing

---

20. Noda Seiko was former Prime Minister Fukuda Yasuo's Consumer Affairs Minister. She went on to serve as Prime Minister Asō's Minister of State for both Science and Technology Policy, and Food Safety.

their support behind the DPJ and the PNP in the 2009 and 2010 elections. To be sure, the postal regime is not nearly as influential as it once was during the early 1980s; postal bureaucrats have lost many of their powers, the postmasters are experiencing a decline in their organizational unity, and it appears that the maturation of institutional changes within the electoral system has permanently weakened the postmasters' electoral clout. But the regime is by no means dead. For as long as the postmasters maintain a semblance of organizational cohesiveness, the FILP persists, and politicians seek the organized vote, elements of the postal regime will survive.

When all is said and done, it was Koizumi's political leadership in the context of new policymaking and electoral institutions that sidelined the postal regime and paved the way for the privatization of Japan's state-run postal system. And it was politics that will enable important elements of the postal regime to survive well into the future—with perhaps negative consequences for Koizumi's political and economic legacies.

ONE

"Making Use of Private Energies":
The Origins and Early Evolution
of the Modern Japanese Postal System

Correspondence is the only means whereby information is spread and communication effected all over the country. Indirectly it promotes the distribution of merchandise at standard prices. We deem it very important, therefore, from administrative considerations as well as from the standpoint of human welfare. Hitherto this matter has been left in the hands of common tradesmen or messengers, so that the delivery of one letter has often taken twelve days for a short distance of about 250 miles. Furthermore, people living in out-of-the-way places could not avail themselves of even such a system as did exist. Messages often remained long in one place and were sometimes lost. We might mention hundreds of other abuses growing out of this imperfect mail system, which tended to hinder good administration and smooth intercourse. Accordingly, we hereby memorialize the [Council of State] that it will be advisable to establish a government postal system whereby letters can be carried all over the country.

—Memorial presented by the Ministry of Public Affairs
to the Council of State, June 1870

In its quest for rapid political and economic modernization, the Meiji state acknowledged very early that a modern postal system was important to the country's long-term survival and economic prosperity. Ac-

EPIGRAPH: Quoted in and translated by Nagao, "Communications in Japan," 344.

cordingly, the 1870s witnessed the introduction of many of the institutions that we now associate with the contemporary Japanese postal services: the mail, money order, and postal savings services, and the network of what was to become the commissioned (*tokutei*) and ordinary (*futsū*) post offices (*yūbinkyoku*). By the end of the nineteenth century, the Japanese postal system was among the largest in the world in terms of the sheer number of financial transactions and letters conveyed.

This chapter traces the historical evolution of the Japanese postal system to the early to mid-twentieth century. I begin with a brief overview of the premodern mail services in Japan and Britain, and then show how elements of both the Tokugawa system of post stations and the post-1840 British postal system helped shape the modernization of postal services in Meiji Japan. I also explain how the near simultaneity of postal modernization and the expansion of the centralized state positioned the Meiji postal system to assume a broader array of communications, financial, and even social services than comparable British institutions—institutions that provided a model for postal "best practices" around the world. I then demonstrate that while the Meiji Restoration created enormous opportunities for change, the trajectory of the modern Japanese postal services owed an enormous debt to the mid-level Meiji bureaucrat Maejima Hisoka. Here, I compare Maejima's impact on postal modernization to that of Rowland Hill, his British counterpart, and illustrate how both men affected—and were affected by—their surrounding environments. The section that follows examines the genesis of the commissioned post office system (*tokutei yūbinkyoku seido*), a Maejima invention that went on to become a significant intermediary institution between the Meiji state and local society. I conclude by chronicling the impact of both the postal system and the commissioned postmasters on the economic, financial, and social development of late nineteenth- and early twentieth-century Japan. As later chapters elaborate, the legacy of these functions helped position the commissioned postmasters to become an important cog in postwar conservative politics.

This chapter also addresses recurring themes in the life of the state-run Japanese postal system: debates about the ideal relationship between state and society as the services grew to embrace both state actors and the "private energies" of the postmasters and private sector businesses; conflicts between the lure of tradition and the demands of modernity;

and the emergence of distinctive values within the postal sphere that permeated both the Japanese public's perceptions about the post office and, by the late 1950s, debates about how best to reform it. As I explain in later chapters, the Meiji period unwittingly spawned a highly politicized postal system, but it also produced many of the features of the Japanese postal services that by the turn of the twenty-first century gave the seemingly arcane subject of postal privatization its political immediacy.

Postal Systems in Pre- and Early Modern History

Japan's postwar postal system was noteworthy for its close association with electoral politics. But the politicization of postal systems was by no means unique to Japan or limited to electoral functions, nor was it necessarily a twentieth-century phenomenon. As both the British and Japanese experiences illustrate, it was not unusual for postal systems to assume a broad array of political functions in accordance with the evolving needs of state authorities. The significance and effectiveness of those functions, I believe, were closely linked to the degree of centralized state control over the postal network.

In Britain, the pre-nineteenth-century "posts" were linked to the expansion of the state and its immediate security requirements. Britain's first "posting stations" were established by the Romans more than 2,000 years ago to facilitate military communications following their conquest of the islands;[1] the stations all but vanished after the Romans withdrew. Until the late middle ages, the posts appeared and disappeared according to the whims of traveling monarchs, following no centralized strategy for expansion. It was not until Elizabethan times that the Crown looked to the postal network as a mechanism for extending its control over the realm, thus granting it a degree of permanency.[2] By the early seventeenth century, when there was reason to suspect that private couriers were being mobilized for seditious purposes, the Crown moved to establish a monopoly over the collection and delivery of mail. It was also at this time that mail censorship was widely introduced to expose political con-

---

1. Beale, *A History of the Post in England,* 1–3, 8.
2. *The Postal History Society Bulletin,* 7.

spiracies and the transmission of treasonous ideas both at home and from abroad.[3] Over the next few centuries, the Crown also attempted to mobilize local postmasters—most of whom were unskilled innkeepers—to collect information about the price of local produce;[4] report on "remarkable" occurrences, including local acts of violence and sedition, worker unrest, and, later, the propaganda campaigns of the political opposition;[5] and serve as a conduit for state proclamations, notices, prayers, and various forms of propaganda.[6] Even after the modernization of the postal system in 1840, the state occasionally instructed postmasters to report on the activities of "suspicious" political groups.[7] In sum, the pre- and early modern British posts were more than just a mechanism for communications and, by extension, economic growth; as the eyes, ears, and mouthpiece of the state at the local level, they performed a host of security functions. In this way, the network helped compensate for the lack of a centralized national security apparatus and no doubt advanced the cause of national unity. That said, the pre-1840 state never fully succeeded in eliminating competition from private couriers and controlling unruly postmasters.[8]

As in Britain, the exchange of letters in Japan began as a function of military rule and imperial expansion. In the decades following the seventh-century Taika Reforms, a system of post stations (*ekisei*) was established along the newly constructed highways to facilitate the travels and correspondence of the court.[9] Loosely based on the Tang Chinese system, the post stations were spaced at far more regular intervals (approximately every sixteen kilometers) than the haphazard British posts

---

3. Joyce, *The History of the Post Office*, 6–7; Austen, *English Provincial Posts*, 1.

4. Joyce, *The History of the Post Office*, 254–55.

5. Austen, *English Provincial Posts*, 1, 125.

6. Joyce, *The History of the Post Office*, 254.

7. During the social and political conflicts of the 1840s, for instance, the postmasters were instructed to open the letters of Chartists, who were campaigning for democratic reforms (Clinton, *Post Office Workers*, 21). And in a document distributed to the postmasters in late 1885, the government decreed that, "In view of the importance of political speeches at the present time the attention of Postmasters is directed to the necessity of reporting all forthcoming political events in their respective towns." (*Post Office Circular*).

8. Ellis, *The Post Office in the Eighteenth Century*, 60.

9. Nagao, "Communications in Japan," 342.

and were administered by station heads (*ekichō*) chosen from among men of "talent and ability" (*saikan*), rather than innkeepers of little social distinction. Like the British innkeepers, the station heads provided horses for traveling officials and tended to the needs of official messengers (eventually known as *hikyaku*, lit. "flying legs"). Unlike the British innkeepers, however, the station heads covered most of their costs from taxes levied on the harvests of neighboring fields, rather than from payments for services rendered.[10]

In subsequent centuries, Japan's official post stations were established and disestablished, private facilities appeared along the Tōkaidō and other major highways for use by commoners as well as officials, and messenger services were introduced (and later dissolved) to service the traveling needs of the samurai class. As in Britain, the system was not always reliable; bandits were a ubiquitous presence on many routes, travelers grappled with cumbersome local checkpoints (*sekisho*) and transit fees levied by the daimyo, and the roads were often impassable during periods of military conflict.[11] Conditions improved rapidly after the Battle of Sekigahara in 1600, when the victorious Tokugawa Ieyasu extended centralized control over the country's main arteries as he sought to expand and solidify his power—something the British Crown was never able to do since its road systems were administered and paid for by local trusts established by Parliament.[12]

Ieyasu's innovations in travel and communications included the expansion and homogenization of a network of post stations (*shukueki*) along the country's five main highways (*gokaidō*). As Constantine Vaporis explains, although each station offered its own distinctive services,

all stations fulfilled the various functions of rest stop, transport center, information communications center, and recreation area. The primary responsibility of post stations was to provide transport services for official travelers and cargo. These services were obtained at the office of the station manager. . . , which was usually located near the center of the station. Many stations had more than one manager and central office, and in those cases duty was rotated

---

10. Kyūshū chihō tokutei yūbinkyokuchōkai, *Kyūshū tokutei yūbinkyokuchōkai shi*, 36–38.

11. Ibid., 39.

12. Vaporis, *Breaking Barriers*, 29.

between men and locations. The manager was assisted by a small staff of men who dispatched horses and porters, kept the official account books, and performed miscellaneous tasks. Stations were also required to maintain at least one designated inn, known as *honjin*, for travelers on official duty, and many maintained auxiliary inns (*waki-honjin*) to handle the overflow of guests. The central location of the *honjin*, as well as their impressive size and construction, signified the political function of the post station.[13]

To ensure that all post stations effectively fulfilled their responsibilities, the shogunate introduced a dizzying array of regulations to guarantee the availability of horses and porters at the stations and to facilitate the movement of soldiers, officials, and official correspondence through and between them.[14] These regulations were strengthened with the gradual introduction of a system of compulsory alternate residence (*sankin kōtai*) in Edo during the first half of the seventeenth century—a system that packed the roads and the post towns with elaborate daimyo retinues and that led to daimyo demands for more effective communication links between their domains and the capital.[15] The political and economic significance of this system of alternate residence and the roads and post stations that enabled it cannot be overstated. In addition to establishing the shogun's political and military control over potentially rebellious lords, they contributed, as Jansen asserts, "to the development of a system of national communications that did more to unify the country than Ieyasu's victory at Sekigahara."[16]

Although the historical record includes plenty of examples of post stations that failed to live up to the shogunate's exacting standards, the network's deficiencies were outpaced by those of the pre-1840 British postal service, in which work stoppages, corrupt practices, and shoddy service were often the norm. The degree of centralized control over postal services explains this discrepancy between the two countries. In Britain, demands for better road conditions and more services were frequently ignored by postmasters general, many of whom were un-

---

13. Ibid., 22.

14. Ibid., 17.

15. The system required daimyo to spend every other year in Edo and to leave members of their families behind as "hostages" when they returned to their domains (*han*).

16. Jansen, *The Making of Modern Japan*, 128.

qualified, self-interested patronage appointees. Those who administered the service on the ground—"farmers" who paid a fee to the Crown in return for control of a portion of the network—cared far more about lining their pockets than serving their communities.[17] From 1677, when the job of administering the British posts was transferred to a government department, bureaucratic incompetence simply added to the deterioration of services.[18] The Japanese system, by contrast, was advantaged by a compulsory relay system for both messengers and official travelers, ensuring that the post stations along a particular route received more or less the same amount of business.[19] As a result, the quality of service varied less from station to station than it did in Britain, which had no such system in place.

Japan's attentive government also ensured a remarkably well-qualified cohort of post station managers. As we have seen, early modern British postmasters were usually innkeepers, few of whom were known for their administrative competence or commitment to public service.[20] By the turn of the nineteenth century, the occupational profiles of local postmasters had diversified to include small shopkeepers, chemists, and other independent small businessmen.[21] (Although the quality of service improved once the innkeepers faded from the scene, the fact that the British system's "eyes and ears" were of such varied socio-economic backgrounds may be one reason why the postal network did not become a consistently effective avenue through which the state could exercise control over local society.) In Japan, the station managers (*ton'ya*) hailed from higher social ranks: village headmen, landlords, and other men of

---

17. There were some notable exceptions to this norm. For example, the famous Ralph Allen, postmaster of Bath, was granted a contract in 1720 that he used to make vast improvements to the postal system in his area (Clinton, *Post Office Workers*, 24).

18. Priest, "The History of the Postal Monopoly in the United States," 36–39.

19. Vaporis, *Breaking Barriers*, 25.

20. One innkeeper-postmaster in seventeenth-century Manchester was less known for supplying horses along a local post road than for his services as master vintner, tavern keeper, and supervisor of "the town's cock-pit, to which the populace and gentry resorted for watching the great matches" (Roeder, *Beginnings of the Manchester Post Office*, 35).

21. Austen, *English Provincial Posts*, 122–23.

local influence.[22] They were also subjected to more intense bureaucratic scrutiny than the English postmasters, many of whom routinely took advantage of the postal system's lax supervision by reneging on their duties and pocketing more than their allotted share of mail profits.

An essential function of the Tokugawa post stations was the conveyance of official—and, eventually, unofficial—correspondence. By the end of the era, three kinds of messenger services were in operation: official express messengers managed by the shogunate; messenger services that carried correspondence for the daimyo between their feudal domains and residences in Edo; and private courier services established by merchants in Edo, Osaka, and Kyoto.[23] As the merchant class expanded, so did the private couriers (*machi-bikyaku*) and the scope of services rendered. In time, the *machi-bikyaku* grew to be quite prosperous—and colorful. The *hikyaku* would travel on foot with their letters stored in a box at the end of a pole. As they hastened along their routes, a wind bell (*furin*) attached to their poles would alert those ahead of their pending arrival. These and other images of the *hikyaku*, together with the ever-expanding daimyo processions along the Tōkaidō and other main highways, were immortalized in the popular wood-block prints (*ukiyoe*) of the day.

While some features of the feudal postal system evoke nostalgia today, others bordered on the grim. Of particular note were the heavy responsibilities shouldered by the residents of communities bordering the post stations—the so-called assisting villages (*sukegō*). Reminiscent of late seventh- and early eighth-century practices, local residents had to contribute to their post station's upkeep by paying taxes on their harvests or, more commonly, supplying horses and human labor. Since working for the post station often meant slave wages and time away from the farm, the *sukegō* system drained local economies and cast

---

22. Many station managers continued in these positions as they carried out their postal duties.

23. Teishin sōgō hakubutsukan, ed., *Kindai yūbin no akebono*, 12–13; Yoshida, "Yūseishō enkaku shōshi," 74; Kyūshū chihō tokutei yūbinkyokuchōkai, *Kyūshū tokutei yūbinkyokuchōkai shi*, 41–42.

Fig. 1.1 An 1873 depiction of a typical private mail courier. It was around this time that the *hikyaku* were banned from carrying the mail. Courtesy of the Teishin sōgō hakubutsukan.

many a peasant into penury.[24] Indebtedness was also a problem for the post stations, since official travelers were authorized to use the facilities for free or at low, fixed rates.[25] Although Ieyasu and his successors provided financial incentives to the post stations, including land grants, rice stipends, salaries, and tax exemptions for the post station managers, they failed to cover costs as the volume of travelers and couriers mushroomed.[26] The post stations tried to compensate for these shortfalls by squeezing the assisting villages even more.

---

24. Jansen, *The Making of Modern Japan*, 138; Westney, *Imitation and Innovation*, 104–5; Hunter, "A Study of the Career of Maejima Hisoka," 76.

25. Vaporis, *Breaking Barriers*, 72–76. Vaporis also notes that many merchants swindled the post stations by passing their wares off as "official" baggage in order to receive lower rates.

26. Ibid., 25.

In contrast to pre-1840 Britain, the Tokugawa system of travel and communications was never a noteworthy source of government revenue. Nor was it a significant means of intelligence gathering and propaganda dissemination—functions that were rendered unnecessary by the system of alternate residence in Edo, which enabled the shogunate to keep a tight rein over outlying areas.[27] (The Tokugawa regime's creative security apparatus also made the private couriers far less threatening to national security than they might otherwise have been.) It can be argued, however, that the feudal posts system did more to contribute to the more innocuous but no less important political goal of national unity than did its pre-1840 British counterpart. Whereas the British system was decentralized and susceptible to habitual mismanagement, the Japanese system, as we have seen, worked reasonably well, thanks in no small part to the shogunate's centralized control over the post stations, the compulsory relay system, and the skills of the carefully selected—and regulated—station heads. Thus, if the British postal system can be likened to the "eyes, ears, and mouthpiece" of the government, the Tokugawa post stations, as Vaporis suggests, resembled "the arms and legs of the realm."[28]

It was clear by the late eighteenth century, however, that the system could no longer meet the needs of a rapidly changing society. As in Britain, high postage rates put long-distance correspondence beyond the reach of ordinary subjects, and road conditions failed to keep up with expanding traffic. The quality and scope of services began to vary from locality to locality, theft grew rampant along some routes, and corruption was on the rise.[29] Meanwhile, the increasing abuse of the *sukego* system by the shogunate and the post stations drove many villagers to protest—sometimes with violence. In the Tenma (Post Horse) Uprising of late 1764, more than 200,000 villagers in provinces surrounding Edo alarmed the shogunate by marching on the capital to protest higher taxes levied in support of post stations along the Nakasendō highway.

---

27. Vaporis detected no evidence that the station managers routinely inspected mail for the Tokugawa government. He attributes this to the sheer volume of mail on the main highways and the already onerous duties shouldered by the station managers (private correspondence, March 17, 2007).

28. Vaporis, *Breaking Barriers*, 17.

29. Yoshida, "Yūseishō enkaku shōshi," 74.

After disbanding, villagers laid waste to the nearby property of wealthy merchants and landowners. As the largest outpouring of peasant protest during the Tokugawa period, the incident highlighted the fundamental relationship between the integrity of the posts network and the stability of the regime.[30] By the time Japan finally embarked on political and economic modernization nearly a century later, Tokugawa communications were ripe for reform.

Nineteenth-Century Postal Innovations

Nineteenth-century postal reform occurred against a backdrop of great political, intellectual, and institutional innovation in both Britain and Japan. Sandwiched between the 1832 Reform Act, which extended the franchise, and the repeal of the repressive Corn Laws in 1846, British postal reform was one of many changes introduced by Parliament to address the communications and economic needs of a country struggling with the transformative effects of industrialization and democratization. As such, postal reform was the product of growing democratic impulses from below. In Japan, postal reform was implemented from above by a newly minted state that was intent on controlling the direction of political, social, and economic change.

Although both the British and Japanese postal systems came to occupy important positions in the lives of their respective populations, their political roles diverged as a result of discrepancies in the timing of their modern institutional development and their historical legacies. In post-1840 Britain, where the modernization of the state—in the form of centralization and bureaucratization—preceded that of the postal system, the postal network developed in many ways into an administrative arm of the state. In post-1868 Japan, state and postal modernization occurred more or less simultaneously, thus enabling the postal network to assume a wide range of tasks relating to state expansion and consolidation. This arrangement was further facilitated by the network's historical legacy of centralization and close association with state authorities. In short, Japan's modern postal system was especially active politically—

---

30. Sippel, "Abandoned Fields," 210–11. For more on the uprising, see Walthall, *Peasant Uprisings in Japan;* and Vaporis, "Post Station and Assisting Villages."

as much an agent of economic, social, and political modernization as a result of those processes.

From the custom of universal service in mail delivery to the basic organizational features of the mail and postal savings services, the British and Japanese postal systems were remarkably similar, not least because the post-1840 British system served as a model for the Japanese reforms three decades later.[31] Particularly striking were the similarities between the ideas that shaped postal reform in each country and the individuals who conveyed them. In each case, postal reform was led by a maverick leader who advocated progressive ideas about education, the social functions of the state, and the ideal relationship between the state and the market. But also noteworthy was the extent to which the institutional and ideational dimensions of the reforms *diverged* as a result of differences in the timing of institutional innovation.

THE "FATHERS" OF POSTAL REFORM

In 1837, a young political activist named Rowland Hill caused a stir in England by publishing a pamphlet advocating an overhaul of the posts.[32] Entitled *Post Office Reform: Its Importance and Practicability*, the pamphlet argued that Britain had a moral obligation to modernize the post office in line with its role as an "engine of civilization."[33] The pamphlet began with scathing indictments against the current system. "It will be found," Hill wrote sarcastically on the opening page, "that the tax on the transmission of letters is the most remarkable for its non-increasing productiveness."[34] Relying on carefully compiled statistics, he illustrated that despite the rising education levels of the population, postal revenue had been decreasing for two decades. At the root of the problem, he argued, were countless instances of error and fraud perpetrated at all levels of the system, but most prominently at the grassroots level: "We have grounds for stating, so far as our scrutiny has extended, that the 'Office Accounts' have most frequently fallen short of the true amounts of

---

31. For an excellent analysis of the institutional similarities and differences between the Japanese and British reform processes, see Westney, *Imitation and Innovation*, Chapter 3.

32. Allam, *The Social and Economic Importance of Postal Reform in 1840*, 13.

33. Ibid.

34. Hill, *Post Office Reform*, 1.

charge as corrected and admitted by the Deputy Post-masters."[35] Postal employees, he warned, were pillaging funds from the system, and the state was poorly equipped to stop them.[36]

Hill's recommendations appear almost quaint today, but in 1837 they bordered on the radical. In weighing the merits of various methods for collecting postage, Hill wrote: "If the postage of all letters were collected *after* their passage through the Central Office, something would be accomplished in simplifying the operations, but how much more would be effected if any means could be devised by which the postage of all letters should be collected *before* their passage through the Central Office!"[37] As for setting postage rates, Hill condemned the practice of pricing according to the weight of a letter and the number of its enclosures, a practice that invited unwelcome intrusions by the postmasters—sometimes by candlelight in the dead of night—into the private correspondence and financial remittances of their patrons. Hill believed that "the charge ought to be precisely the same for every packet of moderate weight, without reference to the number of its enclosures."[38] Nor, he argued, should rates vary according to distance: "If . . . the charge for postage be made proportionate to the whole expense incurred in the receipt, transit, and delivery of the letter, and in the collection of its postage, it must be made *uniformly* the same from every post town to every other post town in the United Kingdom."[39] And so arose the practices of prepaid postage, carried out by affixing postage stamps to the outside of letters or envelopes, and uniform postage rates. These changes, together with other measures designed to make the postal services administratively simple, accessible, and honest, became the guiding principles of postal systems around the world—including Japan's.

Rowland Hill was not the first individual to advocate postal reform in England; the state had tried on several occasions in the past to improve its efficiency, particularly as a revenue-generating institution. Nor did Hill launch the nineteenth-century postal reform movement; this

---

35. Ibid., 56.
36. Ibid., 59.
37. Ibid., 18. Before 1840, postage could be paid either up front or following delivery.
38. Ibid., 14.
39. Ibid.

was a distinction enjoyed by a Glasgow parliamentarian named Robert Wallace, who single-handedly pressured the government into introducing a series of small but important changes during the 1830s.[40] Nevertheless, Hill stood out as the "king" of the modern British postal system,[41] an honor that reflected his zealous commitment to economic and social change.

Hill was a social and political activist from a large family of educators who were steeped in the ideals of laissez-faire economics, representative democracy, and Benthamite utilitarianism. Like Robert Wallace, Hill believed that the high cost of postage constituted a protectionist impediment to commerce that should be reformed according to free trade principles.[42] But to a much greater extent than Wallace, Hill also looked to postal reform as an opportunity to improve the lot of the common man. He felt strongly about the notion of equal opportunity for all and the values of universal education, thrift, and resourcefulness,[43] which could be spread by making the postal system more widely accessible to the public. And the key to serving the interests of both commerce and the public, Hill maintained, was a drastic reduction in the price of postage.

Accordingly, Hill advocated the extension of the pre-existing Penny Post beyond the confines of London to the nation as a whole.[44] The plan eventually found its way into a parliamentary committee that was chaired by Wallace but staffed by hostile MPs.[45] The ensuing hearings highlighted the controversies surrounding the wedding of free trade principles to humanitarian goals in 1830s Britain. Hill's advocates believed that the postal system should respond to market pricing mechanisms, and that the lower the price, the more ordinary citizens would make use

------

40. Daunton, *Royal Mail*, 16; Clinton, *Post Office Workers*, 27.

41. Daunton, *Royal Mail*, 3.

42. Ibid., 15–16.

43. Ibid., 12–15.

44. The Penny Post was the brainchild of a business entrepreneur named William Dockwra. Established in 1680 in London in response to rising public demand for a faster and cheaper postal service, the Penny Post was in gross defiance of the state's professed monopoly over "the mails." But it proved so efficient and lucrative that the General Post Office co-opted it five years later (Joyce, *The History of the Post Office*, 36–41).

45. Allam, *The Social and Economic Importance of Postal Reform in 1840*, 21.

of the system. Others retorted that Hill's plan would deprive the state of much-needed revenue.[46] Skeptical citizens, meanwhile, scoffed that cheap postage was simply a ruse for increasing the profits of wealthy bankers and businessmen.[47] What tipped the balance in the reformers' favor was an outpouring of public opinion. Businessmen and ordinary citizens wrote en masse in support of the national Penny Post, many of them endorsing Hill's argument that postal reform was an essential step toward the social and economic advancement of the nation. In the end, the parliamentary committee approved the plan by a narrow margin.

The Penny Post was introduced at the national level in 1840. But Hill—now employed by the Treasury in a position that permitted him to oversee the entire postal system—was dissatisfied with the reform.[48] At issue was whether the postal service should remain a government monopoly. A staunch believer in free market competition, Hill argued that each branch of the system could be financially self-supporting if faced with competition from private firms. Others, including many civil servants, wished to preserve the government monopoly on the grounds that the government was better positioned than the private sector to provide universal service to all corners of the country.[49] It was a classic debate that was to repeat itself countless times the world over: was the public interest more effectively served by free market principles, or was the state its only viable guarantor? In post-1840 Britain, the defenders of government monopoly prevailed.

Maejima Hisoka, Hill's counterpart in early Meiji Japan, also looked to communications as an "engine of civilization." Born in 1835 to the Ueno family of former low-ranking samurai in what is now Niigata prefecture, the boy lost his father at an early age and was raised by his mother, a fervent advocate of education;[50] when he was in his early thirties, he was adopted into the prosperous Maejima family. At just twelve years old, Maejima traveled by foot to Edo, where he settled for two years to study

---

46. Hill's critics were correct about the initial effects of the scheme on government income; revenues from the national Penny Post dropped by 69.3 percent during its first year and were not to regain their pre-reform levels until 1863 (Daunton, *Royal Mail*, 24).

47. Ibid., 19.

48. Ibid., 26.

49. Ibid., 49–50.

50. Yamaguchi, *Maejima Hisoka*, 11–15.

"Western learning" and medicine.[51] He embarked on another series of tours eight years later, this time to investigate Japan's vulnerable national security following Commodore Perry's fateful arrival in Japan in 1853. His travels took him from Hokkaido to the north to Kyushu in the south, where he immersed himself in "Dutch Learning" (*rangaku*). It was in Nagasaki that Maejima began studying English, a skill that later positioned him to look to Britain as a model for the Meiji postal reforms.[52] It was also in Nagasaki that he spoke to an American missionary about the workings of modern postal systems and purportedly saw his first stamped letter from abroad.[53] By all accounts, these experiences had a formative effect on Maejima's life and career. As Janett Hunter argues, his travels throughout the country and interaction with people from abroad instilled in him a strong national consciousness and awareness of Japan's place in the world.[54] Furthermore, his first-hand knowledge of late Tokugawa Japan's deteriorating road system and messenger services—and of the evils of the *sukegō* system[55]—made him profoundly sensitive to the importance of modern communications systems for the economic, social, and political modernization of a country.[56] Communications, Maejima believed, were the key to enlightenment.[57]

In 1870—two years after the Meiji Restoration—Maejima was appointed to the Ministry of Civil Affairs (Minbushō) as head of both the tax bureau and communications (the latter post was known as *ekitei gonnokami*).[58] That year, the young bureaucrat almost single-handedly

------

51. Ibid., 25; Hunter, "A Study of the Career of Maejima Hisoka," 13.

52. Westney, *Imitation and Innovation*.

53. Yūseishō, ed., *Yūsei 100-nen no ayumi*, 20–21. As stipulated by the treaties concluded after Perry's arrival, foreign governments were permitted to establish post offices in their treaty settlements to convey correspondence between their citizens and the home country.

54. Hunter, "A Study of the Career of Maejima Hisoka," 63.

55. Ibid., 75.

56. Kyūshū chihō tokutei yūbinkyokuchōkai, *Kyūshū tokutei yūbinkyokuchōkai shi*, 47–50. Yūseishō, ed., *Yūsei 100-nen shi*, 56.

57. Hunter, "A Study of the Career of Maejima Hisoka," 143.

58. In addition to postal affairs, the ministry's jurisdiction included taxes, family registers, and mining. Dissolved in 1871, its functions were absorbed by the Finance Ministry (Ōkurashō) and the Public Works Ministry (Kōbushō). When it was established in 1873,

drew up a proposal for a state-run postal system that would eliminate the social abuses of the *sukegō* system and the high costs and inefficiencies of the private courier services. The Council of State (Dajōkan) approved the proposal and work began immediately to implement the new system. Maejima was then abruptly dispatched to Britain to help renegotiate a loan for Japan's first railway line (between Shinbashi and Yokohama),[59] a fortuitous diversion that allowed him to observe Rowland Hill's postal innovations firsthand.[60] During his tour of London (and American) post offices, Maejima studied the postal system's contributions to government revenue as well as the value of postal savings systems for small depositors.[61] Upon returning to Japan in August 1871, he successfully requested reassignment as head of communications and thus presided over the introduction of the new postal system.[62] Within a few years, a national network of post offices had been grafted onto the country's preexisting network of roads and post towns and extended to all corners of the country.[63] In keeping with the British model, postage rates were kept low and, in time, uniform across different geographic regions, postage stamps and universal service were introduced,

---

the Home Ministry (Naimushō) assumed some of these functions, including those relating to the postal system.

59. While Maejima was abroad, the task of overseeing preparations for the establishment of the new postal system fell to another Civil Affairs bureaucrat named Sugiura Yuzuru. Sugiura had made two trips to France before the Restoration and was well acquainted with the postal system there. Sugiura made only a few small changes to Maejima's postal modernization plan (Yūseishō, ed., *Yūsei 100-nen shi*, 62).

60. Maejima greatly admired Hill. Toward the end of his life, Maejima attributed his successful career to three factors: 1) his own personal endeavors; 2) the Meiji government's belief in progress; and 3) Hill's innovations (Hunter, "A Study of the Career of Maejima Hisoka," 143).

61. Beasley, *Japan Encounters the Barbarian*, 143.

62. Kobayashi Masayoshi, *Minna no yūbin bunka shi*, 257–60. In 1934, to mark the founding of the modern postal system in 1871 and the establishment of an independent account for the postal services (see Chapter 4), the Japanese government declared April 20 "Communications Day." Today, postal employees and fans of the post office continue to observe the date with special exhibitions and celebrations.

63. In a telling indicator of the success of the postal system's early expansion, by 1880 Western residents were sufficiently confident in the new system to close their own postal agencies in Japan (Westney, *Imitation and Innovation*, 102).

and service was continuous, rather than activated in response to specific needs.[64]

As Eleanor Westney observes, radical postal reform was probably inevitable in early Meiji Japan given the country's sensitivity to foreign criticisms and the state's concomitant determination to modernize its political and economic institutions. But since most government officials were busying themselves with other concerns at this time—a state of affairs reflected in the relatively low rank of communications within the overall bureaucratic pecking order—Maejima found himself with a unique opportunity to significantly shape the direction of change within the postal sector.[65]

Thus, the postal system bore the imprint of Maejima's views on a number of fronts, including the functions of the post office in modern societies and the ideal relationship between the state and the private sector. Like Rowland Hill before him, Maejima believed in the transformative effects of education and in postal reform as a prerequisite of an enlightened society. But Maejima's vision for the postal system also reflected his—and his compatriots'—indignation over the unequal treaties concluded with the Western powers at mid-century and his conviction that Japan must integrate itself into the international economic system. As William Beasley writes, by establishing a network of post offices, securing Japanese membership in the Global Postal Union in 1877,[66] and negotiating the 1879 withdrawal of British post offices in Japanese treaty ports, Maejima helped the Meiji state restore its sovereignty in the communications sphere.[67] In so doing, moreover, he oversaw the establishment of domestic institutions that facilitated Japanese participation in international communications, commerce, and financial transactions.

---

64. Matsubara, *Gendai no yūsei jigyō*, 99.

65. Westney, *Imitation and Innovation*, 107; Hunter, "A Study of the Career of Maejima Hisoka," 145.

66. An inter-government organization, the Global Postal Union—which changed its name to the Universal Postal Union in 1878—was established in 1874 in Switzerland to introduce international regulations and standards for the exchange of mail, and to administer payments for the delivery of mail between countries.

67. Beasley, *Japan Encounters the Barbarian*, 143. See also Westney, who notes that the establishment of the postal system reflected a broader desire to turn Japan into a modern nation on par with the Western powers (*Imitation and Innovation*, 19).

Fig. 1.2 A Meiji-era commissioned post office, located in the postmaster's home (1909). Courtesy of the Teishin sōgō hakubutsukan.

Both Hill and Maejima recognized the importance of modern postal systems for international commerce, but they disagreed on the proper relationship between the state and the private sector in the communications realm. But as Hill's laissez-faire ideas motivated his suspicion of government monopoly, Maejima faced a dilemma over how best to administer the postal system. Should it be left to officials (*kangyō*)? Or would it suffice to allow the *hikyaku* to expand their services and subject them to a more extensive web of regulations?[68] Although the record is unclear as to what exactly drove Maejima to advocate a state-run system, his writings about state-society relations in the context of railway construction provide some clues:

Where the country is being opened, and equipped with much new knowledge, the government must be the axis of its strength, and where the knowledge of the people is as yet undeveloped, the government must become a kind and strict teacher to them. Although our country is already on the path to civilization, the people as yet possess little knowledge, and so, while they may be aware of opportunities, they cannot themselves make the most of them. Though they

68. Yamaguchi, *Maejima Hisoka*, 118.

may want to establish things themselves, they do not have the strength. Knowing that their own strength is insufficient, they may want to band together, but a mutual distrust prevents them from doing so. This is why great works cannot be achieved. Therefore, the government must become a strict teacher, and by instructing them in the means and teaching them the reasons, will gather the strength of the people, and carry out works of both convenience and benefit.[69]

While Hill had faith in the creative abilities of ordinary people and private enterprise, Maejima expressed much less confidence in his countrymen—at least during the early years of the Meiji period. In the end, Maejima sided with the prevailing views of the day that an activist, paternalistic state was best positioned to lead the country toward "civilization and enlightenment" (*bunmei kaika*)—and to carry the mail.

State paternalism found no better expression than in official directives for using the various postal services. Issued on January 24, 1871, Maejima's "Do's and Don'ts for People Mailing Letters" ("Shojō o dasu hito no kokoroe") was penned in a way that any (moderately literate) Japanese could understand: "mailing rates vary according to size and weight"; "use stamps, which are proofs of purchase"; "stamps can be purchased anywhere."[70] The mere fact that ordinary Japanese had to be taught these simple procedures is testament to the newness of prepaid mail in early Meiji Japan.

Maejima's faith in a paternalistic state should not imply that he opposed private initiative. To the contrary, he introduced a number of creative measures to encourage the growth of the private sector, but in ways that would advance the goals of the emerging state and that harkened back to the Tokugawa era. One such innovation involved the feudal *hikyaku*. Not surprisingly, the courier companies that had controlled Japan's messenger services for so many generations felt threatened by Maejima's introduction of a state-run postal system in 1871. To protest the move and drive the state out of the postal sector, the companies

---

69. Maejima Hisoka, "Tetsudō okusoku," Waseda University, Ōkuma monjo, A2816, c. 1870. Quoted in and translated by Hunter, "A Study of the Career of Maejima Hisoka," 72–73. For more on Maejima's thinking about government investment in railroad construction, see Ericson, *The Sound of the Whistle*, especially 100–102.

70. Kobayashi Masayoshi, *Minna no yūbin bunka shi*, 19–20.

colluded to drastically lower their delivery rates.[71] Maejima appealed to reason. For the sake of Japan's international relations, trade, and social intercourse—and for the overall good of Japan as a "civilized country" (*bunmei koku*)—Maejima advocated a system in which deliveries were cheap, fast, reliable, and open to all. Only the state, he insisted, had the wherewithal to build the roads and establish the nation-wide administrative networks that would make this possible. He then offered his rivals a deal that would establish the state's control over the service while allowing it to take full advantage of the private—and cost-saving—energies of the couriers: if the couriers would merge into a single firm, the state would hire that firm to transport equipment and long-distance mail.[72] The couriers accepted Maejima's offer and in 1872 merged to form the precursor of Nippon tsūun (Nittsū), one of contemporary Japan's leading parcel delivery companies. The arrangement set a precedent within the postal services for a cooperative and mutually beneficial division of labor between the public and private sectors.[73] Two years later, the government enforced a monopoly over the services that would have been the envy of Britain and other countries like the United States, where unchecked private competition posed a considerable threat to government postal functions.[74]

Maejima, who from mid-1871 was in charge of sea transport as well as communications, also orchestrated an innovative partnership between the mail service and the nascent shipping industry. Disappointed by the Meiji state's poor performance in the commercial shipping and international mail transport spheres, but well aware that foreign governments were subsidizing private shipping firms,[75] Maejima spearheaded the transfer of thirteen government-owned ships to the Mitsubishi Trad-

---

71. Yūseishō, ed., *Yūsei 100-nen no ayumi*, 31; Hunter, "A Study of the Career of Maejima Hisoka," 97–98.

72. Kobayashi Masayoshi, *Minna no yūbin bunka shi*, 133–35.

73. As Chapter 4 further illustrates, throughout the history of Japan's state-run postal system, private firms helped service the postal network by transporting the mail, repairing post office machinery, supplying uniforms for postal employees, and so on.

74. Priest, "The History of the Postal Monopoly in the United States."

75. En route to England, Maejima sailed from Yokohama to San Francisco on the Pacific Mail Steamship Line, using the occasion to quiz the ship's captain about the American government's subsidization of the line (Yamaguchi, *Maejima Hisoka*, 125).

ing Company.[76] The state then issued Mitsubishi generous yearly subsidies in return for carrying the mail to points at home and abroad. The arrangement proved a boon to Mitsubishi, which soon achieved regional and then international prominence. It also illustrates that far from being a die-hard advocate of a state-controlled economy, Maejima believed in a flexible approach to economic relations between the state and the private sector. Once again, he was giving practical expression to one of the reigning slogans of early Meiji Japan: "making use of private energies" (*minkan katsuryoku no katsuyō* or *minkatsu*),[77] a slogan that was spawned in part by financial necessity but that also reflected creative business partnerships that lent modern Japanese capitalism so much of its distinctive character.[78]

THE COMMISSIONED POSTMASTERS

Among Maejima's many innovations, none was more illustrative of the emerging state-society partnership in the postal sector than the commissioned post office system.[79] Looking to post-1840 Britain for inspiration, Maejima introduced a multi-tiered postal network that underwent several bureaucratic incarnations before coalescing in 1941 into two groups: large, state-owned facilities that were operated by civil servants as the rough equivalent of Britain's head post offices, and a network of small, privately owned commissioned post offices that were comparable to the British sub-post offices run by small shop owners. But while the sub-postmasters were paid salaries for services rendered, the commissioned postmasters received only small allowances to cover their operating expenses.[80] The unsalaried postmastership was attractive to the cash-

---

76. For an extensive analysis of this transfer, see Wray, *Mitsubishi and the N.Y.K.*

77. Yamaguchi, *Tokutei yūbinkyoku*, 12–13.

78. Maejima also advocated private investment in the expansion of the government railway network (Wray, *Mitsubishi and the N.Y.K.*, 72). Although private firms were unable to deliver, the plan further highlighted Maejima's willingness to take full advantage of private initiative in the fulfillment of state objectives. See Ericson, *The Sound of the Whistle*, 100–102.

79. The arguments in this section are loosely based on my article, "Post Office Politics in Modern Japan."

80. Yamaguchi, *Tokutei yūbinkyoku*, 36.

Fig. 1.3 Maejima Hisoka, architect of modern Japan's mail and postal savings services. Courtesy of the Teishin sōgō hakubutsukan.

strapped Meiji state because it promised to facilitate the expansion of communications without draining public coffers or forcing unpopular increases in postage rates. Officials in the new posts bureaucracy, however, were daunted by the task of recruiting candidates into such a financially unrewarding position.[81]

Maejima's solution to the challenge of recruitment was to portray the commissioned postmastership as a position of status, appealing to the ranks of former post station managers, village headmen, ex-samurai, landlords, trusted local merchants, and other local "men of distinction" (*meibōka*) whose semi-aristocratic ambitions had been frustrated by the rapid breakdown of feudal social hierarchies. Advertisements for the position stipulated that candidates had to be males aged 20 or over, well-educated residents of the communities they were to serve, and "gentle-

81. Westney, *Imitation and Innovation*, 122.

men of means" who could provide the facilities for postal operations.[82] In return for their contributions to the expansion of the postal system, the postmasters could recoup some of their local stature by designating their homes or businesses "government offices" (*oyakusho*). The scheme worked. By advertising the postmastership as a position of prestige, the government attracted well-known and fairly well-qualified candidates, some of whom jumped at the chance to participate in state building and to help lead the movement toward "civilization and enlightenment" at the local level.[83] Those worried about their financial futures, meanwhile, were free to seek supplemental employment elsewhere so long as it did not interfere with their postal duties. As for the state, recruiting well-known local notables not only saved money but also lent an aura of legitimacy and trustworthiness to the emerging postal network.[84]

The postmasters' willingness to serve the state without compensation might strike some as economically irrational, but it made good social sense. As Karl Polanyi reminds us, traditional class behavior is governed far more by "questions of social recognition" than by purely economic considerations, since "the interests of a class most directly refer to standing and rank, to status and security."[85] The genius of Maejima's innovations—and of the Meiji state more generally, given the many instances in which it mobilized traditional social forces to serve distinctly modern aims—was in recognizing that members of this small, social cohort craved a public outlet for their energies and aspirations during the chaotic transition to modernity. (As we shall see in later chapters, political considerations compelled the postmasters to continue their quest for status into the early twenty-first century, well after the *meibōka* had disappeared as a distinct social stratum.)

Thus, whereas the postmasters of larger, state-run post offices were chosen in accordance with their job experience and performance on competitive examinations, the commissioned postmasters were hand-

---

82. Maejima, *Maeijima Hisoka yūbin sōgyōdan*, 75. Unlike in Britain, Japanese women were not permitted to apply for local postmasterships until after World War II (Westney, *Imitation and Innovation*, 123).

83. Yūseishō, ed., *Yūsei 100-nen no ayumi*, 33.

84. Westney, *Imitation and Innovation*, 122.

85. Polanyi, *The Great Transformation*, 160.

Fig. 1.4 A Meiji commissioned postmaster inside his post office. Date unknown. Courtesy of the Teshin sōgō hakubutsukan.

picked by regional postal officials from among local residents and according to such non-meritocratic qualifications as local social standing and personal wealth. In short order, these feudalistic practices were institutionalized through the introduction of the equally feudalistic custom of heredity. In keeping with the stipulation that postal facilities be owned by the individuals who administered them, an increasing number of postmasterships were handed down from generation to generation, subject to the pro forma approval of regional postal officials. By the mid-twentieth century, at least half of all commissioned postmasterships were inherited.[86]

Many commissioned postmasters soon made names for themselves as officials with social standing roughly comparable to that of town and village mayors, school principals, police chiefs, Shinto priests, and the

---

86. Although it was not unusual for postmasterships to be bought and sold in Britain and the United States, Japan may be the only country in modern times in which they were routinely passed down to offspring.

heads of Buddhist temples.[87] As such, they belonged to an expanding stratum of local *meibōka* during the Meiji period that was routinely mobilized by the state to serve as intermediaries between itself and ordinary people.[88] As Carol Gluck notes, these men were periodically praised for donating to the construction of public facilities, promoting local industrial expansion, and encouraging local education. They were also called upon to convey the emperor's wishes to the people while cultivating a sense of community spirit at the grassroots level.[89] Some were even asked to represent the people to the emperor as he traveled through the countryside.[90] At one such event in 1882 in a small rural village, the emperor met with three notables, one of whom was a commissioned postmaster.[91]

Although the "contractual management system" (*ukeoiteki keiei hōshiki*) of hiring private citizens to serve as postmasters was to incite widespread opposition after World War II,[92] from the vantage point of the early Meiji period it was an innovative adaptation of traditional norms to modern ends. Encouraged to run their post offices like businesses (*eigyō*) on behalf of the public interest (*kōeki*),[93] the commissioned postmasters occupied a middle ground between state and society. As the postal system expanded, moreover, these volunteer, contracted government servants became trusted proxies for an activist, paternalistic state. They became, in short, "the arms and legs" of the state, but not so much for reasons of national security. What motivated the postmasters was a sense of social and economic mission inculcated in part by Maejima's views on the functions of the postal services in a modernizing society.

---

87. Katsumata, *Tokutei yūbinkyoku konjaku monogatari*, 45.

88. Ushiki, *Chihō meibōka no seichō*, 7.

89. Gluck, *Japan's Modern Myths*, 95, 202.

90. Ibid., 95.

91. Westney, *Imitation and Innovation*, 123.

92. Ogawa and Takahashi, *Tokutei yūbinkyoku seido shi*, 22. After World War II, the distinctive process of hiring commissioned postmasters was commonly called the "free employment" (*jiyū nin'yō*) system.

93. Yamaguchi, *Tokutei yūbinkyoku*, 13.

Contributing to Modernity

With his image emblazoned on postwar postage stamps commemorating the founding of the postal services, Maejima is best known in contemporary Japan as the "father of mail" (*yūbin no chichi*). What is less known about Maejima is the extent to which he (and his successors) looked to the postal system as a medium not only for the transmission of mail, but also for fulfilling a number of interrelated state objectives: developing Japan's economic and financial infrastructure at the formative stages of the country's industrial development; nurturing key industries; facilitating the social welfare of ordinary Japanese; expanding the reach of the state both at home and abroad; and even contributing to the mass incorporation of ordinary Japanese into the new polity.[94] In short, Maejima and his successors believed that the postal system had a *mission* to perform for Japanese society at this important juncture in its history—a mission that took the Japanese post office significantly beyond what Rowland Hill had envisioned for the post-1840 British postal system. As the remainder of this chapter illustrates, for ordinary Japanese that mission gradually transformed the post office into arguably the most prominent representative of the state at the local level, with far-reaching implications for the acclimation of ordinary Japanese to modern daily life, the modern state, and the country's emerging sense of nationhood.

Among the postal system's most fundamental accomplishments was its impact on the expansion of road and railroad networks. As the Meiji state set out to establish post offices in all major parts of the country—an objective that was more or less achieved within a year of the system's inauguration—it became all the more cognizant of the country's deteriorating road conditions.[95] The state's commitment to extend the postal network thus served as an effective incentive to improve those roads. Comparable trends can be seen in the United States, where the construction of new post roads during the nineteenth century was essential to nation building and the expansion of the frontier. But while new road construction was led by individual congressmen eager to pro-

94. As Westney writes, "The volume of mail in a country is one of the most commonly used indicators of integration and modernization" (*Imitation and Innovation*, 142).

95. By August 1872 post offices had been established throughout Honshu, Shikoku, Kyushu, and even in parts of Hokkaido. Yūseishō, ed., *Yūsei 100-nen no ayumi*, 30.

vide essential services to their expanding constituencies,[96] road expansion in Meiji Japan was controlled primarily by bureaucrats.[97]

The mail service also spurred road expansion in Britain, but the success of this interactive process, which spanned several centuries, was heavily dependent on the whims of local authorities. By 1840, when the nationwide Penny Post was introduced, the postal network was more or less complete and the nation was setting its sights on rail transport. Innovations in the conveyance of mail were thus almost exclusively focused on the emerging rail network.[98]

Although road expansion was the major priority for the early Meiji postal system, Maejima also took great pains to wed the mail service to the country's nascent rail system. Maejima advocated the development of a railroad system on its own merits, arguing that it would spread knowledge, encourage production, and nurture national unity.[99] But he also recognized its utility for the transport of mail, arranging for a mail car to be hitched to the country's first train before it commenced service between Tokyo and Yokohama in 1872. As Westney notes, however, it took nearly twenty years before the railroad system was sufficiently developed to assume the bulk of mail transport. In the interim, the mail was carried from point to point by horse-drawn carriages, uniformed runners, and, eventually, ships.[100]

The postal system also served as the primary avenue for the diffusion of telegraph and telephone services. Japan's first telegraph was a gift from Commodore Perry during his second visit to the country in 1854. The gesture immediately ignited demand for a domestic telegraph service.[101] Recognizing the technology's political and military significance, the Meiji state established Japan's first public telegraph service between Tokyo and Yokohama in 1870. Similar services were introduced between

96. Fuller, *The American Mail*, 44–45; see also Fowler, *The Cabinet Politician*, and Rogers, *The Postal Power of Congress*.

97. During the Taishō period (1912–1926), the Diet assumed more responsibility for overseeing road construction following its enactment of the 1919 Road Law. But I was unable to find evidence that this power was manipulated for electoral purposes.

98. Daunton, *The Royal Mail*, xviii, 36.

99. Hunter, "A Study of the Career of Maejima Hisoka," 71–72.

100. Westney, *Imitation and Innovation*, 120–21.

101. Yūseishō, ed., *Yūsei 100-nen no ayumi*, 13.

Kyoto and Osaka in 1872, and the following year Japan sent its first cable abroad, from Nagasaki to Shanghai.[102] When the Ministry of Communications (Teishinshō) was established in 1885, it assumed jurisdiction over both the postal services and telecommunications.[103] By the end of the decade, local post offices were transmitting cables around the country in much the same fashion as their British counterparts following the nationalization of telegraph services in 1870.[104] But the telegraph was not as popular initially as the mail service among ordinary Japanese. Few could afford to send telegrams, while others viewed them as instruments of the politically powerful or, more ominously, as manifestations of dreaded "Christian magic." Some threw rocks at the telegraph lines, which symbolized yet another unwanted intrusion into their lives.[105] But the Japanese soon grew accustomed to the telegraph, viewing the appearance of poles and wires in their neighborhoods as a sign of prosperity.[106] In short order, local groups were pressuring the authorities to extend the services to their areas.

Once again looking to Britain as a model, Maejima, in his elevated capacity as vice minister of communications, successfully added telephone exchange services to the post offices' expanding roster of responsibilities.[107] Aware of the strategic and economic importance of this new technology and the fact that the private sector lacked the financial wherewithal to install a network nationwide, Maejima helped launch a state-owned service in 1890. With offices in most communities of the country, the postal system was the most cost-effective venue for providing exchange services to ordinary Japanese, as well as direct access to telephones to those who were too poor to acquire instruments of their own. Like the telegraph, the new technology fueled local superstitions; in 1890, it was rumored that telephones had sparked a cholera outbreak.[108]

---

102. Yūseishō, ed., *Yūsei 100-nen shi*, 49–53.

103. For a history of the Japanese telecommunications industry, see Vogel, *Freer Markets, More Rules*, Chapter 7.

104. Yamaguchi, *Tokutei yūbinkyoku*, 42; Daunton, *The Royal Mail*, p. xv.

105. Yūseishō, ed., *Yūsei 100-nen no ayumi*, 18–19.

106. Nagao, "Communications in Japan," 350.

107. Yūseishō, ed., *Yūsei 100-nen no ayumi*, 60–61.

108. Nagao, "Communications in Japan," 354.

Fig. 1.5 Female telephone operators in a large, urban post office (1896). The post office was one the few places where prewar Japanese women could work, but they were not permitted to become postmasters until after 1945. Courtesy of Teishin sōgō hakubutsukan.

But such fears soon subsided as ordinary Japanese came to recognize the telephone's many conveniences.

In time, the local post office also housed the neighborhood radio, giving residents yet another reason to congregate there. On August 15, 1945, it was at the post office that many rural Japanese listened to the emperor's infamous surrender address. In this way, the local post office functioned until well after World War II as a community hub and, in some cases, the village's only link to news from the capital.[109]

The post office's role in disseminating information was further strengthened by its conveyance of newspapers and its contributions to the development of a national newspaper industry. Maejima was eager to promote newspaper publishing and a mass readership, both of which he felt were essential to the development of a modern polity.[110] In reaction to the paucity of Japanese-language newspapers—only one, the

---

109. Maeno, *21-seiki wa Yūseishō no jidai*, 176.
110. Kobayashi Masayoshi, *Minna no yūbin bunka shi*, 147.

Yokohama Mainichi shinbun, existed in 1871—Maejima partnered with a friend-cum-postmaster and amateur publisher to produce, from 1872, the *Yūbin hōchi shinbun* (The Post Intelligence Newspaper). Resembling more a contemporary magazine than a newspaper, early issues of this government-sponsored publication offered information about local products, farming conditions, and natural disasters, as well as gossip and stories of strange goings-on.[111] On the covers were reproductions of colorful wood-block prints, some of them downright tawdry. In time, the newspaper was associated with the politics and thinking of Maejima's mentor and ally, Ōkuma Shigenobu, Ōkuma's political party (Kaishintō), and the Freedom and Popular Rights Movement. But with the movement's decline the newspaper's readership shrank. When the paper changed its name to the *Hōchi shinbun* in 1894, its association with the postal service waned.[112]

The *Yūbin hōchi shinbun* was the first national newspaper in modern Japan to be distributed through the post office at reduced rates—a privilege that was quickly extended to other newspapers. (Similar trends occurred in both Britain and the United States.) Although postmasters and mail carriers alike grumbled about the weight of the papers and the fact that their distribution produced scant income,[113] the expansion of the newspaper industry grew heavily dependent on the postal service. At Maejima's instigation, the postal network conveyed newspaper copy for free. Maejima also took the novel step of publishing official directives to the postal network in one of the newspapers, in lieu of issuing an official—and more costly—gazette (*kanpō*). And so, from July 3, 1883, in yet another innovative example of "making use of private energies," the postmasters throughout the land began reading the *Tōkyō Nichinichi shinbun* each Tuesday.[114] This proved to be a shot in the arm for the newspaper, which later merged with an Osaka-based paper to become the *Mainichi shinbun.*

Another area in which the postal system helped ordinary Japanese transition into the modern world was public finance. In 1875, the gov-

---

111. Yamaguchi, *Maejima Hisoka,* 141.
112. The newspaper still exists today and is devoted to sports coverage (*Sports Hōchi*).
113. Kobayashi Masayoshi, *Minna no yūbin bunka shi,* 150.
114. Ibid., 152.

ernment introduced a British-style postal money order (*yūbin kawase*) service that greatly benefited ordinary Japanese. During the Tokugawa period, special couriers known as "money messengers" (*kane-bikyaku*) conveyed the bulk of financial remittances, but the service was costly, slow, and highly vulnerable to theft.[115] Introduced at Maejima's suggestion, the new money order system promised to ease financial transactions among small businesses and between them and their customers. Although at first only a few urban post offices were able to offer and accept the money orders, since cashing them required substantial reserves,[116] the service soon proliferated in response to public demand.

Also in 1875, Maejima launched a British-style postal savings system. Designed to attract the income of smaller savers at a time when the commercial banking system was still in its infancy,[117] the system helped inculcate a culture of thrift within the population. Postal savings accounts also enabled the Meiji state to reduce its dependence on foreign capital by supplying it with a reservoir of funds for investment in new industries, infrastructural development, and military campaigns.[118]

Shortly after the Meiji Restoration, few Japanese were aware that one's assets could be deposited outside the home for safekeeping. A culture of thrift had been conspicuously absent from among the feudal aristocracy and general public, as illustrated by the popular saying, "trying to get one *sen* to last from one day to the next is shameful."[119] As Sheldon Garon notes, Tokugawa authorities may have encouraged ordinary Japanese to practice frugality in their consumption habits, but they did not promote *savings* per se for fear that the accumulated funds

---

115. Yūseishō, ed., *Yūsei 100-nen no ayumi*, 39.

116. Ibid., 40–41.

117. At first, postal savings was known simply as *chokin,* or "savings." In 1887, it was officially dubbed *yūbin chokin*—postal savings (Matsubara, *Gendai no yūbin jigyō,* 102).

118. Scher and Yoshino, "Introduction," 3. For analyses (in English) of the postal savings system and the prewar savings habits of the Japanese, see Ferber, "'Run the State Like a Business'"; Garon, "'Luxury is the Enemy'"; Garon, "Fashioning a Culture of Diligence and Thrift"; Garon, *Beyond Our Means,* especially Chapters 4 and 5; and Rosenbluth, *Financial Politics in Contemporary Japan.*

119. Yoshino, "Policy Challenges and the Reform of Postal Savings in Japan," 122.

一銭ヲ笑フ者ハ
一銭ニ泣ク

百万ノ富モ
一銭カラ

内務省勤倹奨励中央委員會

Fig. 1.6   One of many savings promotion posters issued by the Japanese government (1914). "Amassing a million begins with the first *sen*." Courtesy of the Teishin sōgō hakubutsukan.

would be used to challenge the standing of local lords.[120] Those who were inclined to save, moreover, had few opportunities to do so. Households could deposit their money with a money exchange (*ryōgaeshō*), but the service was not widely trusted; nor did the deposits earn interest.[121] For lack of a better option, most Japanese stashed their hard-earned cash in a wardrobe (*tansu*) or large jar or pot (*tsubo*).

As a state institution, the postal savings system offered several perquisites to small-scale depositors, namely a small amount of interest and a government guarantee on deposits. Nevertheless, the system was slow to expand during its first year or two. At issue were strict limits on the minimum and maximum amounts that could be deposited, the onerous paperwork and long waiting periods associated with deposits

120. Garon, *Beyond Our Means*, 123–24.
121. Hara and Yamaguchi, *Yūbin chokin*, 128.

and withdrawals, and the small number of post offices that were initially authorized to take part in the system. In 1876–1877, as the government expanded the number of post offices that could engage in postal savings transactions, raised interest rates, lowered minimum deposit requirements, and reduced unnecessary red tape, the number of depositors—as well as total deposits—began to rise. The popularity of postal savings increased even further in the wake of Finance Minister Matsukata Masayoshi's (1835–1924) early 1880s deflationary policies, which forced struggling commercial banks to lower interest rates.[122] Although the system never provided depositors with high returns, it continued to attract substantial deposits from households and small businesses for well over a century.

It appears that the postal money order and postal savings services played a more prominent role in the financial lives of ordinary Japanese than they did in Britain. In nineteenth-century Britain, postal money orders competed with private and other official money order services for the patronage of craftsmen, small shopkeepers, and others not served by the commercial banks;[123] the Post Office Savings Bank competed against other financial institutions for small-scale deposits almost from the start. In Japan, postal money orders were the only viable remittance service available to ordinary people in the decade following the Restoration, just as the postal savings system was the only available savings institution. The cost-effective postal money orders and the postal savings system remained popular even after the expansion of the commercial banking system from the 1880s. This in turn contributed to the post office's stature as the center of local financial transactions—a distinction that the British post offices never quite matched.

As these financial services expanded, so did mail-related services designed to nurture industry, commerce, and agriculture. As Hunter illustrates, Meiji farmers and businessmen benefited from postal regulations that allowed them to send seed samples, commercial samples, and other

---

122. Ibid., 129–35.

123. This does not mean, however, that the English postal money order system floundered; to the contrary, for much of the nineteenth century it was better positioned than private financial services to offer secure and nationwide remittances of small sums of money. See Daunton, *The Royal Mail*, 84–91.

designated items through the mail at reduced rates. Provisions were also introduced to facilitate the exchange of specialized economic information, such as share certificates and industrial and agricultural circulars.[124] Japan was certainly not alone in terms of using the postal services to promote economic development; such practices were also the norm in Britain, the United States, and many other countries. What sets the Japanese case apart is the timing of the postal system's expansion in relation to industrialization. Although statistical data establishing the exact nature of the relationship between the postal system and economic growth are scarce, it is fair to say that had the state not introduced these financial and mail services during the formative stages of rapid industrial and agricultural development, the rate and patterns of Japan's economic modernization might have been notably different.

By the end of World War I, the postal system had also expanded into the social welfare sector with the introduction of a postal life insurance system (*kan'i hoken*, or *kanpo*). Maejima had campaigned long and hard for such a system, but the project languished for lack of reliable death-rate statistics and the inability of ordinary Japanese to purchase life insurance policies.[125] A number of private firms tried to enter the insurance industry from the 1880s, but most were unstable and ultimately failed.[126] In 1902, a Communications official named Shimomura Hiroshi resurrected the idea of a postal life insurance program after observing first-hand the successful Belgian program.[127] (Britain's service did not provide a precedent for Japan in this instance. Shortly after its introduction during the mid-nineteenth century, it succumbed to competition from both private-sector insurance companies and local "friendly societies."[128]) After several years of foot-dragging, the government launched the service in 1916; ten years later, it introduced a small-scale pension program. The insurance service proved immediately accessible to ordinary Japanese, since it offered low premiums and con-

---

124. For a detailed analysis of how postal services contributed to nineteenth-century industrial development, see Hunter, "Understanding the Economic History of Postal Services."

125. Matsubara, *Gendai no yūsei jigyō*, 107.

126. Yūseishō, ed., *Yūsei 100-nen no ayumi*, 104.

127. Matsubara, *Gendai no yūsei jigyō*, 107.

128. Daunton, *The Royal Mail*, 106.

venient monthly payment schemes and did not require its policyholders
to undergo medical examinations. Its popularity can also be attributed
to the willingness of postal employees to pound the pavement in search
of new policyholders, a task the British postmasters and postal workers
were unwilling to undertake.[129] *Kanpo* monopolized the Japanese life insurance sector until 1946, when private companies finally re-entered the
market.[130]

But *kanpo* did far more than offer Japanese low-cost insurance policies. From the early 1920s, the service established a network of social
welfare centers for the insured that functioned as an important arm
of government health policy. Known as "health consultation centers"
(*kenkō sōdanjo*), the facilities—which had no close counterpart abroad—
were designed to fulfill one of the service's primary objectives: lowering
mortality rates.[131] Thus, the centers were mandated during the 1930s to
diagnose infectious diseases like tuberculosis and to distribute information on preventative medicine, while a select number of urban facilities
conducted advanced medical research. By 1939, there were 321 centers
around the country. Those that survived the fire bombings of World
War II went on to provide medical services during the chaotic early years
of the Occupation.[132] Although some of the centers were eventually
closed down, many others were converted into hospitals (*teishin byōin*) for
postal employees, medical clinics for the insured, and local recreation
centers. The recreation centers were especially popular among the elderly as venues for social interaction.

Lowering mortality rates also drove the Ministry of Communication's
decision to launch "radio calisthenics" (*rajio taisō*) in 1928, the year Emperor Hirohito formally ascended the throne. Broadcast by NHK, this
unique Japanese program was aired during the early mornings in community spaces like parks and schoolyards, catering to women, the elderly,
and school children. Participants received special cards from their nearby
post offices that they had stamped after each session. Before long, the

---

129. Ibid., 110.
130. Matsubara, *Gendai no yūsei jigyō*, 108.
131. Kobayashi Masayoshi, *Minna no yūbin bunka shi*, 129.
132. Yūseishō, ed., *Yūsei 100-nen shi*, 657.

健康相談と巡回看護

小兒保險の被保險者も利用出來ます

簡易保險健康相談所

Fig. 1.7   The Postal Insurance Health Consultation Centers performed numerous public health services for those insured by the post office. "Insured children can also use it" (1931). Courtesy of the Teishin sōgō hakubutsukan.

broadcasts were occasions for social interaction as well as physical exercise, and were heavily attended by those who had few other opportunities to exercise.[133] Today, so-called radio calisthenics are supported by an official website that provides information about scheduling as well as detailed illustrations of different exercises.[134]

These information, financial, and health services helped fulfill Maejima's vision of the postal system as a *social* institution that could contribute to the greater public good. But the postal system also played important political and national security functions in pre-1945 Japan. In 1925, the government allowed politicians to mail election materials to their constituents without charge. Ostensibly designed to help cut

133. Kobayashi Masayoshi, *Minna no yūbin bunka shi*, 102–3.

134. For more on radio calisthenics, see http://www.jp-life.japanpost.jp/aboutus/csr/radio/abt_csr_rdo_index.html (last accessed July 25, 2011).

the costs of elections as the franchise expanded,[135] the measure helped ordinary Japanese acclimate themselves to the objectives and practices of modern elections.

The postal system also helped spearhead Japan's territorial expansion both at home and abroad. As Hunter observes, the Meiji state coupled the extension of postal services to its territorial claims in Hokkaido and the Ryukyus (Okinawa). During a dispute with Qing China in the 1870s, for instance, the state pointed to its post offices in the Ryukyus as proof of Japanese sovereignty over the islands. In later years, the post offices eased the state's expansion into Hokkaido and the Ryukyus by serving as a precedent for the introduction of other official institutions in those territories.[136] Ever the patriot, Maejima was an enthusiastic advocate of the postal system as a conduit for the country's territorial ambitions. And while he deeply resented foreign incursions onto Japanese sovereignty, he pressed for the introduction of Japanese postal and other institutions in China, Taiwan, and Korea. Accordingly, Japan established post offices in Shanghai in 1876 and in Taiwan after the Sino-Japanese War (1894–1895).[137] In April 1905, as the Russo-Japanese War drew to a close and just five years before annexing Korea, Japan seized control of the peninsula's telephone, telegraph, and mail systems.[138] For better or worse, the postal system had become an advance man for Japanese imperial expansion.[139] Back home, the postal system helped sell the state's foreign policy to the Japanese people. Many of its prewar commemorative stamps, for example, were issued to mark Japanese victories in battle.[140]

The postal system also contributed to British territorial expansion, but in different ways. Historically, as we have seen, the postal network functioned as a mechanism through which the Crown extended its control over the land, but this process occurred haphazardly over the span of centuries, not years. During the mid- to late seventeenth century, in

---

135. Yūseishō, ed., *Yūsei 100-nen no ayumi*, 132.

136. Hunter, "A Study of the Career of Maejima Hisoka," 116–18.

137. Ibid., 121.

138. Duus, *The Abacus and the Sword*, 185, 187n.

139. Yoshida, "Yūseishō enkaku shōshi," 76.

140. Commemorative stamps also extolled the virtues of the emperor system. Japan's first commemorative stamp, issued in 1894, marked the twenty-fifth anniversary of the Meiji emperor's wedding (Yūseishō, ed., *Yūsei 100-nen shi*, 216, 308).

an effort to improve communications with the colonies, the Crown turned its attention to the colonial posts in America. At first, the Crown contracted the colonial posts to self-interested individuals of dubious administrative ability, resulting in mail services that were costly, inefficient, and largely limited to the conveyance of official communications. In 1711, Parliament passed legislation that subjected the colonial post offices to more direct bureaucratic control, but for largely economic reasons. The move was meant to raise revenue to help defray the costs of British involvement in the War of the Spanish Succession. Benjamin Franklin, who became postmaster of Philadelphia in 1737, balked at the resulting hikes in postage rates, remarking, along with other critics, that the postal system had become yet another form of unjust taxation.[141] Put simply, the British colonial postal system's revenue-gathering functions preempted its transformation into a strategically significant instrument of state expansion, while weakening its effectiveness as an avenue for communications both within the colonies and between them and London.[142]

Closer to home, the late nineteenth-century Japanese post office had become a conduit for the dissemination of modern values, including thrift, patriotism, and even modern conceptualizations of time. While late Tokugawa farmers had come to appreciate the notion of time as they adjusted to the demands of seasonable labor and by-employment,[143] it was not until the Meiji era that they were systematically introduced to the virtues of punctuality. As Gluck writes, instilling a deeper appreciation of time and punctuality among ordinary subjects—particularly in the countryside—was an important component of the Meiji state's broader objective of reforming backward social customs:

---

141. William Smith, "The Colonial Post-Office."

142. The post-independence American post office played a far more active role than its British counterpart in the processes of territorial consolidation. As Richard John explains, since the post office provided Americans on the frontier with a direct link to *both* the federal government and the national economy, citizens actively petitioned their congressmen to have post offices built in their communities. Roughly three decades after the passage of the 1792 Post Office Act, the process of building a national system of post roads was more or less complete (*Spreading the News*, 46–52).

143. Thomas C. Smith, "Peasant Time and Factory Time in Japan," 167.

When local "punctuality associations" [*jishukai*] were formed, the Home Ministry praised them. Clocks, which had been quintessential symbols of civilization in the early Meiji period, were regarded as obvious aids to punctuality. Provincial officials thus encouraged them, landlords sometimes mounted them on the gable ends of their houses to make tenants aware of the time as they worked in the fields, and some village plans counted the number possessed by families in the community.[144]

Historians are less aware that both the post office and the mail service—the success of which rests in part on predictable mail deliveries—were also reminders to ordinary Japanese subjects of the importance of punctuality.[145] In 1871, the government ordered eight-cornered clocks from abroad for use in domestic post offices. Many postal workers had never seen such contraptions and had to be taught how to use them. In 1874, the government required all post offices to have clocks on display. Nine years later, mail carriers were obliged to carry a timepiece; those who were late with their deliveries had their wages docked.[146] With the introduction of telephone services, Japan devised an even more sophisticated way of marking the time: at noon each day, the Central Telephone Office in Tokyo would throw a switch to illuminate a red light in post offices around the country.[147] Meanwhile, ordinary Japanese acquired a heightened appreciation of the rhythms of modern daily life simply by visiting the local post office or keeping an eye out for the postman, who, like postmen in all modern societies, showed up on their doorsteps at roughly the same time each day.[148]

Key to the post office's modernizing influence was the commissioned postmaster. To a significant degree, the postal system's integration into local society and performance of a variety of communications, financial,

---

144. Gluck, *Japan's Modern Myths*, 184.

145. Historians have shown that timepieces were adopted at a much faster rate by public institutions like post offices and railway stations than by households during the early Meiji period. See Uchida, "The Spread of Timepieces in the Meiji Period," 183.

146. Kobayashi Masayoshi, *Minna no yūbin bunka shi*, 53–54, 122.

147. Ibid., 54.

148. In a similar vein, Steven Ericson shows how early Meiji train travel also influenced popular conceptualizations of time and punctuality (*The Sound of the Whistle*, 69–73).

Fig. 1.8 In many prewar rural villages, postal employees served as the sole interface between the state and local residents (1937). Courtesy of the Teishin sōgō hakubutsukan.

and social services rested on the postmaster's elevated position within social networks.[149] Maejima was no doubt aware of this when he instructed the postmasters to collect information about local events and conditions on behalf of the country's nascent newspapers.[150] Even more significant was the postmaster's efforts to instill ideas about modern finance and thrift in local communities. To be sure, the postal savings system's growing popularity owed much to the government's guarantee of postal savings accounts and its carefully orchestrated campaigns to encourage ordinary Japanese to save.[151] But the postmaster's leadership also mattered. Few locals were better situated to convey the state's exhortation to save and to serve as caretaker of the people's hard-earned cash than the local postmaster—a man of repute who, unlike the faceless banking employee, was widely perceived to be working on behalf of the

149. Yamaguchi, *Tokutei yūbinkyoku*, 8.

150. Kobayashi Masayoshi, *Minna no yūbin bunka shi*, 152.

151. For more detailed analysis of these campaigns, see Garon, "Fashioning a Culture of Diligence and Thrift."

public interest, as opposed to his own financial gain. Many postmasters went to great lengths to teach the locals about thrift and why postal savings were essential to the well-being of the nation; some even held public "picture-story shows" (*kamishibai*) about the postal savings system after regular working hours.[152] The postmasters were especially important in this regard during wartime. At the height of World War II, a high-ranking official of the Ministry of Communications counseled a group of nineteen representatives from the national postmasters association that "your work is a battlefield [*senjō*]. Since the success or failure of your efforts to increase savings deposits will have a major influence on wartime finances and thus the outcome of the war, it is absolutely imperative that you meet your targets!"[153]

The postmasters' contributions to the "common good" often carried a stiff financial price, as illustrated by the expansion of the telephone system. During the early 1890s, setting up services in a single village cost as much as 3,000 yen, a hefty sum at a time when the starting salary for most schoolteachers was a mere 10 yen per month.[154] Since the state could provide only minimal financial assistance to establish the necessary facilities, the onus fell on village governments and the postmasters themselves. A few postmasters were able to cover a significant portion of these costs and to eventually recoup some or all of their investments, but others were reduced to borrowing funds or selling off some of their land holdings.[155] Not a few postmasters succumbed to these financial pressures and gave up their postmasterships. In time, more and more postmasters were able to draw on the funds of self-help associations established with the contributions of their colleagues.[156] Some of these "postmasters' societies" (*kyokuchō kyōkai*) obtained legal status as foundations (*zaidan hōjin*)—yet another example of the state's willingness to endorse private solutions to problems in the postal sector.

------

152. Kyūshū chihō tokutei yūbinkyokuchōkai, *Kyūshū tokutei yūbinkyokuchōkai shi*, 95.

153. Ibid. The postmasters were required to fulfill government-designated targets for the sale of life insurance policies and the establishment of postal savings accounts. See Chapter 3 for a description of such targets during the postwar period.

154. Yamaguchi, *Tokutei yūbinkyoku*, 62–65.

155. Kyūshū chihō tokutei yūbinkyokuchōkai, *Kyūshū tokutei yūbinkyokuchōkai shi*, 90–91, 115–16; Yamaguchi, *Tokutei yūbinkyoku*, 64.

156. Yamaguchi, *Tokutei yūbinkyoku*, 174.

The postmaster's reputation as the self-sacrificing caretaker of a trust-worthy institution was dramatically illustrated by the postal system's response to the 1923 Great Kantō Earthquake. In the fires that followed the quake, the Ministry of Communications building in Tokyo suffered damage, scores of postal employees were killed or injured, and 197 post offices were destroyed and many more damaged.[157] But while the Ministry of Finance put a moratorium on withdrawals from the commercial banks, those post offices that remained standing took steps to help local residents. They disseminated official directives and information in an effort to preserve the peace and get medical attention to those who needed it. They also devised an emergency withdrawal procedure for the postal savings system. Two days after the quake, the post offices allowed depositors to withdraw up to 30 yen each day. Those who had lost their passbooks were allowed as much as 10 yen a day.[158] Later, makeshift offices were set up to make payments to the beneficiaries of postal life insurance policies—even though many of those beneficiaries now lacked the necessary documentation.[159] By putting its trust in their depositors, the system enhanced its own trustworthiness.[160]

This is not to conclude that the post offices and the men who led them were paragons of virtue and economic innovation. To the contrary, and as the next two chapters illustrate, the historical record contains numerous examples of postmasters who did not meet acceptable performance standards. This is hardly surprising given the financial pressures confronting the salary-less postmasters. To help make ends meet, the postmasters before 1945 were permitted to hold second jobs, so long as they did not work for the commercial banks—the "competition"—or in occupations that distracted them from their postal duties.[161] Most worked for local companies or established their own small businesses.

---

157. Yūseishō, ed., *Yūsei 100-nen no ayumi*, 424.

158. Hara and Yamaguchi, *Yūbin chokin*, 151.

159. Ibid.; Yūseishō, ed., *Yūsei 100-nen shi*, 420–26.

160. Yūseishō, ed., *Yūsei 100-nen no ayumi*, 122.

161. In time, the postmasters were forbidden to become doctors, lawyers, accountants, notary publics, local or prefectural officials, union officials, employees of insurance or investment firms, or newspaper or magazine publishers/managers. Some of these positions were deemed conflicts of interest; others too time consuming (Yūsei daijin kanbō chōsaka, "Tokuteikyoku no enkaku," 7).

Others—as many as 2,000 out of 13,000 postmasters by the end of World War II—were elected to local (city, town, and village) assemblies.[162] Some postmasters reneged on their postal duties as they focused their attention on more lucrative or politically exciting ventures, ordering their ill-prepared wives or other family members to tend to their official responsibilities.

The postal workers, meanwhile, grew increasingly unhappy. By the turn of the century the post offices were employing women,[163] but postal workers in general complained of low wages, arduous workloads that increased with the expansion of each service, and long work days.[164] (Post offices that offered telegraph services required their employees to make late-night deliveries in all kinds of weather.) Some employees, like the author Tsuboi Sakae (1899–1967), who went to work as the lone employee in a commissioned post office during the 1920s at the age of fifteen,[165] found themselves in charge of just about everything, including the training of other employees after hours with no overtime pay. The following entry from Tsuboi's memoirs, in which she recounts a visit to her former place of employment after a lengthy absence, is a narrow but revealing snapshot of both the everyday contributions of the prewar post office to local life and the burdens shouldered by its employees:

And so, twenty years have passed. Each time I return I see that the line-up of employees has changed. Now that there are telegraph machines in the facility, men are employed. In my day, cables were sent over the phone. Now, I'm surprised by the incessant clatter of the telegraph machine. The post office has

---

162. Zenkoku tokutei yūbinkyokuchōkai, *Tokuteikyoku taikan*, vol. 1, 20.

163. Post office work was one of the few employment opportunities for women during the late nineteenth and early twentieth centuries. Women were first hired as telephone operators during the early 1890s. As the post office's responsibilities grew, women were gradually permitted to work in the mail and financial services; applicants had to be literate and skilled in bookkeeping. But women were not authorized to become postmasters until after World War II (Zenkoku tokutei yūbinkyoku kyokuchō dairikai, *Zenkoku tokutei yūbinkyoku kyokuchō dairikai sanjūnenshi*, 11).

164. In 1925, a government study revealed that a postman earned 58.8 percent of the wages of a railroad conductor (Yūseishō, ed., *Yūsei 100-nen shi*, 563).

165. Tsuboi joined the post office to help lighten her family's financial problems.

Fig. 1.9   The number of female mail carriers increased steadily as men were sent off to war (1944). Courtesy of the Teishin sōgō hakubutsukan.

also grown in size and there's a new postmaster. What hasn't changed, however, is the sight of the young girls at the wickets writing out postcards (*hagaki*) for their customers. The smaller of the two girls, by the name of Miss Otoku, made me feel vaguely nostalgic. . . . She was about the age that I was when I began work there. There were now four employees, two men and two girls. I recalled those days in the past when I had toiled there alone, even while sick, taking in telegrams late into the night.[166]

Conclusion

While the laments of the prewar postal workers bespoke a working environment that fell far short of the labor standards of postwar Japan, they were also indicative of the postal system's multifaceted significance. Serving at once as a bank, insurance company, provider of social welfare services, and conduit for the dissemination of information and correspondence, the postal system helped fuel the growth of commerce, national finance, public health, transportation, and the expansion of state

166. Tsuboi, *Ippon no matchi*, 82–83.

authority. In the process, the local post office helped disseminate and re-inforce many of the values that became synonymous with modern Japan: the prioritization of financial security and risk aversion over long-term profit; state paternalism; thrift; duty to the nation; and an emphasis on mass literacy and education, to mention just a few. To be sure, schools, neighborhood associations (*chōnaikai*), women's groups (*fujinkai*), and the political parties also conveyed these values to the public before 1945. What distinguished the postal system from these other institutions was its penetration into *multiple* spheres—communications, social, financial, political, and even medical.

The postal system's broad reach distinguished it from its British counterpart. This discrepancy can be partly explained by the nature of the system that the Meiji state inherited from Japan's feudal past. Compared to the pre-1840 British system, the Tokugawa network of post stations was considerably more centralized and uniformly regulated, and the qualifications of its postmasters significantly higher. These features created a precedent for the establishment of an even more centralized, state-run system following the Meiji Restoration, and for the appointment of "men of distinction" as local postmasters.

Also important was the timing of the postal system's introduction. That the state and the modern postal system were introduced simultaneously helps explain why the system was mobilized far more frequently than its post-1840 British counterpart to perform tasks of a public and even political nature, such as venturing into uncharted territory and providing medical care and financial services to the general population. Since the post office offered many services for which there was no viable competition from the private sector, moreover, it gradually assumed a more prominent position as a financial, communications, and even social hub than the British post office, which was modernized *after* many competing financial and other institutions had already been established. This is not to underestimate the importance of the British post office for local society; as Martin Daunton notes, by the early twentieth century it had also become "more than a place to mail a letter," providing financial services and pension payments and issuing government licenses.[167] But in Japan, the postal system's birth at the start of the modernization process

---

167. Daunton, *The Royal Mail*, 111–12.

positioned it to offer a broader range of innovative services and to function as a major channel for state influence over the population.

It is important not to overstate the Japanese postal system's significance. One area in which the postal system did not fulfill its potential as a "modern" institution was the public sphere. In the United States, as Richard John explains, the post office's nineteenth-century expansion into the hinterland and conveyance of newspapers at low rates nurtured the development of an independent, democratic public sphere that went on to transform the parameters of American public life.[168] In Japan, the post office functioned as a vehicle for incorporating the masses into the post-1868 polity by educating ordinary subjects on the goals of the state and instilling in them an appreciation for state-sanctioned values. There is virtually no evidence to suggest that the post office contributed to the development of basic freedoms that are the stuff of a vibrant public sphere. Put simply, the post office was an agent of the state, not of the people.

The timing of the postal system's institutional development and its multi-functionality laid much of the groundwork for the politicization of the postal services after World War II. The practice of state investments of postal savings deposits and life insurance premiums was systematized with the postwar establishment of the FILP; as the FILP grew, so did political party maneuverings for a piece of the action. The commissioned postmasters, for their own part, emerged from the war a remarkably homogeneous cohort that was united by pride, a history of personal sacrifice, and a deep-seated commitment to preserve the institutions and values of the commissioned post office system; conservative politicians soon turned to them for electoral support. In short order, as Chapters 2 and 3 explain, these postmasters found themselves at the center of a dense web of political and bureaucratic ties that nurtured LDP rule and served as a brake on postal reform.

---

168. John, *Spreading the News*, 54.

TWO

Public Servants with Private Interests: Postwar Commissioned Postmasters and the Politics of Self-Preservation

The first decade after World War II was a pivotal time in the political history of the postal system.[1] Three-quarters of a century after its establishment, the system was subjected to a host of reforms that promised to both modernize and democratize it. But the period also witnessed the deliberate preservation of key values and practices that had lent the commissioned post offices their semi-feudal aura in the past, and that would continue to do so for decades to come. Moreover, it was during this time that the postmasters established or strengthened institutional ties to both politicians and bureaucrats, laying the groundwork for a triangular relationship that was to influence national elections and policymaking for more than half a century.

This chapter takes another step toward explaining the politicization of the Japanese postal system by chronicling the development of the postwar commissioned postmasters as an interest group. To that end, I explore the pre- and postwar history of the postmasters' representative organizations, the threats and opportunities that shaped their organiza-

---

1. Some of the material in this chapter and Chapter 3 also appears in Maclachlan, "Post Office Politics in Modern Japan."

tional objectives, the nature of their institutionalized links with conservative politicians and bureaucrats, and the sources of their national electoral influence. I pay particular attention to the leadership of Tanaka Kakuei, who welded the commissioned postmasters to the young LDP's electoral machine during the mid- to late-1950s. To further underscore the postmasters' political functions and significance, I analyze them with reference to other Japanese political interest groups.

The Postmasters in Theoretical and Comparative Perspective

A political "interest group" can be broadly defined as a collectivity of like-minded individuals that seeks to influence government decision-making. Through their involvement in both the "input" and "output" sides of the political process, interest groups perform a broad array of functions that can include pressuring and exchanging information with political actors, mobilizing votes behind politicians, and articulating policy proposals. In their capacity as intermediary organizations between state and society, interest groups are widely viewed as important components of liberal democracy.[2]

Essential to any definition of interest groups in democratic polities is the assumption that such groups represent *private*, or non-government, interests. Strictly speaking, then, the postwar commissioned postmasters should not be categorized as an interest group, since they were public servants.[3] As such, the postmasters bore some resemblance to "government-affiliated groups" (*gaikaku dantai*), organized appendages of Japanese ministries and agencies that played key roles in the implementation of public policy. As Aurelia Mulgan notes, some government-affiliated groups behave like private interest groups in terms of their dependence on funds from private as well as public sources and on leaders from both the political and bureaucratic worlds. But Mulgan stops short of including these groups under the analytical rubric of "interest groups":

While it is true that they take on pressure group–type functions when they lobby for subsidies from budgetary and other sources, in almost all cases the

---

2. This view seems most prevalent among American scholars (Tsujinaka, *Reiki shūdan*, 14).

3. The commissioned postmasters lost their status as public servants on October 1, 2007, when the postal privatization process officially began.

gaikaku dantai have been created solely for public purposes, which are specific and narrow, and their membership is dominated by public and semi-public organizations. Their interest representational role is a by-product of their public functioning and not part of their fundamental organizational rationale.[4]

Although it is certainly true that the postwar postmasters' "interest representation was a by-product of their public functioning," we must also recall their historical origins as locally situated, state-contracted citizens with private as well as public interests. Accordingly, while they absorbed the principles of public service, the postwar commissioned postmasters behaved like private citizens; they created a large, politically oriented voluntary organization (*nin'i dantai*) alongside their official, administrative association,[5] and they collaborated with the LDP in ways that further reinforced the private dimensions of their otherwise public persona. So, notwithstanding the postmasters' status as public servants, for analytical purposes this study treats them as private interests.

Borrowing from Mancur Olson's terminology, the postmasters' voluntary association can be viewed as a non-market professional organization that performed lobbying functions, was based on inclusive and compulsory membership, and that sought to secure "collective goods" for its members.[6] In this regard, it resembled the Japan Federation of Bar Associations (JFBA) and the Japan Medical Association (JMA). The postmasters were distinctive, however, in terms of the kinds of collective goods they pursued. Private interest groups the world over are notorious for advancing the interests of their members at the expense of the public good, and the JMA and JFBA are no exception; to cite just one example, the JMA was widely criticized in recent years for trying to block the liberalization of pharmaceutical sales—a policy that benefits patients in many ways but decreases physician income. That said, both the JMA and the JFBA have also lobbied for policies that improve the quality not only of their members' professional lives but also of the services offered

---

4. Mulgan, *The Politics of Agriculture in Japan*, 136.

5. Government-affiliated groups are administrative organizations with legal status and are not normally mirrored by voluntary associations.

6. The concepts and terminology in this paragraph are taken from Olson, *The Logic of Collective Action*.

to their clients.[7] The JMA, for instance, pushes for legal and regulatory changes relating to medical services and insurance schemes that stand to help patients, and the JFBA seeks to reform laws and regulations governing criminal, civil, and administrative lawsuits that advance consumers' and victims' rights. The overriding policy objective of the postmasters, by contrast, was to *prevent* legislative or regulatory changes that might alter the institutional foundations of their profession and jeopardize the survival of the commissioned post office system—even if those changes stood to rationalize state finances or improve the quality of services for post office customers. Chapter 3 explains how this preoccupation with self-preservation (*hoshin*) caused problems for individual postmasters and rendered their voluntary association highly vulnerable to organizational decline. In this chapter, I trace the historical and institutional origins of the self-preservation objective and its implications for Japanese politics.

As public servants with private interests, the commissioned postmasters mirrored Japan's political interest group environment in several ways. First, like other Japanese professional groups and Nōkyō, the national association of agricultural cooperatives, the postmasters' voluntary association was a pyramidal federation of groups extending from the grassroots level to the national level—a structure, as the next chapter argues, that contributed to the association's social and professional cohesiveness.[8] Like other interest groups, moreover, the postmasters association became highly bureaucratized and characterized by significant gaps between the leaders and the led—traits that stemmed from both historical precedent and the difficult task of intra-group coordination.[9]

Second, like the JMA, Nōkyō, and other interest groups with prewar precedents, the postmasters' postwar associations were heavily influenced by their longstanding relationship with the bureaucracy.[10] Although the policy-related influences of political party activism during

---

7. See, for example, Steslicke, *Doctors in Politics.*

8. As Olson argues, interest groups that are constructed as federations of small groups are characterized by the kind of face-to-face relations among members that enhances the effectiveness of social incentives to encourage conformity with group norms. See Olson, *The Logic of Collective Action*, especially 42, 63.

9. For the JMA, see Steslicke, *Doctors in Politics*, 14.

10. Ibid.; Tsujinaka, *Rieki shūdan*, 36.

the Taishō period (1912–1926) should not be underestimated, post-1868 Japan was in many ways a "bureaucratic state" (*kanryō kokka*) characterized by a strong ministerial presence within the policy process.[11] This in turn produced such close ties between the ministries and related interest groups that the latter frequently developed into administrative appendages of the bureaucracy. As Christiana Norgren reminds us, interest groups' efforts to forge links with the political parties were often defeated by the state, which by the early 1940s had emasculated the party system and transformed many organized interests into corporatist control associations (*tōseikai*).[12] In the postmasters' case, these wartime experiences created a strong precedent for top-town leadership within postwar representative organizations and close ties with the bureaucracy.

Close ties with political parties are yet another defining feature of most postwar Japanese interest groups. As Tsujinaka Yutaka has shown, the near revolutionary changes to the constitution and other political institutions during the Occupation (1945–1952) democratized political action and triggered a dramatic upsurge in the formation of new political parties and interest groups in Japan.[13] Harboring demands that were simply beyond the scope of bureaucratic discretion,[14] many interest groups turned to the parties for support; politicians, for their own part, looked to some of these groups as potential vehicles for mobilizing votes and thus compensating for the parties' weak grassroots memberships. As Norgren explains, parties and interest groups were soon forging political "exchange relationships" in which policy benefits were promised in return for votes and other electoral assistance.[15]

Incentives for interest groups to ally with the LDP in particular increased after 1962, when LDP Executive Council Chairman Akagi Munenori and Chief Cabinet Secretary Ōhira Masayoshi introduced the procedure of "preliminary review" (*jizen shinsa*). In an effort to wrest control

---

11. Inoguchi and Iwai, *Zoku giin no kenkyū*, 8.

12. Norgren, *Abortion Before Birth Control*, 14. See also Tsujinaka, *Reiki shūdan*, 74. For more on the Meiji state's delegitimation of political parties, see Gluck, *Japan's Modern Myths*. For an analysis of state-corporatist relationships with prewar interest groups, see Schaede, *Cooperative Capitalism*.

13. Tsujinaka, *Reiki shūdan*, 62.

14. Ibid., 119.

15. Norgren, *Abortion Before Birth Control*, 17–18.

of the policy process from the bureaucrats, the LDP demanded that drafts of bills be approved by the party's executive council (*sōmukai*) before being adopted by the Cabinet for submission to the Diet.[16] Before reaching the Executive Council, these bills were to be scrutinized by the relevant committee(s) of the Policy Affairs Research Council (PARC), the primary locus of power for what were eventually termed *zoku*, or policy tribe, politicians in the LDP. For many interest groups—the postmasters included—establishing ties to relevant *zoku* politicians constituted an important pipeline into the policymaking system.

One curious feature of Japanese political interest groups has been their lack of professional lobbyists.[17] In contrast to American interest groups that tend to employ former bureaucrats or politicians as lobbyists to represent them within the political system, Japanese interest groups normally do the job themselves.[18] Also noteworthy are "interest representative Diet members" (*rieki daihyō giin*), usually interest group leaders or former bureaucrats who are elected to the Diet (mostly the Upper House) as official spokespersons for those groups within the policy process. Their existence significantly blurs the functional demarcations between interest groups and political parties that scholars tend to take for granted in the Anglo-American context.[19]

One side effect of interest groups' close integration into the world of political parties has been a marked tendency to conceal their private lobbying activities from the public eye. As Tsujinaka argues, this is in part because the *zoku* are informal institutions that operate behind the scenes.[20] But we should also note that the concept of "pressure group" (*atsuryoku dantai*) has been a highly pejorative one in Japan,[21] where the political culture historically valorized personal self-sacrifice for the sake of the public good. Thus, to prevent public censure of their very private

---

16. Mulgan, *Japan's Failed Revolution*, 130.

17. Tsujinaka, *Rieki shūdan*, 126.

18. Köllner, "Upper House Elections in Japan and the Power of the 'Organized Vote,'" 118.

19. Ibid., 133. Put differently, these elected politicians combine the roles of legislator and lobbyist—in the American sense. See Curtis, "The 1974 Election Campaign," 64.

20. Tsujinaka, *Rieki shūdan*, 111.

21. Steslicke, *Doctors in Politics*, 12.

(read selfish) activities, many interest groups cast their objectives in terms of the public interest.[22] Physicians, for instance, advertised their efforts to preserve Japan's heavy emphasis on abortion as the primary method of birth control in terms of what was best for women's health,[23] and Nōkyō's continuing quest for state subsidies of agricultural production was cast as part of a mission to preserve the customs and institutions of the country's declining farming sector. And in a creative twist of democratic parlance, the commissioned postmasters portrayed their political activism in defense of their distinctive institutions as part of a selfless quest to preserve the best of Japanese traditional culture. As the next sections illustrate, the postmasters' public interest campaigns were a defensive reaction to a confluence of political developments during the early postwar period that threatened the commissioned post office system with extinction and elevated occupational self-preservation to the top of the postmasters' list of political objectives.

The Rise of Zentei and the Early Postwar Postal Reforms

The postal system emerged from the ashes of World War II with its infrastructure in shambles but its community spirit intact. The post offices had suffered during the latter stages of the war, experiencing steady cutbacks of civilian mail delivery services and severe labor shortages.[24] More than 10,000 postal workers lost their lives while serving as soldiers overseas;[25] many perished in the atomic explosions over Hiroshima and Nagasaki and in the Tokyo fire bombings; more than one quarter of all postal savings accounts were lost;[26] and approximately 90 percent of urban post offices were damaged or destroyed during the final months of the war.[27] After the atomic bombing of Nagasaki, many commissioned postmasters in the area were reduced to sleeping with their customers'

---

22. Ibid.

23. Norgren, *Abortion Before Birth Control.*

24. Hida chiku tokutei yūbinkyokuchōkai kaishi hensan iinkai, ed., *Hida no tokutei yūbinkyoku shi*, 198. Postal workers who were drafted into the armed services were temporarily replaced by women and boys.

25. Kyūshū chihō tokutei yūbinkyokuchōkai, *Kyūshū tokutei yūbinkyokuchōkai shi*, 98.

26. Yūseishō, ed., *Yūsei 100-nen no ayumi*, 170.

27. Civil Communications Section of the Supreme Commander of the Allied Powers, *Report on Survey of Japanese Postal System*, 25.

deposits under their pillows; those who had lost their post offices conducted their transactions on the grounds of nearby temples. Despite these hardships, surviving facilities were opened within a few short days of the blast, allowing even those patrons who had lost their supporting documentation to withdraw their savings and receive insurance payouts as the beneficiaries of those who had perished. As the banks struggled to resume operations, the post offices reaffirmed their reputation as financial and community havens in a manner reminiscent of the aftermath of the 1923 Great Kantō Earthquake.[28] Building on that public trust, the postmasters worked in partnership with the government to rebuild the postal savings, insurance, and pension systems in the months and years following the surrender.[29] Today, older postmasters evoke these accomplishments as evidence of the commissioned post office system's indispensability to local society.

With the onset of the Occupation, the postmasters faced a new set of challenges in the form of a militant labor union and mounting calls for the reform or outright abolition of the commissioned post office system. Japan's first postal unions had been established during the 1920s to secure higher wages and better working conditions for ordinary postal employees.[30] The unions were suppressed by the state during the 1930s and then forcibly subsumed under a state-operated umbrella group.[31] In December 1945, the first postwar postal union was formed at the Tokyo Central Post Office, sparking a wave of unionization efforts in post offices around the country.[32] Five months later, activists established what by 1948 was known as Zentei (Zenteishin rōdō kumiai; Japan Postal Workers Union), a national union that included employees from both the ordinary (*futsū*) and commissioned (*tokutei*) post offices, as well as from the telecommunications service.[33] By the mid-1950s, Zentei was

---

28. Kyūshū chihō tokutei yūbinkyokuchōkai, *Kyūshū tokutei yūbinkyokuchōkai shi*, 96; Tanabe, "Yūseishō ni nozomu," 69.

29. Yūseishō, ed., *Yūsei 100-nen no ayumi*, 183.

30. Rōdō sōgi chōsakai, ed., *Teishin jigyō no sōgi to kumiai undō*, 52–53.

31. Yūseishō, ed., *Yūsei 100-nen shi*, 596–97; Kamiko, *Zentei rōdō undōshi*, 15.

32. Yūseishō, ed., *Yūsei 100-nen shi*, 690.

33. In 1950, with the formation of Nippon Telegraph and Telephone (NTT), telecommunications workers split from Zentei to form their own union, Zendentsū.

closely affiliated with Sōhyō, the radical federation of public sector unions, and the left wing of the JSP.

Zentei's bête noire was the commissioned post office system. Zentei took issue with the methods for hiring commissioned postmasters and the de facto inheritance of postmasterships, the private ownership of post office facilities, and the indirect payment of workers' wages in non-collection and delivery (*mushūhai*) commissioned post offices from government allowances issued to the postmasters (*watarikirihi*).[34] As far as the union was concerned, these practices created an opaque working environment in which the postmasters were free to overwork and underpay their employees. Zentei also maintained that the "free employment" (*jiyū nin'yō*) of commissioned postmasters from among "local men of influence" (*meibōka*) prevented qualified postal workers from being considered for postmasterships. The only way to correct these problems, Zentei concluded, was for the state to assume direct ownership of all post offices and postal equipment, for the postmasters of commissioned post offices to be hired according to the same rational, bureaucratic standards that governed the selection of ordinary postmasters, and for postal workers to be paid directly by the government. In short, Zentei called for the modernization and democratization of the commissioned post office system—processes that would eliminate the very customs and procedures that had come to define the system.[35]

Buoyed by the Occupation's encouragement of the labor union movement, Zentei proceeded to do what unions do best when faced with an intolerable situation: it went on strike. In 1946, postal and telecommunications employees joined forces with railway workers to press for better wages and working conditions for all,[36] organizing wave after

---

34. Unlike collection and delivery (*shūhai*) commissioned post offices, the non-collection and delivery (*mushūhai*) commissioned post offices neither collected mail from mailboxes in their postal districts nor delivered it, and the range of specific services they offered their customers was usually limited. The ordinary post offices were similarly divided.

35. For an overview of Zentei's early history and its position on the commissioned postmasters, see Rōdō sōgi chōsakai, ed., *Teishin jigyō no sōgi to kumiai undō*, especially 315–402.

36. *Asahi shinbun*, February 17, 1946. In the postal sector, worker demands for higher wages could only be met by raising the price of postage. The government took these steps

wave of work stoppages. Zentei also participated in the planning of the February 1, 1947 general strike, and was profoundly disappointed when General Douglas MacArthur outlawed the event and then revoked the public sector workers' right to strike.[37] The era of grand gestures consequently gave way to one of wildcat strikes (*yamaneko sōgi*), mass absenteeism (*shūdan kekkin*), and other ad hoc—but no less disruptive—attacks on the postmasters.[38] As evidenced by customer complaints about delays in mail deliveries and media editorials about the public's declining trust in the postal system, union action had inflicted significant damage on the reputation of the local post office.[39]

The aborted general strike prompted Zentei to sit down with Ministry of Communications (Teishin'in) officials to work out a compromise solution to the problems of the commissioned post office system,[40] a system that it relentlessly condemned as behind the times and a "cancer" (*gan*) on the Japanese communications system.[41] At the time, the Supreme Commander for the Allied Powers (SCAP) was pressuring the ministry to reform and democratize communications.[42] SCAP was concerned that only 4 percent of the post offices in Japan were under the supervision of classified government officials, while 96 percent were managed by individuals of semi-bureaucratic rank who had been selected under the "free employment" system, which SCAP argued was encouraging highly undemocratic practices within the postal network.[43] These features were in marked contradiction to SCAP's ongoing efforts to

---

very reluctantly during the first years of the Occupation, fearing their inflationary effects on the already struggling economy (*Asahi shinbun*, March 5, 1946).

37. Although Zentei's right to strike was never restored, it did regain the right to bargain collectively in 1953 (Zenteishin rōdō kumiai Zentei shi hensan iinkai, ed., *Zentei rōdō undōshi*, 513).

38. Yūseishō, ed., *Yūsei 100-nen no ayumi*, 191.

39. Yamamoto, "Kindaika soku moraru ga gōgi," 46–47.

40. Yamaguchi, *Tokutei yūbinkyoku*, 92.

41. Ibid., 79.

42. SCAP's General Headquarters (GHQ) apparently issued 126 memoranda relating to the democratization of communications in 1945 and 1946. Its objective was to rationalize the administration of communications while expanding and invigorating the scope of services. Ogawa and Takahashi, *Tokutei yūbinkyoku seido shi*, 64; Tokyo chihō tokutei yūbinkyokuchōkai shi henshū iinkai, *Tokyo chihō tokutei yūbinkyokuchōkai shi*, 2.

43. Civil Communications Section, *Report on Survey of Japanese Postal System*, 10.

curb elitism and strengthen merit-based standards of career advancement within the civil service.[44]

In response to SCAP's pressures, the Ministry of Communications proceeded to address some of the most serious flaws in the commissioned post offices, including the postmasters' misuse of operating funds, discrepancies in working conditions between the ordinary and commissioned post offices, and the like. But in a nod to the postmasters, the ministry refused to touch the "free employment" system through which officials from regional postal bureaus used their personal discretion to hire commissioned postmasters from among local authority figures. In round after round of negotiations—some direct, others through intermediary organizations—the ministry maintained that the system was fair and inherently democratic, since choosing commissioned postmasters from among candidates with strong local ties ensured the selection of individuals who were deeply committed and responsive to their communities.[45] What postal officials failed to publicize, however, was their determination to preserve a hiring custom that gave them significant discretion over the selection of the ministry's most important grassroots representatives.

Frustrated by the ministry's refusal to radically reform the commissioned post office system, Zentei turned to the Diet for help. In 1947, the union submitted a petition to the Lower House Communications Committee (Tsūshin iinkai) demanding the complete destruction of the commissioned post office system (*tokutei yūbinkyoku seido teppai no seigan*). The petition included a scathing attack on the "feudalistic" principles of the commissioned post offices and the postmasters' allegedly undemocratic treatment of their employees. Prodded by the besieged postmasters, town and village mayors from Miyagi and Ehime prefectures submitted a petition of their own calling for the retention of the commissioned post office system.[46] Echoing the ministry, the mayors praised the "democratic" characteristics of the commissioned postmasters, noting the enormous costs of converting the commissioned post

---

44. Johnson, *Japan's Public Policy Companies*, 29.

45. Ogawa and Takahashi, *Tokutei yūbinkyoku seido shi*, 81–82.

46. The petitions were known as "Petitions to stabilize the positions of the commissioned postmasters" (*tokutei yūbinkyokuchō no chii no anteika ni kansuru seigan*).

offices into ordinary post offices.[47] Meanwhile, the postmasters put pressure on Diet members to reject the union's demands and elected their first "interest representative Diet member" to the Lower House.[48]

The fate of the commissioned post office system hung in the balance for many weeks in 1947 as the battle between the postmasters and Zentei became increasingly enmeshed in partisan politics. With the pro-Zentei JSP controlling the levers of government, the postmasters had good reason to believe that their days were numbered. Although concrete evidence to corroborate this point is hard to come by, legend has it that what saved the postmasters was an eleventh-hour visit to GHQ by their leader, Yokoyama Hachiji. Viewing the conflict as a strictly Japanese problem, SCAP was initially reluctant to intervene. Yokoyama then reminded the Occupation authorities that if Zentei's demands were fulfilled and the commissioned post office system abolished, more than 13,000 postmasters would withdraw their privately-owned facilities from the national postal network—a move that would have very negative repercussions for the smooth implementation of Occupation policy, not to mention employment levels within the postal services. Yokoyama's entreaty worked. After three days of deliberations, the GHQ instructed Miki Takeo, then Minister of Communications, to persuade the cabinet to throw their lot behind the postmasters. The cabinet then advised the Lower House Communications Committee to vote in support of the pro-system petition, which it did on December 9, 1947.[49] The Upper House followed suit a few months later after deliberating on a similar set of petitions.

Although the commissioned postmasters managed to escape extinction, they were subjected to a number of reforms during the democratization phase of the Occupation that reduced some of the institutional differences between the commissioned and ordinary post offices. Some of those reforms, like the lifting of the ban on female candidates for postmasterships and the direct payment of all employee salaries by the government, had been implemented under SCAP's leadership even be-

47. Ogawa and Takahashi, *Tokutei yūbinkyoku seido shi*, 83–84.
48. Yamaguchi, *Tokutei yūbinkyoku*, 104.
49. Ibid., 105–6; Interview, Zentoku official, Tokyo, March 27, 2003.

fore the petitions had reached the Diet.[50] Others were introduced over the course of the mid- to late 1940s. These included the abolition of the requirement that commissioned postmasters perform their duties within their own homes or private facilities; stricter rules governing the dispensation and monitoring of the postmasters' operating allowances (*watarikirihi*); and the abolition of the postmasters' right to pocket commission from the sale of postage stamps.[51] Not all of the reforms were unwelcome to the postmasters; they benefited, for instance, from the termination of postmaster liability for damages incurred during the performance of postal functions, and from the stipulation that the government pay them rent for the use of their private property.[52] Most importantly, the postmasters were designated "general public servants" (*ippan kōmuin*) under the 1948 National Public Service Law (Kokka kōmuin hō), entitling them to the same salaries and benefits as those enjoyed by other public servants. But the designation also meant that the postmasters could no longer run for any kind of public office or participate in electoral activities. Notwithstanding the government's refusal to touch the traditional hiring procedures of commissioned postmasters, from the perspective of modern bureaucratic theory, with its emphasis on legal-rational authority, the reforms made perfect sense. But the postmasters opposed them as an affront to the very institutions and customs that defined their profession.[53]

As they limped through the reforms, the postmasters faced mounting criticisms from both the media and the general public. Many of the major newspapers covered the standoff between the postal workers and the commissioned postmasters in excruciating detail, frequently siding with the workers. Posters and popular comic books (*manga*) depicted the postmasters as fat, overdressed gourmands who kept their half-

---

50. Few women held commissioned postmasterships—even in the 2000s—and the Ministry of Internal Affairs and Communications did not keep formal track of them. Conventional wisdom has it, however, that roughly 10 percent of contemporary postmasters were women around the time of Japan Post's establishment in 2003 (Interview, Zentoku official, Tokyo, March 27, 2003).

51. Hida chiku tokutei yūbinkyokuchokai kaishi hensan iinkai, ed., *Hida no tokutei yūbinkyoku shi*, 212–13.

52. Ibid.; and Maeno, *Yūseishō to iu yakusho*, 48.

53. Moriyama and Nihei, *GHQ to senryōka no yūsei*, 20.

starved, overworked employees in a state of near penury.[54] One postmaster who lived through the period wrote that the depictions "shook him to the very core of his being."[55] In the context of widespread poverty and democratic unrest, the implications of these depictions were clear: the postmasters had become symbols of the undemocratic excesses of a bygone era in which social status provided a lucky few with opportunities for personal advancement and social influence.[56]

Since the government refused to change the hiring practices that buttressed the postmasters' elevated social position, Zentei remained unappeased by the postwar reforms and continued to campaign for the complete abolition of the commissioned post office system. During the 1950s, the union launched "inspection struggles" (*tenken tōsō*), a grassroots campaign to secure postmaster compliance with the new Labor Standards Law (Rōdō kijun hō) and to stem financial corruption within the post offices. Local groups of postal workers would interrogate suspect postmasters and forcibly inspect their account books, often in the dead of night. These episodes traumatized their victims, a few of whom were driven to suicide. In one well-publicized case during the mid-1950s, a postmaster and his wife in Aichi prefecture strangled their two children and then hanged themselves after being accused—unjustly, some claim—of misappropriating postal funds and mistreating their seven employees.[57] The inspection struggle persisted until the end of the 1950s; Zentei's campaign to abolish the commissioned post office system dragged on until well into the 1980s.

The implications of this ongoing confrontation for both the commissioned post office system and Japanese politics were profound. At one level, the union campaigns punctured the carefully cultivated myth that the postmasters were to a man exemplary public servants and committed citizens. Zentei may have overstated the case of postmaster in-

54. Kyūshū chihō tokutei yūbinkyokuchōkai, *Kyūshū tokutei yūbinkyokuchōkai shi*, 457.

55. Ōmori, *Kyokuchōkai monogatari*, 15–16.

56. The newspapers regularly ran articles about lazy or corrupt postmasters well into the 1950s. In one opinion piece, the employee of a traditional inn (*ryokan*) wrote that her boss ran a post office on the same property as the inn and frequently forced her to deliver his telegrams. These "postmasters in name only" (*namaedake no yūbinkyokuchō*), the author complained, should be fired immediately! (*Asahi shinbun*, December 19, 1954).

57. Yamaguchi, *Tokutei yūbinkyoku*, 151.

transigence, but the fact remains that there were numerous instances of postmaster corruption throughout the prewar and postwar periods.[58] By the same token, Zentei's zealous stance at a time of mounting ideological polarization put the postmasters squarely on the defensive. Within a few short years, the postmasters had strengthened their professional organization and flocked to conservative politicians for support, all in the name of self-preservation. By the late 1950s, the postmasters were ensconced in a partnership with the LDP that was evolving into one of postwar Japan's most powerful—and controversial—political alliances.

The Postmasters Organizations: Historical Precedents

Together with the early Meiji period and the Koizumi administration (2001–2006), the early postwar period was one of the main formative moments in the history of the commissioned postmasters. Facing an uncertain future, the status-conscious postmasters took a series of steps to preserve what was left of their distinctive institutions. They launched local public relations campaigns to improve their tarnished images, explaining in pamphlets and posters the importance of the commissioned post office system for community development and national communications.[59] They rallied local mayors to their defense, pressured prefectural assemblies to adopt resolutions demanding the continuation of the commissioned post office system, and called on national politicians to champion their cause in the Diet. Most significantly for the future of domestic politics, the postmasters built on prewar precedents to establish a powerful network of associations that spanned the national, prefectural, and grassroots levels. That network provided the postmasters with an organizational foundation for their long-term association with both the bureaucracy and the LDP.

The history of the commissioned postmasters associations extends back to the 1870s, when both bureaucrats and postmasters looked to or-

---

58. In my searches for newspaper articles about the commissioned postmasters after World War II, the vast majority of hits pertained to cases of postmaster corruption or suicides. In addition, several postal workers have written books or articles on wayward postmasters. See, for example, Kitagawa, "Zenkindaiteki na mono no saihensei."

59. Zenkoku tokutei yūbinkyokuchōkai, *Tokuteikyoku taikan*, vol. 3, 23–24; Ōmori, *Kyokuchōkai monogatari*, 15.

ganization as a mechanism for solving their respective problems. For the postmasters, those problems were mostly financial in scope. As noted in Chapter 1, the prewar postmasters received no salaries, no rent for their facilities, and inadequate operating allowances. Conscientious postmasters were thus reduced to spending their own funds on the expansion of local postal services and the repair of their facilities.[60] By the late 1890s, the postmasters were allowed to pocket commission from the sale of postage and income stamps (*shūnyū inshi*), but this was small compensation for those in sparsely populated rural areas where the demand for such services was low. The postmasters' liability for damages incurred by their post office employees while carrying out their official duties simply added to their financial woes.[61] For the postmaster preoccupied with his social status and commitment to public service, these monetary problems were a blow to his pride and reputation. They also fueled a profound sense of occupational grievance that was at the heart of the postmasters' collective identity and, in turn, their drive to organize.

While the postmasters brooded about money, the Meiji state carried out a string of institutional experiments to enhance the effectiveness and financial efficiency of the postal services. For the first seventeen years of the Meiji period, the bureaucratic unit in charge of the posts was transferred from one ministerial jurisdiction to another, including the Ministry of Finance and the Ministry of Agriculture and Commerce. With the abolition of the Council of State and the introduction of the cabinet system in 1885, the Ministry of Communications (Teishinshō) was established to oversee both postal and telegraph services, marking the first time that communications had achieved ministerial status.[62]

State efforts to control the rapidly expanding network of commissioned post offices developed alongside these broader institutional in-

---

60. Yamaguchi, *Tokutei yūbinkyoku*, 44, 64.

61. Ogawa and Takahashi, *Tokutei yūbinkyoku seido shi*, 21.

62. The Ministry of Communications existed until 1943, when during a wave of ministerial amalgamations it was temporarily subsumed under the newly formed Ministry of Transportation and Communications (Un'yu tsūshinshō). In 1949, when NTT assumed the bulk of telecommunications functions, the communications bureaucracy was reorganized once again with the formation of the Ministry of Posts and Telecommunications (Yūseishō, MPT).

novations.[63] In 1886, the number of regional communications districts was lowered from 52 to 15—and then to 12 after World War II—and a supervisory bureau (*teishin kanrikyoku*) established in each. The post offices were then divided into three classes, the first (*ittō*) and second (*nitō*) of which were large in scale and administered directly by the ministry. The third class of tiny post offices (*santō yūbinkyoku*) were administered by postmasters with the low bureaucratic rank of *hanninkan*. In 1886, there were 12 first-class post offices in Japan, 45 second-class facilities, and 4,000 third-class post offices.[64] In 1941, the first- and second-class post offices were amalgamated into large, "ordinary" post offices (*futsū yūbinkyoku*), and the third-class facilities became the commissioned post offices that we know today (*tokutei yūbinkyoku*).[65]

From the start, the third-class post offices were difficult for the government to control, in part because of their sheer numbers and geographic dispersal to the remotest corners of the country. But even more problematic was the postmasters' distinctive position as private, contracted servants of the state. Chosen from outside normal bureaucratic channels, the low-ranking postmasters were expected to serve the public interest but think like small businessmen;[66] they were, after all, administering financial and communications services that required meticulous bookkeeping skills. But the combination of official responsibilities with a private sector outlook provided the postmasters with little in terms of material compensation or bureaucratic status. The postmasters, in other words, shouldered the duties of both *kan* (the state) and *min* (the private sector) without reaping the full benefits of either. It is small wonder, then, that the postmasters harbored grievances and, in some cases, reneged on their official duties.

The state's response to the postmasters' potential for trouble was to wrap them in a regulatory web that aggravated their grievances while

---

63. Westney, *Imitation and Innovation*, 127–29.

64. Yamaguchi, *Tokutei yūbinkyoku*, 32.

65. The term *tokutei yūbinkyoku* is literally translated as "special post offices." It is a shorthand usage for "specially designated post offices" (*tokuni shiteishita yūbinkyoku*). I have chosen to translate the term as "commissioned post offices" in order to capture the distinctive contractual relationship between the prewar government and the private citizens who ran the facilities (Yamaguchi, *Tokutei yūbinkyoku*, 2).

66. Ibid., 10 and 13.

forcing them into an uneasy alliance with the state. The Ministry of Communications issued a string of regulations over the postmasters' public and private activities, from minute descriptions of the postmasters' ever-expanding postal duties to prohibitions on certain kinds of private-sector ventures. Postal bureaucrats also took steps to curb the postmasters' political activities. From the postmasters' perspective, it was a matter of course for local men of influence to cultivate political connections and vocalize their opinions about local politics.[67] They also argued that serving in local assemblies positioned them to attract more customers to the post office while contributing more fruitfully to the well-being of their communities.[68] Postal officials felt differently, taking steps almost immediately after the postal system's founding to prevent the postmasters from making political speeches.[69] They also prohibited the postmasters from seeking election to any legislature higher than city, town, or village assemblies on the grounds that this would interfere with the implementation of their local postal duties. By the end of the 1920s, the postmasters were required to resign their commissions immediately upon declaring their candidacy for the national Diet. For many—if not most—postmasters, there was nothing inappropriate about these regulations; like any other public servant, the postmasters were expected to maintain some modicum of political neutrality, avoiding political activities that would either distract them from their official duties or erode the public's trust in the postal system.[70] Regulations designed to control the postmasters' professional organizations, however, proved far more controversial.

The state's initial reason for organizing the commissioned postmasters was to improve the postmasters' financial and administrative skills, which were in short supply among new appointees or, as was sometimes the case, postmasters who were unaccustomed to hard work.[71] When the Meiji postal system was introduced in 1871, supervisors (*ekitei kakari* or *yūbin kakari*) were appointed at the prefectural level to convey work-

---

67. Zenkoku tokutei yūbinkyokuchōkai, *Tokuteikyoku taikan*, vol. 1, 12.
68. Zenkoku tokutei yūbinkyokuchōkai, *Tokuteikyoku taikan*, vol. 2, 21.
69. Ogawa and Takahashi, *Tokutei yūbinkyoku seido shi*, 14.
70. Yūsei daijin kanbō chōsaka, "Tokutei yūbinkyoku no enkaku," 6–7.
71. Ogawa and Takahashi, *Tokutei yūbinkyoku seido shi*, 31.

related directives from central bureaucratic authorities to the post offices. Since the supervisors could not always reach facilities in remote areas, the state, at Maejima Hisoka's behest, encouraged prefectural governments to facilitate communications within the system by organizing the postmasters into groups resembling neighborhood associations.[72] In some instances, the prefectures co-opted postmasters organizations that had organized spontaneously. As a result, the size and organizational structure of these groups varied significantly from prefecture to prefecture. Some were known as "gatherings" (*shūkai*), others as "cooperative associations" (*kyōgikai*) or "study groups" (*kenkyūkai*). Virtually all were designed to promote communication among the postmasters for the purposes of improving the quality of services, preventing crime and accidents during the implementation of postal functions, improving the training of employees, coping with the repair of postal facilities, and, finally, addressing issues not covered by government regulation.[73] From 1886, as the post offices were reorganized and the third-class postal system expanded in size, the number of these groups increased. Eight years later, in a move that underscored its determination to rationalize the postal services and keep close watch over the postmasters, the state ordered the establishment of the national Third-Class Postmasters Association (Santō kyokuchō kyōgikai).[74]

While the postmasters looked to the national association as a forum for airing their financial grievances and nurturing a sense of occupational unity,[75] the Ministry of Communications viewed it as a mechanism for control. Like the pins on a vise, postal officials tightened their grip on the association's conduct. During the mid-1880s, as the Freedom and Popular Rights Movement (Jiyū minken undō) gained momentum, the skittish state ruled that the postmasters association and its local chap-

---

72. Zenkoku tokutei yūbinkyokuchōkai, *Tokuteikyoku taikan*, vol. 1, 19, 148.

73. Ogawa and Takahashi, *Tokutei yūbinkyoku seido shi*, 39; Yamaguchi, *Tokutei yūbinkyoku*, 40.

74. Yamaguchi, *Tokutei yūbinkyoku*, 38–40; Ogawa and Takahashi, *Tokutei yūbinkyoku seido shi*, 30–31; Yūsei daijin kanbō chōsaka, "Tokuteikyoku no enkaku," 6. In 1937, during a comprehensive reform of the third-class postal system, the Santō kyokuchō kyōgikai was renamed the Santō kyokuchōkai. For the sake of simplicity, I have used the same English term, "Third-Class Postmasters Association," for each.

75. Ogawa and Takahashi, *Tokutei yūbinkyoku seido shi*, 31.

ters would have to seek the approval of bureaucratic higher-ups before scheduling meetings and setting their agendas.[76] At the turn of the century, when the postmasters were growing restive in reaction to their expanding duties and the inevitable blows to their prestige caused by their dwindling allowances, the government curbed their ability to discuss these grievances by restricting association meetings to issues that directly related to their postal duties. The government also reserved the right to approve all appointments to the postmasters association's top leadership and to control its budget.[77] The growing importance of postal savings accounts and insurance premiums for funding various military ventures gave the state added incentives to keep the postmasters in line.[78] By 1937, when the third-class postal system was partially reformed in the context of deepening government authoritarianism, the postmasters association was firmly entrenched as a conduit for bureaucratic policing.[79] In the end, the postmasters may have acquired reputations as representatives of the state at the grassroots level, but they were treated just like any other profession or business at the time: as a potentially disruptive private interest that had to be forcibly harnessed to the needs of the state.[80] Straddling that gray zone between public and private, the postmasters emerged from these experiences feeling deeply ambivalent about their close ties with state authority.

Postwar Postmasters Organizations
and the Emergence of a Ruling Triad

In the aftermath of World War II, the commissioned postmasters' financial woes intensified as they grappled with the destruction of their private property and the introduction of land and tax reform, both of which reduced their personal assets.[81] On a more positive note, they

---

76. Yamaguchi, *Tokutei yūbinkyoku*, 40.

77. Ogawa and Takahashi, *Tokutei yūbinkyoku seido shi*, 39.

78. Yamawaki, *Yūsei kōbō*, 179.

79. Yūsei daijin kanbō chōsaka, "Tokuteikyoku no enkaku," 6.

80. Interestingly, the expansion of regulatory controls over the postmasters roughly mirrored those imposed on prewar business associations. This further substantiates the view that while ordinary subjects viewed the postmasters as *kan*, the government treated them just like any other *min*.

81. Ōmori, *Kyokuchōkai monogatari*, 22.

were now in a political environment where they were free to organize as they wished. Accordingly, in 1946 the postmasters established the prototype of the non-statutory Zentoku (Zenkoku tokutei yūbinkyokuchōkai; National Association of Commissioned Postmasters), building on the same organizational units of their prewar associational network.[82] The organization's initial objective was to bargain with the state for solutions to the postmasters' deepening financial problems.[83] But as Zentei's offensive heated up after 1946, the postmasters shifted course. At a milestone retreat in the spa town of Hakone in September 1947, they unanimously agreed that Zentoku's overriding purpose would be to protect and promote their interests (*rieki*) in response to the rise of militant labor unionism, and they vowed to remain vigilant until "Zentei lowered the flag."[84] To be sure, what the postmasters meant by "interests" was the preservation of commissioned postal institutions and the social status that those institutions bestowed. Since it would be another four decades before the union abandoned their campaign against the postmasters, the association remained fixated on this fundamental objective, producing an internal organizational culture that was at once secretive, defensive, and deeply conservative. As later chapters illustrate, this distinctive culture was to color Zentoku's response to all future challenges, including Koizumi Jun'ichirō's drive to privatize the postal services.

Zentoku faced threats from other quarters as well during the Occupation period. In July 1950, just when it appeared that the commissioned postmasters had survived the worst of Zentei's onslaught and SCAP's reforms, General MacArthur abruptly abolished Zentoku. Given that the Occupation authorities had thrown their support behind the commissioned post office system during the 1947 Diet debates, the move left the postmasters feeling bewildered and demoralized.[85] Why did MacArthur take this step? Some postmasters opined that the GHQ had been swayed by the slanderous, biased information disseminated by the

---

82. The postmasters also tried to establish their own labor union during the early Occupation years, but the government forbade the initiative on the grounds that the postmasters were not "workers."

83. Ōmori, *Kyokuchōkai monogatari*, 13.

84. Ibid., 76–80.

85. Zenkoku tokutei yūbinkyokuchōkai, *Tokuteikyoku taikan*, vol.1, 2.

union.[86] Others argued that the GHQ simply lacked knowledge about the association and that its dissolution order was rooted in nothing more than a misunderstanding.[87] Still others suspected that the GHQ had viewed the postmasters' participation in local chapters of the wartime Imperial Rule Assistance Association (Taisei yokusankai) as evidence that Zentoku was a feudal association of local "bosses" and, therefore, an impediment to democratic reform.[88] The problem with this argument is that the timing is off. If the GHQ had indeed branded Zentoku as some sort of black dragon society, why did it abolish the association in 1950, a period of Occupational assaults on left-wing political activists, including several leading members of Zentei, and not in 1946–1947, when right-wing activists were being purged from public office?

If its February 1949 report on the postal services is any indication, SCAP was growing increasingly concerned about the postmasters' bureaucratic influence. Compiled by the Civil Communications Section, the report observed that the commissioned postmasters "are opposing strenuously any move to change or abolish the present system and the Government appears to yield to their demands on all material points. There is every indication that they, as individuals and through their association, exercise strong influence with the Cabinet and the National Diet."[89]

Circumstantial evidence further corroborates the view that the postmasters were exercising considerable sway over the bureaucrats—or, at the very least, that the two sides had developed an unusually close and mutually beneficial relationship. In 1946, the ministry had issued an official notice (*kōtatsu*) endorsing Zentoku, a rather strange step to take given the association's status as a "voluntary" (*nin'i*) organization. The ministry occasionally dispatched officials to work with Zentoku leaders and attend association meetings, and it routinely subsidized the association's coffers. The ministry even sent a thank you letter (*kanshajō*) to one of Zentoku's leaders after the dissolution order, expressing

---

86. Kyūshū chihō tokutei yūbinkyokuchōkai, *Kyūshū tokutei yūbinkyokuchōkai shi*, 109.

87. Zenkoku tokutei yūbinkyokuchōkai, *Tokuteikyoku taikan*, vol. 1, 1.

88. Yamaguchi, *Tokutei yūbinkyoku*, 118; Tōkyō chihō tokutei yūbinkyokuchōkai shi henshū iinkai, ed., *Tōkyō chihō tokutei yūbinkyokuchōkai shi*, 2.

89. Civil Communications Section, *Report on Survey of Japanese Postal System*, 11.

its gratitude for the association's contributions to the recovery of postal services after the war.[90] For their own part, many postmasters welcomed Zentoku's close ties with the ministry as a source of guidance and legitimacy during a particularly troublesome time in their history, while others condemned them as a throwback to prewar state intrusions and an infringement of the association's voluntary status.[91]

In the final analysis, SCAP's move was only a short-term disruption in Zentoku's existence. In January 1953, shortly after the end of the Occupation, Zentoku regrouped with the help of conservative politician Sunada Shigemasa and the ministry's tacit blessing.[92] But rather than turn to the bureaucrats for help during this time of ongoing conflict with Zentei, the postmasters, like other interest groups at the time, sought the advice and assistance of conservative politicians. Their reasons for doing so were clear. Postal officials had an overriding interest in ensuring the smooth and efficient implementation of the postal services, a task that required them to address the needs of Zentei—needs that were usually at odds with those of the postmasters. Officialdom also had a historically well-established tendency to be too controlling. Furthermore, the postmasters recognized that they could not always count on the ministry in a pinch; as recently as 1950, their representatives' efforts to lobby bureaucrats for help in the wake of Zentoku's dissolution had been roundly rebuffed.[93]

Conservative politicians, meanwhile, were on the lookout for supporters against the very same ideological enemies that were plaguing the postmasters. The two sides were natural allies, bound together by their insecure futures and common political values. The political alliance also had prewar and early postwar precedents. There is evidence, for

---

90. Tōkyō chihō tokutei yūbinkyokuchōkai shi henshū iinkai, ed., *Tōkyō chihō tokutei yūbinkyokuchōkai shi*, 4.

91. Ōmori, *Kyokuchōkai monogatari*, 72–78. Voluntary organizations are non-statutory organizations that are not permitted to own buildings or receive government subsidies (Schaede, *Cooperative Capitalism*, 34).

92. Sunada, an ally of Hatoyama Ichirō, was a former Seiyūkai member who had been purged during the Occupation. He recognized in the postmasters a network that could be mobilized to counter the rising influence of Zentei and the JSP (Wada, "Zenkoku tokutei yūbinkyokuchōkai," 121).

93. Kyūshū chihō tokutei yūbinkyokuchōkai, *Kyūshū tokutei yūbinkyokuchōkai shi*, 416.

instance, that postmasters—along with other local bureaucrats of various ranks—were selectively recruited into the Seiyūkai in some parts of the country as part of Hara Kei's long-term effort to build up the party's local support base.[94] During the politically permissive months of the early Occupation period, moreover, many postmasters ran for election to local and prefectural assemblies under conservative party banners or participated in the national election campaigns of conservative politicians. With the promulgation of the National Public Service Law, however, the postmasters' electoral activities were abruptly declared illegal.[95] But rather than sever the emerging ties between the postmasters and their political allies, the new law effectively threw the two sides closer together.

At issue was the postmasters' official bureaucratic status. In the months preceding the enactment of the National Public Service Law, the postmasters and their friends in the conservative parties campaigned hard to have all commissioned postmasters designated special public servants (*tokubetsushoku*), rather than general public servants (*ippanshoku*).[96] While general public servants fall under the political restrictions of the National Public Service Law, including its prohibitions on electoral participation, special public servants, including the prime minister, cabinet ministers, ministerial aides, ambassadors, and the like, do not. The postmasters and the LDP maintained that unlike other national

---

94. Tetsuo Najita mentions in passing that at least one Kyushu governor who was loyal to Hara recruited postmasters into the Seiyūkai (*Hara Kei in the Politics of Compromise*, 227–28; 247–48n20). But the literature, including the postwar postmasters associations' historical materials, gives us very few clues as to the extent of the postmasters' involvement in the party. Although this issue warrants further historical research, it is likely that the postmasters were only mildly attractive to the prewar parties as vehicles for mobilizing the vote, since their activities were so heavily circumscribed by bureaucratic regulations. I would assume, then, that the postmasters' recruitment into electoral politics was a highly localized affair, dependent on the proclivities of local or prefectural political figures.

95. This did not put a stop to postmaster electioneering. In June 1950, for example, fourteen postmasters in Ibaragi prefecture were arrested for taking illegal contributions from the campaign of a candidate for an Upper House seat (*Asahi shinbun*, June 9, 1950).

96. In a 1956 survey conducted by Zentoku, 78 percent of postmasters surveyed wanted special bureaucratic status, while 22 percent were content with regular public servant status (Zenkoku tokutei yūbinkyokuchōkai, *Tokuteikyoku taikan*, vol. 1, 23).

public servants, the commissioned postmasters did not carry out their duties from a position of bureaucratic authority (*kenryoku*); rather, they were semi-private figures who offered public services to local residents in the context of their personal relationships with those residents.[97] The postmasters' distinctive local presence was in turn dependent on the continuation of the free employment system, which valued candidates' "localness" and social ties far more than their prior experience within the civil service. It also depended on their exemption from transfers, which were routinely imposed on general public servants, thereby enabling them to spend their entire careers in one locality. The postmasters further argued that they should be permitted to expand their personal networks and local contributions through elected office;[98] in so doing, they would raise their profiles in local communities and attract more customers to the post office.[99] In sum, the special public service designation would not only reflect the postmasters' "democratic" traditions,[100] but would also allow them to bring the advantages of the commissioned post office system more fully to bear on the public at large. Needless to say, the postmasters were also well aware that political influence resulting from local elected office and alliances with conservative politicians at the national level would strengthen their position vis-à-vis the radical Zentei.[101]

Thanks largely to bureaucratic caution during the Occupation and the JSP's control of government, the postmasters lost their bid for special public servant status in 1947. But the battle was far from over. From the moment the law was passed the postmasters rallied to have their status changed.[102] Their campaign picked up steam at the end of the

---

97. Ibid., 19.

98. The postmasters articulated these preferences in a 1952 public relations pamphlet (Ogawa and Takahashi, *Tokutei yūbinkyoku seido shi*, 110). According to one estimate, as many as 1,700 commissioned postmasters were members of local assemblies when the National Public Service Law was passed in 1947 (Hatagawa, "Tokutei yūbinkyoku wa ika ni arubeki ka," 16).

99. Yamaguchi, *Tokutei yūbinkyoku*, 110 and 143.

100. Zenkoku tokutei yūbinkyokuchōkai, *Tokuteikyoku taikan*, vol. 1, 18.

101. Ogawa and Takahashi, *Tokutei yūbinkyoku seido shi*, 109.

102. The postmasters were not the only ones who fought the stipulations of the National Public Service Law. Workers in other government enterprises, including the

Occupation and then again in 1955, the year the LDP was established and formed its first government. For its own part, the LDP—with Tanaka Kakuei leading the fray—was only too happy to champion the cause. As the party struggled to build up its base of support (*jiban*) in the face of an ominous electoral threat from the JSP, deepening the partnership with the postmasters was an alluring proposition. With their extensive personal networks that stretched from the local to the national levels and their local social status, the postmasters were better positioned than the vast majority of interest groups at the time to mobilize supporters behind the LDP at the grassroots level. Indeed, they were about as attractive to the LDP as the well-organized local agricultural cooperatives, the leaders of which also had cultural roots as local "men of distinction" (*meibōka*).[103] The only impediment to openly recruiting the postmasters for political purposes was the legal ban on electoral participation by general public servants—an impediment that could be removed by simply changing their status. Neither the LDP nor the postmasters openly advertised their ambitions; they instead argued that for the sake of "democratic" community development and the expansion of postal services the postmasters should be permitted to serve in local assemblies.

Neither the media nor the left wing was fooled. When the LDP submitted two bills to the Diet in 1956 to amend the National Public Service Law, the *Asahi shinbun* complained that the LDP was out to transform the postmasters into a base for their electoral activities (*senkyo katsudō no botai*).[104] Meanwhile, the JSP, now the main opposition party, with Zentei's backing, submitted two bills of its own to the Diet calling for the designation of *all* postal employees as special public servants. The bills were subsequently withdrawn to allow the socialists to focus their energies on defeating the government's bills. The left wing's delay tactics were ultimately successful; the Diet session ended before the govern-

---

Japanese National Railways (JNR), opposed the law for denying them the right to strike (Johnson, *Japan's Public Policy Companies*, 30).

103. Bullock, "Nōkyō: A Short Cultural History."

104. *Asahi shinbun*, April 12 and 19, 1956. The newspaper argued that since the inherently conservative postmasters already had considerable social status and local influence, the special designation would greatly advantage the LDP over the opposition parties.

ment bills could be addressed.[105] The battle had been such an ordeal for the postmasters that one of their leaders was publicly reduced to tears.[106]

Undeterred, the postmasters and the LDP held fast to their conviction that each had something to gain in partnership with the other: the postmasters, protection from a militant union; and the LDP, potential access to a loyal electoral machine. Prime Minister Kishi Nobusuke's appointment of the 39-year-old Tanaka Kakuei as Minister of Posts and Telecommunications in July 1957 was just what the two sides needed to formalize their political union. Tanaka saw that together with local politicians, heads of local agricultural cooperatives, and the support organizations of individual politicians (*kōenkai*), the postmasters stood to fill a vacuum in the countryside left by the now dispossessed landlords as gatherers of the vote. The postmasters had the added advantages of running the country's largest institutional network while sitting atop billions of yen per year in government operating allowances (*watari-kirihi*), discretionary funds that could conceivably be put to good electoral use since they were not subject to effective government oversight.[107] In sum, Tanaka recognized the essential contributions that the postmasters could make to the LDP's own survival in the face of the JSP's ongoing electoral challenge. He cultivated the postmasters, moreover, at the same time that the party was converting farmers and small businessmen to the conservative cause and while the processes of local government amalgamation, which were often accompanied by the decline of services in many neighborhoods,[108] were lending the postmasters renewed relevance as local representatives of the state. For the most part, the postmasters were delighted with the partnership, rightfully viewing it as a hedge against future challenges to their profession.

---

105. Yamaguchi, *Tokutei yūbinkyoku*, 145.

106. Kyūshū chihō tokutei yūbinkyokuchōkai, *Kyūshū tokutei yūbinkyokuchōkai shi*, 417.

107. Interview, newspaper reporter, Tokyo, January 23, 2003. *Watarikirihi* were ostensibly earmarked to cover fuel and electricity costs, phone bills, gifts for customers who open new accounts or purchase insurance policies, and the like. But it was an open secret that postmasters also used the funds to pay for everything from private cell phones to business trips and various kinds of meetings (*Asahi shinbun*, June 7, 2001; *Asahi Newspaper*, August 29, 2001).

108. Fukutake, *Japanese Rural Society*, 160.

Ever the astute politician, Tanaka took steps that simultaneously shielded the commissioned post office system from union attacks while greasing the electoral alliance between the postmasters and the party. First, he encouraged the establishment of *more* commissioned post offices, a move that sparked heated debate on the floor of the Diet. In response to accusations from one opposition-party politician that his intention to increase the number of commissioned post offices over the short term by 2,000 was a "careless remark," Tanaka retorted that it was perfectly natural for the state to want to extend its reach throughout the country and in a way that conserved funds. Since many communities still lacked post offices, he continued, it would not be unreasonable to increase the total number of commissioned post offices by 20,000—or even 30,000![109]

As Table 2.1 illustrates, although the number of commissioned post offices increased at a rate much slower than what Tanaka would have liked, his personal endorsement helped put the system on a growth trajectory that contributed to its political influence for years to come. Of particular note was the increasing number of non-collection and delivery (*mushūhai*) post offices relative to that of collection and delivery (*shūhai*) facilities. Non-collection and delivery commissioned post offices, which can have as few as one or two employees, neither collect mail from mailboxes nor deliver it.[110] It is particularly telling that the number of facilities increased in relative terms even in urban areas, which were most efficiently served by larger post offices. Also revealing was the far more modest rise—and, in recent years, decline—in the number of simple post offices (*kan'i yūbinkyoku*).[111] Located mostly in lightly populated mountain and farming areas, the simple post offices were small operations commissioned by the MPT to individuals, agricultural cooperatives,

---

109. Zenkoku tokutei yūbinkyokuchōkai, *Tokuteikyoku taikan*, vol. 1, 50.

110. Although the ordinary post offices were also divided into collection and delivery and non-collection and delivery facilities, I do not highlight this distinction in Table 2.1 since it did not appear to have any significant political consequences. Generally speaking, throughout history the number of collection and delivery ordinary post offices has exceeded that of their non-collection counterparts by large margins.

111. Simple post offices were sometimes referred to as "postal agencies" in English.

or local government entities;[112] those who managed and staffed the facilities did so as private citizens, rather than public servants. If Tanaka's intention was to "save the state money," why were there not more of these cost-effective facilities?[113] Clearly, the overriding objective in prioritizing non-collection post offices was not the rational expansion of postal services but rather the installation around the country of as many well-connected postmasters as possible that could gather the vote behind the LDP. Note, for instance, the fact that LDP politicians often had a hand in establishing these facilities in their electoral districts—and in marked defiance of what should have been a strictly bureaucratic procedure.[114]

Second, Tanaka put Zentei on the defensive. Legend has it that shortly after he became posts minister, Tanaka noticed a sign on one of the ministry's walls with the union's name on it. Viewing this as evidence of the union's expanding access to the corridors of bureaucratic power, Tanaka had the sign removed in what one observer quipped was his first significant act as minister.[115] The move proved highly symbolic of Tanaka's determination to prioritize the interests of the commissioned post office system at the ministry and of his long-term stance toward the postal workers. Although he met regularly with union representatives and openly sympathized with their plight—he was, after all, no stranger to hard labor himself[116]—Tanaka refused to entertain union demands for a radical overhaul of the commissioned post office system.

Tanaka did, however, go through the motions of deliberating on the fate of the commissioned post office system, a task that had already

---

112. Simple post offices offered a reduced range of services. Those operated by agricultural cooperatives, moreover, did not offer postal savings services, since the co-ops had their own banking network.

113. The commissioned postmasters viewed the simple post offices as a threat to the future of their own post offices (Kyūshū chihō tokutei yūbinkyokuchōkai, *Kyūshū tokutei yūbinkyokuchōkai shi*, 255).

114. Some argue that in many parts of the country it was nearly impossible to establish commissioned post offices without the support of LDP intermediaries. See, for example, *Shūkan Daiyamondo* (June 29, 2002): 26–29.

115. Niigata nippōsha, *Za Etsuzankai*, 140.

116. Hayasaka, *Seijika Tanaka Kakuei*, 106.

Table 2.1: Number of Post Offices by Type

Fiscal Year	Total	Ordinary (*futsū*)	Commissioned (*tokutei*)	Collection & Delivery (*shūhai*)	Non-Collection & Delivery (*mushūhai*)	Simple (*kan'i*)
1945	13,281	533	12,748	5,216	7,532	—
1946	13,699	554	13,145	5,237	7,908	—
1950	15,017	665	13,435	5,208	8,227	917
1955	15,566	683	13,646	5,226	8,420	1,237
1960	16,234	797	14,162	5,023	9,139	1,275
1965	18,740	894	15,182	4,871	10,311	2,664
1970	20,643	1,051	16,203	4,696	11,507	3,389
1975	22,043	1,125	17,020	4,690	12,330	3,898
1980	23,005	1,201	17,586	4,590	12,996	4,218
1985	23,633	1,264	17,981	4,295	13,686	4,388
1990	24,107	1,299	18,241	3,922	14,319	4,567
1995	24,587	1,319	18,654	3,692	14,962	4,614
1996	24,638	1,321	18,711	3,682	15,029	4,606
1997	24,693	1,324	18,764	3,655	15,109	4,605
1998	24,736	1,315	18,832	3,656	15,176	4,589
1999	24,764	1,307	18,878	3,651	15,227	4,579
2000	24,774	1,308	18,916	3,641	15,275	4,550
2001	24,773	1,308	18,934	3,627	15,307	4,531
2002	24,752	1,310	18,941	3,563	15,378	4,501
2003	24,715	1,310	18,935	3,530	15,405	4,470
2004	24,678	1,308	18,923	3,465	15,458	4,447
2005	24,631	1,304	18,917	3,438	15,479	4,410
2006	24,574	1,294	18,924	2,418	16,506	4,356
2007	24,523	1,297	18,927	2,405	16,522	4,299

NOTE: Figures relevant until September 30, 2007. Since October 1, 2007, the government no longer recognizes a distinction between ordinary and commissioned post offices.
SOURCES: *Nihon tōkei nenkan* (1949, 1956, 2,000, 2003, 2007); Yūseishō, *Yūsei gyōsei tōkei nenpō* (1995); Japan Post, *Annual Report: Postal Services in Japan: 2007.9* (September 2007).

been delegated to the Commissioned Post Office System Study Group (Tokutei yūbinkyoku seido chōsakai), a fifteen-member advisory council established by cabinet ordinance in May 1957.[117] The MPT had pressed for the council's establishment in response to rancorous debates in the Diet over the objectives and usefulness of the commissioned post offices. Fearing that a ministerial report on the system would over-

117. Yamaguchi, *Tokutei yūbinkyoku*, 163.

politicize the issue, the ministry resolved to solicit the independent opinions of an ad hoc advisory group.[118] Some might find it more than coincidental that the committee's recommendations—issued in January 1958, several months into Tanaka's tenure at the ministry—more or less duplicated the LDP's (read Tanaka's) stance on the commissioned post office system.[119] In keeping with Zentei's demands, the committee recommended that the state establish ownership of all postal equipment, which to date had been owned by individual commissioned post-masters,[120] and of as many commissioned post offices as possible.[121] (Although the state made some progress toward fulfilling the first goal, the majority of commissioned post offices remained the private property of individual postmasters.)[122] More significantly, the report enthusiastically endorsed the defining features of the system, including the hiring of postmasters from among qualified local candidates. In wording that evoked earlier Diet statements on the system, the report stressed that in order for the postal services to benefit all citizens, the commissioned post offices had to combine corporate practices with a spirit of public service; those deemed best suited to achieving this balance, the report maintained, were capable locals with strong ties to their communities.[123]

In a few brief sentences, the study group's report had legitimized customs that would give the LDP long-term access to well-connected political allies at the local level. Although disappointed that the council had refused to recommend the legalization of the postmasters' political activities,[124] Tanaka endorsed the report as a public stamp of approval on the commissioned post office system that precluded the need for further government debate.[125] The report was a major blow to the un-

---

118. Ogawa and Takahashi, *Tokutei yūbinkyoku seido shi*, 113; Hatagawa, "Tokutei yū-binkyoku wa ika ni arubeki ka," 17.

119. Ogawa and Takahashi, *Tokutei yūbinkyoku seido shi*, 120.

120. By 1961, the state had purchased all equipment operated by the commissioned post offices (Yūseishō, ed., *Yūsei 100-nen no ayumi*, 188).

121. The report stopped short of calling for an outright ban on privately owned post offices, acknowledging instead their financial usefulness to the state (Maeno, *Yūsei to iu yakusho*, 49).

122. Maeno, *21-seiki wa Yūseishō no jidai*, 172.

123. Hatagawa, "Tokutei yūbinkyoku wa ika ni arubeki ka," 18.

124. Ogawa and Takahashi, *Tokutei yūbinkyoku seido shi*, 120.

125. Maeno, *21-seiki wa Yūseishō no jidai*, 170.

ion. The postmasters, however, were relieved to be on the winning side of a veritable "Battle of Sekigahara" between the left and the right over the future of the commissioned post office system.[126]

Tanaka served as head of the MPT for only a few short months but continued to exert enormous influence over the postal sector. To ensure party control over the MPT and hence the ministry's continuing support of the commissioned post office system, he controlled top ministerial appointments well into the 1980s.[127] He also took a personal interest in the composition of the PARC's Telecommunications Committee (Tsūshin bukai), which had regular dealings with officials in matters pertaining to the postal system.[128] Predictably, Tanaka's followers went on to dominate that committee; in 1985, it was estimated that a total of 18 (or 56.3 percent) of the committee's 32 Diet members who were considered part of the "postal tribe" (*yūsei zoku*)—an informal but closely-knit group of LDP legislators who had policy expertise in postal affairs and nurtured close ties with the MPT and the postmasters—hailed from the Tanaka faction.[129] The postal tribe served as the nucleus of LDP influence over postal politics and policy, including in the Upper House and Lower House communications committees. But postal affairs attracted the sympathy of politicians beyond the confines of the postal tribe; meetings of the LDP's Postal Services Roundtable (Yūsei jigyō konwakai), an informal organization that promoted the commissioned post office system,[130] were known to attract as many as 300 legislators.[131] Many of Tanaka's close associates, including Kanemaru Shin, Takeshita Noboru, and Nonaka Hiromu, faithfully nurtured his legacy, serving in turn as the "dons" of the postal *zoku* as well as volunteer consultants or advisors (*komon*) to Zentoku.

---

126. Kyūshū chihō tokutei yūbinkyokuchōkai, *Kyūshū tokutei yūbinkyokuchōkai shi*, 114.

127. Calder, "Linking Welfare and the Developmental State," 47.

128. Ibid.

129. The only other policy tribe in which the Tanaka faction was more dominant was the construction tribe, controlling 22 (or 68.8 percent) of 32 members (Inoguchi and Iwai, *Zoku giin no kenkyū*, 150, 302).

130. Maeno refers to the study group as "the nucleus of postal-system support organizations" (*Yūsei to iu yakusho*, 68).

131. Calder, "Linking Welfare and the Developmental State," 48.

All the while, the LDP welcomed the postmasters—as private citizens—into the ranks of the party membership,[132] and as members and financial patrons of the Liberal National Congress (Jiyū kokumin kaigi), a party support organization established in 1977 with chapters throughout the country.[133] The party rarely missed an opportunity to praise the postmasters' many virtues, a point that was nicely underscored by Takeshita's speech to a Zentoku meeting in the late 1970s: "When I was growing up," he reminisced, "there was only one postmaster in my town. His personality represented the trustworthiness of the postal services that in turn embody the history and traditions of the Japanese people. To me, the postmaster conjures up images of the cherished hometown [*furusato*]." Takeshita went on to include himself and the postmasters as representatives of a true conservatism that signified courage in rapidly changing times.[134] Another LDP politician later remarked that Zentoku was one of the party's "big three" (*gosanke*) supporters—a provocative allusion to the three powerful branch families that had supported the Tokugawa regime.[135] The postmasters, grateful for their second chance, were quick to thank their political benefactors, Tanaka being chief among them. "We'll never forget Tanaka," they gushed in 1962. "He increased the number of non-collection post offices and breathed new life into the entire postal system."[136]

While the LDP worked steadily to cement its partnership with the postmasters, the MPT struggled to shore up its own influence over the commissioned post office system in ways that both strengthened and complicated the triangular relationship among the postmasters, LDP politicians, and the ministry. In late 1956, after several years of bureaucratic experimentation, it launched Tokusuiren (Tokutei yūbinkyokuchō

---

132. Maeno, *21-seiki wa Yūseishō no jidai*, 178. A majority of commissioned postmasters had joined the LDP by the mid-1970s.

133. Kyūshū chihō tokutei yūbinkyokuchōkai, *Kyūshū tokutei yūbinkyokuchōkai shi*, 412. For an overview of this ideologically conservative organization, see its official website at http://www.jiyukk.jp/jiyuu.html (last accessed July 20, 2011).

134. Tōkyō chihō tokutei yūbinkyokuchōkai shi henshū iinkai, ed., *Tōkyō chihō tokutei yūbinkyokuchōkai shi*, 188.

135. Kyūshū chihō tokutei yūbinkyokuchōkai, *Kyūshū tokutei yūbinkyokuchōkai shi*, 452. The other two supporters would be farmers and the construction industry.

136. Zentoku tokutei yūbinkyokuchōkai, *Tokuteikyoku taikan*, vol. 2, 53.

gyōmu suishin renrakukai; Liaison Association for the Promotion of the Commissioned Postmasters' Duties). In theory, Tokusuiren was an administrative vehicle for the smooth functioning of postal services— a system of "group administration" (*shūdan kanri hōshiki*), in the words of one member, led by the state.[137] Subject to ministerial ordinance, it was a pyramidal organization that stretched from the ministry down to the grassroots level. Evoking the prewar "study groups," this elaborate set-up enabled the ministry to expedite the flow of information to the farthest reaches of the system, thereby contributing to the more efficient provision of services.[138]

In practice, Tokusuiren was a politicized body that straddled the boundaries between public and private. Established in the immediate aftermath of the LDP's ill-fated attempt to change the bureaucratic status of the postmasters, which was opposed by many MPT bureaucrats,[139] Tokusuiren was originally intended to strengthen ministerial control over a body of civil servants that was becoming increasingly politicized.[140] At first, the ministry tried unsuccessfully to extend its influence over Zentoku, following its formal re-establishment in September 1953. But as a partial concession to angry postal workers, who viewed any form of ministerial interference in the affairs of the commissioned postmasters as an act of empowerment for their adversaries, the ministry decided to create a second organization that would separate the administrative functions of the postmasters from their private interests as represented by Zentoku, which is not rooted in legislation.[141] Within a few years of Tokusuiren's establishment, however, the two organizations had become closely intertwined. Zentoku's local and regional organizations duplicated those of Tokusuiren and there was an almost complete overlap between the leaders of the two organizations. For much of the postwar era, newly chosen leaders of Zentoku went on to assume parallel posts in Tokusuiren, a move that helped strengthen

---

137. Interview, Zentoku official, Tokyo, March 27, 2003.

138. Yamaguchi, *Tokutei yūbinkyoku*, 151.

139. *Asahi shinbun*, September 25, 1956. Many bureaucrats believed that changing the status of the postmasters to enable them to participate in political activities would have drawn the postmasters' attention away from their official duties.

140. *Asahi shinbun*, September 23, 1956.

141. Interview, Zentoku official, Tokyo, March 27, 2003.

the hand of the postmasters and their political allies vis-à-vis the bureaucrats. It was also not unusual for the two organizations to place former bureaucrats in their more prominent leadership positions. Zentoku justified these arrangements by pointing out that while Tokusuiren's leaders were chosen by the ministry and, at the regional level, by the postal bureaus, Zentoku's representatives were ultimately endorsed through democratic elections among rank-and-file members.[142] (Never mind that these two sets of leaders were virtually the same.)

This elaborate institutional arrangement involved trade-offs for both the ministry and the postmasters. As far as the ministry was concerned, the organizational overlap between its administrative arm and Zentoku allowed it to keep closer tabs on the commissioned postmasters, who remained a highly cohesive group with strong local roots and who had the capacity to resist bureaucratic directives. But it also rendered the ministry more vulnerable to interference from LDP politicians who worked closely with Zentoku leaders both during and between election campaigns. And while some postmasters resented the ministerial interference and duplication of functions,[143] most welcomed the arrangement as another hedge against threats to their existence insofar as it folded bureaucrats, politicians, and the postmasters into a dense institutional network of overlapping interests.

The Electoral Functions of the Ruling Triad

The LDP benefited from the organizational integration of Tokusuiren and Zentoku because it facilitated ministerial participation in electoral politics. Although we may never know the exact mechanisms of the ministry's electoral involvement, some inside observers claimed that MPT officials routinely used the two associations to help organize the postmasters into vote-mobilizing teams behind individual LDP candidates.[144] There are some smoking guns to support this observation, such as the

---

142. Ibid.

143. Interviews with various commissioned postmasters, Tokyo and Kitakyūshū, 2002 and 2003.

144. Interview, newspaper journalist, Tokyo, January 23, 2003. This journalist explained that most of the MPT's electoral work was carried out by non-career bureaucrats so as not to jeopardize the futures of career-track officials.

leadership overlap between the two associations, the presence of former bureaucrats in the leadership ranks of the two organizations, and the fact that Zentoku actively supported the electoral campaigns of former postal officials running for the Diet under the LDP banner.[145]

For several decades, the electoral activities of the commissioned postmasters were informally known as the "fourth service" (*daiyon jigyō*), after mail delivery, postal savings, and postal insurance. Although a few postmasters openly carried out these tasks, which were orchestrated by top Zentoku leaders in consultation with the LDP and bureaucrats, others were more mindful of the statutory ban on political activities by public servants and thus assumed a more low-key political posture. These postmasters tended to delegate their electoral duties to two auxiliary organizations: the *fujinkai* (women's groups) connected to local and regional chapters of Zentoku, and Taiju zenkoku kaigi, an association of retired commissioned postmasters. These organizations resembled Nōkyō's political leagues, which are auxiliary or "front" organizations that help the cooperatives circumvent legal restrictions on financial contributions to political parties and other electoral activities.[146]

Unlike the women's groups linked to business associations, which usually function as informal friendship societies, those connected to Zentoku were large, well-organized, and very active politically. Virtually all Zentoku wives belonged to these groups, which had their own leadership structures and operating customs. And since the spouses of active postmasters did not fall under the jurisdiction of the National Public Service Law—so long as they themselves were not postal employees— they were free to participate openly in political activities. As Chapter 3 further explains, *fujinkai* members were pressured to recruit new members to the LDP and the support groups (*kōenkai*) of individual conservative politicians. They also worked on the campaigns of conservative candidates for the Diet, manning the phones in their regional offices, getting out the vote, and so on.

Taiju, which consisted of both *fujinkai* members and retired postmasters (postal OB, or "old boys"), also served as a kind of dummy political association for Zentoku that fell outside the purview of the

---

145. *Asahi shinbun*, November 21, 2001.
146. Bullock, "Nōkyō: A Short Cultural History."

National Public Service Law.[147] The organization's first manifestations were as local groups of retired postmasters who banded together in the 1970s to carry out *kōenkai* activities and lend their support to politicians at election time, all in concert with active postmasters in their areas. Some of these groups, like the "Tokyo OB Association of Commissioned Postmasters" (Tōkyō tokutei kyokuchō OB kai), openly defined themselves as a "directly affiliated branch [*shokuiki shibu*] of the LDP engaged in political support activities."[148] In 1982, local and prefectural OB associations formed a loosely organized association at the national level.[149]

The postmasters were particularly influential during the 1970s and early 1980s as the LDP's electoral machine matured and the rate of increase in the number of postmasters in Japan reached its peak.[150] Although they were active in Lower House elections, the commissioned postmasters and their spouses and retired colleagues focused their efforts on Upper House elections, and for good reason: given their lack of geographic concentration they were in a better position to mobilize supporters in the larger constituencies of the Upper House than in either the pre-1994 multi-member districts or current single-member districts of the Lower House. Since 1947, the Upper House electoral system has consisted of a proportional representation (PR) national constituency and multi-member prefectural constituencies. Elections are held every three years for half of the chamber's seats (now 126 of 252 seats), and voters cast two votes each time, one in the national constituency and one in the prefectural constituency. The postmasters focused most—but certainly not all—of their vote mobilizational energies on the national tier. For many years this involved mobilizing potential voters into the support organizations (*kōenkai*) of the postmasters' preferred candidates and then persuading them to vote for those candidates at election time. In 1982, the rules governing the national constituency were changed so that voters now had to cast their ballots for a party, rather than an in-

---

147. Enō, *Jitsuroku*, 229–30.
148. Tokyo chihō tokutei yūbinkyokuchōkai shi henshū iinkai, *Tokyo chihō tokutei yūbinkyokuchōkai shi*, 228–29.
149. Kyūshū chihō tokutei yūbinkyokuchōkai, *Kyūshū tokutei yūbinkyokuchōkai shi*, 462.
150. Yamamura, "Tokutei yūbinkyokuchōkai no shōtai," 96.

dividual. (The candidates were arranged in rank order on closed lists drawn up by the parties in advance of the election.) This meant that in addition to mobilizing voters behind the LDP, the postmasters faced the difficult task of pressuring the party to place their favorite candidates high enough on the list so that they would be guaranteed seats. As a result of these reforms, the electoral influence of the postmasters— and of other organized interest groups—on Upper House elections began to decline.

In 2000, the government of Mori Yoshirō attempted to reverse this trend and its negative effects on the party's electoral machine by reforming the Upper House electoral system yet again.[151] Now, voters can cast their ballots for *either* an individual *or* a party in the national constituency. Votes for individual candidates are then translated into votes for the party, and seats are distributed according to the party's portion of the total vote. Those who occupy the seats are chosen not according to their relative position on a pre-determined list, but rather to their total number of votes. Organized interest groups like the postmasters preferred this system because it allowed them to focus on mobilizing votes behind individual candidates rather than manipulating the candidate's position on a party list. Analysts have observed that voters will tend to choose parties over individuals when the latter are not recognizable to them,[152] which means that the 2000 reforms may not have had as big an impact on shoring up the significance of the organized vote as some might have hoped. The fact that the number of votes credited to the postmasters' mobilizational efforts declined in the 2001 and 2004 Upper House elections would seem to corroborate this point.

For years, the electoral activities of Zentoku and its companion associations were carried out behind the scenes and with only occasional media scrutiny—and with virtually no interference from the police or regional postal authorities. But in the aftermath of the July 29, 2001 Upper House election, the inner workings of this secretive ruling triad were revealed in a sensational scandal. At the center of the maelstrom was Kōso Kenji, the head of the Kinki Postal Bureau between 1998–1999 who had just won election in the national constituency as the post-

---

151. Hashimoto et al., *Zukai Nihon seiji no shōhyakka*, 100–101.
152. *Asahi Newspaper*, July 23, 2004.

masters' "interest representative Diet member." Kōso, it was revealed, had been involved in an illegal vote-gathering scheme involving Taiju, the postal bureau, and local postmasters.[153] Top-ranking postal officials, including Kōso's successor at the bureau, were accused of collecting electoral contributions from both their colleagues and individual postmasters and channeling them into the Postal Services Agency (Yūsei jigyōchō; PSA),[154] and of paying for meetings at which the postmasters discussed electoral tactics.[155] As many as 3,100 commissioned post offices were allegedly involved in this pyramidal vote-mobilization scheme,[156] and there is evidence that many postmasters channeled funds from their government-allotted discretionary funds (*watarikirihi*) into the campaign.[157] Bureau officials allegedly participated in the campaign in order to secure themselves lucrative post-retirement jobs in public corporations connected to the postal bureaucracy. In late September 2001, Kōso succumbed to pressure from top LDP leaders and resigned his Diet seat, and no fewer than fifteen high-level officials in the Kinki Postal Bureau and the postmaster of the Kinki Central Post Office, an ordinary post office, were arrested for electoral violations.[158] Several were later convicted and given suspended sentences.[159]

The Kōso incident was the largest electoral scandal in the history of the postwar Japanese postal system and led to the most detailed media accounts of involvement by postal bureaucrats in electoral affairs. The sheer scope of the scandal was attributable to at least two factors, the first of which was Prime Minister Mori's Upper House electoral reforms.

---

153. The Public Office Election Law (Kōshoku senkyo hō) states that if a former government official runs as a candidate in a national election within three years of leaving his position, any electoral violations committed by his successor (to the government post) at the candidate's request would invalidate the candidate's election. Kōso had vacated his position in the Kinki Postal Bureau only two years before the election (*Japan Times*, September 17, 2001).

154. *Mainichi Daily News*, August 28, 2001. The PSA assumed many of the administrative functions of the postal system in 2001. It was dissolved in 2003 and replaced by Japan Post, a public corporation. See Chapter 5 for more details on these changes.

155. *Japan Times*, September 1, 2001.

156. *Asahi Newspaper*, September 1, 2001.

157. *Asahi Newspaper*, August 29, 2001.

158. *Japan Times*, September 7, 2001.

159. *Mainichi Daily News*, January 17, 2002.

Although legal violations were not uncommon after 1982 as interest groups pressured the LDP to get their preferred candidates placed toward the top of the party lists (the postmasters, however, were not openly accused of such violations), they were more likely after 2000 as many of those groups opted to throw their lot behind individual candidates, rather than the party. For the postmasters, this meant employing tried and tested tactics as they struggled to mobilize ever widening swaths of first postal personnel and then local residents behind their best bet, Kōso Kenji. The postmasters and their bureaucratic allies were further motivated in 2001 by the increasingly pro-reform political atmosphere of the new Koizumi administration. Fearing the kind of changes that might jeopardize the defining institutions of their profession, the postmasters turned to Kōso, a kindred soul who campaigned vehemently against Koizumi's postal reform proposals.[160] In the end, the Kōso affair turned many Japanese against the postmasters, lending added credibility to Koizumi's crusade against the state-run postal system and the political interests that buttressed it.

The Postmasters in Perspective

The Kōso scandal offers insight into the structure and activities of one of Japan's most secretive but politically significant ruling triads. Established during a period of institutional flux and consciously nurtured by Tanaka Kakuei, early postwar Japan's foremost political entrepreneur, it was a relationship that facilitated the mobilization of votes behind the LDP and shielded the commissioned post office system from outside threats. At the center of that ruling triad was an interest group that was in many ways typical of Japan's interest group environment.

All of this, of course, begs an important question: just how important were the postmasters to the electoral longevity of the LDP? A comparison of the vote mobilizing capabilities of different interest groups provides some clues. As Inoguchi Takashi illustrates, Taiju mobilized approximately 1.03 million votes in the 1980 Upper House election, but this performance was surpassed by that of the construction industry (1.74 million votes) and the agricultural cooperatives (1.12 million).

---

160. *Japan Times*, September 26, 2001.

Clearly, the LDP was less dependent on the postmasters than on these other two groups. If we examine the performance of these same groups in the 2001 election, we see that the vote mobilizing capacity of all interest groups had declined; the number of votes collected by the postmasters, the construction industry, and the agricultural cooperatives was estimated to be 480,000, 270,000, and 160,000, respectively. Significantly, the postmasters were the top vote gatherers among these three sets of interest groups in that fateful election. Also noteworthy is the proportion of LDP rank-and-file members constituting each of these groups in 2001. While 180,000 hailed from construction and only 10,000 from the agricultural cooperatives, the postmasters comprised 230,000 LDP members. (At 150,000, the third largest group of LDP members came from the association of war veterans.)[161] Interestingly, while the 1990s in particular witnessed a steady weakening of *all* organized interests in Japanese electoral politics—a weakening that can be attributed to several interrelated developments, including the 1994 Lower House electoral reforms, the expansion of the floating vote, and the decline of LDP factions—the postmasters' decline was less precipitous. This is not to suggest that the postmasters were indispensable to the LDP; had they severed their ties with the LDP at the height of their influence, the party no doubt would have continued to win elections. But it does seem safe to say that for as long as the organized vote mattered to the LDP, the postmasters were among the party's top three supporters.

This is remarkable, because the commissioned post office system and the associations that represented it had no economically or administratively rational reason for being. The commissioned post office's functions could have been easily performed by other entities, including the simple post offices or large ordinary post offices that enjoy significant economies of scale. By the late 1950s, moreover, the wealthy Japanese state no longer had grounds to argue—as Maejima Hisoka had done so persuasively three-quarters of a century beforehand—that the commissioned post office system was an essential cost-minimizing en-

---

161. Inoguchi, "Japan's Upper House Election of 29 July 2001," 48. Inoguchi's figures were drawn from the *Nihon keizai shinbun*, August 5, 2001. Other observers estimated that region by region, Taiju comprised as much as 10 percent or more of LDP membership at the time of the 2005 Lower House election (*Asahi shinbun*, September 4, 2005).

terprise. The postmasters were hired according to highly subjective standards exercised at the discretion of individual officials at the regional level, rather than objective, merit-based requirements that were rooted in law. Their authority, moreover, was based far less on legal-rational authority, as is the norm in most modern bureaucracies, than on social status and hierarchy. Simply stated, the postwar commissioned post office system made poor economic and bureaucratic sense.

It was thanks largely to Tanaka Kakuei's deft leadership that the postmasters were able to survive for so many years. And it was thanks in part to the postmasters' dogged efforts to protect their interests that they managed to suffer a somewhat less precipitous decline in the face of electoral change than the LDP's other interest group patrons. But in the end, the postmasters were indeed in decline. In fact, as the next chapter illustrates, developments within the profession were rendering the profession highly inflexible and vulnerable to collapse.

THREE

The Commissioned Postmasters:
The View from Inside

Yoshimura Takeshi, a retired commissioned postmaster from Kamakura, has a most unusual business card (*meishi*).[1] Affixed to the front is a one-yen postage stamp adorned with Maejima Hisoka's image; on the back is a map of Maejima's burial site in Kanagawa prefecture. As the director of what amounts to a Maejima fan club, Mr. Yoshimura helps lead a pilgrimage of retired postmasters to the site every April to pay homage to the architect of Japan's modern postal system on the anniversary of his death. Mr. Yoshimura is also an amateur historian who has conducted extensive research on Maejima's legacy and the history of the commissioned post offices—including his own.

Mr. Yoshimura's post office typifies the historical trajectory of the commissioned post office system. Established in 1904, the tiny non-collection and delivery (*mushūhai*) facility was first headed by a local resident named Nakano Jitarō, who later handed his position to a male relative. In succession, the two postmasters presided over their facility's expansion into the postal insurance, telephone, and telegraph services. Since there was no family heir to carry on the Nakano tradition after the early 1930s, the postmastership was transferred to Mr. Yoshimura's father, who witnessed the near total destruction of his home and post

---

1. The names of individual postmasters have been changed to protect their privacy.

office during the final months of World War II. In 1968, Mr. Yoshimura assumed the position, serving his community until his retirement during the early 2000s at the age of 68—three years beyond the official retirement age for ordinary postmasters.[2] Since none of Mr. Yoshimura's family members coveted the position, the post office is now run by one of his four former employees—a woman. Mr. Yoshimura continues to live with his wife in the family home, just a stone's throw from the post office, and remains active in his research. He also attends periodic meetings of the area's Taiju chapter, as well as year-end parties and weekend outings with his retired colleagues.

Mr. Yoshimura is part of a dying breed. Dignified and deeply conservative, he is proud of his accomplishments as a postmaster and of the postal system's traditions and contributions to modern Japan. While reticent about the postmasters' electoral activities, he worries about Japan's changing political environment, the shortage of candidates to take over vacant postmasterships, and the idea of postal privatization. To Mr. Yoshimura, these changes mark the decline of postal customs that combine the very best of Japanese tradition with modern institutions. "The postmasters' traditional allies are disappearing," Mr. Yoshimura observed sadly in 2002, "and the future of the commissioned post office system is uncertain."[3]

My purpose in this chapter is to look inside Mr. Yoshimura's changing world to more fully illuminate the postmasters' social and electoral influence on the eve of postal privatization. Until recently, understanding the occupational and political lives of the postmasters was all but impossible given the shroud of secrecy that surrounded them and their relations with the LDP. Thanks to heightened media scrutiny since the 1990s, the postmasters' increasing willingness to grant interviews, and the publication of revealing memoirs by former postmasters, their lives are now more accessible. Drawing on these sources, I explore the postmasters' interests and aspirations, the nature of their participation in representative organizations, the origins and ramifications (both social

---

2. Under the state-led postal system, the government permitted the commissioned postmasters to extend their commissions for three years past their official retirement age of 65. The postmasters of ordinary post offices enjoyed no such privilege.

3. Interview, Kamakura, August 15, 2002.

and political) of their community stature, and the extent of their electoral activities. In so doing, I provide a snapshot of the postmasters in their workaday environments and of their contributions to contemporary Japanese life—contributions, as we shall see, that were closely integrated with their electoral functions. Finally, I show how the internal dynamics of their representative organizations rendered them inherently vulnerable to decline even before Koizumi came on the scene and threatened them with occupational extinction.

The Enduring Traditions of the Commissioned Post Office System

As Chapters 1 and 2 have shown, the Japanese commissioned post office system underwent several transformations after its establishment during the 1870s. Thanks to the reforms of the immediate postwar period and the late 1950s, the postmasters finally received salaries and benefits for their services, were no longer required to provide the buildings in which those services were offered, were subject to more predictable hiring procedures, and were banned from engaging in political activities—just like any other Japanese bureaucrat. In practice, however, many of the informal institutions of the commissioned post office system survived the reforms, giving rise to a distinctive set of interests that came to define the postmasters' collective identity and partnership with the LDP.

Among the more significant Occupation reforms was the abolition of the requirement that the commissioned postmasters provide their own private facilities as post offices. Although the original purpose of private ownership was to relieve some of the financial pressures on the Meiji state, postwar critics viewed it as the primary source of corruption within the commissioned post office system. In response to the recommendations of the 1958 report on the system issued by the MPT, the state proceeded to purchase both post offices and postal equipment from individual postmasters. But while the state established nearly complete ownership of postal equipment by the early 1960s, the same cannot be said for the buildings themselves. As Table 3.1 illustrates, state ownership of the commissioned post office facilities never reached 10 percent, and this is precisely what the postmasters preferred.

In 1960, Zentoku established Zenkyōren (Zenkoku tokutei kyokuchō kyōkai rengōkai; Alliance of Commissioned Postmasters Associations)

Table 3.1: State-Owned Commissioned Post Offices

Year	# of commissioned post offices	# of state-owned post offices	% of state-owned post offices
1951	13,496	378	2.80
1955	13,651	544	3.99
1965	15,201	1,093	7.19
1975	17,019	1,378	8.10
1980	17,587	1,388	7.89
1985	17,979	1,423	7.91

SOURCE: Yamaguchi, *Tokutei yūbinkyoku*, 177.

to promote and protect the private ownership of post offices. A legal foundation (*zaidan hōjin*), Zenkyōren and its local chapters issued the postmasters low-interest loans to build or purchase new facilities and occasionally assumed ownership of struggling post offices.[4] The postmasters' reason for going to such lengths was simple: if the custom of private ownership were to disappear, so too would many of the other customs that gave the commissioned post office system its distinctive character. In response to these trends, the state quietly loosened its efforts to increase the number of state-owned facilities.[5]

One custom that survived because of the private ownership of postal facilities was the handing down of postmasterships through generations of offspring or other close relatives. Even at the turn of the twenty-first century, it was not uncommon for postmasters to head post offices that had been established by their great-grandfathers, a heritage that many proudly recounted to curious customers. To be sure, inheritance practices helped preserve the popular appeal of many of Japan's older commissioned post offices—tiny, architecturally-significant structures tucked away in remote villages or urban side-streets that were often

---

4. Yamaguchi, *Tokutei yūbinkyoku*, 176. Some postal facilities were located in privately owned buildings and local government facilities.

5. The Kyushu chapter of Zentoku reported that the national rate of private ownership of commissioned post offices rose from 51.6 percent in 1990 to 64.7 percent in 1995—a significant increase given pressures from the postal workers and other critics to increase state ownership of the facilities (Kyūshū chihō tokutei yūbinkyokuchōkai, *Kyūshū tokutei yūbinkyokuchōkai shi*, 330).

named after neighborhoods or landmarks that had long since disappeared. In a quaint testament to the cultural significance of these entities, Japanese post office aficionados would travel from post office to post office as they would to temples or shrines, taking pictures, purchasing postage stamps that depicted the region, and collecting the distinctive seals of each post office visited. As their owners were quick to point out, had these entities been passed on to "outsiders," they may not have been kept up as well as they were.

Officially, the postmasters' inheritance practices did not exist. The Ministry of Internal Affairs and Communications (Sōmushō; MIC) publicized no statistics on it, claiming that the custom had been eliminated by the postwar introduction of "rigorous" hiring procedures for new recruits.[6] The postmasters, for the most part, avoided the word inheritance (*seshū*) altogether for fear of provoking public criticism, insisting that they had attained their positions on the basis of personal merit.[7] But while the number of inherited postmasterships declined significantly after the war, the custom persisted, by 2001 affecting one-quarter to one-third of all positions.[8]

The nature of the hiring process also facilitated the inheritance of postmasterships. As I illustrated in Chapter 1, prewar candidates for vacant postmasterships were chosen at the discretion of regional postal bureau officials according to the guidelines introduced by Maejima during the 1870s: candidates had to be long-term residents of the communities they were to serve, as well as men of intellectual ability and financial means who could provide the facilities for the post office. Unlike their counterparts in the ordinary post offices, candidates did not have to be experienced postal employees, nor were they required to take examinations. Needless to say, the process heavily favored the offspring of existing postmasters. In response to Zentei's criticisms, the government tried to bring the hiring process in line with that of ordinary postmasters as the postwar decades unfolded. Before long, candidates had to take a

---

6. Interview, two MIC officials, Tokyo, March 3, 2003.

7. Interviews, three commissioned postmasters, Kitakyūshū, August 8–9, 2003.

8. There was disagreement on the extent of this practice, but these figures were commonly cited in my interviews with commissioned postmasters and other informed observers of the system. Conventional wisdom has it that at least 50 percent of all commissioned post offices were subject to inheritance around 1945.

written examination that tested their administrative skills, write an essay that demonstrated their personal qualities, and submit to an interview with postal bureau officials.

One might conclude that the rationalization of the hiring process would ensure the selection of only the most qualified candidates. But several customs worked at cross-purposes to this objective. First, as the Japan Post website clearly stated as late as September 2007, just days before the official start of postal privatization, local residents were still heavily favored as candidates to lead commissioned post offices, the success of which depended on their "close ties to local communities."[9] Second, the exams for postmasterships were only announced once a position became vacant, and in many cases only one applicant would sit for it—more often than not the son or other relative of a retiring postmaster who had received a personal recommendation from Zentoku.[10] The exams themselves were often dismissed as empty formalities that produced unqualified "back-door public servants" (*uraguchi kōmuin*).[11] One disaffected former postmaster revealed that the hiring process reinforced a sense of entitlement among the scions of postmaster families, some of whom audaciously referred to themselves as "lords" (*otonosama*). Inheritance, he wrote, "is all fine and well if [the candidate] is an exemplary, insightful individual, but if an idiotic lord is hired, it means nothing but toil for the employees."[12]

The third distinctive feature of the commissioned postmasters that persisted more or less unchanged since the early Meiji period was their exemption from periodic transfer. Virtually all national, career-track bureaucrats in Japan, including the postmasters of large, ordinary post offices, are subject to transfer from time to time, a practice that gives them the experience to become generalists within their administrative jurisdictions. The commissioned postmasters escaped this custom be-

---

9. After the privatization process officially began, postal authorities dropped the residency requirement for prospective postmasters. But candidates for the position must still demonstrate an ability to earn the trust of the community, a requirement that is likely to privilege local residents. See http://www.jp-network.japanpost.jp/employment/career/index02.html (last accessed July 18, 2011).

10. Enō, *Jitsuroku*, 200.

11. *Nikkei Business*, June 18, 2001.

12. Enō, *Jitsuroku*, 46.

cause of the private ownership of postal facilities and the local residency requirement for new recruits. Thus, since the vast majority of commissioned postmasters spent their entire careers at a single post office, they were far better positioned to become important personages within their neighborhoods than ordinary postmasters. This in turn helped them cultivate *chiensei*, the social capital that was at the root of their social, professional, and political standing in Japanese communities.

A term used by the commissioned postmasters for generations, *chiensei* can be simply defined as the territorial bonds that develop during the postmaster's long association with a community. But in much the same way that blood ties (*ketsuen*) bind together otherwise disparate members of an extended family, *chiensei* includes an emotional dimension that valorizes nostalgia for and loyalty to a geographical place and its people. Thus, the postmaster with *chiensei* was one who served his neighborhood not merely as an appointed state representative, but also as a loyal son of the community—one who went above and beyond the call of duty by providing his customers with personalized financial advice and serving as a community volunteer.

Once acquired, *chiensei* had a number of practical uses. For example, a commissioned postmaster with *chiensei* found it much easier than the transient ordinary postmaster to convince residents to deposit their money into postal savings accounts and purchase postal life insurance policies. This was reason enough for the commissioned postmasters to zealously work on expanding their *chiensei*, recognizing in their social capital the potential to compensate for the inefficient size and operating deficits that plagued the vast majority of commissioned post offices.[13]

The product of their localness and the currency of their influence, *chiensei* was cultivated in ways that further reinforced the distinctive features of the postwar commissioned post office system. Since *chiensei* was difficult for outsiders to acquire, the postmasters and their representa-

---

13. It is a telling point that the commissioned post offices, which comprised about three-quarters of the total number of post offices in Japan on the eve of postal privatization, collected approximately 75 percent of postal savings accounts and postal insurance policies. The commissioned postmasters often commented that it was their *chiensei* that allowed them to compete so effectively with the ordinary post offices, which, given their economies of scale, should have grabbed a disproportionate share of new savings accounts and insurance policies.

tive organizations went to great lengths to ensure local hires for vacant postmasterships and to convince the sons of retiring postmasters to step up to the plate.[14] All told, preserving the institutions of the commissioned post office system and the social capital these institutions generated—and depended on—was at the heart of Zentoku's existence, a subject to which we now turn.

The Postmasters in Organizational Context

The postmasters participated in inclusive, well-institutionalized organizations for two sets of reasons: to facilitate and monitor the administration of postal services and to preserve and promote the status of the postmasters and the institutions they administered. After several years of experimentation, in 1956 the MPT launched Tokusuiren to accomplish the first objective, and the postmasters established Zentoku in 1953 to fulfill the second. As we observed in Chapter 2, although the first organization was an official, bureaucratic association and the second a "voluntary" one, the two overlapped almost completely in terms of organizational structure and leadership. They were, as the postmasters themselves observed, "two sides of the same coin."[15]

Both Zentoku and Tokusuiren focused most of their energies on presenting a united front to the social and political worlds. But they also spent a great deal of time cajoling the postmasters into fulfilling their professional responsibilities—responsibilities that grew more and more burdensome as the twentieth century unfolded. From 1934, when an independent postal account was established and the postal services could no longer rely on the government to bail them out in a pinch,[16] the services were required to become financially self-sufficient.[17] This put added pressure on the postmasters to increase revenues. By the early postwar era, however, the social rewards for hard work and self-sacrifice

---

14. Kyūshū chihō tokutei yūbinkyokuchōkai, *Kyūshū tokutei yūbinkyokuchōkai shi*, 294–95; Enō, *Jitsuroku*, 46–49.

15. Kyūshū chihō tokutei yūbinkyokuchōkai, *Kyūshū tokutei yūbinkyokuchōkai shi*, 17.

16. Yūseishō, ed., *Yūsei 100-nen shi*, 572.

17. According to the guidelines governing the independent account, the salaries of postal employees had to be covered by income generated by the services. Only *watari-kirihi*, government allowances issued to commissioned and ordinary postmasters to cover operating expenses, were funded from the general account.

had begun to dwindle. Whereas prewar postmasters generally hailed from the stratum of well-regarded local notables, that stratum had all but disappeared by the end of World War II, taking with it much of the prestige that was once automatically associated with the postmastership. The profession's allure suffered additional blows from the postwar decline of public trust in state institutions and increasing media attention to the postmasters' improprieties. Put simply, the postmasters could no longer count on elevated social status just by assuming their positions. Nor could they expect to enhance their prestige by running for local elected office, thanks to the restrictions of the 1948 National Public Service Law. For professional, social, and political reasons, status still mattered to the postwar commissioned postmasters, but it now had to be *earned*—largely through the time-consuming process of cultivating *chiensei*. Not surprisingly, as their professional and social lives grew more demanding, some postmasters reneged on their duties, pilfered public funds, or left the profession altogether.

The structure and customs of Zentoku and Tokusuiren worked to keep these defections to a minimum and ensure that the postmasters complied with the standards of the profession. They made membership in the associations compulsory, just as a lawyer is obliged to join the Japan Federation of Bar Associations (Nihon bengoshi rengōkai; JFBA) upon passing the bar examination.[18] But while lawyers are required by law to join the JFBA, compulsory membership in the postmasters associations was the product of both bureaucratic ordinance and happenstance. MPT regulations stipulated that all commissioned postmasters be automatically admitted to Tokusuiren, the ministry's supervisory organization. But given the almost complete overlap between the two organizations' leadership and constituent local chapters, which sometimes led to discussions of Zentoku business at Tokusuiren meetings,[19] once a postmaster entered Tokusuiren, he was inducted almost by default into Zentoku, the postmasters' political lobbying organization.[20]

---

18. The analysis in this paragraph is inspired by Olson, *The Logic of Collective Action*, especially 68.

19. Enō, *Jitsuroku*, 204–5.

20. Female postmasters participated in Zentoku along with their male colleagues, but also had their own subcommittee within the association.

The composition of Tokusuiren and Zentoku conforms to Olson's observations about the effectiveness of federations in nurturing close relationships between the leaders and the led in an interest group.[21] With tiers stretching from the national level to the grassroots level, where groups of ten individual post offices were organized into *bukai* (sections), the two associations went to great lengths to encourage group conformity. In the *bukai*, the postmasters engaged in face-to-face interactions and monitored one another in a manner reminiscent of the wartime neighborhood associations (*tonarigumi*). Older colleagues and *bukai* chiefs would keep a close watch on their younger colleagues,[22] dropping in on them at the post office or after hours in their homes to discuss postal business and other issues.[23] It was also at this level that the postmasters evaluated one another's professional performance, set objectives for serving the community, and established divisions of labor for group projects.[24] By enveloping each postmaster in a web of social contacts and mutual obligations, association leaders at the regional and national levels were well poised to issue directives to rank-and-file members and to force compliance with those directives.

Tokusuiren and Zentoku also provided the postmasters with social and psychological "selective incentives" to adhere to the profession's rules and norms.[25] As a result of the *bukai* structure and the frequency of official meetings at all levels of the organizational hierarchy, many postmasters grew to know one another well, forming friendships that persisted well beyond retirement. Membership within these networks also presented young postmasters with opportunities for marriage— a custom, as a later section explains, that reflected electoral, as well as social, incentives.[26] Lastly, the postmasters and their families were en-

---

21. Olson, *The Logic of Collective Action*, 62–63.

22. *Asahi shinbun*, June 7, 2001.

23. Honma, *Tokutei yūbinkyokuchō ni natta boku no rakudai nikki*, 208.

24. Enō, *Jitsuroku*, 24–25.

25. As Olson explains, selective incentives are offered to individual members to encourage them to join or remain in a particular group or to participate in collective activities (*The Logic of Collective Action*, 51).

26. One third-generation postmaster whom I interviewed in Kitakyūshū in 2002 and 2006 married the daughter—herself a postal employee—of one of his older colleagues.

couraged to socialize. At Zentoku's yearly national meetings, for instance, participants were treated to several days of lavish banquets and entertainment, with fleets of tour buses at the ready to shuttle them to nearby tourist sites.

The postmasters associations and their affiliated organizations offered or channeled a number of other selective incentives to their members, including professional advice, pensions and other social services for retired postmasters, loans for the repair and rebuilding of postal facilities, and government rents for those facilities. Although these perquisites certainly made the postmasters' job easier, they did not always compare favorably with those of many other large interest groups. Nōkyō, for example, serves as a conduit for state subsidies to the farming sector and as the sole collector and distributor of rice and other farm products. Nōkyō also functions as a bank, insurance provider, technical assistant, supplier of farming inputs, and even a real estate broker for its members.[27] The postmasters associations were never in a position to deliver comparable benefits to rank-and-file members since there were few such benefits to deliver in the first place. While the state-run postal system offered banking and insurance services, the postmaster's role was to *administer*, rather than receive, those services. The postmasters' social-welfare benefits, moreover, were no better than those offered in most other large professions. Had the postmasters been private actors operating in a more competitive market setting, perhaps the non-salary economic perquisites of their profession would have been more substantial. As it stood, their legal status as public servants effectively denied them access to many forms of state or market largesse.

With relatively few carrots at their disposal, the postmasters associations depended heavily on sticks, or "negative incentives," to keep their less compliant members in line. These incentives borrowed heavily from Japan's traditional shame-based culture. For instance, Tokusuiren cooperated with regional postal bureaus to impose quotas (*noruma*) on the postmasters for the sale of postage stamps, New Years' greeting

---

This postmaster arrived at our first meeting with another local postmaster in tow; the two were such close friends that they felt comfortable finishing one another's sentences.

27. Mulgan, *The Politics of Agriculture in Japan*, 207.

cards (*nengajō*), "hometown packages" (*furusato kozutsumi*),[28] postal life insurance policies, and new postal savings accounts. Tokusuiren and the bureaus would then publicize the results of the postmasters' performance, singling out those who had fallen short of their quotas. In the case of postal savings accounts and insurance policies, postmasters and postal workers who met or exceeded their quotas received cash awards; one government study revealed that successful postal employees were awarded approximately 380,000 yen each at one point during the mid-1980s.[29] Those who failed to make the grade received official warnings to shape up.[30] To avoid these humiliations, postmasters and their employees would form special teams to devise more effective sales tactics.[31] Some even resorted to secretly buying up large quantities of greeting cards or hometown packages, a practice known among postal employees as "self-destruction" (*jibaku*).[32] The pressure on the postmasters and their employees to increase the volume of postal transactions was no more dramatically illustrated than in 2000 and 2001, when high-interest ten-year time deposits issued in 1990 and 1991 reached maturity. The postmasters and their employees hit the streets in droves, calling on local

---

28. Hometown packages consist of specialty foods and manufactured items from specific localities that customers can order through the postal system. See Chapter 4 for more details about this program.

29. The practice of awarding the postmasters and postal workers "encouragement allowances" (*shōrei teate*) began in 1937 to promote the sale of war bonds. Private sector critics complained that it was inappropriate to award public servants for doing their jobs. According to one estimate, awards connected to postal savings amounted to roughly 0.5 percent of the total amount of savings deposits collected within a given period (*Shūkan Tōyō keizai*, September 7, 1997).

30. *Shūkan Daiyamondo*, June 29, 2002.

31. The postmasters and their employees would also set up special small-scale groups (*shōshūdan*) to improve the overall quality of postal services (Yūseishō yōin kun-renka, *Tokutei yūbinkyoku*, 185–89).

32. *Shūkan Daiyamondo*, December 22, 2007; Enō, *Jitsuroku*, 270. In 2000, the MPT revealed that one postmaster in Hyōgo prefecture had forged 245 postal life insurance contracts in order to improve his sales record (*Japan Times*, April 17, 2000). On a lighter note, young postal workers have been wont to complain about the cloying scent of *udon* and curried rice in their dormitories at certain times of the year, all purchased by their colleagues in a frantic effort to meet their quotas for "hometown packages" (*Shūkan Daiyamondo*, June 29, 2002).

residents to roll their deposits back into the postal savings system rather than the riskier, higher-yield offerings of private financial institutions.[33]

Zentoku also took steps to control entry into—and exit out of—the profession. To ensure that only sympathetic individuals were admitted into the commissioned post office system, Zentoku would hand pick the candidates for vacant postmasterships and then recommend them to regional examination authorities—often through the good offices of local Diet members.[34] Some Zentoku chapters even tried to prevent "early retirements" by requiring postmasters to obtain the association's permission before resigning their positions. According to one former postmaster, it was not uncommon for Zentoku to take several years to grant such requests.[35] It is also likely that financial indebtedness to Zen-kyōren acted as an additional deterrent to premature exit.

One wonders whether Zentoku needed to go to such lengths to limit defections, given traditional Japanese employment practices and the postmasters' mobility prospects. Until recently, Japan offered few second chances to most white-collar employees, who tended to remain in a single company for their entire working lives. Even if the labor market had been more flexible, there were few employment opportunities for the disgruntled postmaster looking for a career change.[36] Although the functions of the postal system overlapped with those of private parcel delivery companies, the telecommunications industry, and the private banking and insurance sectors, many postmasters lacked the skills to do well in these fields. Add to this the fact that many postmasters owned their own postal facilities, which were not easily transferred to other

---

33. It was also not unusual for postal employees to lie about deposits in order to meet their postal savings targets. Since the targets were based on the size of deposit transactions rather than account balances, some employees would issue fake deposit and withdrawal documents to make it look as if many (and large) deposits were being made over time—even though no money was actually changing hands. Some employees would also use their own money to open accounts under fictitious names or the names of friends or relatives. In late 2003, Japan Post investigated 47 employees nationwide for such fraud (*Asahi Newspaper*, November 26, 2003).

34. *Shūkan Daiyamondo*, June 29, 2002.

35. Enō, *Jitsuroku*, 253.

36. One exception to this was job opportunities offered by private or semi-public firms connected to the postal network, the so-called postal family firms (*yūsei fuamiri kigyō*).

sectors or industries, and the implication was clear: most commissioned postmasters were all but locked into their professions.

In his classic work on organizational life, Albert Hirschman observed that organizations can stave off decline by responding to two signals: the "exit" of members from the organization and "voice," an attempt by members to "change, rather than to escape from, an objectionable state of affairs."[37] Exit from Zentoku and Tokusuiren, and hence from the profession, was clearly not an attractive option for most postmasters. But neither was voice—at least not from within the commissioned post office system. Although the federal structure of the two associations encouraged communication among the postmasters, their rigid, top-down hierarchies discouraged constructive criticisms from rank-and-file members. Furthermore, there was no institutional mechanism in place for reform-minded postmasters to assume top leadership positions, virtually all of which were filled by experienced—and highly conservative—postmasters or former bureaucrats in a seniority-based system of promotion. In response to mounting discontent within Zentoku at the turn of the twenty-first century over the quota system and other issues, association leaders invited progressive postmasters to express their complaints and suggestions to higher ups. Many complied, but their communications fell largely on unresponsive ears.[38]

Limited opportunities for exit and voice deprived the postmasters associations of what Hirschman called "recuperation mechanisms," democratic decision-making processes and organizational dynamism that would have given Tokusuiren and Zentoku the tools to resolve internal problems and adapt to change.[39] But even as the associations slipped into organizational rigidity, most—if not all—postmasters remained loyal to the commissioned post office system as their only viable avenue for earning a good, respectable living. And they expressed their loyalty by engaging in community service, partnering with the LDP in the electoral sphere, and pressuring the government to preserve the postal status quo.

---

37. Hirschman, *Exit, Voice, and Loyalty*, 30.
38. Enō, *Jitsuroku*, 212.
39. Hirschman, *Exit, Voice, and Loyalty*, 97.

Building Social Capital:
The Postmasters and Community Service

The commissioned postmasters had long been regarded as important individuals in their communities. During the Meiji period they helped build telegraph and telephone facilities while tending to their post office duties. Many also volunteered in local community development projects, and wealthier postmasters helped finance recreation parks and other local amenities. To be sure, there were economic incentives behind these seemingly selfless acts of charity and voluntarism. After the postal system's direct link to state coffers was severed in 1934, the postmasters were under increasing pressure to raise revenues by increasing postal transactions; one way to do this was to nurture the local population's trust in the post office by voluntarily contributing to community development.[40]

As the postwar period unfolded, the commissioned postmasters found new incentives to prioritize "community activities" (*chiiki katsudō*), as they were known inside the profession. First, as the decline of the *meibōka* class in local society deprived them of their innate social status, the postmasters sought new ways to strengthen their local "charm" (*miryoku*) and expand their *chiensei*. To that end, Zentoku issued a new internal "vision" during the mid-1970s that included guidelines for how the postmasters should think, conduct themselves, and face their futures. The overriding message was that the postmasters needed to do more to win the hearts and minds of local residents by expanding the scope of their local volunteer activities.[41] The report touched off an intensified phase in Zentoku's ongoing public relations campaign to elevate the commissioned post office's status in local society.

These and subsequent campaigns helped shape the official parameters of "good conduct" among the postmasters by drawing on traditional notions of leadership and morality. In the words of Mr. Kitaoka, a commissioned postmaster from semi-rural Kyushu,

---

40. Hida chiku tokutei yūbinkyokuchokai kaishi hensan iinkai, ed., *Hida no tokutei yūbinkyoku shi*, 273.
41. Yamaguchi, *Tokutei yūbinkyoku*, 194.

The post offices have traditionally had a good image among the people. Therefore, the postmasters feel it is important to "lead" local residents, to educate
them, increase their knowledge. . . . The postmasters feel a certain obligation
in this regard in part because they accept money from local residents and also
because they realize that economically, their situation is often more secure than
that of many of their customers.

Mr. Kitaoka went on to compare the postwar commissioned postmasters to high-ranking Buddhist priests (*jūshoku*) during the feudal era
who would build reputations for themselves as intellectuals (*chishikijin*)
by teaching the locals how to read and use the abacus. In addition to
helping local residents, he explained, these activities strengthened the
temple's standing within the community. The same can be said for the
commissioned post offices: through upright conduct and community
service, the postmasters hoped to secure the trust and confidence of
their neighbors.[42]

Another reason for the postmasters' intensifying interest in community service was the postwar commissioned post office system's declining role as the "arms and legs of the state." From the early Occupation
period, local governments challenged the post office's stature as a key
intermediary between the state and local society. The postal system met
that challenge in part by gradually co-opting local government functions.
By the early 2000s, post offices in many local jurisdictions were legally
authorized to provide residents with official copies of important documents, dispense welfare payments, and offer a host of other services that
would normally fall under the jurisdiction of the village government or
ward office. But since there were limits to the postal system's encroach-
ment on local government jurisdictions, the commissioned post office
system had to look for other ways to preserve its local stature. Once
again, community service fit the bill. While Zentei, the postal workers
union, continued to evoke the past by using the "arms and legs" metaphor in their public discourse about the post office's local significance,[43]
the postmasters set out to transform the commissioned post offices into
the "face of the community" (*chiiki no kao*)—a wellspring of voluntarism

---

42. Interview, commissioned postmaster, Kitakyūshū, August 9, 2002.
43. Kano, *Chiiki to kurashi o posuto ga tsunagu*, 58.

and innovative social services that responded to the specific needs of the locality.[44]

The postmasters' desire to become the "face of the community" also fueled their quest for self-preservation in the context of their ongoing battle with the radical Zentei. By proving to local residents that they were upright public servants, the postmasters hoped to discredit Zentei's campaign to abolish the commission office postal system. By the late twentieth century, however, this proved no longer necessary. Zentei's militancy gradually lost its punch as the postmasters' ties with the LDP deepened and the state upheld its implicit pledge to preserve the status quo within the postal system. Meanwhile, factions among postal workers deprived the union of its ability to speak with a unified voice. In 1965, two rival labor organizations merged to form Zen'yūsei (Zen Nippon yūsei rōdō kumiai; All Japan Postal Labor Union), a union consisting primarily of commissioned post office workers.[45] In 2007, the politically moderate union encompassed a membership of approximately 86,000—considerably less than Zentei's 140,000.[46] From the start, Zen'yūsei opposed its rival's militant labor tactics and frequently worked alongside the postmasters to defend the commissioned post office system.

Much to the postmasters' surprise, mounting exogenous threats to the state-run postal system turned their enemies into allies. In 1981, as the government of Suzuki Zenkō launched administrative reform—a campaign that targeted postal reform during its early stages—Zentei began to rethink its opposition to the commissioned post office system. With the specter of radical reform and even privatization looming, the union fixed its sights on the long-term job security of its members, a goal that was intricately tied up with the survival of the postal network. Later in the decade, the union quietly abandoned its decades-old campaign to destroy the commissioned post offices and resolved to cooperate with the postmasters on behalf of select causes. In a nod to the

---

44. Enō, *Jitsuroku*, 168.

45. The union also attracted workers from ordinary post offices and communications hospitals (*teishin byōin*). Japan's seventeen or so communications hospitals originally served postal employees and their families, but are now open to the general public.

46. In response to postal privatization, the two rival organizations merged in October 2007 to form the Japan Post Group Union (Nihon yūsei gurūpu kumiai), a private sector union. See http://www.jprouso.or.jp/ (last accessed July 25, 2011).

postmasters' quest to strengthen their network's social legitimacy, one such cause was transforming the local post office into a "community center." In 1988, these and other policies were endorsed and publicly articulated at Zentei's annual rally.[47] The postmasters, meanwhile, stepped up their efforts to improve relations with the postal workers and to create an environment in which both sides could benefit from their cooperative contributions to society.[48] Although relations between Zentei and the commissioned postmasters were to remain testy, for the first time in four decades the two sides were more or less on the same page.

Community contributions by the postmasters and their erstwhile enemies, the postal workers, ranged from the independent initiatives of individual post offices to regional and national campaigns. Many postmasters found creative ways to transform their facilities into "post offices that customers could love."[49] For some, this meant as little as offering candy to visiting children. Others sponsored small art exhibitions in their post offices or set up karaoke corners. One postmaster converted the lobby of his postal facility into a "salon" for the elderly, complete with a tea wagon, and organized weekend bus trips to a nearby hot springs resort for post office patrons.[50] Some postmasters volunteered for local crime prevention programs,[51] while others chaired or participated in local neighborhood associations (*chōnaikai*)—work that involved the planning of seasonal festivals and other local events. By putting the postmasters in contact with individuals ranging from ordinary residents to heads of local government, these and related activities were invaluable to the cultivation of *chiensei*.

Children became a major focus of community activism, particularly among younger postmasters.[52] Some postmasters served as the coaches of local children's sports teams, and many more were members or chairs of parent-teacher associations. Some also met with elementary school students to teach them letter-writing etiquette and the history of the

---

47. Yamaguchi, *Tokutei yūbinkyoku*, 222–25.

48. Yūseishō yōin kunrenka, *Tokutei yūbinkyoku*, 3.

49. Honma, *Tokutei yūbinkyokuchō ni natta boku no rakudai nikki*, 175.

50. Ibid., 178.

51. Segawa, *Koizumi Jun'ichirō to tokutei yūbinkyokuchō no arasoi*, 34–35.

52. Interviews, commissioned postmasters in Kitakyūshū and Kamakura, August 2003.

postal system; these sessions were frequently held in the postal facilities themselves. Finally, many partnered with their employees to provide the equivalent of "neighborhood watch" services for local children (*kodomo no 110 ban*) as they walked to and from schools and community playgrounds.[53]

The most noteworthy of the post office's community activities were the social welfare services offered to housebound elderly residents in many rural and semi-rural communities. In what was perhaps the best known service, mail carriers on their daily rounds would collect the postal savings deposits of needy elderly residents, returning their updated passbooks the next day. But the services did not stop there; many local post offices also partnered with local governments, social welfare councils (*shakai fukushi kyōkai*), and other local organizations to tend to the health-related needs of their older clients. Known collectively as *himawari* services, constituent activities included procedures for checking on the safety and well-being of the elderly, programs for delivering medicines and groceries to the incapacitated, and so on. Some localities even organized campaigns in which local schoolchildren and other residents provided cheerful messages of encouragement to their elderly neighbors (*fureai yūbin*, or *koekake yūbin*; "contact mail"),[54] while others experimented with meal delivery services.[55] Residents requesting assistance would put a small flag on their windowsill to alert the local mail carrier, who would then network with participating merchants and local authorities to have grocery orders delivered and prescriptions filled.

These social welfare services were significant on a number of fronts. Most fundamentally, they illuminated the extent to which post offices had become integrated into the warp and woof of community life. They also serviced basic humanitarian objectives, since visits by "Mr. Himawari" (*Himawari-san*) were often the only human contact experienced by elderly invalids living alone. Furthermore, the post offices' welfare services helped compensate for severe budgetary constraints on local government welfare programs and a shortage of welfare providers in

---

53. Kano, *Chiiki to kurashi o posuto ga tsunagu*, 64–65.

54. In FY 2007, 151 rural and semi-rural communities were experimenting with "contact mail" (Japan Post, *Annual Report: Postal Services in Japan: 2007*, 88).

55. Matsubara, *Gendai no yūsei jigyō*, 127.

many rural communities.[56] And while few postal employees or politicians would admit this openly, the *himawari* services helped deter the post office's most prized customers—and the LDP's most loyal voters—from moving to larger communities where they could obtain the assistance of family members.[57]

Community service underscored the commissioned post office system's ability to adapt to changing local needs and, in so doing, to enhance the relevance of the postal system to local residents. But it is important to remember what ultimately motivated these programs. As even union representatives acknowledged, the commissioned post offices intensified their volunteer activities during the 1980s because they were worried about their futures in the event of postal reform or privatization.[58] Talk of privatization, in other words, had prompted the postmaster and the mail carrier alike to devise new survival tactics under the guise of philanthropy. As the product of the very human urge for self-preservation, however, these innovations did little to change the internal dynamics of the postmasters associations. They also masked the more secretive practices of the commissioned postmasters—their electoral activities being foremost among them.

The Postmasters' "Vote-Gathering Machine"

In its 1988 "Manual for Community Activities" (*chiiki katsudō no tebiki*), Zentoku's Kyushu branch explained why the postmasters needed to cultivate political power: since the commissioned post office system was not rooted in—and hence protected by—law, the postmasters had no choice but to link up with the LDP in opposition to "social structural change" (*shakai kōzō no henka*).[59] Only *politics*, one postmaster explained,

---

56. The National Association of Towns and Villages was quick to point this out when Koizumi came to power in 2001 on a platform of postal privatization. Privatization, the association claimed, would force many post offices to abandon their welfare programs, thus putting unwanted pressure on the localities to pick up the slack (*Japan Times*, April 6, 2001).

57. *AERA*, November 25, 1995.

58. Kano, *Chiiki to kurashi o posuto ga tsunagu*, 205.

59. Kyūshū chihō tokutei yūbinkyokuchōkai, *Kyūshū tokutei yūbinkyokuchōkai shi*, 411.

would ultimately determine if the commissioned post office system lived or died.[60]

As far as the LDP was concerned, the alliance was *good politics*. As Tanaka Kakuei maneuvered to build up the party's base of support, he recognized the many advantages of partnering with the national network of commissioned postmasters. First, the postmasters could be mobilized behind conservative candidates with de facto impunity. Even though the postmasters' electoral activities were forbidden under the National Public Service Law, they were rarely the targets of official scrutiny. Had regional postal officials or the Public Prosecutors Office taken it upon themselves to enforce the law, more than 18,000 postmasters would have to be arrested.[61] Thus, until the Kōso scandal of 2001 overshot the public's tolerance of corruption within the postal system, routine electoral violations were by and large ignored.

Second, the postmasters had access to *watarikirihi* that covered non-salary operating expenses and promotion campaigns for the sale of products or services like commemorative stamps, New Year's greeting cards, postal insurance policies, and postal savings accounts.[62] Authorized under the 1947 Accounting Law (Kaikeihō), the sums were appropriated from the general account and quietly distributed to the postmasters. Since they were never subjected to strict accounting procedures, *watari-kirihi* could be siphoned into electoral projects. Finally, the postmasters' dearth of positive selective incentives proved to be an asset for the party. As Prime Minister Obuchi Keizō once remarked to the head of Zentoku, the LDP leadership was relieved that the postmasters put virtually no demands on the government budget.[63] In short, the postmasters were amongst the LDP's most valuable—and cost-effective—allies.

Zentoku orchestrated the postmasters' electoral obligations through an almost ritualistic set of procedures. For the individual postmaster, initiation into the political world took place within two or three years of joining the profession and usually involved an unannounced visit

---

60. Enō, *Jitsuroku*, 235.

61. Nikkei Business, *Daremo shiranai yūsei teikoku*, 39.

62. According to one estimate, the commissioned postmasters received a total of more than 9 billion yen in *watarikirihi* in FY 2001. "Tōhoku tokutei yūbinkyoku chōkai de uraganezukuri ga hakkaku," 8.

63. *Asahi shinbun*, November 21, 2001.

from a Zentoku official. Since the postmasters' employees were usually within earshot, the official would state the purpose of his visit in vague terms: "It is time for you to leave the business of the post office to the employees so that you can devote yourself to 'general policy.'"[64] Zentoku's phrase of choice since 1995,[65] "general policy" (*sōgō seisaku*) was a euphemistic reference to the wide gamut of electoral and political activities that comprised the postal system's "fourth service" (*daiyon jigyō*), after mail delivery, postal savings, and postal life insurance.

In keeping with Tokusuiren's tradition of establishing strict controls over the professional and voluntary activities of the postmasters, Zentoku set quotas for each electoral activity. Among the more important of these activities was the recruitment of new members into the *kōenkai* of "interest representation Diet members" (*rieki daihyō giin*) and other members of the postal *zoku*, a task that sometimes involved mutual strategizing between the postmasters and their political patrons.[66] In any given year, the postmasters were instructed to take advantage of their *chiensei* and recruit as many as 130 *kōenkai* members each. The names of the new members were then carefully noted, along with their personal seals, and submitted to Zentoku.[67] Also known as "special savings" (*tokubetsu chokin*), the task of *kōenkai* recruitment was often compared to cajoling new customers into the postal savings system.[68]

The postmasters were also required to recruit new party members for the LDP in between official election campaigns. In many instances, the postmasters would gather new members on behalf of their "interest representation Diet member," thereby improving that Diet member's chances of being ranked high on the LDP's PR list.[69] The task often

---

64. Enō, *Jitsuroku*, 223.

65. Kyūshū chihō tokutei yūbinkyokuchōkai, *Kyūshū tokutei yūbinkyokuchōkai shi*, 411.

66. In the fall of 1973, for example, the Kantō Friendship Society of Communications Retirees (Kantō teishin taishokusha dōyūkai) met with Upper House Diet members in one of their Nagatachō office buildings to discuss *kōenkai* recruitment strategies (Tōkyō chihō tokutei yūbinkyokuchōkaishi henshū iinkai, ed., *Tōkyō chihō tokutei yūbinkyokuchōkai shi*, 228.

67. Enō, *Jitsuroku*, 235.

68. Honma, *Tokutei yūbinkyokuchō ni natta boku no rakudai nikki*, 118.

69. Köllner, "Upper House Elections in Japan and the Power of the 'Organized Vote,'" 123.

proved challenging, however, because new members had to be cajoled into paying membership dues.[70] It was also illegal, since the LDP is a "political organization"—unlike the *kōenkai*, which are not officially recognized as such. To circumvent this problem, the postmasters relied heavily on the *fujinkai* (women's associations) and Taiju (the association of retired commissioned postmasters and the spouses of active postmasters) to do the work for them. *Fujinkai* and Taiju members were also active during election campaigns, openly volunteering in their candidates' local offices, canvassing votes on street corners, and visiting their neighbors at home. It was precisely because of the *fujinkai*'s special electoral role that Zentoku put heavy pressure on young postmasters to wed.[71] After all, only by acquiring a spouse could the postmasters remain within the letter of the law while fulfilling their "general policy" functions.

While the postmasters associations performed a number of other political functions, such as donating funds to their favorite candidates' campaigns or *kōenkai* and recruiting local residents to attend Diet members' speeches,[72] their *kōenkai* and party and vote mobilization responsibilities consumed the bulk of their time. These activities caused great stress for a good many postmasters, given the ethical questions involved and Zentoku's strict quotas. One former postmaster complained about having to recruit 120 new members for a particular *kōenkai*—an all but impossible task for someone who was new to his job, lived in a small village, and did not yet know his customers well.[73] Electoral responsibilities were particularly onerous for "hired postmasters" (*yatoware kyokuchō*; young postmasters who did not inherit their post offices or carpetbaggers who moved into the jurisdictions of their facilities upon assuming their positions) and "commuting postmasters" (*tsūkin kyokuchō*; those who lived outside the neighborhoods they served). With few or no

---

70. Ibid., p.147.

71. Enō, *Jitsuroku*, 228–29.

72. Taiju in particular was a major source of funds for LDP candidates. According to government documents, individual members of Taiju donated a total of 48 million yen in 2004 to LDP Upper House Diet member Hasegawa Kensei, a former MIC official (*AERA*, September 30, 2005).

73. Honma, *Tokutei yūbinkyokuchō ni natta boku no rakudai nikki*, 146.

local connections, these "outsiders" (*tozama*) lacked the social capital—the *chiensei*—to effectively meet their electoral targets.[74]

It was therefore not uncommon for the hired or commuting postmaster—and even the weary veteran—to resort to cheating. Some would cajole friends and family members into joining the LDP in return for paying their membership dues. Others would concoct fictitious *kōenkai* membership lists. The fact that the postmasters went to such lengths underscores the extent of the association's control over its members, not to mention the postmasters' lack of opportunities to "exit" the profession. Zentoku leaders would not hesitate to visit individual postmasters to discuss their electoral performance, while postmasters who failed to meet their quotas experienced the shame of seeing their names in print in the association's internal publications. In the past, postmasters who did not live up to their electoral responsibilities suffered from virtual ostracism (*mura hachibu*), a most undesirable fate within this proud group.[75]

Although the postmasters were involved in the electoral activities of both Lower House and Upper House lawmakers, their ultimate goal was to elect "interest representation Diet members" to the Upper House—former postmasters or retired MPT officials who had intimate knowledge of the postal system and could be trusted to defend the system's interests within both the LDP and the bureaucracy. In this regard, the postmasters were no different from other Japanese interest groups that lobbied the government from within the corridors of power. The postmasters themselves certainly saw nothing untoward about this: "We just like to have people in the Diet who are looking out for us," explained one postmaster. "Isn't this just human nature?"[76]

On a few occasions, Zentoku would pressure a favored bureaucrat to resign his position and then run for an Upper House seat in the national PR district. If elected, that Diet member, like other members of the postal *zoku*, would become an advisor/consultant (*komon*) to Zentoku, a position that involved regular attendance at the association's national and regional meetings, writing introductions or "greetings" (*aisatsu*) for

---

74. Enō, *Jitsuroku*, 256; *Shūkan Daiyamondo*, June 29, 2002.
75. *Asahi shinbun*, May 29, 1983.
76. Interview, commissioned postmaster, Kitakyūshū, August 9, 2002.

official association documents or commemorative histories, providing the postmasters with unobstructed access to his Diet office, and lobbying bureaucrats and other lawmakers for favorable policy. One of the postmasters' favorite interest representative Diet members was Teshima Sakae, who served for many years as an MPT official before resigning his position at the postmasters' behest to run for a seat in the 1956 Upper House election. A few years later, Teshima was appointed Minister of Posts and Telecommunications, thus fulfilling his ultimate ambition. Sadly for the postmasters, Teshima died in 1963 after less than a year in that position.[77] According to a former Zentoku president, the association succeeded in electing only five "OB" to the Diet before 2001; Kōso Kenji, elected in summer 2001, was the sixth.[78] By the end of Koizumi's term as prime minister, there was only one postal OB in the Diet: Hasegawa Kensei.[79] This is not to suggest that the postmasters were short of allies in the Diet; numerous lawmakers since 2001 trumpeted the postmasters' cause, including Nonaka Hiromu, the don of the postal *zoku* until his retirement in 2003; Watanuki Tamisuke, speaker of the Lower House between 2000 and 2003; and Kamei Shizuka, the Lower House member from Hiroshima who grew increasingly sympathetic toward the postmasters' cause as the postal reform movement gathered steam.

Their systematic participation in electoral activities notwithstanding, the postmasters were frequently troubled by the ethical ramifications of their activities. But while younger generations of postmasters appeared more and more reluctant to conform to Zentoku's electoral customs, the association's traditionalists recalled the postmasters' many sacrifices in the past and concluded that they were honor-bound to preserve the institutions of the commissioned post office system by quietly nurturing their political power.[80] Zentoku's control mechanisms were designed to ensure that the traditional view prevailed.

---

77. Segawa, *Koizumi Jun'ichirō to tokutei yūbinkyokuchō no arasoi*, 40.

78. *Asahi shinbun*, November 21, 2001.

79. The postmasters found it difficult to convince postal bureaucrats to run for elected office. But this was unsurprising. As career advancement grew more routinized—and drawn out—within the ruling LDP, fewer and fewer mid- or senior-level bureaucrats were attracted to the notion of spending their last working years as lowly backbenchers.

80. Kyūshū chihō tokutei yūbinkyokuchōkai, *Kyūshū tokutei yūbinkyokuchōkai shi*, 418.

Many postmasters tried to alleviate their personal discomfort by developing elaborate rationales for their involvement in electoral affairs. For most, this involved drawing a fine line between what was inherently "political" and what was not. As Mr. Kitaoka, the commissioned postmaster from Kyushu, explained: "Postmasters are government officials, so officially, we're not supposed to support [*shien*] the LDP. But speaking for myself as an individual, I can express my views—so long as I do it after hours. Also, we're prohibited from engaging in electoral activities, but outside the actual campaigns, it's OK."[81] Other postmasters reasoned that while they could not run for elected office, solicit votes during working hours or official campaign periods, or use their social status for overtly electoral purposes,[82] as "private citizens" they were free to attend political lectures and meetings and attract new members into the inherently "apolitical" *kōenkai*. (To be sure, few would openly admit that the *kōenkai* constituted a vast reservoir of likely voters for their patrons at election time.)

Meanwhile, Zentoku devised a number of tactics to keep the postmasters' electoral activities under wraps, not least of which was relying on wives and retired postmasters to carry out the more overtly political functions of the postmasters' fourth service. The postmasters also went to great lengths to mask their activities in a web of euphemistic terminology. In addition to "general policy," electoral functions were sometimes referred to as "community contributions" (*chiiki kōken*) or "basic issues" (*kihon mondai*),[83] innocuous terms designed to minimize the public's awareness that the postmasters were engaged in anything but the business of the post office and their vaunted volunteer activities. To fend off the nosy media, Zentoku instructed new postmasters to avoid taking notes during political training sessions and to commit the details of those discussions to memory. Manuals on various electoral tactics did exist, but Zentoku forbade the postmasters from photocopying them or disclosing their contents to journalists.[84]

---

81. Interview, commissioned postmaster, Kitakyūshū, August 9, 2002.
82. Kyūshū chihō tokutei yūbinkyokuchōkai, *Kyūshū tokutei yūbinkyokuchōkai shi*, 412.
83. Enō, *Jitsuroku*, 202.
84. Ibid., 241–42.

In the final analysis, Zentoku's clandestine tactics did little to deflect the media's attention; in 2001 the Kōso Kenji affair exposed many of the organization's inner workings and attracted the kind of public censure that the postmasters had worked so hard to avoid. Even before 2001, those tactics had given Zentoku—and Taiju—the dubious reputation of being among Japan's most mysterious interest groups. Many complained that in contrast to other Japanese interest groups, it was almost impossible to discern who Zentoku's leaders were at any given time.[85] One newspaper reporter who had spent several years on the MPT beat confessed that he was often frustrated by Zentoku's unwillingness to respond to his queries. He went on to liken the association's opulent headquarters in the Roppongi area of Tokyo to a "ghost building" (*obake biru*);[86] Zentoku's top leaders, he claimed, were more likely lodged within the bowels of MPT itself—a valid claim, since those men were also running Tokusuiren, the official bureaucratic organ. At the end of the day, while the secretiveness that shrouded Zentoku may have facilitated the postmasters' participation in electoral activities, it also worked at cross-purposes to their quest for prestige.

The Kōso Scandal and Its Aftermath

As we observed in Chapter 2, the scandal involving former Kinki Postal Bureau director Kōso Kenji's election to the Upper House caused a major media stir and tested the public's tolerance of electoral corruption in the postal sector. In the past, the postmasters were able to mobilize behind their preferred candidates with virtually no legal repercussions. In the aftermath of Kōso's July 2001 election, fourteen Kinki Postal Bureau officials and one postmaster were arrested; several were later convicted of electoral violations. When the LDP finally forced Kōso to give up his Diet seat, it was clear that the postal regime had lost its de facto legal immunity.

The scandal also focused the public's attention on the problem of *watarikirihi*. Interestingly, the postal system consumed far more of these

---

85. Interview, two *Asahi shinbun* reporters, Tokyo, February 17, 2003.

86. Interview, newspaper journalist, January 23, 2003. Since Zentoku could not rent or own facilities in its capacity as a voluntary organization, it established a non-profit organization that became the legal owner of their Roppongi headquarters.

funds than even the Ministry of Foreign Affairs, which distributed them to its embassies abroad. By the late 1990s, the public was catching on to the controversies surrounding *watarikirihi* as the opposition parties questioned the practice in the Diet and citizens groups investigated it under information disclosure provisions at the national and local levels. Just a few weeks before the Kōso scandal broke, opposition party members of the Lower House's General Affairs Committee (Sōmuiinkai) produced statistics showing that Tokusuiren was spending the funds on entertainment and food—as much as 75,000 yen on any given day.[87] Shortly after the 2001 election, the Japanese Communist Party (JCP) posted an article on its *Shinbun Akahata* (Red Flag Newspaper) website complaining that there were no strict accounting rules governing the usage of these funds and urging the Koizumi government to address the issue in its postal reform program.[88]

The Kōso scandal prompted the government to take action against the excesses of *watarikirihi* expenditures. In spring 2002, a PSA study revealed that out of 238 commissioned post offices investigated, 16 had fabricated a total of 28.72 million yen in *watarikirihi* expenses. The PSA suspended one postmaster for six months, reduced the paychecks of eight others, and issued official warnings to an additional four. Minister of Internal Affairs and Communications Katayama Toranosuke subsequently apologized to the public for the postmasters' misuse of public funds.[89] Later in 2002, the Accounting Law was quietly amended to abolish *watarikirihi* and the MIC began transferring operating allowances to the post offices in accordance with more stringent accounting procedures. The postmasters' secret reservoir of political funds had dried up.

Meanwhile, key postmasters broke their vows of silence as they scrambled to repair their tarnished reputations. In a rare but revealing interview with the *Asahi shinbun*, Takeuchi Kiyoshi, director general of Zentoku, acknowledged the public's criticisms in the wake of the scandal by speaking openly about the history of his association's electoral

---

87. See transcript at http://www.shugiin.go.jp/itdb_kaigiroku.nsf/html/kaigiroku/009415120010619023.htm#p_honbun (last accessed October 3, 2007).

88. http://www.jcp.or.jp/akahata/aik/2002-07-31/2002-0731faq.html (last accessed October 3, 2007).

89. *Kyodo News*, March 29, 2002.

functions. In the past, he explained, Zentoku had not been a "political group" per se; the association's involvement in politics was limited to defending its existence and conveying the postmasters' wishes to the state. "But before we knew it," Takeuchi observed, "it seems we were leaning too much into electoral activities." Takeuchi stopped short of acknowledging Zentoku's reputation as an "electoral machine" (*shūhyō mashīn*): "We are not," he asserted, "branch organizations of the LDP or the Hashimoto faction." He also skirted the question of whether Zentoku would back another "postal OB" in the next election by stating that he had no opinion on the matter. Takeuchi then admitted that mobilizing behind another OB would be challenging, since there were no potential candidates waiting in the wings.[90]

Inside Zentoku, a number of young postmasters hoped that the association would finally sever its ties to the LDP and put an end to electioneering. But this was not to be. In 2002, Zentoku sponsored a series of "general dialogue campaigns" (*sōtaiwa undō*) at the regional level to encourage the "free exchange" of ideas among the postmasters, but the leadership refused to entertain suggestions that electioneering should end; instead, they urged their underlings to be more discreet in their electoral activities. Some leaders portrayed themselves as victims of the government, arguing that postmasters and postal bureaucrats should not be prosecuted for engaging in *kōenkai* activities.[91] And while they agreed to rank-and-file demands to lower the postmasters' 2004 election quotas,[92] association leaders held fast to their conviction that their political links to the ruling party had to be maintained. For as long as Zentoku's traditionalists prevailed, the association proved incapable of adapting to the changing political winds.

The Postmasters at the End of the Twentieth Century

After an LDP candidate backed by the postmasters won a seat in the national constituency of the 1980 Upper House election with 1,030,000 votes, the media announced that Zentoku and its affiliate organizations

---

90. *Asahi shinbun*, November 21, 2001.

91. Enō, *Jitsuroku*, 247–48.

92. Ibid., 248. See also the *Nikkei Business* special edition on postal privatization, June 18, 2001.

represented "one million votes."[93] In 2001, Kōso Kenji was elected with 480,000 votes, less than half the 1980 total. Although other interest groups appeared to be doing even more poorly, it was clear that the postmasters' electoral clout was in decline even before Koizumi's privatization crusade had gathered steam. A number of factors contributed to that decline, some of which were specific to the postmasters and their representative organizations, and others to the broader institutional environment in which they operated. But first, it is important to recall the postmasters' inherent weaknesses as an interest group— weaknesses that are illuminated through comparison with Nōkyō, one of Japan's most politically significant interest groups.

Nōkyō, like Zentoku, developed into an essential cog in the LDP's electoral machine, mobilizing votes at election time, recruiting new members into the *kōenkai*, contributing campaign funds to the LDP, and populating its grassroots membership. Also like Zentoku, Nōkyō has been constrained by laws governing its political activities; as a statutory organization that receives state subsidies, the association is barred from making political donations and faces restrictions on participating in national elections. To circumvent these legal stipulations, Nōkyō siphons off some of its political activities to the so-called farmers' political leagues,[94] auxiliary organizations that in some ways function like Taiju and the *fujinkai*.

These similarities notwithstanding, Nōkyō had several advantages over Zentoku. First, Zentoku appears to have been more institutionally rigid than Nōkyō, a result of its fixation on self-preservation, heavy reliance on negative selective incentives, and lack of opportunities for ordinary postmasters to "voice" their needs and concerns within the organization. But Nōkyō's advantages extended to the electoral realm as well. First, individual Nōkyō executives in their official capacities were permitted to seek and hold elected office; not even rank-and-file postmasters enjoyed this right, given their status as public servants. Con-

---

93. In the July 1995 Upper House election, a candidate backed by the Japan Medical Association amassed more votes than any other LDP candidate. Okano Hiroshi, a Zentoku advisor, received the second highest number of votes (*Shūkan Tōyō keizai*, September 7, 1996).

94. Mulgan, *The Politics of Agriculture in Japan*, 82.

sequently, Nōkyō had an easier time establishing a foothold in the Diet. Robert Bullock has shown that 5.9 percent of all Diet members between 1949 and 1983 were from Nōkyō, that 7 out of 46 Nōkyō prefectural chairmen held Diet seats in 1970, and that 140 local cooperative chairs occupied prefectural assembly seats.[95] Zentoku executives, by contrast, had to retire their positions before running for office. These differences help explain why Zentoku's "interest group representatives" had to be recruited from outside and totaled only six or so between 1955 and 2001.

Second, Zentoku lacked the electoral advantage of sheer size. Nōkyō consisted of approximately 8.5 million members in 1990, a total that included virtually all farming households.[96] Even if only one-quarter of Nōkyō's members were to vote for the LDP, this would still constitute a significant voting bloc. Zentoku consisted of only as many members as there were commissioned postmasters at any given time—a total that never exceeded 19,000—and Taiju consisted of an additional 230,000. And since those numbers were spread thinly across the country, the postmasters associations' electoral clout was largely confined to the national PR constituency of Upper House elections and depended heavily on their ability to mobilize non-members. Nōkyō, which operated in the countryside where Lower House electoral constituencies were heavily malapportioned in the LDP's favor, was an influential electoral force in both houses of the Diet.

The two associations also differed in terms of their control over the political functions of their respective members. One reason for this is, again, size, but Zentoku may have had the advantage in this regard. As Japan's largest "political" organization, Nōkyō was left with little choice but to tolerate political diversity within its ranks; as Bullock and Aurelia Mulgan have both shown, local co-ops and affiliated organizations were permitted to support whichever political party they pleased, although Nōkyō as a whole clearly leaned toward the LDP.[97] At only a fraction of Nōkyō's size, Zentoku forbade such diversity, requiring all members to perform a wide range of functions on behalf of the LDP.

---

95. Bullock, "Nōkyō: A Short Cultural History."
96. Ibid.
97. Ibid.; Mulgan, *The Politics of Agriculture in Japan*, 102.

(Of course, we will never know just how many postmasters cast their votes for opposition parties in defiance of the leadership's directives.)

In addition to its more manageable size, Zentoku's reliance on negative incentives enabled it to force rank-and-file members to mobilize en masse behind the LDP. Unlike Nōkyō, Zentoku established quotas for its members' electoral functions and threatened negative publicity for those who failed to meet them. The result was a far higher political participation rate within Zentoku. Mulgan has observed that while roughly 10 percent of Japanese citizens participate in some sort of political activity, the figure approaches 50 percent for Nōkyō members.[98] Although comparable figures do not exist for Zentoku, given the legal restrictions on public servants in the electoral realm, I would estimate that as many as 90 percent of Zentoku members complied with Zentoku's electoral directives at the height of their influence during the early 1980s. Some postmasters, of course, abstained from these activities. By doing so, however, they risked losing the few positive perquisites of Zentoku membership, such as access to low-interest loans for the repair or rebuilding of post office facilities.

There is good reason to conclude that by the late twentieth century, defections from Zentoku were increasing despite the postmasters' relative lack of alternative employment opportunities. As the recent memoirs of disgruntled former postmasters attest,[99] more and more postmasters appeared willing to leave their profession before retirement and to break age-old taboos against speaking about their experiences in public. Generational changes were one driving force behind this trend. Deprived of the formative experiences of hardship and self-sacrifice that shaped the postmasters' culture until the early postwar era and buoyed by a more flexible labor market, these younger postmasters were more likely to oppose the demanding community service and electoral requirements of the profession. Attitudes toward postal privatization also shifted, in part along generational lines. During the 1960s, 1970s, and 1980s, the vast majority of postmasters reacted to talk of privatization with alarm and disbelief. In a more market-oriented postal system, the postmasters might receive higher salaries but would no longer enjoy

---

98. Mulgan, *The Politics of Agriculture in Japan*, 386.

99. Honma, *Tokutei yūbinkyokuchō ni natta boku no rakudai nikki*; Eno, *Jitsuroku*.

property tax exemptions and high government rents for their facilities. The postmasters also stood to lose the distinctive institutions of the commissioned post office system, and with them, their local social standing. But by the early years of the Koizumi administration, an increasing number of postmasters—perhaps as many as 25 percent—were resigned to the inevitability of postal privatization. A few postmasters even welcomed privatization in the hopes that it would make the struggling local post office more competitive and attractive to its customers.[100]

As the specter of privatization grew, many postmasters were doubtful that the profession could weather the storm. Of 400 postmaster respondents to an unscientific survey conducted by Zentoku's Kyushu chapter in 1994, 77 percent noted that their futures looked "grim."[101] Of particular concern was the problem of succession. While 41 percent of respondents claimed that they wanted one of their children to succeed them, they were pessimistic that their offspring would comply with their wishes.[102] Their pessimism was well founded. As the postmasters' finances stabilized in the wake of the early postwar reforms, many proudly sent their sons off to the University of Tokyo or other prestigious institutions. But their generosity was wont to backfire. Attracted to urban life and to corporate or government careers, many offspring were loath to return to their *furusato* (home town) and take over the family post office.[103] Running a commissioned post office during the postwar period had never been an easy proposition; now, it was becoming less so.

As far as the postmasters were concerned, the implications of the succession problem for Zentoku's political functions were profound. As association leaders explained, a postmaster hired from beyond the post office's neighborhood could not possibly understand why "general policy" was so important to the future of the profession.[104] Outsiders who were willing to conform to the association's political culture, meanwhile, had a hard time cultivating the local social capital—the *chiensei*—that was so integral to Zentoku's ultimate political influence. Accord-

---

100. Enō, *Jitsuroku*, 244.
101. Kyūshū chihō tokutei yūbinkyokuchōkai, *Kyūshū tokutei yūbinkyokuchōkai shi*, 393.
102. Ibid.
103. Interview, newspaper journalist, January 23, 2003.
104. Kyūshū chihō tokutei yūbinkyokuchōkai, *Kyūshū tokutei yūbinkyokuchōkai shi*, 450.

ingly, Zentoku established committees and study groups to address the so-called succession crisis, and a great deal of attention was devoted to the issue at local meetings and national conferences.

Other factors were at work to weaken the ties that bound the post-masters to the LDP. The first and most obvious was Upper House electoral reform. As we observed in Chapter 2, changes introduced to Upper House electoral rules in 1982 had diluted the electoral influence not just of the postmasters but of all organized interests. Although subsequent reforms introduced in 2000 worked in the postmasters' favor, the postmasters never fully recouped their pre-1982 influence.

The postmasters also worried about the effects of the 1994 changes to the Lower House electoral system. While Zentoku historically focused most of its energies on Upper House elections, it still paid close attention to and participated in the Lower House constituencies of LDP politicians in the postal tribe. Primed to mobilize the vote behind individual candidates rather than parties more generally, the postmasters benefited from the old multi-member district system that pitted LDP candidates against one another in the same constituencies. Zentoku and its affiliates would stand behind the postmasters' preferred candidate, applying all the mobilizational tactics described earlier. Although Zentoku continued to back their LDP patrons after 1994, they, like other interest groups, worried that their influence would be significantly diluted under the winner-take-all system of the new single-member districts. As expected, while the LDP continued to court the organized vote, it now had to cast its net wider in order to attract a more diverse swath of the local voting population. Consequently, as Mr. Yoshimura observed in 2002, LDP politicians were no longer nurturing the personal relationships that were at the root of their exchange relationship with the postmasters:

At one time, LDP politicians who were sympathetic to the postmasters established personal relations with them at the local [*jimoto*] level. Our political patrons attended local Zentoku meetings, paid their respects at the funerals of prominent postmasters, and even visited the postmasters' homes at New Year's. But with these new single-member districts, politicians no longer have the time to make these personal visits. *The postmasters' traditional allies are disappearing and the future of the commissioned post office system is uncertain.*[105]

105. Interview, Kamakura, August 15, 2002.

Changes in the nature of common threats also contributed to the decline of the Zentoku-LDP exchange relationship. Until the early 1980s—and particularly during the 1950s and 1960s, when Japanese politics was split along ideological lines—the postmasters and the ruling party found common cause in their opposition to the partnership between Zentei and the JSP. Fully aware of the electoral importance of the postmasters for conservative party rule, the socialists mounted the LDP's most formidable electoral challenge and threw their support behind the union's crusade to abolish the commissioned post office system. During the 1980s, however, this ideological threat to the conservative alliance quickly ebbed as a new challenge arose from within the LDP: the movement to promote postal reform. That movement was sufficiently strong by the Nakasone era (1982–1987) to divide the LDP on postal issues and throw the union into the postmasters' camp. By the early 2000s, the postmasters had become distrustful of what they termed their "two-tongued" (*nimaijita*) LDP patrons, some of whom pledged their support to the postmasters while backing Koizumi—the postmasters' archenemy—at election time.[106] Gone were the days when the postmasters could count on unconditional support from the ruling party.

The LDP's increasing tolerance of postal reform in turn reflected the declining influence of Tanaka Kakuei's legacy within the party. After laying the groundwork for many of the customs that linked the postmasters to the party within the electoral sphere, Tanaka went on to influence key appointments to the MPT and relevant Diet committees until well into the 1980s. His role as "don" of the postal tribe was later assumed by a succession of protégés, including party bigwigs like Takeshita Noboru, Kanemaru Shin, Obuchi Keizō, and Nonaka Hiromu. By 2004, all of these men had either died or retired. Meanwhile, and as Chapter 5 illustrates, Hashimoto Ryūtarō, one of Tanaka's successors as factional leader, defied his mentor's lead by pressing for postal reform while serving as prime minister (1996–1998), a move that invited strong opposition from his faction members. The Hashimoto faction's reputation as the last bastion of support for the postmasters slipped further during the early 2000s when Hashimoto was implicated in a major political corruption scandal. In the end, Hashimoto's downfall

---

106. Enō, *Jitsuroku*, 251.

dealt a major blow to what remained of machine-style politics and the party's electoral alliance with organized interests like the postmasters.

A string of social and political changes at the local level coalesced to further weaken the postmasters' vote-gathering clout during the 1980s and 1990s. One such change was the decline of community cohesiveness. Mulgan argues that as the farming community shrank in size as a result of urbanization and the rise of corporate agriculture, the social bonds between farmers and local cooperatives loosened. These changes in turn weakened Nōkyō's ability to influence the voting decisions of local residents.[107] Similar dynamics were at play among the postmasters. In the past, Zentoku—like Nōkyō—lent credence to the so-called network model of voting behavior, which assumed that local residents were motivated less by rational considerations when casting their votes than by their social ties and obligations.[108] In this context, the postmasters, like the leaders of local agricultural cooperatives, small-business associations, firefighting associations, politicians at the town and village level, neighborhood association leaders, and other local "men of influence" (*yūryokusha*) acted as "opinion leaders"—individuals who, by virtue of their local leadership positions, were in a position to help shape the voting decisions of otherwise apolitical residents.[109] But as small communities lost their social cohesiveness, and alternative sources of electoral information proliferated,[110] the postmasters' persuasive powers declined.

The postmasters' vote-gathering potential was strongest in rural and semi-rural Japan, but whatever powers they had in the cities were eroded by the rise of urban (or suburban) floating voters. These young, well-educated professionals are more attentive to politics and far less susceptible to the persuasive overtures of opinion leaders like the postmasters. As Chapter 6 further explains, the floating voters proved decisive in Koizumi's Lower House electoral victory in September 2005, which cleared the path toward the passage of postal privatization legislation.

---

107. Mulgan, *The Politics of Agriculture in Japan*, 455–56, 473.
108. Richardson, "Social Networks, Influence Communications, and the Vote," 333.
109. Ibid., 336.
110. Amyx, Takenaka, and Toyoda, "The Politics of Postal Savings Reform in Japan," 33.

The power of interest groups, Katō Kōichi commented in 2003, has long been exaggerated in Japanese politics.[111] And so it was with the postmasters. After functioning as important electoral partners of the LDP for most of the postwar period, the postmasters' relevance declined as a result of demographic, electoral, and other political changes. That they managed to survive as influence peddlers for as long as they did is testament to their thick institutions and dogged perseverance. But their inherent conservatism—both institutional and ideological—prevented them from radically transforming their institutions in ways that might have enabled them to weather some of these changes. All other things being equal, the commissioned post office system's legitimacy crisis and electoral decline would have continued no matter who occupied the Prime Minister's Office. But the postmasters' future grew even more tenuous with Koizumi's rise to power in 2001—a development that sparked the most decisive battle in their 130-year history.

---

111. Interview, Katō Kōichi, Tokyo, March 24, 2003.

FOUR

The Postwar Postal Regime

and the Failure of Reform

For much of the postwar period, social stability trumped competition as an objective of Japanese economic development. Industry developed complex distribution systems and generous wage scales to keep employment levels high. Large firms reduced bankruptcies by encouraging corporate interdependence and risk sharing. Consumers tolerated high prices in exchange for protected markets, and investors traded high returns for long-term financial security. For many Japanese, this distinctive form of capitalism was the natural order of things. Economic growth must serve a higher social purpose; if achieving that purpose meant modifying free market principles, then so be it.[1]

The state-run postal services both reflected and contributed to these broader economic values and practices. The postal savings system nurtured a culture of thrift in Japanese society while generating funds for government investment not only in industrial development, but also in public works projects designed to soften the negative side effects of rapid economic growth. At the grassroots level, the commissioned postmasters and their employees performed social welfare functions that

---

1. As the economist Ogata Shijurō writes, Japanese government officials historically justified their control of market trends on the grounds that markets do not always produce "the socially optimal result" ("Financial Markets in Japan," 176).

helped stabilize rural communities in the throes of depopulation. All the while, the postal services generated vast institutional networks that spanned the divide between the public and private sectors and provided employment to tens of thousands of Japanese. The postal services may have produced economic inefficiencies that are the bane of classical economists, but they did much to enhance the social well-being of the Japanese people.

The vested interests that emerged from the postal system were quick to extol these social benefits as they opposed the evolving movement to liberalize, corporatize, or privatize the postal services. Reformers, they argued, were advocating unfettered competition and other free-market principles that had no place in modern Japan's distinctive social and economic trajectory. If the postal savings system were abolished, ordinary Japanese would lose a safe and convenient haven for their deposits. If private actors were to enter the mail delivery service, they would neglect sparsely populated areas in their quest for profits. By driving small, unprofitable post offices out of business, moreover, competition would increase unemployment and inconvenience count-less citizens, particularly in vulnerable rural areas. In short, advocates of the status quo framed postal reform as an attack on some of the last defining institutions of Japanese-style capitalism and its underlying values. The message was clear; if radical postal reform were to succeed, a distinctive way of life would be lost.

The purpose of this chapter is to explain why friends of the post office managed to keep the reformers at bay—at least until the early 1990s. To put the story in context, I begin by exploring the postwar postal system's significance in both local society and the broader political economy, focusing on its relationship to the Fiscal Investment and Loan Program (FILP). I then identify the institutional networks that evolved out of the postal system. Whereas Chapters 2 and 3 examined the his-torical evolution and political power of the triangular alliance among the commissioned postmasters, LDP politicians, and postal bureaucrats, this chapter casts its net more broadly to identify other actors—both public and private—connected to the postal system and the FILP that had vested interests in the continuation of the state-run postal system. Together, these actors constituted a veritable "postal regime" that transcended specific LDP governments as it simultaneously contributed to the longevity of conservative party rule.

In the second half of the chapter, I trace the origins and subsequent evolution of the postal reform movement from the late 1950s to the early 1990s. Here, I explain how members of the postal regime took advantage of institutional and political opportunities to dramatically slow the pace of reform. To make sense of the changes that *were* introduced, I identify two orders of reform: those that merely tinkered with the programs and management principles of the state-run services (second-order reform) versus those that transformed the very institutional and political foundations of the services, as well as the basic economic and social principles that supported them (first-order reform). As a result in part of the postal regime's unrelenting resistance, changes to the postal system until the early 1990s occurred largely within the second order of reform. As the next chapter explains, it was not until later in the decade—in the midst of political and economic uncertainty and under the leadership of Prime Minister Hashimoto Ryūtarō—that the reform camp acquired the political wherewithal to introduce changes that fell within the first order of reform. As Chapter 6 illustrates, this political about-face culminated in the stunning 2005 passage of Koizumi Jun'ichirō's postal privatization legislation.

The Postal Services in Japanese Society

As the country's largest institutional network, the state-run postal system formed an essential part of the "lifestyle infrastructure" (*seikatsu infura*) of ordinary Japanese, particularly in rural areas.[2] Not least among the network's many conveniences was sheer geographic proximity. Fans of the post office took pride in the fact that while many communities lacked commercial bank branches, every town, village, and city ward had a post office within a child's walking distance. More significantly, while the banks catered to the financial needs of corporate Japan, the

---

2. This chapter focuses primarily on the social and political implications of the postal services. For more about their financial structure, see Cargill and Yoshino, *Postal Savings and Fiscal Investment in Japan*; and Japan Center for Economic Research, "Postal Privatization in Japan and the Future of Banks and Life Insurers."

Table 4.1: Principal Interest Rates on Ordinary Savings Deposits: Commercial Banks and Postal Savings

Fiscal Year	Banks	Postal Savings
1946	1.830	2.640
1950	1.830	2.760
1955	2.190	3.960
1960	2.560	3.960
1965	2.190	3.600
1970	2.250	3.600
1975	2.500	3.840
1980	2.750	4.080
1985	1.500	2.880
1990	2.080	3.480
1995	0.100	0.250
1996	0.100	0.250
1997	0.100	0.250
1998	0.100	0.150
1999	0.050	0.080
2000	0.100	0.120
2001	0.020	0.020
2002	0.003	0.005
2003	0.001	0.005
2004	0.001	0.005

SOURCE: Ministry of Internal Affairs and Communications, *Historical Statistics of Japan*, 2010, Table 14-1.

postal system focused on small-scale depositors like households and individuals. The post office's financial remittance services were cheaper, covered more destinations both at home and abroad, and were easier to use than those of the banks. As Table 4.1 illustrates, the postal savings system also offered higher interest rates than the commercial banks on its savings accounts, although the gap between the two rates was significantly narrowed from 1998. And while both the postal system and the banks were authorized to offer ten-year time deposits (*teigaku chokin*) at fixed interest rates compounded semi-annually, only the postal system allowed depositors to withdraw their funds after six months without penalty. From the 1980s, the postal savings system established yet another competitive edge over the banks by offering ATM services that were free of charge. The post office also offered a wider variety of savings instruments, including special accounts for post-retirement, college tuition, and home purchases.

The postal savings system's most important advantage was the government's guarantee of deposits, a feature that made the system especially popular during periods of financial uncertainty. The rate of increase in postal savings deposits overtook that of commercial bank deposits by large margins in the years immediately following the 1907 and 1927 financial panics and the 1973 "oil shock," and during the early 1990s following the collapse of the real estate and stock market bubbles.[3] By the late 1990s, the volume of postal savings totaled one third of all savings deposits. But the Japanese were by no means unique in their penchant for financial security. In their study of cross-national savings trends, Mark Scher and Naoyuki Yoshino discovered that depositors everywhere tend to value security over other perquisites, including higher interest rates.[4] But the Japanese showed signs of being particularly cautious, exchanging higher returns for zero risk.[5] Consider, for instance, the fate of the 27 trillion yen in ten-year postal savings time deposits that matured in 1999 and 2000.[6] Purchased when interest rates were high, the accounts came due while interest rates were much lower, the financial sector was diversifying, and opportunities to invest abroad at competitive interest rates were expanding. Many pundits predicted that households would transfer their deposits into these lucrative ventures, wreaking havoc on the postal system's ability to cover the withdrawals. Instead, 84.9 percent of the deposits were rolled back into the postal system.[7] As Scher and Yoshino explain, Japanese depositors had opted for safety over higher returns;[8] they were encouraged, I might add, by the postmasters' grassroots campaign to keep their clients within the postal system's protective embrace.

Convenience and safety were the operative principles of the postal life insurance system as well. Designed to help stabilize the financial lives

---

3. Cargill and Yoshino, *Postal Savings and Fiscal Investment in Japan*, 36–41.

4. Scher and Yoshino, "Introduction," 3–4.

5. Lincoln, *Arthritic Japan*, 174–75.

6. *Japan Times*, August 26, 1999.

7. Scher and Yoshino, "Policy Challenges and the Reform of Postal Savings in Japan," 142.

8. Ibid.

of ordinary Japanese by helping them to "help themselves,"[9] the voluntary system required low monthly fees that could be automatically withdrawn from a policyholder's postal savings account. Unlike commercial life insurance plans, the system did not discriminate on the basis of age or occupation,[10] nor did it require applicants to undergo medical examinations. For all intents and purposes, it was a universal and affordable plan that performed a useful service for ordinary Japanese, especially low-income groups and the elderly. And its policies were guaranteed by the state, a feature that reassured many Japanese during the late 1990s as several small private insurance providers succumbed to bankruptcy.[11] The public's trust in the postal insurance system was reflected by its size: in 1999, with 40 percent of the total life insurance market, the system was 3.7 times larger than Nihon Seimei, the private sector's largest provider.[12]

In addition to its basic mail and financial services, the postwar postal system spawned a number of supplementary services and institutions that served the common good, most notably at the local level. Toward the end of twentieth century, for example, the post offices had assumed a number of local government functions, including the provision of official documents and the sale of transportation passes. These functions expanded more rapidly during the early 2000s as many local government offices shut down following a wave of mergers among village, town, and city governments. The postal system also helped nurture feelings of local identity among the population. For decades, the mail service issued "hometown postage stamps" (*furusato kitte*) and "hometown postcards" (*furusato hagaki*) adorned with enticing images of specific cities or regions. These stamps and postcards were meant to evoke a pride of place in

---

9. As SCAP observed, "The Government's motive in undertaking the enterprise is said to be solely the promotion of the welfare of the masses" (Civil Communications Section of the Supreme Commander of the Allied Powers, *Report on Survey of Japanese Postal System*, 20).

10. Matsubara, *Gendai no yūsei jigyō*, 185.

11. By the end of the twentieth century, Japan was the only country in the world that still had a postal life insurance system in place. In many other countries, including England, post offices serve as retail agents for the policies of private insurance corporations (Yamawaki, *Yūsei kōbō*, 206).

12. Mizuno, "Yūsei min'eika e no nagaki michinori," 173.

much the same way that pre-1945 stamp issues stoked nationalist senti-ments by commemorating imperial anniversaries and military victories abroad. Also noteworthy was the 1983 introduction of the "hometown packages" (*furusato kozutsumi*) service, in which the post offices func-tioned as a national network for the purchase and distribution of local agricultural or manufactured products.[13] A complement to the "one village, one product movement" (*isson ippin undō*) that had begun a few years earlier, the service aimed to increase employment levels in local industry and agriculture.[14] Expanding rapidly during its first decade,[15] the program was embraced by local postmasters as a useful tool for "building post offices that people could love."[16]

The postal system offered a host of other services designed to nurture national communications, help the disadvantaged, and encourage vol-untarism. In the spirit of Maejima Hisoka's efforts during the early Meiji period to promote mass literacy and communications, for instance, the postwar mail service charged low fees for the distribution of newspapers, magazines, and materials for correspondence courses. Many financial and mail services were offered in Braille, and the handicapped received a number of services free of charge. Fees for many services were sus-pended following natural disasters; postage was waived for postcards sent into and out of stricken areas, as were fees for transferring dona-tions from postal savings accounts to disaster victims. For many years, individual savers enjoyed tax exemptions on deposits of up to 3 million yen (the *maruyū* system); the elderly, and, for a short time, single mothers, continued to enjoy this perquisite even after 1988, when the government eliminated this exemption. The postal savings system also helped ordi-nary citizens engage in international philanthropy. Established in 1991, the "international volunteer savings accounts" (*kokusai boranchia chokin*) automatically set aside 20 percent of interest earned on deposits. These

---

13. Today, the service is operated by Japan Post Network Co., Ltd. Information can be accessed at http://www.postal-jp.com/psc/ws010d01.html (last accessed July 14, 2011).

14. Matsubara, *Gendai no yūsei jigyō*, 145–46. It is doubtful, however, that this pro-gram has had a significant impact on local employment levels.

15. Ibid.

16. Hida chiku tokutei yūbinkyoku chōkai kaishi hensan iinkai, ed., *Hida no tokutei yūbinkyoku shi*, 285.

proceeds were transferred to NGOs that planted trees, purchased text-books, built wells, and provided food and medical care to disadvantaged communities in the developing world. By 1995, the Japanese had donated approximately 2.8 billion yen through the service.[17]

Finally, the postal savings and insurance systems constructed and managed two networks of facilities that provided recreational and welfare services to local residents. The national network of postal insurance inns (*kanpo no yado*), the successors to the prewar "health consultation centers" (*kenkō sōdanjo*) described in Chapter 1, offered rest and recuperation opportunities for the ill and elderly, medical clinics, recreation facilities, assembly halls, and hotel services. By 1996, roughly 12 million postal insurance policyholders were making regular use of the more than 70 facilities, reaping social as well as health benefits.[18] Meanwhile, a network of 19 Mielparque (Meruparuku), formerly known as Postal Savings Halls (Yūsei chokin kaikan), offered low-cost hotel services, wedding and banquet facilities, and meeting quarters. Although both the Mielparque and the postal insurance inns attracted intense criticism for intruding on a private sector domain, they did seem to occupy a significant space in the social lives of many local residents.

Together, these formal and informal programs helped develop the postwar postal system into a multi-functional, paternalist entity that attended to everything from the individual's financial needs to his or her medical problems. It was largely for these reasons that proposals to radically reform the postal system were met with dismay by many Japanese citizens and their local governments—particularly in small, rural communities where the post office remained the people's only direct link to the state.

Administering the Postal Services

Although the postal system's social benefits were rarely contested—even by critics who wished to see the system privatized—its institutional structure was hotly debated. From the 1870s, when the mail and postal savings services were introduced, until the present, bureaucrats,

---

17. Matsubara, *Gendai no yūsei jigyō*, 181.
18. Ibid., 199.

scholars, and postal employees have wrangled with one another over how the services should be organized, paid for, and run. At stake was the quality of communications, the health of the Japanese financial system, employment levels, and, as many would have it, the country's social well-being.

Between 1870 and the early 1930s, policymakers were bitterly divided over Maejima's proposal to establish an independent or "special" account (*tokubetsu kaikei*) for the postal services.[19] While Maejima was on his official visit to Britain in 1870, the state opted to link the mail service directly to the general account (*ippan kaikei*). Maejima and many postal bureaucrats later complained that the arrangement fettered the services by making them overly dependent on politically motivated Diet members for access to government subsidies. (The fact that many commissioned postmasters were reduced to funding the network's local expansion from their own pockets must have lent added weight to these complaints.) They further argued that by making the mail and postal savings services financially independent—the postal insurance and pension systems had independent accounts from the start—the services would be better incentivized to maximize profitability and expand.[20]

In what proved to be one of the earliest battles in the so-called Hundred Years War between two of Japan's leading ministries, the Ministry of Finance (MOF) held firm throughout the Meiji and Taishō eras against pressure from the Communications Ministry (Teishinshō) for an independent account for all postal services. The MOF defended the status quo by defining it in the postal system's best interest; moving to an independent accounting system, the ministry maintained, would violate the postal system's mandate to perform important "public services" (*kōeki jigyō*) by forcing it to focus on profits and losses. (As later chapters illustrate, the argument that "profit" had no place in government or public enterprise would later be appropriated by the opponents of postal privatization.) The MOF was also concerned about the lack of foreign precedent for such a move. But it appears that the MOF's

---

19. Japan has long had a custom of establishing special accounts to manage specific government programs. By 2000, there were 38 such accounts in existence (Wright, *Japan's Fiscal Crisis*, 212).

20. Yūseishō, ed., *Yūsei 100-nen no ayumi*, 143.

position was primarily motivated by revenue concerns; for instance, although proceeds from the mail service were meager, the ministry was determined to keep them flowing into the general account at a time when state finances were tight. If the service required extra resources for expansion, then tax revenues should be appropriated.[21] The ministry was also determined to maintain its control over the investment of postal savings deposits. For the first time in its history, the MOF was openly treating the postal network as a source of government income.

By the 1920s, the conflict had intensified as communications budgets failed to cover costs within the services—even though postal revenues were now rising. But the campaign to establish an independent account for the postal services met with a series of false starts, one of them the fault of none other than Koizumi Matajirō, grandfather of contemporary Japan's most famous postal reformer. Serving as Prime Minister Hamaguchi Osachi's communications minister between 1929 and 1931, Koizumi took little interest in his underlings' campaign in his preoccupation with a revolutionary but ill-fated plan to privatize the telephone and telegraph services.[22] It would be another few years before the Communications Ministry's efforts to bring the MOF to the negotiating table finally bore fruit.

In time, the MOF finally agreed to grant its rival accounting independence. In return, the Communications Ministry was to transfer fixed yearly sums from mail service proceeds into the general account, postal savings funds would continue to flow into the MOF's Deposit Bureau,[23] and the MOF would retain the authority to set postal savings interest rates, with only small percentages of interest earned returning to the postal system.[24] A resentful but overpowered Communications Ministry agreed to these requirements, and an independent umbrella account for the communications services (*teishin jigyō tokubetsu kaikei*) was approved

---

21. Yūseishō, ed., *Yūsei 100-nen shi*, 574.

22. Ibid., 576.

23. The MOF established the Deposit Bureau in 1925 to rationalize the management of proceeds from the postal savings and insurance programs (Park, *Spending Without Taxation*, 66).

24. Yūseishō, ed., *Yūsei 100-nen no ayumi*, 145.

Fig. 4.1   Koizumi Matajirō, Minister of Posts and Telecommunications under Prime Minister Hamaguchi, advocated the privatization of telecommunications. His grandson went on to become Japan's most famous postal reformer. Courtesy of the Teishin sōgō hakubutsukan.

by the Diet in 1933 and launched the following year.[25] (In 1949, with the establishment of NTT, the account was split in two: one account for the telegraph and telephone services and the postal services special account, *yūsei jigyō tokubetsu kaikei*.)

From the Communications Ministry's perspective, the new account allowed it to lower costs and enhance services by introducing private-sector accounting principles to the administration of the postal services. The system also came with some new responsibilities; in order to expand and maintain the postal network's infrastructure, the services

25. Japan was a pioneer in the timing of its decision to make the postal services financially self-sufficient. A similar policy was not introduced in the United States until 1970, when the United States Postal Service (USPS), an independent federal agency, was established (Sherman, "Competition in Postal Service," 193).

had to generate their own capital—through loans and bond issues, if necessary.[26] The system, in short, could no longer depend on public funds as heavily as it had in the past to finance its operations.

The new accounting procedures spawned some improvements within the services. Coupled with a series of reforms introduced during the 1930s and early 1940s to reorganize the network of post offices, the independent account enabled the mail service and hence the postal system more generally to generate significant surpluses. But since the mail service was required by law to transfer 2 million yen each year into the general account, it struggled to finance new infrastructure and services in response to demands generated by rapid mobilization for war. To help make ends meet, the mail service on several occasions raised postage rates,[27] which the already strained population could ill afford.

By August 1945, the postal services were deeply in the red as they struggled to raise funds to repair or replace the system's war-torn infrastructure.[28] Although finances stabilized by the mid-1950s following the introduction of a series of small accounting reforms and the economy's recovery from the war, the mail service remained handicapped by the 1934 requirement that fixed sums be transferred each year into the general account. The system as a whole continued to run a deficit and required occasional subsidies from the general account.[29] It was not until 1961 that the MOF agreed to drop the transfer requirement and to raise interest rates paid on postal savings proceeds that were transferred into the Trust Fund Bureau (the postwar successor to the Deposit Bureau).[30] The fiscal health of the postal system over the next two decades or so improved as a result of these changes, although occasional deficits within specific services—particularly mail—were certainly not uncommon.

---

26. Until 2003, postage increases had to be approved by the Diet (Yūseishō, ed., *Yūsei 100-nen shi*, 578).

27. Ibid., 578, 593–94.

28. Ibid., 689, 695.

29. Kinoshita, "The Economics of Japan's Postal Services Privatization," 7.

30. Ibid.; Yūseishō, ed., *Yūsei 100-nen no ayumi*, 210.

Postal System Weaknesses and (Dis)Incentives to Reform

Until 2003, when it was transformed into a public corporation, the postwar postal system was owned by the government but managed within an accounting framework that enabled the services to achieve independent profitability.[31] Within the framework of the system's independent accounting system, each postal service had its own discrete account. Although the three services were prohibited from directly subsidizing one another, they nevertheless enjoyed a synergistic relationship. Since the postal financial services contributed the lion's share of the postal system's overall revenue, they helped compensate for frequent shortfalls in the mail service. Synergies were also important for the financial health of individual post offices. In areas where the volume of mail was in decline, for example, post offices depended heavily on customer traffic for savings, insurance, and other financial services like money orders and remittances (Giro transfers).[32]

While the postal savings and insurance systems generated profits for much of the postwar era, the weakest link in the postal system was consistently the mail service. As in most countries, a large proportion of the mail service's operating expenses was eaten up by labor costs; in 1985, labor-related expenditures peaked at 74.2 percent of total costs.[33] Although the gradual mechanization of tasks like mail sorting helped to reduce these costs, there was only so much that machines could do. When all is said and done, human beings must collect and deliver the mail. To complicate matters, the legal requirement of universal mail service meant that even post offices in very sparsely populated (read unprofitable) communities had to hire workers. Furthermore, the presence of a powerful union of postal workers (Zentei) made it difficult for the state to trim costs by reducing what by the early 2000s was a workforce of approximately 250,000 full-time employees.[34] Granted, profits from

---

31. Matsubara, *Gendai no yūsei jigyō*, 129–30.

32. Interview, Yoshino Naoyuki, Faculty of Economics, Keiō University, Tokyo, July 3, 2010.

33. Matsubara, *Gendai no yūsei jigyō*, 130–32.

34. Yūsei jigyō kenkyūkai, *Nihon no yūsei*, 199. Part-time workers within the postal services brought the total number of employees to nearly 400,000 (Yamawaki, *Yūsei kōbō*, 20).

more lucrative urban areas could be used to cover less profitable regions, but as the mail service began to stagnate in reaction to mounting competition from mobile telephones and electronic mail, this became less and less feasible. By the 1990s, the service was suffering from deep and recurring deficits that were alleviated only by the occasional postage rate increase.[35]

As in other countries, solving the mail service's weaknesses by breaking the government's monopoly on mail collection and delivery posed a dilemma for both the government and potential private carriers. All other things being equal, if private competitors are allowed to enter a national market, they are likely to neglect (costly) rural communities and to crowd the government out of lucrative urban areas by offering lower postage rates; this, in turn, would deprive the government provider of profits that could compensate for heavy losses incurred in less populated areas, where the government is likely to remain the sole provider.[36] To avoid taking such a heavy financial hit, the government would have to impose universal service requirements on private competitors, but this would be a costly proposition for carriers who lacked access to national distribution networks.[37]

Also at issue by the 1990s was the administrative efficiency and financial health of the national network of post offices. As illustrated in Table 2.1, the vast majority of postal facilities in Japan were small commissioned post offices, most of which did not collect letters from mail boxes or deliver them. Nearly all of these tiny, non-collection and delivery (*mushūhai*) entities ran operating deficits due to high fixed costs and low revenues. However, the commissioned postmasters, their LDP sympathizers, and other defenders of the postal status quo resisted ef-

---

35. By law, the system can only raise postage rates if the total debt in any give year equals more than 5 percent of total income (Matsubara, *Gendai no yūsei jigyō*, 155).

36. Urban areas are far more profitable than rural areas because of denser distribution networks and high mail volume (OECD, *Promoting Competition in Postal Services*, 7).

37. Britain's Royal Mail has exemplified these problems. Although the 2006 lifting of the public corporation's monopoly over the conveyance of letters resulted in cheaper and higher quality service for businesses, the process also sparked a wave of worker strikes and post office closures. Critics continue to question the negative effects of mail competition on universal service, employment within the postal network, and the Royal Mail's rising debt (*Guardian*, February 23, 2009).

forts by handfuls of enterprising bureaucrats in the MPT to enhance network efficiency by shutting down or amalgamating unprofitable post offices. The postmasters and their allies worried about the ramifications of such measures for employment—both theirs and that of their employees. Rural residents fretted about their access to financial and social services. Conservative politicians dwelled on the possible impact of closures on voter support at election time. As a result of these pressures, the number of inefficient, non-collection commissioned post offices actually *increased* during the recession-prone 1990s, while that of more cost-effective ordinary post offices eventually dropped.

The long-term integrity of the postal network was a major consideration among those who defended the postal status quo. The postmasters and their allies feared that privatization—or even just the introduction of more competition into the services under the rubric of a public corporation—would prioritize the profit motive, leading to closures of loss-generating post offices. They also argued that separating mail, savings, and insurance into separate corporate entities in a more market-oriented environment would precipitate a decline in such services in unprofitable regions, thereby putting added pressure on struggling post offices to close. This, in turn, would be bad for the well-being of small local communities, particularly those that lacked easy access to commercial banks. It was for these reasons that advocates of the state-run postal system held firm to the principle of "state administered, unified services" (*kokuei de san jigyō ittai*) throughout the long evolution of Japan's postal reform debate.

The Postal System and the FILP

While defenders of Japan's state-run postal system focused primarily on the positive effects of the postal network and services on households and local communities, advocates of corporatization or outright privatization dwelt on the impact of the post office's financial services on the financial system as a whole. Reformers were quick to point out that the postal savings and insurance systems were by far the largest competitors within their respective sectors; in its capacity as the world's largest bank, moreover, the postal savings system raised serious moral hazard concerns. Reformers also argued that under the state's protective wing, the bloated postal services had caused serious distortions within the private financial sector that slowed the pace of recovery among the beleaguered commercial banks during the 1990s.

Equally controversial was the postal system's connection to the FILP.[38] Established in 1953, the FILP was "a plan for loans and expenditures to be made from the government's various savings accounts and annuity programs" that were earmarked primarily for industrial and infrastructural development.[39] Valued at approximately 70 percent of the general budget in FY 2001,[40] many scholars referred to the FILP as Japan's "second budget," since it was dispensed largely at the state's discretion. But this term was somewhat misleading; although general budgetary expenditures involved Diet-approved subsidies, grants, and other direct payments to targeted recipients, FILP expenditures were mainly in the form of loans that in theory had to be repaid.[41] As others have observed, Japan was by no means the only country to develop government-sponsored loan programs for economic development. What distinguished the FILP was its massive size.[42]

The FILP was fueled by a number of sources including national welfare and pension premium payments and postal life insurance premiums. But the largest source by far was postal savings deposits. These funds were channeled into the Trust Fund Bureau of the MOF, while postal insurance proceeds found their way into the FILP via the Postal Life Insurance Reserve Fund.[43] FILP funds were then moved into sev-

---

38. Although the FILP still exists, it has undergone significant changes since the late 1990s. I therefore refer to the pre-reformed FILP in the past tense.

39. Johnson, *Japan's Public Policy Companies*, 82. Cargill and Yoshino's definition is also illustrative: "The FILP is not so much an institution or government agency as it is a process of decision making concurrent with the formulation of the national budget that directs financial resources under the government's control to targeted sectors of the economy" (*Postal Savings and Fiscal Investment in Japan*, 9). In a similar vein, Gene Park refers to the FILP as "policy finance": a financial instrument for carrying out public policy that enables the state to keep tax rates low (*Spending Without Taxation*, 18).

40. Matsubara, *Gendai no yūsei jigyō*, 96.

41. Interview, Yoshino Naoyuki, Faculty of Economics, Keiō University, Tokyo, January 8, 2007.

42. Doi and Hoshi, "Paying for the FILP," 37.

43. Cargill and Yoshino, *Postal Savings and Fiscal Investment in Japan*, 9.

eral dozen FILP-financed entities including special accounts,[44] government financial institutions that lent funds to niche constituents at competitive interest rates,[45] special corporations,[46] and local governments.[47]

The custom of government investment of proceeds from the postal system's financial services dates back to the early Meiji period, but it was not until 1953—shortly after Japanese sovereignty over domestic budgetary matters had been restored—that the FILP acquired its formal, postwar structure.[48] The ultimate recipients of FILP funds varied according to the policy objectives of the state at any given time. During the 1930s and 1940s, FILP expenditures targeted national public policy companies like Japan Steel, munitions firms, and control associations, as well as other strategically important entities.[49] After the Occupation, funds were channeled into the postwar reconstruction of electric power, iron and steel, shipping, and coal mining. By the 1960s, the emphasis was on catching up with the advanced economies of the West by targeting industries with significant growth potential: electronics, machinery, oil refining, synthetic fibers, and nuclear power generation.[50] But the FILP did not focus exclusively on winners; it also allocated funds to sectors

---

44. Seven special accounts were funded by the FILP in 2000, including those for hospitals, schools, and airport development.

45. A total of eight government financial institutions were connected to the FILP: Development Bank of Japan; Japan Housing Loan Corporation; National Life Finance Corporation; Japan Finance Corporation for Small Business; Japan Bank for International Cooperation; Okinawa Development Finance Corporation; Japan Finance Corporation for Municipal Enterprises; and Agriculture, Forestry, and Fisheries Finance Corporation of Japan.

46. Most semi-governmental organizations that received FILP funds were connected to transportation, energy, and technological development.

47. Cargill and Yoshino, *Postal Savings and Fiscal Investment in Japan,* 9. A portion of these funds was also set aside to purchase government bonds.

48. For more on the FILP's prewar precedents, see Cargill and Yoshino, *Postal Savings and Fiscal Investment in Japan*; Ferber, "'Run the State Like a Business'"; Johnson, *Japan's Public Policy Companies*; and Wright, *Japan's Fiscal Crisis*. For a comprehensive analysis of the FILP and its significance for postwar politics and public finance, see Park, *Spending Without Taxation*.

49. Johnson, *Japan's Public Policy Companies*, 86.

50. Scher and Yoshino, "Policy Challenges and the Reform of Postal Savings in Japan," 126.

that had been left behind by rapid economic development,[51] and to special corporations like the Housing Loan Corporation that served public welfare goals.[52] Ten years later, social welfare and environmental concerns spurred allocations to the construction of welfare facilities, residential land development, and pollution prevention plans. By the 1980s, funds were used to promote alternative sources of energy.[53]

In the context of the post-bubble recession and the decline of industrial policy, FILP allocations shifted course once again. Now, the aim was to maintain employment levels and promote structural adjustments in key industries so they could compete more effectively in response to slower growth rates and mounting global competition.[54] Following the liberalization of land use policies during the 1980s, moreover, funds were increasingly devoted to building infrastructure—a goal that proved a boon to the construction industry. At this time, large portions of the funds earmarked for developmental purposes were channeled directly into special corporations (*tokushu hōjin*) rather than through governmental financial institutions,[55] a trend that created even more vested interests in Japan's already saturated public works programs.

The FILP, in short, was at "the heart of industrial policy"[56] as a financial engine and policy instrument that helped generate Japan's postwar economic miracle. In principle, the FILP bore the imprint of Japanese capitalist values in that funds were to be allocated not to narrow economic interests but to grand, national projects relating to economic development, environmental protection, and social welfare that, in some cases, private firms could not afford to implement.[57] FILP investments were also meant to eliminate risks to postal savings depositors and postal insurance policy holders by emphasizing loans issued through govern-

---

51. Cargill and Yoshino, *Postal Savings and Fiscal Investment in Japan,* 54.
52. The Housing Loan Corporation helped make housing more available to ordinary consumers.
53. Scher and Yoshino, "Policy Challenges and the Reform of Postal Savings in Japan," 126.
54. Scher and Yoshino, "Introduction," 10.
55. Scher and Yoshino, "Policy Challenges and the Reform of Postal Savings in Japan," 127.
56. Lincoln, *Arthritic Japan*, 173.
57. Doi and Hoshi, "Paying for the FILP," 37.

ment financial institutions, rather than outright subsidies that would never be repaid.[58] The FILP, in other words, was supposed to use the people's money for the people's benefit, and without increasing their tax burden.

In practice, however, the FILP often failed to live up to these principles. From the start, the fund was politicized as a result of bureaucratic turf battles and, during the postwar era, its contributions to the perpetuation of LDP rule. The FILP was at the center of a protracted conflict between the MOF and the MPT and its pre-1949 incarnations over the control of postal savings accounts—the so-called Hundred Years War. Since the early Meiji period, the MPT's predecessors had been responsible for collecting postal savings deposits, which at first were transferred to a commercial bank. From 1878, amidst increasing banking instability, the MOF laid claim to a portion of those deposits; after the Matsukata Deflation of the early 1880s, it controlled the entire amount.[59] It was at this time that the practice of making postal savings funds available for government investment in the economy was introduced.[60] By the end of the nineteenth century, the MOF had assumed control of channeling those funds to the private sector through government-affiliated financial institutions.[61] And so evolved an informal division of labor between the two ministries in which postal bureaucrats collected postal savings deposits and life insurance premiums and the MOF dispensed them. The postal bureaucrats resented this arrangement and put relentless pressure on its rival to grant it more autonomy over the postal savings system, including setting interest rates and controlling the investment of deposits. The MOF, which viewed its competitor as a second-tier ministry, refused to give up its prerogatives.[62]

In the wake of World War II, the bureaucratic "tug-of-war" (*kōbōsen*) moved from behind the scenes into the open.[63] As Frances Rosenbluth explains, the MPT's quest for greater control over the investment of postal savings and insurance funds was partly motivated by its desire to

---

58. Wright, *Japan's Fiscal Crisis*, 212, 219–20.

59. Kuwayama, "Postal Banking in the United States and Japan," 36–37.

60. Ferber, "'Run the State Like a Business,'" 142.

61. Kuwayama, "Postal Banking in the United States and Japan," 37.

62. Jin, *Ōkura kanryō*, 183.

63. Ibid.

underwrite the projects of key conservative politicians in return for political support for its various bureaucratic projects. The MOF refused
to give in to these demands, and was backed by both SCAP and local
governments that depended heavily on a flow of loans from postal savings accounts. (Clearly, the MOF was not the only entity that distrusted
the MPT.) When the Occupation ended, the division of labor between
the two ministries was formalized; the MPT would continue to collect
postal savings deposits and postal insurance premiums, and the MOF
would exercise full authority over their investment.[64] It would be several decades before this arrangement was significantly altered.

In both its prewar and postwar manifestations, the FILP was prone to
political mischief. During World War I, Prime Minister Terauchi Masa-
take tried to coax Chinese warlords into Japan's political orbit by extending them a series of bank loans. After all but a handful of the warlords defaulted on the loans, the MOF used postal savings funds to bail
out the banks. The incident sparked a major public outcry and eventually
led to the introduction of more stringent regulations on the use of postal
savings funds.[65] From the early 1970s, when FILP budgets were first
subjected to Diet approval,[66] FILP investments in politically motivated
projects increased. By the 1990s, FILP funds were being lavished on
countless public works projects—bridges leading to nowhere and roads
and railway lines in sparsely populated areas that were ultimately designed to enhance the popularity and electoral fortunes of conservative
party incumbents.[67] To be sure, these expenditures helped keep ordinary
Japanese employed and had positive spin-off effects for other sectors
of the economy. But as Japan entered the recession years of the 1990s,
they were increasingly criticized as symptoms of official corruption and
financial wastage, as well as an impediment to economic recovery.[68]

---

64. Rosenbluth, *Financial Politics in Contemporary Japan*, 172–74.

65. Johnson, *Japan's Public Policy Companies*, 85–86.

66. Yearly FILP plans are now submitted to the Diet as an attachment to the budget
bill (Doi and Hoshi, "Paying for the FILP," 41).

67. Park provides convincing statistical evidence that FILP investments in public
works and other projects may have helped the LDP win seats in Lower House elections
(*Spending without Taxation*, Chapter 5).

68. Doi and Hoshi estimate that by the early 2000s, as much as 75 percent of FILP
loans were non-performing (ibid., 56).

The postal financial services and, more broadly, the FILP system, reached the end of the twentieth century with a mixed record. On the one hand, these interrelated systems served a number of public interest goals: the postal savings system encouraged higher household savings rates, and the FILP supplied the MOF with a steady flow of funds for investment in industry and reduced the country's reliance on foreign capital.[69] The FILP also enabled the state to fulfill social welfare goals by funding the construction of public housing and local infrastructure, loans for small- and medium-sized businesses, and the introduction of environmental protection programs. As such, the FILP was a positive manifestation of what is otherwise pejoratively known as "financial socialism"—state functions that go well beyond their stated economic or financial purposes to provide (costly) social services to the public.

On the other hand, the FILP had some deep flaws that became all too apparent once the rapid growth period drew to a close. The system was not subject to normal budgetary processes and its disbursements were opaque and susceptible to political interference. It frequently supplied funds for projects that served narrow political objectives.[70] Finally, the FILP nurtured a host of special corporations that competed—many say unfairly—with the private sector and helped keep retired bureaucrats employed. As the next section illustrates, the vested interests that grew around these functions were important components of the movement to oppose postal reform.

The Postal Regime

Taking our cue from T. J. Pempel, we can interpret the various institutions and interests that developed within and around the postal system as a "regime": "a middle level of cohesion in the political economy of a nation-state" that "transcends several specific administrations." Regimes, according to Pempel's definition, are composed of three inter-

---

69. Cargill and Yoshino, *Postal Savings and Fiscal Investment in Japan*, 70–72.

70. Rosenbluth, *Financial Politics in Contemporary Japan*, 179. Several scholars have found that the dispensation of FILP funds tended to increase following electoral losses by the LDP. Often, those increases would target key constituents like small businesses. See Amyx, Takenaka, and Toyoda, "The Politics of Postal Savings Reform in Japan," 27; and Patterson, "Electoral Influence and Economic Policy."

dependent elements: "socioeconomic alliances, political-economic institutions, and a public policy profile."[71] But while Pempel's subject of
inquiry was the postwar regime that underpinned the political economy
as a whole, the postal regime was more of a subset of that broader
entity—a system of public and private institutions, political alliances,
and policy preferences specific to the postal sector. As such, the postal
regime both reflected and contributed to the broader regime.[72]

At the heart of the postwar postal regime was the triangular alliance
among the postmasters, postal bureaucrats, and LDP politicians, particularly members of the party's postal tribe, which was based in the
Telecommunications Committee (Tsūshin bukai) of the LDP's Policy
Affairs Research Council (PARC). Since the early 1960s, membership
in parliamentary organizations connected to the postal system, including
the Diet's communications committees (*teishin iinkai*) and the informal
but multi-partisan Postal Services Roundtable (Yūsei jigyō konwakai),[73]
increased steadily as conservative politicians sought reliable mechanisms
for mobilizing votes and politicians of all stripes tried to edge closer
to the postal savings trough. These units functioned as conduits for the
LDP's linkages with both the postmasters and the postal bureaucrats.

By the late 1980s, in response to mounting calls for postal reform,
that triangular alliance expanded to embrace Zentei, Japan's largest and
most powerful postal union, its supporters in the JSP, and Zen'yūsei,
the smaller postal union consisting mostly of conservative-leaning commissioned post office employees.[74] A decade later, many members of the
Democratic Party of Japan (DPJ) jumped on board after the party replaced the Socialists as the Zentei's main political patron. Underpinning
the alliance's widening appeal was nonpartisan support for the postal

---

71. Pempel, *Regime Shift*, 20.

72. Some Japanese newspapers have referred to what I call the "postal regime" as the
"postal family" (*yūsei ikka*), but none, to my knowledge, has clarified exactly who belongs
to it. Although I have used the term myself in earlier writings, my extensive reading on
the postal system has since revealed rather imprecise usages. I have therefore refrained
from using "postal family" in this book.

73. Roundtable chairmen all hailed from Tanaka Kakuei's faction or its successors:
Kanemaru Shin, Obuchi Keizō, and Nonaka Hiromu.

74. Zen'yūsei, gravitated first toward the Democratic Socialist Party and then, like
Zentei, the DPJ.

savings system and the various perquisites it generated for politicians and the public.[75] Although ideological differences impeded regular cooperation between the alliance's conservative and progressive interests, the two sides often backed one another from the mid-1980s as they battled the advocates for postal privatization.[76]

Although the mass media had long acknowledged the existence of the triangular alliance among the postmasters, LDP politicians, and postal bureaucrats, as well as the supporting role played by the unions and progressive parties, other interests that developed around the postal system received less attention. Of particular note were networks of private firms and public corporations that helped knit the public and private sectors into a web of mutually beneficial interests and obligations. What bound these entities to the postal regime were practices that characterized the postwar political-economic regime more broadly, namely, rent-seeking, *amakudari*,[77] and bid-rigging.

The postal system spawned a number of special corporations (*tokushu hōjin*) that carried out specialized functions for the postal bureaucracy and the postal network.[78] Foremost among them were the three organizations that merged during the mid-2000s to form Postal Welfare (Yūsei fukushi). Founded in 1952 and administered by the MPT, the Postal Benefits Association (Yūsei kōsaikai) provided relief to postal network employees and MPT bureaucrats, including benefits for the dependents of deceased employees, disaster relief, and the like. The association also supported individual post offices by supplying them with cleaning services, copiers, safes, signboards, air conditioners, mail bags, surveillance machines, and other equipment—all for a fee. With about 3,000 employees, in 2000–2001 the association's income was roughly equivalent to that of a typical medium-sized enterprise. It also functioned as a prime

---

75. Calder, "Linking Welfare and the Developmental State," 45.

76. Interview, Zentoku official, Tokyo, March 27, 2003.

77. *Amakudari* (lit., "descent from heaven") refers to the custom of bureaucrats landing lucrative postretirement positions, usually in private or special corporations that were under the jurisdiction of their former ministries. The practice is widely condemned as a vehicle for corrupt relations between the bureaucracy and the public and private sectors.

78. According to one observer, by 1999 these entities had a range of different legal designations, including *kōeki hōjin*, *tokushu hōjin*, *zaidan hōjin*, and *shadan hōjin* (Ikeda Minoru, *Yūbin'yasan ga naiteiru*, 24–25).

landing spot for retiring MPT bureaucrats and Zentei officials;[79] in 1994, 19 of the organization's 40 executives were former MPT bureaucrats.[80]

In 1954, the MPT founded the Postal Mutual Aid Society (Yūsei gojokai), also a foundation, to supply additional social services to retired employees of the postal network. The society administered a fund fueled by employee paycheck deductions that provided benefits to the families of deceased employees and helped cover the costs of employee weddings and funerals.[81] By the early 2000s, the society boasted an estimated 350 billion yen in assets, thanks largely to its construction and ownership of postal facilities and, before 2003, its tax-exempt status.[82] In March 2001, it owned 1,566 (mostly commissioned) post offices and 179 postal bureau facilities; these were leased to the ministry in return for rents that were significantly higher than what the market would have offered.[83] The society also owned employee dormitories—approximately 6,600 individual apartments as of 2005—that it leased to the ministry.[84] Like the Postal Benefits Association, the Mutual Aid Society provided post-retirement job opportunities to many MPT bureaucrats. It also delved into business ventures outside of the postal sphere. Under Minister of Posts and Telecommunications Suzuki Zenkō's tenure, for instance, the society helped finance the founding of the Tōhoku Institute of Technology (Tōhoku kōgyō daigaku) in Sendai; in subsequent years, both society executives and retired MPT bureaucrats served on the institute's board of directors.[85]

The third component of Postal Welfare, the Postal Welfare Association (Yūsei fukushi kyōkai), was established during the early 1960s to provide social services to retired postal employees and their families—in this instance through group insurance schemes. It, too, functioned as a landing spot for retired bureaucrats.

---

79. Matsuda, "Yūsei sanjigyō ni 'kisei' suru gaibu dantai, famirī kigyōgun," 99–102.

80. *Mainichi shinbun*, April 16, 2000.

81. http://www.yuseifukushi.or.jp/service/youing/index.html (last accessed July 11, 2011).

82. *Asahi shinbun*, February 27, 2007.

83. Matsuda, "Yūsei sanjigyō ni 'kisei' suru gaibu dantai, famirī kigyōgun," 105–6.

84. Inose, *Kessen*, 12.

85. Matsuda, "Yūsei sanjigyō ni 'kisei' suru gaibu dantai, famirī kigyōgun," 105–6.

Numerous other public and semi-public organizations serviced the postal network. By the end of the 1990s it was estimated that as many as 230 special corporations were connected to the MPT. Most operated within the telecommunications sector; several were deemed dummy corporations (*meimoku hōjin*). Of those linked to the postal system, many employed fairly large numbers of people. One such organization was the Postal Savings Promotion Association (Yūbin chokin shinkōkai), which, as its name suggests, was established in 1969 to promote postal savings among the general population. To that end, it sponsored public seminars and other educational programs, conducted research on savings trends and products, and carried out public opinion surveys. From the late 1970s, the association also administered the aforementioned Mielparque.[86] Managed in part with proceeds from postal savings, the typical Mielparque consisted of hotel rooms, banquet and wedding facilities, restaurants, and, for good measure, corners for disseminating public information on the postal savings system. Some Mielparque had swimming pools, movie theaters, and concert halls; one luxurious facility in the resort area of Nikkō sported an outdoor spa (*rotenburo*), a water park, and astronomy facilities.[87] The Postal Savings Promotion Association's top executives were heavily skewed toward retired MPT bureaucrats, and many of the general managers of individual Mielparque were former postmasters, few of whom were experienced hotel administrators. In 1983, the Second Ad Hoc Commission for Administrative Reform (Daini rinji gyōsei chōsakai or Second Rinchō)[88] ruled that bureaucrats should not be in the business of running hotels, not least because these government-run facilities unfairly undercut the prices of private-sector hotels.[89] But it was not until the 2005 passage of postal privatization that the Mielparque network was streamlined in any meaningful way; by late

---

86. The association was reorganized in 2003 as Yūsei zaidan. See http://www.yu-cho-f.jp/ (last accessed July 21, 2011).

87. Inose, *Kessen*, 28.

88. The Second Rinchō and its role in postal affairs will be examined later in this chapter in the section on postal reform during the 1980s.

89. Ikeda, *Yūbin'yasan ga naiteiru*, 25–27. The MPT was not alone in running its own network of hotels. The national pension system, for instance, ran a similar network known as the *kōsei nenkin kaikan* under the auspices of the Ministry of Health and Welfare.

2007, when postal privatization began, the number of facilities had been reduced from nineteen to eleven.

The comparable entity for the postal insurance system was the Postal Life Insurance Welfare Corporation (Kan'i hoken fukushi jigyōdan). Established in 1962, the corporation served as a prized landing spot for retiring bureaucrats, particularly from the MPT bureau in charge of the postal life insurance system. From the late 1980s, after the postal system was permitted to retain small portions of postal savings and insurance funds, the corporation oversaw the funds' investment. Its record on that score was poor; according to the MIC, it recorded losses of 3.86 trillion yen in mid-2001.[90] The corporation also oversaw the construction and administration of the "postal insurance inns"; the approximately 70 structures that remained by the end of the twentieth century included not only medical and recreational facilities, but also opulent tourist hotels equipped with spas (*onsen*) and gourmet restaurants. Like the Mielparque, the inns were exempted from paying rents and taxes; this in turn enabled them to undercut the prices of private hotels. Despite these perquisites, the network of inns ran significant budget deficits by the end of the century.[91]

Also noteworthy was the Postal Services Center, a special corporation established in 1967 to administer the "hometown packages" service.[92] The center helped set prices for the various goods distributed through the service and made explanatory pamphlets available to customers through the post offices. Customer orders were forwarded by the post offices to the center, which then dealt directly with local manufacturers in return for substantial commissions. According to one estimate, by the early 2000s more than 70 percent of the 90 individuals who worked for the center were former postal bureaucrats.[93] In keeping with the customs of other special corporations connected to the postal system, the center provided a valuable social service by promoting local manufacturers, especially in rural areas ravaged by depopulation and economic decline. In so doing, however, it constituted a vested interest

90. *Nikkei Weekly*, July 16, 2001.
91. Mizuno, "Yūsei min'eika e no nagaki michinori," 162; Inose, *Kessen*, 21.
92. *Japan Times*, October 21, 2002.
93. Ibid.; *Shūkan Daiyamondo*, June 29, 2002.

in the state-run postal system.[94] It was also immersed in scandal after failing to declare nearly 120 million yen in profits over a three-year period ending in March 2001.[95]

In addition to these and several other special corporations, scores of private firms were involved in the day-to-day administration of the postal network. Small, local companies—many of them linked to the Mutual Aid Society—were contracted to help build post offices, clean their interiors, supply and maintain equipment and worker uniforms, collect mail from mail boxes, maintain the postal network's ATM machinery, service postal computer systems, and so on. In several instances, single companies came to dominate the market for specific services. For example, Japan Postal Transport (Nippon yūbin teisō; Nittei), with approximately 50,000 employees, monopolized the market for transporting mail from mailboxes to the post offices,[96] and Japan Online Maintenance (Nihon onrain seibi) controlled the market for servicing the system's ATM network. Since these were private entities, information about their operations is hard to come by. There is good reason to conclude, however, that the firms reaped significant profits through their association with the postal network and offered lucrative positions to retired postal bureaucrats and former Zentei officials.[97] In 2007, the *Yomiuri shinbun* estimated that roughly one-third of Nittei's executives were former postal bureaucrats.[98]

In the past, individual post offices would draw up their own contracts with gasoline suppliers. But in the name of rationalization, the MPT ruled in 1991 that each regional postal bureau should control the distribution of supplier contracts and grant those contracts to the private

---

94. Critics claimed that were it not for the quotas levied on postal employees for the sale of "hometown packages," the Postal Services Center would have been far less successful (*Shūkan Daiyamondo*, June 29, 2002).

95. *Japan Times*, October 21 and 29, 2001.

96. Inose, *Kessen*, 36.

97. Matsuda, "Yūsei sanjigyō ni 'kisei' suru gaibu dantai, famirī kigyōgun," 106–8; *Asahi Newspaper*, October 22, 2002. According to the National Personnel Authority, 90 commercial businesses connected to the postal services hired 300 ex-postal employees between 2001 and 2003. *Japan Close-Up* (July 2004).

98. http://www.yomiuri.co.jp/e-japan/miyagi/kikaku/007/2.htm (last accessed October 15, 2007).

firm(s) of its choice. This trend soon led to the establishment of General Materials Service (Sōgō shizai sābisu), a national company that went on to control the supply of gasoline and some machinery for much of the network. Of its approximately 100 employees in 2000, 80 percent were retired bureaucrats. Although individual post offices could still negotiate their own contracts with gas stations and equipment providers in their areas, payments to those entities had to be made through General Materials Service. All the while, the postal system maintained the façade of a competitive bidding process for new gasoline contracts. In practice, however, private firms that wished to service the postal network had to provide proof of preexisting contracts with the post offices before they could tender a new bid; not surprisingly, only the General Materials Service consistently fulfilled this requirement.[99]

Retired bureaucrats were not the only ones who benefited from these firms' hiring practices; several politicians also took advantage of them. Okada Yūji, for instance, served a combined total of 21 years as the director of a private enterprise that supplied equipment to the network. A member of the LDP's Tanaka faction, Okada had been a high-ranking member of the postal tribe, a former speaker of the Upper House, head of the chamber's LDP caucus, and of course, one of the postmasters' "interest representation Diet members." Before entering politics, he had served for many years as an MPT bureaucrat connected to the postal services.[100] Okada's long-term position in a "postal family enterprise" was just one more link in the complex web of interrelationships among bureaucratic, private sector, and political party units that constituted the institutional foundations of the postal regime.

As with other sectors of the Japanese economy, bid-rigging among postal family enterprises positioned many firms to extract large rents from the public sector. After remaining under the radar screen for decades, these incidents began to attract more and more attention during the 1990s as the movement to reform the postal services gathered steam. In 1999, for example, Matsushita Communications Corporation, Ltd. was publicly censured for tendering an unreasonably low bid to supply the MPT with a database for tracking national postcard and postage

---

99. Matsuda, "Yūsei sanjigyō ni 'kisei' suru gaibu dantai, famirī kigyōgun," 117–18.
100. Ibid., 113–15.

stamp sales.[101] In an even more widely covered scandal, Toshiba and NEC were implicated in an MPT-led bid-rigging scheme to build machines for reading the system's seven-digit postal codes (*yūbin bangō*). The resulting set-up enabled Toshiba to supply machines to half of the country at inflated prices, and NEC to the other half. The companies' subsidiaries, many of which employed former MPT bureaucrats and postmasters and were already servicing the postal network, were to be put in charge of inspecting and maintaining those machines. Several post offices had placed their orders before the bidding process had begun, thereby prompting the Japan Fair Trade Commission to issue a cease and desist order. Although the flow of *amakudari* bureaucrats into these subsidiaries was reduced in the wake of the scandal, neither the firms nor the ministry admitted to the bid-rigging.[102]

As Edward Lincoln reminds us, "quasi-government organizations" have always been a feature of Japan's postwar economic system, as well as a contributing factor behind Japan's high employment rates.[103] In short, the positive impact of Postal Welfare's predecessors and other special corporations connected to the postal network on overall employment rates was by no means unusual. We should also remember that the overlap between the public and private sectors in the postal sphere had deep historical roots. Recall, for instance, the early Meiji commissioned postmasterships, which were filled by private subjects to carry out public responsibilities. Consider, too, Maejima Hisoka's arrangement with the feudal messenger services (*hikyaku*) following their displacement by the state's monopolization of mail collection and delivery. Amalgamated into a single private firm (Nihon tsūun; Nittsū), the services went on to enjoy a privileged and profitable relationship with the postal network as a conveyor of machinery, the mail, and eventually packages. These and similar public-private relationships gave concrete expression to the Meiji slogan, "Making use of private energies"; comparable arrangements could be found in many other sectors of the Meiji economy. In sum, the practice of contracting with private actors to carry

---

101. *Mainichi shinbun*, November 21, 1999.
102. Matsuda, "Yūsei sanjigyō ni 'kisei' suru gaibu dantai, famirī kigyōgun," 109–12.
103. Lincoln, *Arthritic Japan*, 104.

out the business of the state was a widely accepted norm in nineteenth- and twentieth-century Japan.

But by the mid- to late twentieth century, political calculations had begun to displace efficiency considerations as the driving force behind these public-private alliances within the postal sector—and at the price of institutional flexibility. By underwriting the network of commissioned post offices, for example, the Mutual Aid Society nurtured the mutually beneficial electoral relationship between the postmasters and LDP politicians. By providing bureaucrats and postal union officials with post-retirement work, these public and private entities strengthened the stake of MPT and Zentei in the survival of the state-run postal system. Meanwhile, many of these organizations posed a threat to competition in the private sector; the Mutual Aid Society's control over the construction of new postal facilities crowded out private competitors,[104] while the postal insurance inns and the Mielparque gained unfair competitive advantages over private hotel chains. Finally, some of the special corporations, including those that later merged to form Postal Welfare, were mired in ethical—if not legal—controversies. Should public-sector foundations be permitted to engage in rent seeking and other for-profit activities, even if those activities ultimately served a broader social purpose?

Since the blurred boundaries between the public and private sectors, mutually-beneficial political and economic relationships, and institutionalized rent-seeking were typical not only of the postal regime but also of the Japanese political economy more generally, they cannot be singled out as the sole source of the postal regime's remarkable staying power. Also important was the regime's position within a *single, large sector* and that sector's performance of important functions for both the economy and the public; this in turn lent the regime a significant degree of cohesiveness. Second, the dependence of LDP politicians on the postmasters for votes and bureaucrats on the post-retirement employment opportunities provided by postal family enterprises and public corporations constituted disincentives for either group to tamper with the system. Third, multi-partisan participation within the regime helped diminish the chances that opposition to its continued existence would arise along ideological lines. Fourth, the postal sector was distinctive in that

---

104. Enō, *Jitsuroku.*

it generated a massive reservoir of funds for investment in industry, small- and medium-sized enterprises, public works, and other projects of electoral significance. This feature alone made it all but certain that threats to the institutions of the postal regime would be fought tooth and nail by both those within the regime and by those who benefited from the postal system's largesse. Finally, to a much greater degree than the construction or telecommunications industries, for example, the postal services and the regime that buttressed it had the wherewithal to apply postal proceeds to the broader social welfare of Japan. The system's "social embeddedness" no doubt encouraged many ordinary Japanese—those who valued Japan's distinctive, humanistic approach to capitalism and who feared the impact of postal reform on traditional economic values—to turn a blind eye to the economic inefficiencies and political pathologies of the regime itself. As we shall see, the social and cultural significance of the postal system transformed the question of postal reform into a veritable culture war.

Early Attempts at Postal Reform

The question of postal reform grew increasingly important with each passing decade of the postwar period as the need for a state-administered postal savings system diminished, the scope of the system's financial resources expanded, and the mail service slipped deeper and deeper into the red. Before Koizumi came to power, however, pressure from the postal regime drastically slowed the pace of reform. As the remainder of this chapter illustrates, the regime viewed even small administrative changes to the three postal services as threats to the very institutions that helped guarantee the regime's longevity.

THE 1950S–1960S

As Patricia Kuwayama writes, the "problem" of the postal savings system rested not so much on the fact that it was a "postal" service; the problem was that it was a government bank "backed by the full faith and credit of the national authorities."[105] The postal savings system enjoyed numerous advantages over commercial banks, including government

---

105. Kuwayama, "Postal Banking in the United States and Japan," 9.

guarantees on deposits (both the principal and interest), corporate and property tax exemptions, and exemptions from the Bank of Japan's capital reserve requirements. Unlike the banks, the postal savings system did not have to pay dividends to shareholders; nor did it have a pressing need for deposit insurance, since the bulk of its investments were channeled into safe government bonds.[106] These advantages might have made good economic sense when the banks were underdeveloped or the state required vast reservoirs of funds for investment in rapid military or industrial development, but economists and policymakers found them increasingly unnecessary—and even damaging—as the economy matured. Economists pointed out, for example, that the competitive advantages enjoyed by the postal savings system made it difficult for credit associations and other regional banks to attract deposits.[107] (By the same token, friends of the status quo maintained, the postal system should be credited for being more receptive to consumer demand.[108])

Postal reform first became a topic of political debate in postwar Japan during the late 1950s. While the "postal savings problem" (*yūcho mondai*) did not capture the full attention of the government at this time, some economists and bank representatives were voicing concerns that were only to intensify in subsequent years: as postal savings rates rose in relation to those of the banks, they were unfairly dampening the latter's ability to compete. Although calls for reform were surfacing, the emerging political consensus never extended beyond support for a more equitable balance between the postal savings system and the banks. There were, in short, no concerted demands for changes to the administrative structure of the postal services,[109] let alone to the political interests that were emerging out of the services at that time.

---

106. Scher and Yoshino, "Policy Challenges and the Reform of Postal Savings in Japan," 16.

107. Okina, "Japan's Financial System Since the Bursting of the Bubble," 10.

108. Scher and Yoshino, "Policy Challenges and the Reform of Postal Savings in Japan," 17. The authors point out that since the bulk of the commercial banks' individual accounts were "captive employee accounts"—that is, held by the employees of firms with which they had main bank relationships—the banks had few incentives to innovate in ways that would attract new accounts (20–21).

109. Matsubara, *Gendai no yūsei jigyō*, 213–14.

Government foot-dragging on the postal reform issue continued into the 1960s as the economy reached maturity. Government advisory councils were quick to recommend the rationalization of the postal services, with one such recommendation by the First Ad Hoc Commission for Administrative Reform (Daiichi rinji gyōsei chōsakai or First Rinchō) in 1964 leading to the gradual mechanization of the postal services;[110] however, it was not until 1967, with Prime Minister Satō Eisaku's encouragement, that the debate deepened to include the management practices of the services. That year, the Minister of Posts and Telecommunications instructed the Postal Services Council (Yūsei shingikai) to explore the option of converting the postal services into a public corporation.[111] The council failed to produce a consensus behind the proposal.

Why would the MPT encourage debate on postal reform? It should be noted that not all MPT bureaucrats were dead set against change; to the contrary, many favored changes that would enhance the performance of the services, particularly those that negated the need for privatization. It is also likely that pro-reform postal bureaucrats had been influenced by foreign trends; the United States had abolished its postal savings system during the late 1960s and the British postal system, which had long been a governmental department, was poised to become a state-owned corporation.

In 1969, after announcing that he wanted the postal system to operate more like a business, the Minister of Posts and Telecommunications sent the Postal Services Council back to the drawing board. Surprisingly, the council's subcommittee on postal reform went on to express some support for corporatization. Members of the postal regime viewed the recommendations with great trepidation, but their worries were for naught. Although the *Nihon keizai shinbun* and other newspapers favored corporatization, the banks ultimately opposed it on the grounds that extant plans did not include provisions to eliminate the tax exemptions and other state supports that had given the postal savings and insurance systems a leg up over the banks.[112] The MOF, for its own part, suggested

110. Hida chiku tokutei yūbinkyoku chōkai kaishi hensan iinkai, ed., *Hida no tokutei yūbinkyoku shi*, 268; Yamaguchi, *Tokutei yūbinkyoku*, 202.

111. Matsubara, *Gendai no yūsei jigyō*, 215.

112. Ibid., 215.

that it was reluctant to let go of its control over the postal system's financial resources. Since a public corporation would have more freedom to raise user fees as an antidote to the system's perpetually high personnel costs, the ministry argued, the Japanese people would ultimately suffer. The "people's treasury" and the postal insurance system, the ministry concluded, could only be administered by the state.[113] Officials in the MPT harbored a separate set of concerns. What would happen to the ministry if the postal system were corporatized and the ministry's responsibilities reduced? Would the MPT become an agency? Would it be pressured into merging with another ministry?[114]

The postmasters also responded negatively to the notion of corporatization. Would a public corporation be able to carry out its functions properly? How would corporatization affect the public welfare (*kōkyō-sei*)? And what would happen if the postal system were broken up into its component services, as some reformers were recommending? In a formal statement to the ministry opposing corporatization, the postmasters argued that a public corporation would be economically unsound and would greatly inconvenience the people. They went on to insist on the retention of all three services under a single administrative roof,[115] a stance that was to define their position for decades to come.

THE 1970S

Throughout the 1970s, the volume of postal savings deposits expanded in response to the popularity of ten-year time deposits (*teigaku chokin*).[116] (The public was clearly taking advantage of the postal savings system following the first oil shock.) At the same time, the debate over postal reform reached new levels. From 1975, the Bank of Japan upped its criticisms of the system on the grounds that it interfered with monetary policy and complicated banking reform.[117] It was also at this time that

---

113. Ibid., 216.

114. *Shūkan Tōyō keizai*, September 6, 1997.

115. Tōkyō chihō tokutei yūbinkyokuchōkai shi henshū iinkai, ed., *Tōkyō chihō tokutei yūbinkyokuchōkai shi*, 84–88.

116. In late FY 1970, the share of postal savings in individual savings was 18.9 percent; ten years later, the total reached 29.8 percent (Matsubara, *Gendai no yūsei jigyō*, 62–63).

117. Cargill and Yoshino, *Postal Savings and Fiscal Investment in Japan*, 76.

an argument appeared among some reformers in favor of both privatizing and breaking up the services (*min'ei/bunkatsu ron*). The basic tenets of this argument were that: 1) the postal savings system had grown too large because of its unfair tax and legal advantages; 2) the state-run postal savings and insurance systems were impediments to financial deregulation at a time when Japan was under pressure from the United States to liberalize; 3) the postal system's financial services were distorting private sector finance; and 4) the postal system was contributing to government debt by feeding the FILP and purchasing government bonds.[118]

During the late 1970s, the debate was increasingly focused on the postal savings system's linkages to the FILP. Many critics contended that Japan should rethink its overall financial system as growth rates slowed, and that postal savings would have to be a major part of that rethink. Meanwhile, as government advisory commissions continued to churn out reports recommending limits on postal savings deposits, the Japan Bankers Association (Zenkoku ginkō kyōkai rengōkai, or Zengin-kyō) stepped up its calls for a reevaluation of the postal savings system, advocating identical interest rates for postal savings and commercial bank accounts.[119]

These demands can be interpreted as early rumblings in Japan's gradual ideological shift toward greater economic liberalism. But before the early 1980s, there was insufficient support for postal reform from where it mattered most, namely, the MOF and the banking sector. The MOF favored financial liberalization but was loath to relinquish its control over the investment of postal savings deposits, the source of so much strategic government investment. For their own part, advocates for postal reform within the banking sector lacked the political sponsors to make a real difference within the policy process.[120] Officials elsewhere in the government were also holding their breath, fearing that significant postal reform would decrease FILP support for the many special corporations that offered attractive job opportunities to government re-

---

118. Matsubara, *Gendai no yūsei jigyō*, 221.
119. Ibid., 66.
120. Cargill and Yoshino, *Postal Savings and Fiscal Investment in Japan,* 18.

tirees.[121] Last but not least, the public seemed to have little interest in changing the postal status quo. Insofar as the postal savings system was concerned, ordinary Japanese saw little need to tamper with a service that was far more attentive to their needs than the commercial banks, which paid lower interest rates on deposits and charged user fees.[122] To the postmasters and other members of the postal regime, this lack of cohesion within the so-called reform camp and elsewhere in the bureaucracy was welcome news; it also precluded a concerted counter-offensive—at least for the time being.

THE 1980S

The postal reform debate gained momentum during the 1980s as administrative reform became a top government priority. The debate was punctuated by three key developments: the 1980 introduction of a "green card" system for tracking postal savings depositors; the 1988 abolition of the postal system's tax-exempt (*maruyu*) status; and sandwiched between these two events, as a later section illustrates, the Second Rinchō's limited deliberations on postal reform. What distinguished this decade from the previous ones was the intensity of postal regime activism against threats to the customs and formal institutions of the postal network.

In March 1980, with the MOF's support, the Diet quietly passed an amendment to the Income Tax Law (Shotokuzei hō) that included the introduction of a "green card" system for small-scale depositors. Scheduled to begin in January 1984, the system was intended to prevent depositors from setting up multiple accounts under fictitious names, a practice that had mushroomed during the 1970s as depositors tried to take full advantage of tax exemptions on savings accounts under 3 million yen. On the surface, the new plan seemed a reasonable solution to the mounting problem of tax evasion among small-scale depositors that was particularly troublesome within the postal savings system.

In the months following the amendment, members of the LDP's postal tribe—responding in part to pressures from the postmasters—

---

121. Amyx, Takenaka, and Toyoda, "The Politics of Postal Savings Reform in Japan," 30.

122. Ibid., 31.

expressed their growing opposition to the green card plan on the grounds that it would "dampen incentives to save and thus harm the foundations of the free economic system." In May 1981, under Kane-maru Shin's leadership, the tribe organized a loose, multi-partisan fed-eration of Diet members (*taisaku giin renmei*) that launched a massive petition drive to reverse the measure.[123] Zentoku launched a similar campaign, flooding the MPT and the MOF with written protests. These campaigns culminated in the passage of a government-sponsored bill in 1983 to postpone the implementation of the system by three years.[124]

The MOF, which had strongly supported the green card program, took its "Hundred Years War" with the MPT to new heights by pro-posing other steps to expand government revenue.[125] The MOF wanted to eliminate tax exemptions on interest for both postal and commercial bank savings accounts under 3 million yen—the *maruyū* system.[126] Al-though the commercial banks were unhappy about the proposal since they, too, were authorized to offer tax-free accounts,[127] they recognized its potential to weaken the popularity of the postal savings system. It had long been assumed that the commissioned postmasters were en-couraging their depositors to open multiple tax-exempt accounts, an accusation that is supported by a simple statistical observation; by the 1980s, the number of postal savings accounts had exceeded the pop-ulation of Japan. By eliminating the tax exemption, depositors would have one less incentive to open multiple accounts.[128]

The MOF's proposal provoked an outcry from key interests in the postal regime, including the MPT, which argued that the postal savings system deserved special treatment because of its distinctive history.[129] Eliminating the *maruyū* system, regime representatives argued, would re-

---

123. Inoguchi and Iwai, *Zoku giin no kenkyū*, 239.

124. Yamaguchi, *Tokutei yūbinkyoku*, 218–19.

125. Jin, *Ōkura kanryō*, 183–85.

126. Tax exemptions for interest on postal savings accounts had been in place from 1920. Commercial banks introduced similar measures in 1963 (Maeno, *21-seiki wa Yūsei-shō no jidai*, 93).

127. Jin, *Ōkura kanryō*, 183–85.

128. Anderson, "The Political Economy of Japanese Saving," 88; Kuwayama, "Postal Banking in the United States and Japan," 45.

129. Maeno, *21-seiki wa Yūseishō no jidai*, 93.

sult in huge losses for the postal savings system while undermining user confidence in the commissioned post office system. As the LDP's Tax Committee (Zeisei chōsakai) explored the issue, the commissioned post-masters persuaded nearly every local and prefectural assembly around the country to pass resolutions in support of the *maruyū* system. In December 1984, the LDP's Postal Services Roundtable formed a committee to research the issue that included LDP Diet members, 500 postmasters and Zentoku leaders, and 100 citizen representatives. Predictably, the committee recommended that the tax-free system be preserved. That same month, several top LDP leaders recommended that the "green card" system be abolished once and for all, and that the government take stronger regulatory actions against abuses of the *maruyū* system rather than abolish the system outright. But in October 1985, amidst mounting support for financial reform both within and outside of the party, the PARC shocked the regime by recommending that the *maruyū* system be scrapped. Two years later, the Diet passed an amendment to the Income Tax Law that effectively eliminated key components of the system. The resulting changes went into effect in April 1988.[130]

The MOF had won the day, but not before granting a number of concessions to the anti-reform camp. First, it agreed to let the postal savings system exercise control over the investment of a small portion of postal savings deposits and insurance premiums, instead of channeling the entire amount into the MOF's Trust Fund Bureau. It also agreed to retain a revised *maruyū* system for accounts held by the elderly and, for a time, single mothers and the handicapped;[131] the interest on funds in excess of the 3 million (later 3.5 million) yen limit would be subject to a 20 percent tax. This was a significant concession in the context of Japan's aging society and a boon to the LDP's vote-mobilizing efforts, not to mention a nod to the social functions of the postal savings system. The compromise enabled the postal regime to emerge from the reforms more or less unscathed.

Although the reform of the *maruyū* system contributed to a declining postal savings rate during the late 1980s, the commissioned postmasters quickly found ways to bypass the new restrictions. Under pressure from

130. Ibid., 220–21.
131. Rosenbluth, *Financial Politics in Contemporary Japan*, 167.

Tokusuiren (the MPT-led association of postmasters) to meet their personal quotas (*noruma*) for new postal savings accounts, many postmasters neglected to report taxable income to the appropriate authorities. In 2004, the Board of Audit estimated the total loss of taxable income between 1993 and 2002 from such accounts at 11 billion yen.[132]

While the postal regime grappled with the green card and *maruyū* issues, another movement was afoot that threatened far more extensive changes to the postal system and hence the postal regime. At the center of that movement was the Second Rinchō, the powerful advisory council (*shingikai*) established by Prime Minister Suzuki Zenkō in 1981 within the Prime Minister's Office that answered directly to the prime minister. The Second Rinchō differed from past reform-oriented councils in terms of its broad deliberative mandate, the strong support of the big business community and reformist politicians in the LDP, the stature of its leader—Dokō Toshio, the highly respected chairman of the Japan Federation of Economic Organizations (Keidanren) and former president of Toshiba—and its role as an instrument for the leadership aspirations of Nakasone Yasuhiro, who assumed the prime ministership in 1982.[133] In contrast to advisory councils in the past, which were normally attached to specific ministries and hence susceptible to pressures from interest groups in their jurisdictions, the Second Rinchō was far more than a rubber stamp for the preconceived policies of Japanese bureaucrats.[134] Instead, it stood outside of normal bureaucratic channels and their affiliated vested interests and encouraged decisive leadership by requiring the prime minister to act on its recommendations.[135] The Second Rinchō's mandate was to recommend ways to reduce state interference in the economy in the context of slower economic growth rates, revise outmoded administrative institutions, and conserve resources.

The Second Rinchō's very existence marked a sea change in attitudes about the state's relationship with the private sector. As Lonny Carlile explains, by advocating a reduced role for the state and self-help on the part of consumers and businesses, the Second Rinchō seemed to be

132. *Japan Times*, October 13, 2004.
133. Carlile, "The Politics of Administrative Reform," 78–81.
134. Schwartz, "Of Fairy Cloaks and Familiar Talks," 234.
135. Samuels, "Leadership and Political Change in Japan," 12.

walking down the path of neoliberal economics as defined by trends in both Britain and the United States;[136] at the very least, it was abandoning demand-side Keynesian economics.[137] But there were some important differences between the Japanese and Anglo-American approaches to reform. First, while the neoliberal experiment in the Anglo-Saxon world sought to streamline the welfare state, the Second Rinchō left the Japanese welfare system more or less alone.[138] This refusal by both the Suzuki and Nakasone governments to exclude welfare from the scrutiny of reformers underscores Gregory Kasza's argument that social welfare had been an important corollary of the ruling LDP's advocacy of industrial policy and a source of the party's electoral longevity.[139] It also made it unlikely that any reform attempts would target the welfare functions of the postal services.

Japan's approach to invigorating the private sector during the 1980s also differed from that of its Anglo-Saxon counterparts. Whereas the United States trumpeted the virtues of deregulation, which would expand the scope of private sector freedoms in the market, the Japanese advocated a partnership between the public and private sectors that resonated well with historical precedent. In a remarkable evocation of the Meiji period's slogan of "Making use of private energies," Nakasone praised the virtues of *minkatsu* (*minkatsu katsuryoku no katsuyō*; the mobilization of private sector vitality).[140] Like the Meiji slogan, *minkatsu* signified the practice of contracting with private sector actors to perform functions that might otherwise be assumed by the state.[141] In practical terms, *minkatsu* found expression in the introduction of more cost-effective land use policies during the 1980s that expanded private sector participation in public works projects while perpetuating tight, triangular relationships between private firms, the bureaucracy, and the LDP.[142] For the postal regime, these trends could be read as a tacit endorsement

---

136. Carlile, "The Politics of Administrative Reform," 79.
137. Matsubara, *Gendai no yūsei jigyō*, 67.
138. Carlile, "The Politics of Administrative Reform," 79.
139. Kasza, *One World of Welfare*.
140. Carlile, "The Politics of Administrative Reform," 79.
141. Ibid.
142. Ōtake, "The Rise and Retreat of a Neoliberal Reform," 251–52.

of the long-standing relationships among state-run postal institutions, special corporations, and private enterprises within the postal sector.

Notwithstanding these developments, the Second Rinchō's March 1983 final report was cause for concern within the postal regime. Stating unequivocally that "the bureaucracy should complement the private sector" (*kangyō wa mingyō o hokan*), the report supported the continuation of the state-run postal system while advocating a reevaluation of its long-term fixed savings instruments, the unification of interest rates for postal savings and bank deposits,[143] and a freeze on ceilings for postal savings deposits. The report also recommended that the postal savings system be denied the authority to invest its deposits (*jishū un'yō*). These were essentially the same recommendations that had been advocated two years earlier by the controversial Kin'yūkon (Kin'yū no bunya ni okeru kangyō no arikata ni kansuru kondankai; Committee to Review the Government Administration of the Financial Sector), an informal, intra-governmental group that prioritized the preferences of the MOF and the banking sector.[144] It appeared, in short, that the Second Rinchō was siding with the banks.

Recognizing the political futility of pursuing major postal reform in the face of strong, concerted opposition from the postal regime, Nakasone and the Second Rinchō eventually focused their sights on privatizing JNR, NTT, and Japan Tobacco (JT). Consequently, subsequent councils that were established to finish the work of the Second Rinchō paid scant attention to the postal system. Established in July 1983, the Gyōkakushin (Daiichiji rinji gyōsei kaikaku suishin shingikai; First Ad Hoc Advisory Council to Promote Administrative Reform) called for more research on the postal savings system and the FILP. The Second Gyōkakushin made a series of rather vague recommendations in April 1990 that simply reinforced the Second Rinchō's liberal economic principles while endorsing the postal system's contributions to the public welfare. The Third Gyōkakushin addressed the sensitive issue of reducing the scope of postal savings, but was interrupted by the 1993 Lower House election and the formation of Hosokawa Morihiro's coalition

---

143. Although the interest rates for the two systems were never fully streamlined, the gap between then narrowed during the late 1990s.

144. Yamaguchi, *Tokutei yūbinkyoku*, 202–5; Machida, *Nihon yūsei*, 114.

government. In October of that year, the council did little more than echo its predecessors' recommendations by advocating the reduction of postal savings bloat and making the postal system more "attentive to the people's welfare."[145] None of these councils proposed corporatization in any meaningful way, let alone the privatization and breakup of the services. Nor did they follow through on the Second Rinchō's more limited recommendations for postal reform. Although the gap between the interest rates for postal savings and bank accounts narrowed during the late 1990s, they were never fully streamlined. The commercial banks were allowed to offer long-term fixed savings instruments, but those of the postal system remained untouched, and the ceiling on postal savings accounts continued to rise until the early 2000s, when it reached 10 million yen.

Explaining the Pace of Postal Reform

A number of factors explain the slow pace of postal reform before the early 1990s. First, and most simplistically, the post office never became mired in the kinds of crises that can lead to rapid change. Although the mail service experienced deficits after the oil shocks and its fixed costs remained high, the resumption of economic growth during the 1980s helped mask these problems. Furthermore, as the bubble economy deepened and consumers increased their spending and invested more in private sector financial ventures, the postal savings system's challenge to the commercial banking sector appeared less ominous. The assets of the postal system may have increased in absolute terms in some years and public awareness of that system's many inefficiencies intensified, but these "problems" never touched the pocketbooks of ordinary Japanese or threatened to put private firms out of businesses. For all intents and purposes, postal reform remained largely a technocrat's issue.

Second, postal reform during the 1980s was overshadowed by the privatization of JNR and NTT, and for good reason; the latter two processes were simply more politically "doable" than substantial postal reform. Tackling the JNR, with its massive debts, and NTT, which was struggling to keep up with international competition, seemed far more

---

145. Matsubara, *Gendai no yūsei jigyō*, 68–71.

pressing than reforming a postal system that in relative terms appeared to be working fairly well. At the risk of understating the enormity of NTT and JNR privatization, moreover, it bears keeping in mind that reformers in these two cases could look to comparable British and American reforms for guidance, while postal reformers—many of whom were daunted by the Japanese system's massive size and inter-service synergies—lacked that advantage. It was not until the late 1980s and 1990s, with the advent of postal privatization in Germany and a handful of other European countries, that anything approaching an international precedent for Japanese postal reform had materialized. Last but not least, reforming the postal sector, with its vast financial assets, had far greater repercussions for the financial and other sectors of the economy than the privatization of NTT and JNR ever did.

Third, although it would be a mistake to reduce the success or failure of postal reform to the outcomes of narrow interest group politics, it is significant that a strong, cohesive constituency in favor of reform never materialized at this time. (There is reason to conclude that such a constituency was lacking even in 2005, but that story will appear in a later chapter.) Rumblings in favor of change were intensifying in the MOF and the banking community, but disagreement continued over what kinds of changes should be introduced. And for as long as those disagreements remained, the forces opposed to reform retained the upper hand.

Fourth, the structure of the anti-reform camp proved highly advantageous. At the heart of that network was the tightly knit alliance of LDP politicians, postal bureaucrats, and commissioned postmasters, the last of whom were at the height of their political power during the early 1980s. Thanks to the electoral relationship between the postmasters and the LDP, the close administrative relationship between the postmasters and postal bureaucrats, and the long-standing, consensus-oriented partnership between the LDP and the bureaucracy within the postal policy sphere, each set of players had institutional mechanisms through which to effectively articulate its interests to one another. On the issue of postal reform, all were more or less in agreement: any changes that decreased MPT control over postal savings, enhanced competition within the postal network, divided the services into their constituent parts, jeopardized political party access to FILP investments, or reduced the postmasters' vote-mobilizing role must be avoided at all costs. These and related concerns were routinely expressed in the LDP's postal tribe, the Diet's communications committees, the Postal Services Roundtable, and within a policy process that from the 1960s required LDP approval for all bills drawn up by the bureaucracy prior to receiving the cabinet's endorsement.[146]

Yamaguchi Osamu writes in his analysis of the commissioned post office system that a deal was struck between the reformers and postal regime representatives on the eve of the Second Rinchō's establishment. The agreement was cobbled together by Chief Cabinet Secretary Miyazawa Kiichi, Kanemaru Shin—the era's leading postal tribe "don," friend of the postmasters, and chairman of the Postal Services' Roundtable—and Takeshita Noboru, in his capacity as representative of the reformist Liberal Economics Roundtable (Jiyū keizai konwakai). Within two weeks, the ministers of both the MPT and the MOF were on board, and PARC and the Executive Council followed suit within days. In a nutshell, all agreed to leave the postal system alone during the government's push toward administrative reform—at least for the time being.[147] That this agreement ultimately survived the administrative reform process is testament to even the Second Rinchō's vulnerabilities to pressure from the postal regime.

Other interests within the postal regime helped further the agenda of the anti-reform camp. Since the many public corporations, private firms, union members, progressive political parties, and other beneficiaries of the state-run postal system were far more diffuse than the core conservative players of the postal regime, their opposition to postal reform did not translate into direct influence within the policy process. By the same token, the sheer breadth of these interests meant that postal reform had the potential to become deeply politicized, as evidenced by the outpouring of local assembly opposition to the abolition of the *maruyū* system.

Postal reform may have failed to produce more than "second-order" changes during the 1970s and 1980s, but it did gain momentum as a result of the administrative reform movement of the 1980s. As Lonny

---

146. Mulgan, *Japan's Failed Revolution*, 130–31.
147. Yamguchi, *Tokutei yūbinkyoku*, 205.

Carlile notes, the Second Rinchō lent administrative reform an "aura of ideological hegemony" that persisted into the 1990s.[148] Richard Samuels, meanwhile, observes that the successes of the Rinchō era created an atmosphere within the LDP in which reform became the primary platform through which up-and-coming politicians could distinguish themselves from their predecessors.[149] This did not bode well for the postal regime. In a political climate like this, it was only a matter of time before the massive postal system—Japan's last significant government enterprise—was targeted as the next reform frontier. In the context of the post-bubble economy of the 1990s, with its near-zero growth rates, deepening credit crunch, and rising postal savings rate, postal reform finally attained the urgency it needed to become a political reality.

---

148. Carlile, "The Politics of Administrative Reform," 89.
149. Samuels, "Leadership and Political Change in Japan," 27.

FIVE

Setting the Stage:
The Hashimoto Reforms

Entrust to the private sector what the private sector can do.
—Slogan of the Hashimoto Government

From the commissioned postmasters' point of view, Hashimoto Ryūtarō was a most unlikely postal reformer. As a protégé of Tanaka Kakuei and, in later years, the leader of his deceased mentor's faction, to which most members of the postal tribe still belonged, Hashimoto seemed to represent the kind of machine-style politics that had entrenched the postal regime in postwar Japanese politics. From 2001, after losing the LDP presidency to Koizumi Jun'ichirō, Hashimoto was true to his factional heritage, siding with the "forces of resistance" against his rival's plan for postal privatization. As prime minister between January 1996 and July 1998, however, Hashimoto shocked the postmasters by championing postal privatization as an integral step toward comprehensive administrative and financial reform.

It is ironic that while Hashimoto ultimately failed in his bid to privatize the postal savings and insurance services, his accomplishments lent Koizumi some of the political, institutional, and ideological ammunition to succeed. By terminating the automatic flow of postal savings deposits and postal life insurance premiums into the FILP and giving postal authorities independent investment authority, Hashimoto's 1998 reforms helped lower the perceived financial risks—and political stakes—of privatization. In a similar vein, the reforms laid the groundwork for the transformation of the state-run services into Japan Post, a public corporation that performed sufficiently well within its first year of operations (2003–2004) to convince many naysayers that further market-oriented reform might actually work. Finally, the reforms facilitated Koizumi's efforts to overcome the resistance of vested interests by strengthening the prime minister's decision-making authority. In sum, Hashimoto's legacy helped legitimize the idea of postal privatization and weaken the postal regime's stranglehold over the policymaking process. Although the 1998 reforms were by no means sufficient to guarantee the passage of postal privatization in 2005—as Chapter 6 illustrates, much depended on institutional incentives, creative leadership, and some old-fashioned political horse-trading—without them, it is doubtful that Koizumi would have traveled as far as he did on the road to privatization.

My purpose in this chapter is to explore the economic and political developments that precipitated Hashimoto's accomplishments, including Koizumi Jun'ichirō's ascent as Japan's most committed postal reformer, and the significance of the 1998 Basic Law for the Reform of Central Ministries and Agencies. The fate of the FILP figures prominently during this stage of the postal reform saga, for as the fund ballooned during the post-bubble years to incorporate new public works projects, the financial and political significance of postal reform increased. The chapter also touches on some of the long-standing political conflicts that surrounded postal reform, including battles over the ideal relationship between the state and the private sector in the marketplace, the effects of financial reform on the future of rural Japan, and the fate of the postal system's social welfare benefits. Although many observers during the late 1990s viewed Hashimoto's postal reforms as something of a failure, when analyzed in combination with changes to the executive branch of government, it is clear that they fell within what I identified in Chapter 4 as "first-order" reforms that transformed the institutional and political foundations of the services as well as their underlying economic and even social principles. As such, they constituted an integral step toward reducing the financial reach of the postal services as well as the political power of the postal regime.

The International Context

Given the impact of foreign pressure (*gaiatsu*) on policy change in postwar Japan, it is perhaps not surprising that many Japanese from the 1990s assumed that *gaiatsu* was driving their government's investigation of radical postal reform: why else would Tokyo seriously consider "Americanizing" the postal system? But while the American Chamber of Commerce in Japan (ACCJ) occasionally voiced concerns about the size of the Japanese postal savings and insurance systems,[1] there is little evidence to suggest that the United States—or any other country, for that matter—was applying consistent pressure on Japan to reform its postal services.

This is not to suggest that foreign models did not matter. For decades, bureaucrats had been traveling abroad to observe foreign postal systems—from Maejima Hisoka in 1870 to Takenaka Heizō in 2005. The Japanese also took careful note of international trends. They noticed, for instance, that while they were among the first countries in the world to separate telecommunications from postal services, they were the only major country by the late 1990s to maintain all postal services under a single, state-administrated roof.[2] They were well aware that their postal savings system was the largest in the world, that they were the only country with a postal insurance system at the end of the twentieth century,[3] and that the size of the FILP dwarfed that of comparable state-run financial programs abroad. Japan paid close attention to the conversion of Britain's postal services in 1969 into a statutory corporation, the reorganization of its postal savings system into the National Savings Bank,[4] and the reduction of the Royal Mail's monopoly on mail collection and

---

1. In late 2004, for example, the ACCJ complained that Koizumi's postal privatization plan would disadvantage international competitors, particularly in the insurance sector (ACCJ, "ACCJ Concerned About LDP's Proposal on Postal Reform," Press Release, December 22, 2004).

2. Matsubara, *Yūsei min'eika de kō kawaru*, 66.

3. France, Germany, and Britain have no postal insurance systems, but they do sell private-sector insurance policies through their post offices.

4. The bank was later renamed National Savings and Investment. It remains a state-owned entity.

delivery by the early 2000s.[5] The establishment of the United States Postal Services (USPS) in 1970 as an independent government agency that monopolized the mail and postal money order services was another international development that influenced Japanese postal reform debates. (To be sure, American postal reform fell far short of the radical overhaul that many Japanese might have expected given their tendency to associate the United States with capitalist excess.) Also important were attempts to significantly reform or even privatize all or portions of postal systems in Sweden, Germany, the Netherlands, Italy, Belgium, Australia, and New Zealand. And while Deutsche Post was upheld as an example of how radical postal reform could produce highly competitive mail delivery systems, New Zealand's ill-fated attempt at mail liberalization served as a useful cautionary tale.[6] In short, international trends were frequently evoked in government, scholarly, and media writings on postal reform in Japan,[7] providing intellectual ammunition to all sides of the debate.

But for all their careful tracking of international developments, the Japanese ultimately debated postal reform on their own terms, measuring various options for change against the financial, economic, and political contingencies of the day. By the late 1990s, it was the recession and Hashimoto's commitment to comprehensive financial reform that put postal privatization toward the top of the government agenda.

The Post-Bubble Economy and the Challenge of the Postal Financial Services

As the 1990s unfolded, it became increasingly clear that the Japanese economy, the postal services, and the FILP were at a turning point.[8] After the collapse of the stock market in 1990 and of the real estate market

---

5. As of 2011, 57 licensed operators were competing in Britain's mail delivery market (http://www.psc.gov.uk/postallicencesandoperators/licensedoperators [last accessed July 12, 2011]). For more on the history of British postal reform, see R. Campbell, *The Politics of Postal Transformation.*

6. After the abolition of the state-run mail monopoly in 1998, both workers' wages and the quality of service in New Zealand suffered precipitous declines.

7. See, for example, Hoshino, *Sekai no yūbin kaikaku;* and Mizuno, *Doitsu posuto vs. Nihon yūsei kōsha.*

8. Matsubara, *Gendai no yūsei jigyō,* 33.

the following year, Japan entered into a period of financial and economic stagnation marked by a protracted credit crunch,[9] price deflation, unemployment, and mounting government debt. Many analysts and policymakers viewed the financial crisis as a blip on the landscape that would eventually disappear if the country patiently adhered to convoy capitalism, government financial intermediation, industrial policy, and the other ingredients of the country's postwar recipe for economic growth. Rooted primarily in the LDP, key government ministries (including Construction and the MPT), and their affiliated interest groups, these advocates of "Japanese-style capitalism" found common cause with reform-minded officials, politicians, and scholars who advocated increased government spending to loosen the credit crunch and lower unemployment. Both sides agreed that the FILP should serve as a vehicle for such spending. Consequently, by FY 1996 annual FILP expenditures reached a staggering postwar high of 40.5 trillion yen; three-quarters of that total was earmarked for special corporations, many of which were involved in housing and public works projects (see Table 5.1).

As the FILP ballooned, politicians reveled in the flow of public works funds into their electoral districts. Critics, however, fretted over the government's disregard of the country's long-term financial needs in the context of a rapidly aging society and the economy's declining international competitiveness.[10] To generate the funds to meet these challenges, they argued, Japan would have to nurture a savings system with higher rates of return;[11] this in turn would require the wholesale reform of the FILP and the postal savings and insurance systems, which were diverting much-needed funds from the commercial banking and private insurance sectors, respectively. Recognizing that financial liberalization since the 1970s had done little to shrink the size of either the postal savings system or the FILP, reformist MOF officials, LDP politicians

---

9. The long-term banking crisis, caused primarily by non-performing loans, penetrated the public consciousness in 1995 with the liquidation of several housing loan corporations (*jūsen*) affiliated with commercial banks, and then again in 1997–1998, following the bankruptcy of Hokkaido Takushoku Bank and Yamaichi Securities. For a definitive account of the banking crisis, see Amyx, *Japan's Financial Crisis.*

10. Kowaguchi, *Yūsei no Sekigahara,* 21–22.

11. Cargill and Yoshino, *Postal Savings and Fiscal Investment in Japan,* xi.

Table 5.1: FILP Budgets (in trillions of yen)

Fiscal Year	Total FILP Budget	FILP Budget for Public Corporations
1988	25.3	19.4
1989	26.3	20.9
1990	27.6	22.3
1991	29.1	23.6
1992	32.3	26.2
1993	36.6	29.5
1994	39.4	31.5
1995	40.2	31.7
1996	40.5	30.1
1997	39.3	28.7
1998	36.7	27.3
1999	39.3	29.9
2000	37.5	28.2
2001	32.5	23.1
2002	26.8	17.7
2003	23.4	14.2
2004	20.5	11.8
2005	17.2	11.3
2006	15.0	10.2
2007	14.2	10.0
2008	13.9	——
2009	15.9	——
2010	18.4	——

SOURCES: Ministry of Finance, *FILP Report: 2007* and *FILP Plan (Proposal) for 2010*. The MOF's annual FILP reports stopped publicizing allocations of FILP funds to public corporations in 2008.

like Koizumi, and many economists stressed that new rounds of financial liberalization would be all but meaningless if the bloated postal and FILP systems were not added to the agenda. The media also jumped onto the financial reform bandwagon. In 1995, the pro-banking *Nihon keizai shinbun* repeatedly referred to the postal savings system as an egregious example of financial socialism, and the *Tōyō keizai* called for the complete abolition of both postal savings and the FILP.

Meanwhile, as Japan's financial morass deepened during the 1990s, problems in the postal services intensified. The mail service was particularly hard hit, after struggling for nearly two decades to rid itself of recurrent deficits. In 1981, the Diet had moved to reverse these deficits by jacking up postage rates, only to trigger a major drop in the demand for mail. The government then tried to cut costs by switching from rail to truck transport, pressing local post offices to campaign more aggressively for new business, and introducing a number of new products, including the "hometown packages" service. These efforts yielded a partial turnaround in the service's financial fortunes, thanks in part to the postal workers' willingness to comply with recovery plans.[12] But by the early 1990s, the positive effects of internal reform had been all but erased by another round of cost increases within the service and further drops in demand. At mid-decade, many analysts were calling for sweeping reform of the mail service—if not outright privatization.

The bloat within the postal savings system was also growing painfully evident around this time. Few disputed its causes. The system had long been advantaged by a loose division of labor that left industrial finance to the city and regional banks and individual/household finance largely to itself and small, local credit associations. After the collapse of the financial bubble, the *jūsen* debacle, and the failure of several large financial institutions and credit associations during the 1990s, many Japanese lost their trust in the banking system and flocked to the post office. As a result, postal savings deposits expanded from approximately 135 trillion yen in 1989 to 213 trillion yen in 1995, and to 260 trillion yen just four years later—a rate of increase that surpassed that of commercial bank deposits by a significant margin.[13] Japan's system for collecting small deposits had morphed into a Godzilla that was trampling on the interests of the private financial sector.[14]

The expansion of deposits notwithstanding, the postal savings system was experiencing some significant financial setbacks during the 1990s. Interest rates were largely to blame. While postal savings funds deposited into the Trust Fund Bureau yielded fixed interest over seven-year contract periods at rates slightly higher than that of ten-year government bonds, ordinary depositors of *teigaku* (time deposit) accounts

---

12. Kinoshita Nobuyuki argues that postal workers may have been motivated to cooperate with management after the JNR's failure to convince labor to accept much needed cost-cutting measures ("The Economics of Japan's Postal Service Privatization," 10–11).

13. Cargill and Yoshino, *Postal Savings and Fiscal Investment in Japan*, 40.

14. Mizuno, "Yūsei min'eika no nagakimichi nori," 174.

could withdraw their funds without penalty. This proved problematic for the system during the low-interest years of the early 1990s, when it had to make payments on mature *teigaku* accounts that had been established a decade beforehand when interest rates were high.[15] Meeting these obligations had adverse effects on the system's profitability.

For the *kanpo* postal insurance system, the main problem from the 1990s was not declining profitability but rather an overall competitive advantage that struck many as grossly unfair. *Kanpo* enjoyed many of the same perquisites that pertained to the postal savings system: the cost advantages of operating within the massive postal network, tax exemptions, lax government oversight, and a government guarantee. Like the postal savings system, *kanpo* also benefitted from a committed staff that was obligated to meet rigorous sales quotas; in 2002, postal employees each sold five times more life insurance policies per month than their individual counterparts in the private sector. Other perquisites of the postal system contributed more to the competitiveness of postal life insurance than to that of the postal savings system. For instance, while the advantage of a government guarantee on postal savings deposits was partially offset by the 1971 introduction of a deposit insurance system for commercial banks, the fact that there was no corresponding obligation for private insurers before 1998 put the postal life insurance system—which was also covered by a government guarantee—in an unusually strong competitive position. Finally, *kanpo* may have offered more modest coverage to policyholders than private insurers, but its hospital riders were more generous.[16] Together, these advantages not only enabled *kanpo* to offer favorable terms to its policyholders,[17] but also to acquire larger capital reserves than its private competitors.[18] After the collapse of several private insurers by the end of the 1990s, the postal life insurance system constituted 40 percent of its respective market.

---

15. Kinoshita, "The Economics of Japan's Postal Service Privatization," 8.

16. Aketa, "Issues in the Privatization of Postal Life Insurance," 2–5.

17. As noted in Chapter 4, these terms included low premiums, easy payment plans, lax eligibility requirements, and a waiver on physical examinations. Kinoshita writes that this last feature "obliged the postal life insurance business to limit risk by constraining the size of death benefits for an individual policyholder" ("The Economics of Japan's Postal Service Privatization," 4).

18. Aketa, "Issues in the Privatization of Postal Life Insurance," 5.

Table 5.2: Bank and Post Office Branches

End of Fiscal Year	# of Banks (City, Regional Trust, Other)	# of Post Offices
1990	16,595	24,103
1995	16,954	24,583
2000	15,315	24,774
2002	14,415	24,752
2003	14,060	24,715
2004	13,823	24,678
2005	13,617	24,631
2006	13,522	24,574
2007	13,534	24,094

NOTE: Statistics provided by the Japan Bankers Association and Japan Post. Bank figures exclude ATMs. For 1990 and 1995, post office figures for the 2010 issue of *Nihon tōkei nenkan* conflict with those presented in earlier editions; 2010 figures are used here.
SOURCE: Sōmushō, *Nihon tōkei nenkan*, 2010.

The post office's ubiquitous presence at the local level must have made its financial services all the more attractive to nervous households. Although the ratio of post offices to bank branches had been gradually decreasing over the years, as Table 5.2 illustrates, post offices still out-numbered bank branches by a significant margin during the 1990s and early 2000s. It was not until the establishment of Japan Post in 2003 that the number of post offices began to decrease, but at first only by a few facilities per year. While the banks struggled to stay afloat, the post offices remained a dependable presence at the grassroots level.

To be sure, the postal system's many advantages reflected its com-mitment to "serve the people." As defenders of the system liked to point out, the objectives of the 1947 Postal Savings Act had remained constant over the decades: to create a savings system that was safe and easy to use, and that enhanced the stability (*antei*) of the national economy and the welfare of ordinary Japanese.[19] (Article 1 of the Postal Life Insurance Act included a similar statement.[20]) Since the postal system had fulfilled

---

19. Machida, *Nihon yūsei*, 105.

20. Article 1 stated: "The purpose of this law is to provide the public with life in-surance that is easy to use, managed with certainty, and whose premiums are as low as

these objectives quite well through the generations, it is understandable that many Japanese failed to see that the services needed fixing. Takenaka Heizō, a young Keiō University economist, discovered this the hard way in 1997. An avowed advocate of sweeping financial reform who went on to become Koizumi's financial and postal-privatization czar, Takenaka had a tiff with his aging mother-in-law about the merits of privatizing the postal savings system. Why, she complained, would anyone want to tamper with this prized financial institution and risk putting it out of business?[21]

Early 1990s Postal Reform and the Koizumi Factor

Unfortunately for the advocates of postal privatization, their politically entrenched opponents were asking the same question during the 1990s as a succession of governments toyed with the notion of reform. Although a number of noteworthy changes were imposed on the system before Hashimoto became prime minister in 1996, the anti-reform camp ensured that they were fairly small in scope.

Perhaps the most important reform of the early 1990s was the 1994 agreement between the MOF and the MPT to partially liberalize postal savings interest rates by setting them closer to those of private-sector banks. Around the same time, the commercial banks were authorized to offer ten-year time deposits.[22] Together, these changes narrowed the postal savings system's comparative advantage.[23] Anticipating a reduced flow of traffic into local post offices, the postmasters and their employees ramped up their efforts to remind their customers of the risks inherent in commercial savings bank accounts, which were covered by a deeply flawed deposit insurance system and no government guarantees;[24] postal authorities put a stop to these tactics for fear that they would unfairly disadvantage the banks.[25]

---

possible, so as to stabilize their economic activity and enhance their welfare." Quoted in Aketa, "Issues in the Privatization of Postal Life Insurance," 2*n*3.

21. *New York Times*, November 18, 1997.

22. Matsubara, *Gendai no yūsei jigyō*, 4, 106; Cargill and Yoshino, *Postal Savings and Fiscal Investment in Japan*, 20.

23. Kuwayama, "Postal Banking in the United States and Japan," 46.

24. By 1994, the deposit insurance system was insolvent and had to be reconstituted.

25. Cargill and Yoshino, *Postal Savings and Fiscal Investment in Japan*, 28.

In theory, the level of competition between the postal savings system and the commercial banks had been ratcheted up; in practice, however, the post office retained the upper hand thanks to its popular fixed-interest, ten-year *teigaku* accounts, which by the mid-1990s made up 80 percent of total postal savings deposits.[26] Introduced by the government in 1941 as part of its wartime campaign to encourage individual savings,[27] the service had an edge over private-sector time deposits because of the government guarantee on deposits and the ability of depositors to withdraw their funds without penalty after six months and reinvest them—often in a new *teigaku* account—at higher interest rates. The commercial banks were unwilling to offer this latter perquisite, which was accompanied by considerable financial risk.[28] Since the early 1990s reforms failed to address this fundamental imbalance between the postal savings system and the banks, many analysts dismissed them as meaningless.

It was also around this time that Koizumi, a well-known "anti-postal system" (*han yūsei*) Diet member, stepped up to the plate and began changing the terms of the postal reform debate. In December 1992, Prime Minister Miyazawa Kiichi appointed Koizumi his Minister of Posts and Telecommunications, a move that sent shock waves through the postal regime. Koizumi hailed from a political family that had established close ties with the postmasters. Known for his ill-fated campaign to privatize telecommunications during a stint as Minister of Communications between 1929 and 1931, Koizumi's grandfather, Matajirō, mobilized the postmasters in his Kanagawa prefecture constituency to help improve telecommunications services. Koizumi's father, Jun'ya, was a former director general of the Defense Agency who carefully cultivated electoral ties with this powerful interest group.[29] But Koizumi defied family tradition following his father's death in 1969 by setting himself on a path to become Japan's most committed—and irreverent—postal reformer.

---

26. Kuwayama, "Postal Banking in the United States and Japan," 45; Cargill and Yoshino, *Postal Savings and Fiscal Investment in Japan*, 21.

27. Rosenbluth, *Financial Politics in Contemporary Japan*, 172.

28. Cargill and Yoshino, *Postal Savings and Fiscal Investment in Japan*, 50–51.

29. Machida, *Nihon yūsei*, 81.

Koizumi learned of his father's death shortly after graduating from Keiō University and while studying in London. At the funeral, the 27-year-old surprised both his family and his father's *kōenkai* leaders by announcing that he would run for his father's Lower House seat in Kanagawa prefecture's second district in the next (1969) Lower House election. Competition for the district's four seats proved fierce, as the Kōmeitō, Socialist, and Democratic Socialist candidates vied for the first three seats, leaving Koizumi and one other LDP candidate in a dead heat for the fourth. In the end, Koizumi won 103,335 votes, 97 more than what his father had received in the previous election, but approximately 4,000 less than his conservative rival, Tagawa Seiichi. It was a humiliating loss, especially given the respectable performance of other second- and third-generation politicians in the election and the fact that the LDP had done well overall, increasing its total number of seats from the last election by 11 to 288, and then to 300 as 12 independents later joined the party.[30]

Legend has it that what brought Koizumi down in 1969 was a rebellion by local commissioned postmasters—a legend that Iijima Isao, Koizumi's long-time private secretary, adamantly denies.[31] A local postmaster and relative of Tagawa's apparently took the lead in the postmasters' revolt, cajoling fourteen of his local colleagues to shift their allegiance away from Koizumi.[32] Some analysts are skeptical that the postmasters managed to manipulate enough votes to tip the balance in Tagawa's favor, but when we consider the substantive vote-gathering quotas (*noruma*) that the postmasters routinely shouldered, the accusation is certainly not without merit.[33]

Another formative experience in Koizumi's early political career was his close association with Fukuda Takeo, one of the LDP's top faction leaders and prime minister between 1976 and 1978. Shortly after his electoral defeat, Koizumi went to work at Fukuda's home in Tokyo's Setagaya ward, receiving petitioners, managing correspondence, and the like. Fukuda's close ties to the MOF and intense dislike of Tanaka Ka-

---

30. Ibid., 85–86.
31. Yamawaki, *Yūsei kōbō*, 46.
32. Machida, *Nihon yūsei*, 85–86.
33. Yamawaki, *Yūsei kōbō*, 46.

kuei's machine-style politics evidently made a strong impression on the young Koizumi. When Fukuda lost the LDP presidency to Tanaka in 1972 after a bitter contest, Koizumi was stunned. As far as the two men were concerned, Tanaka had plucked the presidency for himself by distributing massive amounts of money to his politically well-placed supporters,[34] many of them from the postal regime. And if that were not enough, Tanaka and Zentoku later cooperated to mobilize party votes behind Fukuda's archrival, Ōhira Masayoshi, in the 1978 LDP presidential primary; it appears that Zentoku played a pivotal role in securing Ōhira's victory and ascension to the prime ministership.[35] In sum, although we may never know for certain if Koizumi's stance on postal reform was motivated by a personal grudge against the postmasters, he most certainly viewed them as symbols of long-standing political practices that he had come to despise.

In 1972, Koizumi was elected to the Lower House and immediately joined the chamber's Finance Committee (Ōkura iinkai).[36] Several years later, he was appointed parliamentary vice minister (*seimu jikan*) to the MOF, a position that left him with nagging worries about Japan's ballooning government debt.[37] With the establishment of the Second Rinchō during the early 1980s, Koizumi publicly championed the downsizing of government and the invigoration of the private sector.[38] He was also an outspoken critic of the FILP, calling for the reform of the special corporations that received FILP funds and criticizing the FILP's financial linkages to the postal savings and insurance systems.[39] "Postal savings and postal insurance are like extraterritorial areas in the financial sector," Koizumi reportedly remarked in 1979. "They collect money from the public on more advantageous conditions than the private sector, and the money flows into public corporations and is wasted there. It is not fair."[40]

------

34. Ibid., 50–51.
35. Segawa, *Koizumi Jun'ichirō to tokutei yūbinkyokuchō no arasoi*, 64.
36. Yamawaki, *Yūsei kōbō*, 47.
37. Iijima, *Koizumi kantei hiroku*, 211.
38. Yamawaki, *Yūsei kōbō*, 47.
39. Kowaguchi, *Yūsei no Sekigahara*, 22.
40. *Daily Yomiuri*, October 16, 2005.

Whatever possessed Prime Minister Miyazawa to appoint an anti-postal politician as his Minister of Posts and Telecommunications in 1992? It appears that Miyazawa felt compelled to appoint someone from outside of the postal regime in the wake of the Sagawa kyūbin scandal, a politically debilitating incident that implicated Kanemaru Shin, a self-proclaimed "don" of the postal tribe. Second, although it is un-clear whether Miyazawa was thinking carefully about competition between the banks and the postal savings system when he made his decision, as a finance expert, he was deeply concerned about the state of the economy following the recent collapse of the real estate and stock market bubbles. As such, he favored policies that would stimulate growth rather than promote more savings—policies that Koizumi also advocated. Finally, Koizumi had a well-established reputation as a tough-minded reformer who was willing to stand up to vested interests,[41] a trait that appealed to younger members of the LDP who were pressuring the party leadership to adopt a more reformist policy stance. In short, the times proved propitious for the likes of Koizumi, and Miyazawa felt he had more to gain than to lose by ending the postal regime's longstanding stranglehold on the MPT.

Although Koizumi failed to fully satisfy the reformist members of the LDP and prevent their eventual defection from the party, he immediately lived up to his reputation as a serious advocate of liberal-economic change. At a press conference shortly after his appointment as Minister of Posts and Telecommunications, Koizumi shocked postal bureaucrats and many of his party colleagues by announcing that he would block the MPT's proposal to raise the ceiling on tax-exempt postal savings accounts (*maruyū*) held by the elderly. Koizumi explained that by operating as a social welfare service for aging Japanese, the *maruyū* system worked at cross-purposes to Miyazawa's and the MOF's pledge to simulate consumption;[42] it was, he maintained, a prime example of both "financial socialism" and the political excesses of the postal system. Koizumi's announcement triggered a backlash from the postal regime; the LDP's parliamentary vice minister to the MPT resigned in protest and members of the postal tribe in both houses of the Diet engaged in round after round

41. Machida, *Nihon yūsei*, 123.
42. Ibid., 94.

of "Koizumi bullying."[43] In the end, Koizumi succumbed to pressure by increasing the ceiling on *maruyū* savings accounts, but the increase was far less than what the bureaucrats had hoped for.[44]

As Minister of Posts and Telecommunications, Koizumi routinely annoyed the postal regime. In a move that foreshadowed his actions in the spring of 2005, he fired two bureaucrats who had refused to follow his directives.[45] He also focused attention on the postal savings system's impact on the long-term health of the commercial banks, touting the virtues of postal privatization and accusing the MPT of serving its own interests rather than those of the nation. All told, Koizumi's actions sparked a series of protests from the postmasters and a tremendous loss of face for postal bureaucrats who were used to working with members of the postal tribe and getting their way in the policymaking sphere.[46]

The postmasters, for their own part, trudged through the early 1990s on high alert, searching for ways to hedge against the threat of privatization. Although Koizumi's political ascent and many years of government deliberations on postal reform had yielded little in the way of significant change before the late 1990s, embarrassing questions were being raised in the public sphere about the postmasters' inheritance practices and political activities. In reaction, the postmasters tried to burnish the reputation of the "town post office" (*machi no yūbinkyoku*) and earn the sympathy of local governments by stepping up their public relations campaigns and volunteer activities. They also upped their efforts to increase the rate of private ownership of post office facilities, decrease the number of "commuting postmasters" (*tsūkin kyokuchō*) by promoting more local hires for vacant postmasterships,[47] and address other problems that could potentially weaken the commissioned post office's standing in local communities.[48] In short, the postmasters embarked on a protracted

---

43. Ibid.

44. Yamawaki, *Yūsei kōbō*, 49–51.

45. Machida, *Nihon yūsei*, 125.

46. Yamawaki, *Yūsei kōbō*, 49–51.

47. Commuting postmasters were not residents of the neighborhoods they served. Their increasing presence within the postal network highlighted the declining allure of the commissioned postmastership for younger Japanese.

48. Kyūshū chihō tokutei yūbinkyokuchōkai, *Kyūshū tokutei yūbinkyokuchōkai shi*, 321, 326.

battle for the hearts and minds of ordinary Japanese as the movement to privatize the postal system gained momentum.

DEBATING POSTAL SAVINGS AND FILP REFORM

Koizumi may have incurred the wrath of the postal regime, but subsequent developments reveal that his message of financial and postal reform was gaining traction, particularly after the LDP's temporary fall from power in 1993 and the intensification of the political-economic reform movement more broadly. In 1994, Socialist Prime Minister Murayama Tomiichi established the Administrative Reform Commission (Gyōsei kaikaku iinkai) within the Prime Minister's Office to deliberate on such topics as deregulation and information disclosure. In the subcommittee on the relationship between *kan* and *min*, discussions revealed substantial support for postal privatization or, at the very least, enhanced competition within the postal services.[49]

Hashimoto Ryūtarō's ascent to the prime ministership in July 1996 intensified these debates. A lone wolf within the former Tanaka faction who lacked close ties to the postal regime, Hashimoto set the reformist tone of his new government almost immediately. Under the slogan of "entrust to the private sector what the private sector can do" (*minkan ni dekiru mono wa minkan ni yudaneru*), Hashimoto vowed to shrink the size of government and make it more accountable to the people, and to introduce long-overdue financial reforms.[50] These objectives logically embraced postal privatization, which promised to stimulate private-sector finance and reduce the number of government employees.[51] By championing these goals, Hashimoto became the first prime minister since Nakasone Yasuhiro to wholeheartedly embrace emerging global norms based on liberal-economic ideals.[52]

---

49. Mizuno, "Yūsei min'eika no nagaki michinori," 135–39.

50. Matsubara, *Yūsei min'eika de kō kawaru*, 56.

51. As Chapter 6 elaborates, the argument that privatization would shrink the size of government was misleading. Although privatization would strip approximately a quarter million postal employees of their public-servant status, since the postal services were financially self-supporting, it would make virtually no difference to the general account.

52. Hashimoto's reformist credentials were shaped in part while serving as Minister of Transportation in the third Nakasone cabinet. While occupying that position, he helped orchestrate the privatization of JNR.

Hashimoto's early stance on postal reform was shaped in part by his rivalry with Koizumi. During their 1995 race for the LDP presidency, Koizumi pressed for postal privatization and smaller government.[53] Hashimoto then one-upped his opponent by pledging not only to privatize the postal services but also to reform the FILP.[54] The postmasters erroneously interpreted Hashimoto's proclamations as mere political posturing and concluded that their futures would be more secure under him than the incendiary Koizumi. So they threw their lot behind Hashimoto and convinced several LDP Diet members to do the same. The besieged Koizumi then softened his stance, claiming that a vote for him would not necessarily translate into a vote for postal privatization.[55] But the about-face was not enough to clinch the presidency; Koizumi lost roundly to Hashimoto by a vote of 87 to 304.[56]

Hashimoto's subsequent behavior indicates that he was well aware of the dangers posed by postal privatization to one's electoral fortunes. Although the issue had been a major component of his June 1996 "Hashimoto Vision," it was conspicuously absent during the October 1996 Lower House election. Analysts observed that in this first test of Japan's post-1994 single-member district, "winner-takes-all" system, LDP candidates feared that championing postal privatization would alienate the postmasters and other (vote-gathering) beneficiaries of Japan's postwar financial model.[57] Instead, Hashimoto focused on the less politically divisive goals of financial reform and reducing the number of government ministries that were backed by many in the business and policymaking communities as stepping-stones to structural reform.[58] In time, however, circumstances enabled Hashimoto to once again set his sights on postal privatization.

But first, Japan's troubling economic circumstances forced the newly installed prime minister to tackle financial liberalization. In 1997, the Diet passed a series of bills to strengthen the transparency of financial

---

53. *New York Times,* June 22, 1998.

54. Noble, "Front Door, Back Door," 111.

55. Yamawaki, *Yūsei kōbō,* 52.

56. Iijima, *Koizumi kantei hiroku,* 215.

57. *Shūkan Tōyō keizai,* September 6, 1997.

58. Mishima, "The Changing Relationship Between Japan's LDP and the Bureaucracy," 968.

institutions, reduce state involvement in the financial sphere, and tighten the government's financial regulatory regime. The resulting financial "Big Bang" ushered in a reduction of the MOF's functions, enhanced the independence of the Bank of Japan, and established the Financial Supervisory Agency, an independent financial regulatory organ that was later renamed the Financial Services Agency. Together, these changes marked both a step toward freer financial markets that were more accepting of financial risk and bankruptcy and a shift away from convoy capitalism and some of the other trappings of the old financial order.[59]

Ultimately, Hashimoto's "Big Bang" legislation failed to prevent yet another financial downturn—this one precipitated by an ill-timed consumption tax increase, fallout from the 1997 Asian financial crisis, and a string of failures among the banks and securities firms. Although the government introduced measures to reverse the crisis, including massive injections of public funds into the banking sector, the nationalization of two banks, and stricter transparency requirements for nonperforming loans, the financial system was slow to recover.[60] Against this backdrop, the financial inefficiencies of the postal financial services and the FILP became the targets of intense debate. As the postal savings rate expanded in response to growing public disillusionment with the commercial banks, critics complained that the postal system and the FILP were impeding the growth of capital and money markets by slowing the flow of funds into the private financial sector. This was unacceptable, many argued, given Japan's need to increase growth rates and the national tax base in the context of a rapidly aging society. Put simply, it was no longer politically possible for the postal savings system and the FILP to remain outside of the liberalization agenda.[61]

The financial and demographic justifications for postal and FILP reform were not enough to trump the entrenched resistance of the postal regime, or for that matter, the misgivings of the general public. At the end of the day, few Japanese outside of academia and the policymaking world bought the argument that the post office and the FILP system were in any way responsible for Japan's ongoing financial and economic

59. Cargill and Yoshino, *Postal Savings and Fiscal Investment in Japan*, 7.
60. Ibid., 23.
61. Ibid., 147, 151.

woes; to the contrary, many praised these quintessentially Japanese institutions for helping to offset the late 1990s credit crunch.[62] (Koizumi and his allies retorted that there would have been less of a credit crunch in the first place had funds destined for the postal savings and insurance systems been channeled into private financial markets.) More to the point, the postal savings system was still very popular among ordinary Japanese. The postal savings rate may have slipped following the reforms of the *maruyū* system during the 1980s, but it had risen steadily during the troubled decade of the 1990s. Many Japanese still viewed the postal savings system as a friend of the people—as the safest and most convenient destination for their hard-earned income.[63]

Postal employees, politicians, postal bureaucrats, postal family enterprises, and other members of the postal regime took advantage of these public misgivings to launch an all-out assault on the postal reform movement. Far better organized than their adversaries, who were scattered throughout the polity and private sector, these beneficiaries of the FILP and the state-run postal services sang the praises of Japan's "traditional" financial model, with its emphasis on risk minimization, full employment, and paternalistic state leadership. Underscoring their support for the status quo was a faith in government and public enterprise as the only institutions capable of promoting the public interest within the financial and economic systems. Regime representatives relied on public opinion data to strengthen their positions.[64]

Meanwhile, some critics—including not a few economists who supported a degree of reform—voiced fears that postal privatization would cause widespread financial instability by terminating the flow of postal savings and insurance funds into the FILP and hence diminishing the FILP's role as a major purchaser of government bonds. Extremists in

---

62. Ibid., 28.

63. Ibid., 45.

64. Not all of that data was reliable, however. In one 1996 poll commissioned by the Postal Services Council (Yūsei shingikai), a whopping 94 percent of the 6,000 citizens and local assemblymen surveyed expressed support for continuing government ownership of the postal services. It was later revealed that postal officials, rather than an independent third party, had conducted the poll. Many of the questions were so biased that the responses supporting MPT interests were the only viable choices (Machida, *Nihon yūsei*, 131–32).

this group predicted that the disruption would wreak havoc on Japan's already fragile system of public finance and bring the economy to a standstill.

Other opponents of radical reform played to the public's fears that postal privatization would result in serious social dislocations. They commended the state-run system for guaranteeing universal service and contributing to the people's welfare, while warning that privatization would make small post offices less profitable and force them to shut their doors at great inconvenience to poorer, rural areas.[65] These arguments reflected a perhaps simplistic understanding of the benefits of public enterprise in monopoly situations. But they meshed well with the views of leading consumer organizations during the 1980s and 1990s that deregulation and the privatization of basic social services threatened economic and social stability—values that were considered far more important than lower prices and enhanced consumer choice.[66] In sum, while the anti-reform camp may have paid little heed to rational economic theory, it effectively appealed to Japanese during the turbulent 1990s who were skittish about rapid economic and social change and the pressures of globalization.[67]

THE ADMINISTRATIVE REFORM COUNCIL'S INTERIM REPORT

Shortly after forming his second cabinet, Hashimoto established the Administrative Reform Council (Gyōsei kaikaku kaigi) to deliberate on government reform, naming himself as head.[68] By this time, Nakasone Yasuhiro was urging Hashimoto to prioritize postal privatization in the deliberations, but Hashimoto was skeptical that the move would suc-

---

65. Hida chiku tokutei yūbinkyokuchōkai kaishi hensan iinkai, ed., *Hida no tokutei yūbinkyoku shi,* 270.

66. I elaborate on these points in *Consumer Politics in Postwar Japan,* esp. 177–78, 187–88.

67. The public's high regard for the postal savings system, the social importance of the postal network, and the political influence of the anti-reform movement help explain why simply abolishing the postal savings system was never a serious option for Japanese policymakers.

68. This was not a council that simply reported to the prime minister; Hashimoto was an integral part of the deliberations and took his own notes during the proceedings (Matsubara, *Yūsei min'eika de kō kawaru,* 144).

ceed given the depth of opposition within the LDP. At first, the prime minister intended for the council to simply present arguments for and against postal privatization, but he shifted course after the media criticized the council for soft-pedaling on financial reform. In August 1997, Hashimoto reluctantly instructed council members to make bold recommendations on postal reform.[69]

On September 3, the council dropped a bombshell. In its interim report, it recommended the immediate privatization of the postal insurance system, the eventual privatization of the postal savings system, and a break-up of the three services into separate companies. The mail service was to remain a state-run entity and its functions transferred to a semi-independent postal services agency (*yūsei jigyōchō*). The council also urged the post offices to promote "one-stop services" and pressed for an end to both the postal system's tax-exempt status and the automatic transfer of postal savings deposits to the MOF's Trust Fund Bureau.[70] All told, the interim report constituted the most radical government proposal for postal reform to date.

The postal regime, which lacked representation on the council, had worked feverishly behind the scenes to prevent just this sort of outcome; after September 3, it focused on reversing the council's recommendations. Three months before the interim report was released, the MPT's Postal Services Council (Yūsei shingikai; PSC) issued a report on the commissioned post office system that recommended the introduction of more market-friendly management techniques but tacitly endorsed the controversial system's continuation. The postmasters interpreted the report as an unequivocal statement of the ministry's support for the postal status quo.[71] The PSC later shocked those who were worried about the mail service's now chronic deficit by recommending a seven-year freeze on postage increases. Since a market-oriented mail service would require the freedom to set postage rates at will, the rec-

---

69. Yamawaki, *Yūsei kōbō*, 80–81.

70. The expression "one-stop services" connoted the post office's assumption of local government functions, as well as a variety of postal services.

71. Kowaguchi, *Yūsei no Sekigahara*, 33–34.

ommendation was received as a ministerial ploy to constrain and discredit the privatization movement.[72]

Meanwhile, Zentoku put relentless pressure on its allies and members of the Administrative Reform Council to oppose postal privatization.[73] At its annual meeting in Yokohama in May 1997, the LDP's Obuchi Keizō and Nonaka Hiromu, two old-guard members of the postal tribe, were on hand to welcome the postmasters and express their misgivings about the privatization movement. Also present was Katō Kōichi, a potential prime ministerial candidate who was not normally associated with the postal regime but who was critical of postal privatization.[74] In his address, Katō acknowledged the LDP's appreciation of the postmasters, a not-so-veiled admission of the party's electoral exchange relationship with one of the country's most well organized vote-gathering machines.[75]

Nonaka's presence at the Zentoku gathering was especially significant. Forty years earlier, while serving as speaker of a small-town assembly in Kyoto prefecture, Nonaka had traveled to Tokyo to confer with Tanaka Kakuei, then Minister of Posts and Telecommunications, about securing governmental financial support for struggling post offices in his area. Tanaka granted the request and went on to support Nonaka's rise through the ranks of local, prefectural, and then national government. Both men were deeply committed to nurturing rural Japan and believed that developing the postal network was a fundamental step toward that goal.[76] By the 1990s, Nonaka was well ensconced as a leader of the postal tribe—a position first occupied by his now deceased mentor—and widely recognized as Japan's "shadow prime minister" (*kage no sōri*).

In his address to the assembled postmasters, Nonaka announced that while he did not have the power to salvage the MPT as a discrete ministry as the government explored ways to reorganize the bureaucracy, he would fight hard to defend the three postal services as a government-

---

72. Matsubara, *Yūsei min'eika de kō kawaru*, 148.

73. Kowaguchi, *Yūsei no Sekigahara*, 27.

74. *The Economist*, October 18, 1997.

75. *New York Times*, November 18, 1997.

76. Yamawaki, *Yūsei kōbō*, 77–78.

run entity under a single administrative roof. An MPT official sitting close by looked nonplussed by the announcement, but the postmasters responded with thunderous applause.[77] Nonaka had hit on the crux of the postal regime's position. Assuming that only the government could guarantee universal postal service, the postmasters and their LDP and bureaucratic allies had long insisted on "state administered, unified services" (*kokuei de sanjigyō ittai*).[78] Driving this position was the belief that the more the three services were exposed to market forces, the more commissioned post offices would be threatened with bankruptcy; this in turn would jeopardize the exchange relationship between the postmasters and the LDP. State management, conversely, would shield the services from dangerous competitive forces, as would the inter-service synergies that were only possible when the mail, savings, and insurance services were run by a single administrative entity.

As the summer unfolded, the MPT rallied regime members to crush the council's recommendations for privatization, the MPT and Zentoku working through the LDP and the unions through the Social Democratic Party of Japan (SDPJ) and the newly formed Democratic Party of Japan (DPJ). Each group insisted that the council defend government ownership of the postal services.[79] Zentoku officials, for their own part, faxed the association's regional and local leaders to rally the public to the cause; to prevent delays in communications while they were off at work, the postmasters had their wives handle the correspondence. The postmasters went on to launch a massive grassroots campaign to convince local residents of the need to protect the postal savings system in particular—"the people's asset" (*kokumin no zaisan*)—and the postal services more generally.[80] They mounted posters in their communities soliciting the public's support, channeled approximately 20,000 letters of protest from the public to the Administration Reform Council, pressured all but two prefectural assemblies to adopt resolutions opposing privatization, and, together with the postal workers, lobbied Diet mem-

---

77. Ibid., 73–74.

78. Machida, *Nihon yūsei*, 132.

79. Matsubara, *Yūsei min'eika de kō kawaru*, 69–70.

80. Kyūshū chihō tokutei yūbinkyokuchōkai, *Kyūshū tokutei yūbinkyokuchōkai shi*, 124–25.

bers.[81] And in a move that could not have been more unsettling to their party patrons, in August 1997 the postmasters stopped paying their membership dues to the LDP.[82] Desperate times called for desperate measures; if the posts were to "fall to the enemy" (*yūsei rakujō*) at the hands of the LDP,[83] the postal system's exposure to market forces would in all likelihood spell the end of the commissioned post office system.

On August 27, 120 LDP Diet members gathered at party headquarters for an emergency meeting of the Telecommunications Committee of the PARC. Many fretted about their future electoral prospects; now that nearly 19,000 postmasters had withheld their party membership fees, could they be trusted to rally voters behind the party? The question was particularly pressing now that Prime Minister Hashimoto's approval ratings were hovering around 35 percent.[84] As the LDP's reformist image deteriorated, lawmakers found themselves all the more dependent on the organized vote to get them safely through the next election.

Poll numbers revealed public disenchantment not only with the Hashimoto cabinet but also with the notion of privatization itself. Shortly after the interim report was released, newspaper surveys showed that approximately 60 percent of the public was content with the postal status quo. One Kyodo News poll commissioned by Zentei, the leading postal union, indicated that as many as 69.4 percent of Japanese wanted state control of the postal services to continue. And while several newspapers sided with the commercial banks and were generally positive about postal privatization, not a few social commentators opined that privatization would hurt the public interest by reducing the number of post offices in sparsely populated areas. Some even questioned why postal savings should be targeted for reform, since it served the needs

---

81. Mishima, "The Changing Relationship Between Japan's LDP and the Bureaucracy," 977; Kowaguchi, *Yūsei no Sekigahara*, 32, 35. Citing newspaper sources, Mishima writes that postal employees contacted each Diet member at least three times about the postal privatization plan.

82. Yamawaki, *Yūsei kōbō*, 82.

83. Kowaguchi, *Yūsei no Sekigahara*, 20.

84. Yamawaki, *Yūsei kōbō*, 82–83. Hashimoto's support rate declined in part because of his appointment to the cabinet of Satō Kōkō, who had been convicted of accepting bribes during the 1976 Lockheed Scandal.

of ordinary people while top executives at the commercial banks reaped higher and higher salaries.[85]

By early October 1997, it looked like the forces of opposition were about to stop postal reform in its tracks. And then Koizumi entered the fray.

TOWARD A COMPROMISE SOLUTION

In November 1996, shortly after the LDP's Lower House election victory, Hashimoto appointed Koizumi his Minister of Health and Welfare. Although the portfolio had nothing to do with postal affairs, Koizumi used it as a platform to criticize the postal savings system and the FILP and to press for a number of reforms. He was particularly adamant about privatizing the postal savings system, arguing that the system's mere presence stood in marked contradiction to Hashimoto's preference for heightened competition in the financial sphere.[86]

At a press conference on October 12, 1997, when it seemed that postal reform of any kind no longer had a future, Koizumi shocked his LDP elders by announcing that he would resign his cabinet position if the three postal services remained under a single, state-run roof. ("What kind of 'reform' is that?" he scoffed.)[87] He also called on cabinet members who had opposed the Administrative Reform Council's September 3 privatization recommendations to tender their resignations. The move was unprecedented; although Japanese cabinet members occasionally resigned because of scandal, they certainly did not do so over policy disagreements. Nor did cabinet members speak out publicly on important policy issues without first securing the support of the ruling party and the government.[88] For Hashimoto, whose standing in the polls was steadily slipping, the timing could not have been worse. If Koizumi made good on his threat, the government might very well collapse.[89]

Koizumi's preferences were by no means supported by a coherent alliance of reform-oriented groups. Nor, for that matter, did those pref-

---

85. Kowaguchi, *Yūsei no Sekigahara*, 32–33.

86. *New York Times*, November 18, 1997.

87. Kowaguchi, *Yūsei no Sekigahara*, 49; *Japan Times*, October 13, 1997.

88. Machida, *Nihon yūsei*, 146.

89. Yamawaki, *Yūsei kōbō*, 84.

erences always resonate with their likely beneficiaries. Take, for instance, Koizumi's demand for independent investment authority for the postal services. One would think that postal bureaucrats would have championed an objective that had, after all, stood at the center of the ministry's "Hundred Years War" with the MOF. But such was not the case; with so little investment experience behind them, MPT officials actually dreaded the responsibility. The MOF was also ambivalent. Although some MOF officials had come to accept the notion of independent investment authority for the postal system by the 1990s as a logical corollary of comprehensive financial reform,[90] others were reluctant to relinquish the ministry's powers over this politically significant reservoir of funds.[91] MOF officials were also worried about what the transfer of investment authority—or worse yet, postal privatization—would mean for the future of the FILP.

Although Koizumi's resignation threat struck many as the destabilizing act of a troublemaker, it was, in retrospect, a stroke of political genius. By mid-October 1997, it appeared that postal reform deliberations had become so stalemated that the Administrative Reform Council would have no choice but to back away from virtually all of its September 3 recommendations. In a move that foreshadowed his daring exploits of 2004–2005, Koizumi had linked the fate of postal reform to the longevity of the Hashimoto government and thus the LDP's prospects in the July 1998 Upper House election. Although it is unlikely that voters would have focused on the failure of postal reform per se during the election campaign, given their support for the state-run services and interest in other issues, they most certainly would have dwelled on the LDP's inability to take a strong stand on reform more generally at a crucial period in Japan's economic history. For a party that had just suffered the ignominy of falling from power after nearly four decades of uninterrupted rule, this was not a risk worth taking.

The LDP thus faced the difficult task of forging a compromise on postal reform that would bring both Koizumi and the postal regime on

---

90. By the mid- to late 1990s, many economists were advocating independent investment authority for the postal system and the introduction of a special bond system to finance the FILP.

91. Yamawaki, *Yūsei kōbō*, 53–54.

board. Koizumi's conditions were stiff; although he soft-pedaled on his demand for the privatization and breakup of the postal services, he insisted on independent investment authority for the postal savings and insurance systems and the introduction of competition into the mail service.[92] He also supported the eventual corporatization of the postal system. All the while, he complicated the delicate negotiations process by breaking political taboos and publicly condemning the postal regime's electoral functions and defense of the postal status quo.[93] True to form, Koizumi relished the resulting outcry from the postal regime. "Dying in battle," he dramatically proclaimed, "does not mean dying in vain."[94]

Top LDP leaders—none of them fans of either Koizumi or radical postal reform—were left to broker the peace between Koizumi and regime representatives as the party's rank-and-file railed against reform. By late October, Yamasaki Taku and Katō Kōichi, two members of the supra-factional YKK triad that included Koizumi, began negotiations with their colleague, and former Prime Minister Takeshita Noboru joined forces with Yamasaki to work on Nonaka. The group produced an uneasy compromise between Koizumi and his opponents: the three postal services were to be subsumed under a new public corporation in which postal employees would retain their status as public servants, independent investment authority for the postal savings system would be introduced, and the government would be obligated to explore the liberalization of the mail service.

Nonaka's support for the compromise plan should not be interpreted as a mere by-product of intra-party pressure; he in fact had reasons of his own to back the plan. For instance, corporatization was compatible with his pledge to Zentoku to preserve the administrative unity of the three main postal services. Nonaka also welcomed a degree of competition within the postal services on the grounds that it would help the troubled services meet the challenges of globalization. Moreover, he liked the idea of decreasing the bureaucracy's control over the postal services. Nonaka never held bureaucrats in high regard or cultivated close ties with them. (This may, incidentally, be one reason why he re-

---

92. Matsubara, *Yūsei min'eika de kō kawaru,* 70.
93. Machida, *Nihon yūsei,* 146.
94. Kowaguchi, *Yūsei no Sekigahara,* 39.

fused to defend the MPT against the reformer's ax.[95]) Finally, never wedded to the notion of state ownership of monopoly enterprises that served the public interest, Nonaka was easily persuaded to support independent investment authority for a corporatized postal system. In the final analysis, Nonaka was dead set against privatization for fear that it would damage rural communities. But corporatization was an acceptable compromise that stood to invigorate the postal services while preserving the postal network's social functions.[96]

The compromise plan eventually appeased rank-and-file members of the LDP and the party's two coalition partners, the Sakigake Party and the SDPJ. At first, politicians of all political stripes opposed postal reform of any kind, issuing a barrage of protests against the Administrative Reform Council's interim report. Convincing both the LDP rank-and-file and other coalition parties to throw their support behind the corporatization plan proved difficult and time-consuming,[97] but by late November a sufficient number of politicians had concluded that corporatization and the other proposed reforms would be far less threatening to the postal network—and hence to their individual electoral futures—than privatization.

Reduced to the status of mere figurehead in the deliberations,[98] the Administrative Reform Council dutifully released a final report on December 3, 1997, that incorporated the results of the compromise. Hashimoto revealed the report's contents to the public in a press conference on December 2. Noting that he fully understood the importance of the post office to local communities, he announced that the government would not seek postal privatization but rather the transformation of the services into a public corporation within five years. He also announced the government's intention to establish independent investment authority for the corporatized postal system and to pave the way for deliberations on the introduction of private participation in the mail service. And while postal employees would remain public servants (a

95. Yamawaki, *Yūsei kōbō*, 89.

96. Ibid., 87–88.

97. *Japan Times*, November 19, 1997.

98. Mishima, "The Changing Relationship Between Japan's LDP and the Bureaucracy," 974.

major concession to the postal regime), private sector accounting rules and stricter transparency and disclosure practices would be applied to the services, which would now be subject to FSA oversight.[99] In the end, Hashimoto reassured his audience, the changes would enhance the postal system's responsiveness to public demand.[100]

In June 1998, the Diet passed the Basic Law for the Reform of Central Ministries and Agencies (Chūō shōchō tō kaikaku kihon hō), which included the Administrative Reform Council's final recommendations on postal reform. The law also reduced the number of government ministries and agencies from 22 to 12, with major implications for the MPT. At the Administrative Reform Council's recommendation, parts of the ministry were merged with the Management and Coordination Agency to form the MIC.[101] The law also established the semi-independent Postal Services Agency to directly administer the postal services, and a supervisory bureau within the new ministry. But the Postal Services Agency was destined to be short-lived; launched in January 2001 along with the MIC, the law laid the groundwork for the agency's transformation into Japan Post, a public corporation, in 2003.

Both the advocates and opponents of postal reform had mixed feelings about the law. For many of the advocates, Hashimoto's reforms marked a significant departure from the status quo but fell fall short of the ultimate objective of privatization. For those who favored government enterprise, corporatization was preferable to privatization since postal employees would retain their status as public servants, the services would not be broken up into their component parts, and the government would continue to play a substantial role in the services. The postal regime was also reassured by the Basic Law's stipulation that "privatization is not to be revisited" (*min'eika nado no minaoshi wa okonawanai*), an unprecedented nod to those who wished to close the book for good on the privatization debate. It was a provision, as we shall see in the next chapter, that Koizumi was only too willing to ignore.

---

99. Scher and Yoshino, "Policy Challenges and the Reform of Postal Savings in Japan," 135.

100. Iijima, *Koizumi kantei hiroku*, 223–24.

101. Other proposals were considered as well. Some LDP lawmakers, for instance, wanted to merge the MPT with the Ministry of Transportation.

Assessing Hashimoto's Postal Reforms

To some analysts, the establishment of a public corporation (*kōsha*) contradicted the very essence of "reform." The economist Matsubara Satoru observed that whereas a public corporation should in theory establish some distance from the state, Japan Post would be controlled both from on high and on the ground by public servants. It was, he pointed out, a "state-administered public corporation"—a contradiction in terms,[102] not to mention a reflection of the postal regime's lingering power.

The postal regime emerged from the reform process limping but intact. Privatization had been avoided, universal service would be preserved under the new corporation,[103] and the postmasters and their employees would remain public servants. The commissioned post office system had been left untouched, and Tokusuiren and Zentoku, which tied the postmasters to the bureaucrats and the LDP, respectively, had weathered the reform process with nary a scratch. The postal *regime*, as a set of "socioeconomic alliances, political-economic institutions, and a public policy profile,"[104] had survived the process with most of its basic pillars still in place. The postal regime was in relative decline due to generational changes in the LDP and problems within the commissioned post office system; and indeed, the MPT was about to lose some of its bureaucratic powers as the postal services were siphoned off to first an independent agency and then a public corporation. But the regime had suffered no other direct blows from the reforms. In the words of Zentoku's Kyushu chapter, "the crisis had, for the time being been overcome" (*kiki o ichiō kokufukushita*).[105]

Although traumatized by the reform process, the postmasters were quick to identify the positive ramifications of the ordeal. Some postmasters observed that corporatization might eventually enable them to seek election to local assemblies, as per the pre-1948 custom.[106] This proved to be wishful thinking. More importantly, the postal reform movement provided the postmasters with opportunities to expand their

---

102. Matsubara, *Yūsei min'eika de kō kawaru*, 69–70.
103. Interview, Zentoku official, Tokyo, March 27, 2003.
104. Pempel, *Regime Shift*, 20.
105. Kyūshū chihō tokutei yūbinkyokuchōkai, *Kyūshū tokutei yūbinkyokuchōkai shi*, 125.
106. Ibid., 448.

web of conservative party contacts. Motivated by a fixation on self-preservation, the postmasters in the past had confined their most intimate dealings to members of the LDP's postal tribe—particularly those who served as close Zentoku advisors (*shimon giin*). As the threat of privatization intensified, the postmasters sought the support of other LDP Diet members as well. The collaboration proved mutually beneficial; conservative politicians were, after all, worried about the negative effects that a deteriorating postal network could have on their political futures, especially in the post-1994 era of increasing electoral uncertainty. In sum, the postmasters had found common cause with a broader— if not deeper—swath of Diet members on an issue greater than themselves.[107] This in turn helps explain why many LDP politicians who supported some degree of postal reform after Koizumi came to power were reluctant to voice their views in public.

When measured against Hashimoto's initial aspirations, the outcomes of the 1997–1998 postal reform process were disappointing. But when measured against past attempts to reform the postal services, Hashimoto's accomplishments were truly remarkable. This was, after all, the first major *institutional reorganization* of the postal services since 1941, when the prewar post offices were reorganized to form the ordinary (*futsū*) and commissioned (*tokutei*) post offices. (Some might argue that it was the most significant institutional change within the postal sector since the 1870s, when Maejima Hisoka established the modern, state-owned postal system.) It is also worth noting that by severing the postal savings system's formal ties to the FILP, the Hashimoto government ended in a single stroke the "Hundred Years War" between the MOF and the MPT that had colored postal politics for generations.

The Hashimoto reforms appear all the more remarkable when we consider the forces that were aligned against them. Long used to controlling the flow of funds into Japan's "second budget," the MOF was slow to support the delinking of postal savings and the FILP. The MPT, for its own part, was unenthusiastic about independent investment authority and fearful of the diminishing effects of corporatization on its jurisdiction. The postmasters and other representatives of the postal regime fought tooth and nail to protect the status quo; the decline of

---

107. Ibid., 411.

government enterprise, they believed, meant a deterioration of Japan's distinctive economic and social institutions and values. Finally, the postal regime was still larger and better organized than the pro-reform camp, which was a small and eclectic group spread thinly across the polity. The odds, in short, seemed firmly stacked against Hashimoto.

How, then, can we explain Hashimoto's accomplishments? Part of the answer has to do with the changing balance of power between the postal regime and the pro-reform camp. As earlier chapters illustrated, the postal regime reached the peak of its political power during the 1980s and then began to decline. Several factors contributed to that decline: the dampening effects of Upper House electoral reform on the organized vote; simmering dissention within the ranks of the postmasters as they struggled to preserve the institutional customs of their profession in the context of generational change; the declining susceptibility of voters to the persuasive powers of the postmasters and other local opinion leaders; and the deaths of Tanaka Kakuei and Kanemaru Shin and the deterioration of Tanaka's political machine.

As the postal regime grappled with decline, the movement in favor of postal reform was on the rise. During the early postwar period, economists and a small group of conservative politicians had questioned the need for a state-run postal savings system. The movement grew in the context of Nakasone's neoliberal reforms and picked up speed during the recession years of the 1990s. Although the reform movement was still eclipsed by the postal regime in terms of sheer size, the ongoing banking crisis and a widely perceived need for comprehensive financial reform strengthened its legitimacy. To be sure, this shifting balance of power between contending interests was not enough to guarantee meaningful change. It did, however, elevate postal privatization as a major focus of government deliberations—deliberations that in turn culminated in the Administrative Reform Council's groundbreaking interim report of September 3, 1997.

Institutionally, little had changed in 1997–1998 compared to previous eras in which postal reform had been on the government agenda. Indeed, the deliberative process tended to conform quite closely to policymaking customs established during the 1960s,[108] with the LDP's

---

108. See Mulgan, *Japan's Failed Revolution*, 131–33.

PARC and Executive Council exercising their informal prerogative of "preliminary review" (*jizen shinsa*) before the Hashimoto plan was formally adopted by the cabinet and submitted to the Diet.[109] Hashimoto tried to transcend these policymaking patterns by drawing on precedents set by the Second Rinchō during the early to mid-1980s and relying on the Administrative Reform Council to set the terms of the policy debate. As a result of pressures from the postal regime, however, the council failed to preserve its independence through the latter stages of the policy process. All other things being equal, the Administrative Reform Council proved incapable of finalizing a meaningful blueprint for postal privatization. Council politics had succumbed to interest group pressures.

What made a difference in 1997–1998 was the exercise of creative leadership at strategic points in the policy process. Although Hashimoto was skeptical about the future of postal reform, he must be credited for championing a difficult cause and presiding over a painstaking process of negotiations and consensus building. But even more critical to the reform process was Koizumi. By threatening to resign if certain reforms were not introduced, Koizumi transformed an unpopular issue into a litmus test of the government's overall commitment to political-economic reform. Koizumi's advantage during those fateful weeks of autumn 1997 was the increasing importance of reform as a source of conservative party legitimacy. Before the 1980s, reform of any kind was of minor significance to the LDP's longevity. But as Richard Samuels explains, the situation changed dramatically in the wake of Nakasone's administrative reforms as the "division between mainstream and anti-mainstream conservatives was replaced by a divide between reform and anti-reform groups within the LDP and among conservative politicians in general." [110] After younger, reformist politicians fled the LDP in 1993, the party faced even stronger incentives to position itself as the vanguard for change.

------

109. For an overview of "traditional" policymaking patterns involving the LDP and the bureaucracy, see Mishima, "The Changing Relationship Between Japan's LDP and the Bureaucracy"; and especially Mulgan, *Japan's Failed Revolution*, Chapter 5.

110. Samuels, "Leadership and Political Change in Japan," 27.

For much of 1997, postal reform was just one item on Hashimoto's vast reform agenda. Koizumi, however, transformed the issue into one that was too big to fail, leaving Hashimoto with no choice but to broker a compromise with the postal regime in favor of change. It was a tactic that Koizumi was to pursue on numerous occasions in the future—recast the terms of the political debate in defiance of LDP and policy-making customs and then threaten to quit if he did not get his way. Without Koizumi, Hashimoto's postal reforms may have never seen the light of day.

Conclusion

Although the 1998 Basic Law for the Reform of Central Ministries and Agencies ostensibly slammed the door on future debate about postal privatization by stipulating that the issue was not to be revisited, several of the law's provisions actually *increased* the likelihood that privatization would eventually succeed.

First, and as the next chapter further explains, the law's provisions for the establishment of a public corporation produced divided opinions among postal bureaucrats about the merits of privatization. In turn, this weakened the MIC's clout as a spokesperson for the postal status quo, not to mention the unity of the postal regime. Bureaucrats from the MIC and other ministries who were dispatched to Japan Post from 2003 developed personal stakes in the successful operations of the new corporation. In short order, many began to chafe at the economic and financial limitations of the new entity and to clamor for more economic and regulatory freedoms; some eventually concluded that these goals could only be fulfilled through privatization.

Second, the postal system's record in exercising independent investment authority after 2001 convinced many that privatization might actually work. No longer could naysayers convincingly argue that privatization would devastate the public financial system by dampening the postal system's appetite for government bonds and hence weaken the government's ability to service its debt. From 2001, the FILP and affiliated institutions had to raise their own funds in part through bond issuances.[111]

---

111. These consisted of FILP-agency bonds with and without government guarantees, as well as FILP bonds issued by the MOF (Cargill and Sakamoto, *Japan Since 1980*, 199).

The risk-averse postal services invested the bulk of their proceeds in these relatively safe offerings, which meant the de facto continuation of the financial relationship between the post office and the FILP. Although economists predicted that the postal services would gravitate more toward the stock market once interest rates increased, for the time being at least, the fear that postal privatization would lead to widespread financial instability appeared unfounded. Another stumbling block on the road to postal privatization had been loosened.

Third, and peripherally to the processes of late 1990s postal reform, the Basic Law enhanced the powers of the executive over the policy-making process in ways that proved integral to Koizumi's achievements after 2001. For years, LDP politicians in the relevant policy tribes worked in concert with concerned bureaucrats to dominate issue-specific policymaking. Although these practices produced broad consensuses that allowed for smooth policy implementation, they did not leave much room for innovative prime ministerial or cabinet leadership. As Aurelia Mulgan wrote in 2002, "The result is that Japan does not have cabinet government, it has party-bureaucratic government. It is a system in which the executive is left out of the loop."[112]

The Basic Law—along with the accompanying Law to Amend the Cabinet (Kaisei naikaku hō)—established several new organs and positions that strengthened the potential for executive leadership (*kantei shudō*) within the policy process.[113] First, the Cabinet Secretariat (Naikaku kanbō), which assists the prime minister, was expanded to include enhanced powers of policy coordination, and the prime minister was given the authority to create new positions within the organ and to fill them with individuals from both outside and inside government. These changes helped strengthen the Cabinet Secretariat's independence from the bureaucracy.[114] Second, the prime minister was granted a larger personal staff, including five personal assistants who were not subject to the normal salary restrictions of public servants.[115] He also gained the authority to appoint what might be termed "ministers without portfolio"

---

112. Mulgan, *Japan's Failed Revolution*, 146.
113. See Itō, "Kantei shudōkei seisaku kettei to Jimintō."
114. Mulgan, *Japan's Failed Revolution*, 178–79.
115. Noble, "Political Leadership and Economic Policy in the Koizumi Cabinet," 24.

(*tokumei tantō daijin*). In the past, such individuals were judged to be little more than counselors. But as cabinet members directly answerable to the prime minister, these new appointees—including, under Koizumi's watch, a minister in charge of postal privatization—were able to escape the control of bureaucrats and, for Koizumi at least, become part of the "front line of structural reform."[116] Third, a more powerful Cabinet Office (Naikakufu) was created to replace the old Prime Minister's Office (Sōrifu) and was placed under the direct control of the prime minister. This policy-initiating organ helps with the planning and coordination of cabinet policy and is relatively immune to outside pressures.[117] Fourth, as the ministries were reorganized and efforts to create more horizontal linkages between them introduced, the number of political appointees to each ministry was substantially increased. Together, these innovations were designed to reduce the power of bureaucratic officials relative to that of politicians and the prime minister.[118]

Fifth, the law established four new advisory councils within the Cabinet Office. Unlike the advisory councils of old, these entities enjoy institutional perks such as office space and permanent secretarial assistance that help strengthen executive authority within the policymaking process.[119] Of particular note was the Council on Economic and Fiscal Policy (Keizai zaisei shimon kaigi; CEFP), which was headed by the prime minister and played a central role in the establishment of broad fiscal and economic policy. The eleven-member council, which was eventually dubbed the "control tower of reform,"[120] consisted of the Minister of State for Economic and Fiscal Policy, the ministers of key economic ministries, the governor of the Bank of Japan, and four private sector representatives. By pulling the government's main economic and fiscal decision-makers out of their ministerial contexts and into a high-level forum with leading thinkers from the private sector, the CEFP strived to overcome bureaucratic localism and inter-ministerial competition— something that neither standing nor ad hoc advisory councils (*shingikai*)

---

116. Iijima, *Koizumi kantei hiroku*, 23–24.
117. Mulgan, *Japan's Failed Revolution*, 180–81.
118. Pempel, "Learning to Lose is for Losers," 122.
119. Noble, "Political Leadership and Economic Policy in the Koizumi Cabinet," 25.
120. Uchiyama, *Koizumi and Japanese Politics*, 26.

like Hashimoto's Administrative Reform Council were ever able to fully achieve. By posting the minutes of CEFP meetings on the Internet, moreover, the council was incentivized to concentrate on substantive policymaking rather than political deal making;[121] this provision also served as a disincentive for individual policymakers to push their private agendas against the wishes of the council. Although the effectiveness of the CEFP depended in part on capable leadership, its very presence marked a major milestone on the road to stronger executive authority in Japan.

The ultimate irony of the Hashimoto reforms was that while interest groups in the postal regime congratulated themselves for negotiating a postal reform package that had once again defeated the specter of privatization, the corporatization of the postal services and their assumption of full investment authority, along with the institutional empowerment of the prime minister, carried within them the seeds of more radical change. Had the postmasters and their allies paid closer attention to these provisions as they were being debated, they might have stood a fighting chance against the Koizumi government's privatization crusade, a subject to which we now turn.

---

121. Ibid., 24.

SIX

Koizumi Jun'ichirō
and the Politics of Postal Privatization

Political-economic reform involves far more than simply rewriting the rules of economic conduct. It can also reflect and influence changes in the basic values of the nation-state, including conceptualizations of the public interest and state-society relations and, ultimately, visions of what constitutes an "ideal society." And so it was in Japan between 2001 and 2005, when Prime Minister Koizumi Jun'ichirō's crusade to privatize the postal services once again raised questions about the fate of institutions now more than 130 years old—institutions that began as harbingers of modernity but that now symbolized the best (or worst, as some might have it) of Japanese social and economic tradition.[1] As Koizumi's crusade unfolded, interests allied against privatization launched their biggest political campaign to date, evoking Maejima Hisoka's legacies as they lobbied hard against change. "It is no exaggeration to say that this is the biggest crisis Zentoku has faced since its establishment," the head of the organization wrote on the occasion of its 50th anniversary in 2003, urging his colleagues to continue their "mission" (*shimei*) to protect this fundamental component of Japan's distinctive way of life.[2]

---

1. Some of the arguments and information presented in this chapter also appear in Maclachlan, "Storming the Castle" and "Two Steps Forward, One Step Back."

2. Zenkoku tokutei yūbinkyokuchōkai, *Zentoku 50-nen no ayumi*, preface.

Zentoku ultimately failed in its mission and is now witnessing the gradual privatization of the postal services—a process that Koizumi proudly called "the biggest reform since the Meiji Restoration."[3] How did it come to this? After decades of keeping the postal privatization movement at bay, what was it about the Koizumi years that led to the postal regime's political defeat and the end of the state-administered postal system?

The answer, as this chapter illustrates, is a complex one. The most dramatic source of change was Koizumi himself, who seemed to have an uncanny ability to push his agenda forward while marginalizing his enemies, all the while paying little heed to the many taboos of party and interest-group politics. Koizumi had demonstrated these skills during the 1990s while serving as a cabinet minister in the Miyazawa and Hashimoto governments; as prime minister, he learned to perfect them. But at the risk of underestimating the significance of Koizumi's remarkable leadership talents, it is unlikely that they would have yielded as much as they had were it not for institutional, political, and ideological developments that had been set in motion well before he reached the pinnacle of power. As others have illustrated, structural changes introduced during the Hashimoto administration to the executive branch of government strengthened Koizumi's hand vis-à-vis his adversaries, as did the 1994 reform of the Lower House electoral system.[4] But also noteworthy were two developments that weakened the relative influence of the postal regime: the long-term deterioration of the exchange relationship between the beleaguered postmasters and the LDP old guard, and the defection of many postal bureaucrats from the postal regime following the establishment of Japan Post, a public corporation, in 2003. All of this occurred as the state-run postal system faced a deepening legitimacy crisis in the context of economic globalization and mounting demographic and financial pressures at home. Together, these developments enhanced Koizumi's leverage over the postal regime and enabled his daring leadership exploits to bear fruit.

This chapter travels Koizumi's remarkable road to postal privatization in three stages: 1) the period culminating in the 2002 passage of

---

3. Iijima, *Koizumi kantei hiroku*, 247.

4. See, for example, Estévez-Abe, "Japan's Shift Toward a Westminster System."

legislation to flesh out the details of Japan Post and partially liberalize the mail service; 2) the months stretching from the formulation of Koizumi's privatization plan in 2004 to the Diet's defeat of his legislative package in August 2005; and 3) the September 2005 Lower House election and the subsequent passage of the postal privatization bills. These milestones mark a progression in Koizumi's ability to learn from past mistakes and to take full advantage of new institutional and political opportunities for policy innovation. The end result was unprecedented change within both the postal sector and the political system.

Koizumi's Rise to Power and the Postmasters' Decline

After two failed attempts during the 1990s, Koizumi clinched the LDP party presidency in April 2001 in a manner that revealed the postmasters' deteriorating political power. Koizumi's main contender for the position, former Prime Minister Hashimoto Ryūtarō, played to a traditional script by appealing to organized interests,[5] including the postmasters associations. In keeping with his reputation as chief power broker between the postmasters and LDP leaders, Nonaka Hiromu had convinced the postmasters and their retired colleagues to throw their support behind his faction boss in return for a "cool" stance on postal privatization.[6] After campaigning for the LDP presidency in 1995 on a platform of bold financial reform and then ushering in the most significant postal reforms to date, Hashimoto's reversion to machine-style conservative politics must have been deeply reassuring to the postmasters. Koizumi, by contrast, assumed an even more aggressively reformist stance than he had in the 1995 presidential race, upholding postal privatization as his number one policy priority and the "citadel of reform" (*kaikaku no honmaru*).[7] Koizumi won the contest handily, collecting 298 votes to Hashimoto's 155.[8] Asō Tarō came in a distant third with 31 votes.[9]

----

5. *Wall Street Journal*, June 29, 2001.

6. Nikkei Business, *Daremo shiranai yūsei teikoku*, 36.

7. Yamawaki, *Yūsei kōbō*, 90. Koizumi's slogan symbolized the view that postal privatization was essential to Japan's administrative, financial, and economic health.

8. Iijima, *Koizumi kantei hiroku*, 217.

9. Kamei Shizuka was also in the running, but withdrew shortly before the final vote after cutting a deal with Koizumi on policy and cabinet-appointment issues. Koizumi

The postmasters had proved all but impotent in 2001 in the context of a revised LDP presidential selection process. In the past, factional maneuverings controlled the selection of party presidents in ways that privileged organized interests. This was certainly true in 1978, when the party's brief experiment with a presidential primary system led to Ōhira Masayoshi's surprise win over Fukuda Takeo after the Tanaka faction amassed throngs of new party members, including many recruited by the postmasters,[10] to vote for Ōhira.[11] In 1995, the electorate was expanded, but not enough to significantly dilute the influence of factional and interest group politics on the primaries.[12] In 2001, following a public backlash against LDP factions for their backhanded selection of the highly unpopular Mori Yoshirō as party president, the primary system was revised once again. In addition to votes from all sitting LDP Diet members,[13] the number of prefectural votes was raised from 47 to 141.[14] In theory, the new system had empowered the party's rank-and-file voters. In the context of the decline of factions in response to the post-1994 electoral and campaign finance rules,[15] as well as the Lower House's new "winner-takes-all" single member districts, primary voters now faced

---

failed to honor the deal, which included a pledge to tone down his position on postal privatization.

10. Segawa, *Koizumi Jun'ichirō to tokutei yūbinkyokuchō no arasoi*, 64.

11. As Chao-Chi Lin explains, LDP rank-and-file members were given the right to vote in the 1978 primary in the expectation that they would overpower "factional bloc voting." To increase their chances of finishing amongst the top two vote-getters and proceeding to the second stage of voting, presidential candidates—or representatives of their factions—recruited supporters as party members. In many cases, the factions paid for the recruits' membership fees. "Far from eliminating factional maneuvering in the presidential election, the introduction of the primary ended up factionalizing the grassroots of the party" ("How Koizumi Won," 111).

12. Ibid., 111–12.

13. *Japan Times*, April 13, 2001. In this particular election, 346 LDP Diet members were eligible to vote.

14. Except for Osaka, each prefecture adopted a winner-takes-all system whereby the top vote-getter in the presidential primary would receive all of that prefecture's votes (Estévez-Abe, "Japan's Shift Toward a Westminster System," 643).

15. The 1994 Lower House electoral reforms encouraged competition between parties rather than individual LDP politicians backed by factions, and stricter campaign finance regulations and the new government electoral subsidies for individual politicians weakened the faction boss's control over the flow of funds to his supporters.

strong incentives to select presidential candidates who could appeal to broad swaths of the electorate, as opposed to candidates backed by special interests.[16]

Despite these changes, Nonaka and other LDP leaders seemed confident that the factions would still reign supreme in the 2001 presidential race.[17] But it was not to be. A majority of the party's prefectural chapters decided that the charismatic Koizumi, with his weak factional base, anti-establishment rhetoric, and outstanding media skills, was far better positioned to shore up the party's public image and electoral prospects than candidates backed by the likes of the postmasters.[18] Reluctant to defy this outpouring of public opinion, far more LDP Diet members than expected cast their votes for Koizumi.

The 2001 presidential election gave Koizumi an unprecedented mandate within the LDP to exercise strong, decisive leadership in pursuit of his reformist agenda. Once in the prime minister's seat, Koizumi's political powers were further enhanced by Prime Minister Hashimoto's 1998 institutional reforms. These reforms imbued the prime ministership with a more independent and powerful image after decades of being held hostage to factional alignments and interest group pressures.[19] With an initial public support rate of approximately 80 percent—more than that of Prime Minister Hosokawa Morihiro at the height of his popularity—Koizumi manipulated that image to great effect, leading the LDP to a comfortable victory in the Upper House election of July 29, 2001. As the story of postal privatization further illustrates, moreover, by defying LDP customs and hence freeing the prime ministership from the shack-

---

16. Since it takes more votes to win an election in a winner-takes-all single-member district than what organized interests can provide, candidates have to appeal to a broader cross-section of the electorate. But the post-1994 electoral system did not render the mobilizational efforts of organized interest groups completely obsolete; the presence of highly restrictive campaign rules and other challenges incentivized candidates to continue their dependence on these groups as they struggled to attract as many voters as possible. See Krauss and Pekkanen, "Reforming the Liberal Democratic Party," 25.

17. Lin, "How Koizumi Won," 116–17.

18. For more on the presidential election results and their significance, see ibid.; and Kabashima and Steel, "The Koizumi Revolution," especially 79–80.

19. For more on the sources of the Hashimoto reforms and their broader implications for executive leadership, see Noble, "Political Leadership and Economic Policy in the Koizumi Cabinet," especially 24; and Shinoda, *Koizumi Diplomacy*, especially 63.

les of ruling party control, Koizumi managed to use his executive powers to their fullest potential (or at least close to it) within the policymaking process.[20]

The 2001 Upper House election further highlighted the postmasters' deteriorating electoral influence. This is not to suggest that the organized vote no longer mattered in Diet elections; as the *Asahi Newspaper* estimated, approximately half of the 27 LDP candidates running in 2001 in proportional-representation (PR) districts had been backed by special interests like the postmasters.[21] But the data also suggest that the country's nearly 19,000 postmasters and their retired colleagues were much less powerful than they had once been. The postmasters gathered about 480,000 votes behind their candidate, Kōso Kenji, the most of any other interest group mobilized behind the LDP but less than half their postwar high of 1 million votes.[22] The downward trend was only to continue. The vote-rigging scandal that eventually engulfed Kōso and the postmasters led Zentoku leaders to predict at the association's May 2004 convention that the postmasters would fall far short of their vote-gathering quotas (*noruma*) of 50 votes each during the 2004 Upper House election.[23] Sure enough, the postmasters mobilized only 280,000 votes that year behind Hasegawa Kensei,[24] fewer than 15 votes per postmaster.

In sum, Koizumi's selection as LDP president and the 2001 Upper House election and subsequent scandal both highlighted and accelerated the postmasters'—and the postal regime's—long-term electoral decline. Thanks to that decline, and to new institutions in the party and the executive branch of government, it would seem that Koizumi was in a strong position to implement his vision for postal privatization.

---

20. Estévez-Abe, "Japan's Shift Toward a Westminster System."

21. *Asahi Newspaper*, July 27, 2001.

22. According to Patrick Köllner, the construction industry ranked second with approximately 180,000 votes and the war veterans third, with roughly 150,000 votes ("Upper House Elections in Japan and the Power of the 'Organized Vote,'" 130).

23. *Japan Times*, June 8, 2004.

24. *Asahi Newspaper*, July 23, 2004.

The Koizumi-Takenaka Line and Its Detractors

Koizumi may have staked his political fortunes on postal privatization, but his views on the subject are difficult to convey. Not one to dwell on the specifics of policy, Koizumi focused instead on some of the broader implications of privatization in his speeches and "email magazine" (*merumaga*) postings, leaving it to colleagues and sympathetic economists to fill in some of the blanks. The result was a series of slogans and sweeping statements that on the surface, at least, struck many Japanese as intuitively very appealing. Those who wanted to know more about privatization, however, were left feeling ambivalent or confused. Intentional or otherwise, Koizumi's rhetorical strategy had two important consequences. First, it allowed the postal regime to set many of the terms of the privatization debate during the early Koizumi years, transforming the economic issue of postal privatization into an ideological battle over the traditions and values of the political economy. Second, the very simplicity of Koizumi's "sound bite" rhetoric allowed him to portray postal privatization to ordinary Japanese as a black-and-white choice between change and stagnation—a strategy that in 2005 was to reap extraordinary electoral and legislative benefits for the proponents of change.[25]

Focusing on the postal system's implications for the broader economy, Koizumi borrowed from the language of neoliberal economics to highlight the alleged absurdity of the government's continuing hand in the postal services and to make the case for privatization. In 1999, as Japan's post-bubble recession neared the ten-year mark, he argued that financial reform must address the pressures of Japan's rapidly aging society on an already over-indebted government. How, he asked rhetorically, should these challenges be met—by invigorating the economy via structural reforms like postal privatization or by raising the consumption tax?[26] Given that consumers already shouldered a heavy tax burden and that the economy still required demand-led stimulus, the answer was obvious.

---

25. For more on Koizumi's media style, see Uchiyama, *Koizumi and Japanese Politics*, 6–12.

26. Koizumi, "Forward," 3.

Koizumi was fond of evoking the taxpayer's plight while trumpeting the need for privatization. On June 11, 2002, at a meeting of the Lower House's Internal Affairs and Communications Committee (Sōmu iinkai), he had this to say in response to a committee member's observation that the postal system's financial self-sufficiency rendered privatization unnecessary:

> If you think about it, doesn't all that money that's collected from postal savings and postal insurance put a tax burden on the people? [I]f the postal system falls into the red, it'll inevitably mean (higher) taxes. Postal savings, postal insurance, the FILP system, special corporations—think about it! It's very important that these all be reformed. And postal reform must be the first step.[27]

Koizumi had adopted a similar rhetorical style in 2001 when campaigning for the LDP presidency. He pointed out that despite the dour predictions of the anti-privatization camp, the newly privatized Japan Railways Group (JR) had developed into a viable corporate taxpayer and Nippon Telegraph and Telephone (NTT) managed to preserve universal service in telecommunications. If JR and NTT could accomplish these feats, why not the postal services?[28] Why, he asked, was it necessary for the state to monopolize these services, with their tax-exempt status and wasteful use of resources? Japan must strive for smaller, more effective government by paring bureaucratic functions down to a minimum and delegating the rest to the private sector (*kan kara min e*).[29] In what amounted to a usurpation of former Prime Minister Hashimoto's pet slogan, Koizumi argued that, "The private sector should do what the private sector can do!" (*minkan no dekiru koto wa minkan de yarubeki desu*).

Koizumi came to power determined to reduce deficit financing, resolve the nonperforming loan crisis, reduce government expenditures, and either reform or privatize public corporations.[30] The last two goals

---

27. Sōmu iinkai meeting transcript, no. 22, 154th session, June 11, 2002. http://kokkai.ndl.go.jp/SENTAKU/syugiin/154/0094/main.html (last accessed July 14, 2011).

28. Iijima, *Koizumi kantei hiroku*, 216. Koizumi made similar arguments in his Koizumi Cabinet email magazine postings. See, for example, Koizumi Cabinet email magazine, no. 151, August 5–19, 2004, http://www.kantei.go.jp/foreign/m-magazine/backnumber/koizumi/2004/0805.html (last accessed July 14, 2011).

29. Koizumi, "Forward," 2.

30. Noble, "Political Leadership and Economic Policy in the Koizumi Cabinet," 26.

were linked to the more ambitious objective of shrinking the FILP—an instrument of government policy that Koizumi roundly criticized for producing serious market distortions in Japan's mature economy.[31] The public financial system had to be changed, he argued, not only by reforming the government institutions and public corporations at the receiving end, or "exit" (*deguchi*), of the FILP system, but also by severing the FILP once and for all from the postal savings and insurance systems, the so-called "entrance" (*iriguchi*) to the system. In an autumn 2004 email magazine posting, Koizumi conceded that ordinary Japanese were far more concerned about pension reform and other social security issues than they were about postal privatization. But "the privatization of the postal services is at the heart of reform," he wrote. Without it, the reinvigoration of the private banking sector and broader financial restructuring would not be possible.[32]

As far as Koizumi and many economists were concerned, the postal savings system had long since "completed its historical mission" to enable economic modernization and growth. With the decline of industrial policy, postal savings deposits were no longer needed as capital for government investment in growth industries. The convenience of the post office—once the only financial institution in town—was losing its allure as private banking networks expanded. Government guarantees of postal savings accounts were less attractive now that commercial banks were backed by a deposit insurance system. As of 2001, the FILP was no longer completely dependent on automatic transfers of postal savings and insurance funds into its coffers. Finally, as the Japanese economy relied increasingly on profitable "investment" opportunities, the postal savings system—as a haven for safe, low-interest "savings"—had grown antiquated.[33] The postal savings system, Koizumi firmly believed, had lost its relevance.

Postal privatization served Koizumi's political goals as well. In an effort to destroy the last vestiges of Tanaka Kakuei's political machine,

---

31. Inose, *Kessen*, 86.

32. Koizumi Cabinet email magazine, no. 160, October 21, 2004, http://www.kantei.go.jp/foreign/m-magazine/backnumber/koizumi/2004/1021.html (last accessed July 14, 2011).

33. Okina, "Japan's Financial System Since the Bursting of the Bubble," 12.

Koizumi vowed to loosen the grip of vested interests on the LDP. Foremost among those interests were the postmasters and their retired colleagues who had helped mobilize the vote behind LDP candidates for more than half a century. By eliminating the postmasters' privileges as public servants and exposing them to market forces, Koizumi hoped to reduce the occupational cohesiveness that fueled their vote-gathering powers. This, in turn, would help sever their ties to the LDP, thus paving the way toward more meaningful political-economic reform. These goals were encapsulated in one of Koizumi's favorite slogans: "Change the LDP, change Japan" (*Jimintō o kae, Nihon o kaeru*).

Lastly, Koizumi upheld postal privatization as a mechanism for reducing the size of the civil service by approximately one-third and for weakening the bureaucracy's overall influence. Shrinking the bureaucracy had been a widely held political goal since the deregulatory movement of the 1980s, a time when scandal-ridden bureaucrats were becoming unpopular and politicians were on the lookout for new ways to enhance their relative power within the policymaking system.[34] During the post-bubble years, decreasing the size of the civil service also promised monetary gains for the state's beleaguered coffers. Transforming the postal system's approximately quarter million public servants into private citizens would appear to accomplish all of these goals,[35] while appealing to the public's growing preference for a leaner and less corrupt bureaucracy. But the argument that postal privatization could serve as a mechanism for civil service reform was, in fact, highly misleading. Since the salaries of both the postmasters and the postal workers were covered by the services themselves, rather than by the general account, postal privatization would make nary a dent in the government's ballooning debt. Be that as it may, many in the pro-privatization camp continued to trumpet postal reform as a major step toward civil service reform and, more broadly, a more market-oriented political economy.[36]

---

34. Dore, *Stock Market Capitalism*, 158.

35. Koizumi liked to state in public that the postal services had far more employees—full and part time—than the national police force (250,000) or the Self-Defense Forces (240,000). *Asahi shinbun*, September 6, 2005.

36. During the 2005 Lower House election campaign, many voters were convinced that the postmasters' salaries were covered by tax revenue (*Asahi shinbun*, September 3, 2005).

In Takenaka Heizō, Koizumi found a kindred soul with the economic and financial expertise to sell the need for postal privatization in more concrete terms. He also gained a key advisor whom he consulted on postal reform more than any other scholar or bureaucrat.[37] A Keiō University economist with diverse academic and government experience, Takenaka was also a well-known television personality who had a knack for clarifying complicated economic issues.[38] Throughout Prime Minister Koizumi's tenure, Takenaka occupied cabinet posts: Economic and Fiscal Policy and Postal Privatization, both of which were rooted in the 1998 Basic Law for the Reform of Central Ministries and Agencies, and, eventually, Internal Affairs and Communications. For the first few years of his cabinet career, Takenaka performed his duties without simultaneously holding a seat in the Diet. This arrangement helped shield him from the pressures of vested interests, but not from the criticisms of LDP colleagues who resented his meteoric rise to the top echelons of power.[39] Takenaka later surprised his detractors by running—at Koizumi's urging—for a seat in the 2004 Upper House election and winning more votes than any other LDP candidate on the PR list.

Takenaka believed that the postal services were on the road to destruction.[40] In addition to advocating much smaller postal savings and insurance systems, he and other economists argued that competition through privatization would reduce wasteful costs within the services, enhance the effectiveness of the postal network, and diversify postal services.[41] Like Koizumi, he viewed the privatization and breakup of the postal services as an integral component of broader financial and economic reform, arguing that it was "socialistic thinking" to assume that the state should carry out functions that could just as easily be performed by the private sector.[42] Also like Koizumi, he had one eye on the FILP as he pushed the government's postal privatization agenda forward. As Gregory Noble notes, Takenaka saw the FILP as an obstacle not only

---

37. *Asahi Newspaper*, January 22, 2005.
38. Yamawaki, *Yūsei kōbō*, 132.
39. Ibid., 138.
40. Takenaka, *Yūsei min'eika*, 176–77.
41. Keiichiro Kobayashi, "The Points of Contention Surrounding Postal Services Reform."
42. Takenaka, *Yūsei min'eika*, 21.

to full financial recovery, but also to corporate restructuring, since FILP financing by government financial institutions was keeping many so-called zombie companies afloat.[43] But both men understood that re-forming the FILP and the postal system at the same time would be a hard political sell, since so many influential firms and interest groups were tied to the FILP system. They therefore resolved to begin at the FILP's source: the postal system.[44]

One of the most controversial elements of the Koizumi-Takenaka line was the breakup of the postal system into its constituent parts. Ko-izumi honed his views on this point in May 1999, when he formed the Postal Privatization Study Group (Yūsei min'eika kenkyūkai) in part-nership with the DPJ's Matsuzawa Shigefumi. Consisting of seventeen Diet members who were disappointed by the narrow scope of Prime Minister Hashimoto's postal reforms, the non-partisan group conducted extensive research on postal privatization and held a series of hearings with interested parties, including representatives from parcel delivery firms like Yamato Transport. The study group eventually produced a proposal that called for the abolition of the government's monopoly on mail collection and delivery, the breakup of the postal system into service-specific joint-stock companies, and in an effort to encourage free and fair competition between the postal financial companies and the pri-vate sector, a further breakup of each financial firm into regional com-panies (ten for postal savings, two or three for insurance).[45] Koizumi and later Takenaka were convinced that the separation of services was neces-sary to prevent losses in one service from negatively affecting the other services—a safeguard that was at least partially achieved under the state-run system by the establishment of discrete accounts for each service. They also believed that if forced to chart their own independent corpo-rate paths, each service would face more incentives to reduce costs and enhance profitability.[46] Although the division of the postal system into

---

43. Noble, "Front Door, Back Door," 111.

44. Inose, *Kessen*, 49–50. Takenaka argued that the two sides of the FILP equation were closely connected. Once the ties that bound the postal savings system to the FILP were fully severed, he argued, special corporations would weaken as their primary fund-ing source dried up.

45. Matsubara, "Yūsei min'eika 'Koizumi gen'an' to wa nani ka," 17–19.

46. Takenaka, *Yūsei min'eika*, 41, 58.

three separate services eventually carried the day, intense pressure from the postal regime forced Koizumi and Takenaka to abandon their preference for multiple, region-specific postal savings and insurance firms.[47]

The Koizumi-Takenaka line stood in stark contrast to the postal regime's views of how best to serve the public interest. Skeptical of the market's capacity to address the common good, postal employees and their party and bureaucratic patrons looked to the state as the only entity that could simultaneously offer public goods like universal postal service and absorb the financial costs that universal service entailed. Some even argued that the state should prioritize the provision of public goods over balancing the books,[48] since the common good was so much more important than the narrow pursuit of profit. This is not to suggest that the postal regime was oblivious to the postal system's financial health; in fact, one of the reasons the regime favored a unified postal system was that it produced positive financial synergies among the three services that would disappear if the postal system were broken up into its component services. In slogan-speak, the regime's goal was "state administered, unified services" (*kokuei de sanjigyō ittai*). Koizumi and Takenaka, by contrast, were primarily interested in Japan's overall economic health and ability to compete in an increasingly globalized economy. The common good was certainly a concern, but the two men saw no reason why it could not be fulfilled in a competitive market where each service was its own, discrete firm. If telecommunications firms could provide universal service in their privatized, more competitive environment, so too could each of the postal services.

In his 2006 memoirs, Takenaka confessed that the government had done a poor job of selling privatization to the public before early 2005.[49] As Aurelia Mulgan argues, market-oriented reforms invariably face concerted opposition from those most likely to lose from them, while their immediate beneficiaries—consumers and businesses that stand to gain from lower prices and an expanded range of choice—are often too dif-

---

47. Koizumi's critics preferred national, rather than regional, postal savings and insurance firms on the grounds that proceeds from urban areas, where the volume of transactions was expected to be quite heavy, could be used to compensate for shortfalls in sparsely populated regions.

48. Matsubara, *Yūsei min'eika de kō kawaru*, 98–99.

49. Takenaka, *Yūsei min'eika*, 3.

fuse to rally behind them.[50] As Koizumi stuck to his script that privatization would expand the services available to consumers, postal regime representatives, heads of rural local governments,[51] and other privatization skeptics raised some troubling questions. What exactly *could* the private sector do for the postal services? What would happen to the social functions performed by the postal network if the services were privatized? More to the point, how would postal privatization affect the daily lives of ordinary people and the health of small communities? By appealing to risk-averse Japanese who were struggling with the effects of economic restructuring, unemployment, local government budgetary constraints, and a decline of community in the countryside, Koizumi's opponents tried to make the case that postal privatization would hurt local residents by putting individual post offices out of business, increasing unemployment among local postal employees, shrinking the postal system's social safety net, and even opening the floodgates to unwelcome foreign investment in the postal service firms and a flow of postal savings and insurance proceeds to destinations abroad.[52] Koizumi, they concluded, had embraced the worst of American-style capitalism and was poised to sacrifice Japan's distinctive social and economic values to the lowest bidder.

Stage I: The 2002 Legislation

Prime Minister Koizumi's first foray into postal reform was riddled with mixed messages, institutional roadblocks, and strategic mistakes. On April 25, 2001, shortly after forming an LDP government in coalition with the Conservative Party and the Kōmeitō, Koizumi announced

---

50. Mulgan, *Japan's Failed Revolution*, 10.

51. A Kyodo News survey revealed that in late 2001, more heads of local governments supported postal privatization than opposed it (38.1 percent and 32.8 percent, respectively). But nearly half of the mayors of towns and villages with populations of 5,000 or less were opposed to privatization; many others were undecided. In April 2001, the National Association of Towns and Villages stated its opposition to privatization on the grounds that it could deprive rural elderly residents of valuable social welfare services and thus put pressure on cash-strapped localities to fill in the gap (*Japan Times*, April 6, 2001 and January 8, 2002).

52. Interview, Arai Hiroyuki, Tokyo, March 26, 2003; Oshita, *Kamei Shizuka*, 309. For more on these arguments, see Arai, *Yūbinkyoku o Amerika ni uriwatasu na*.

that he would enact legislation to facilitate the replacement of the Postal Services Agency (Yūsei jigyōchō) with a public corporation in 2003 and to allow private-sector participation in the mail service. Both measures were in keeping with the stipulations of the 1998 Basic Law for the Reform of Central Ministries and Agencies. Koizumi's adversaries, however, correctly assumed that the prime minister had more ambitious plans up his sleeve. In a thinly veiled warning to Koizumi to tow the party line, Nonaka Hiromu defiantly proclaimed at Zentoku's annual meeting in late May that "Further reforms to the three postal services will not be carried out!"[53]

Undeterred, in early June Koizumi announced the establishment of the Roundtable on Postal Services Reform (Yūsei sanjigyō no arikata ni tsuite kangaeru kondankai),[54] an informal advisory group consisting of ten private-sector representatives and scholars and headed by Tanaka Naoki, a well-known economics commentator and Koizumi ally.[55] The roundtable met monthly to discuss not corporatization but privatization, a move that proved damaging to the immediate task at hand. To be sure, the group lacked the legal status to do anything more than provide the prime minister with advice. But the nature of its deliberations challenged the Basic Law's stipulation that privatization was not to be revisited. (Koizumi's solution to the gag order was to demand—unsuccessfully—that the 1998 stipulation be repealed.[56]) More practically, the roundtable's mandate to discuss the privatization option caused confusion among both roundtable participants and key actors in the policy process. MIC bureaucrats in charge of deliberating on and drafting the 2002 legislation found themselves at loggerheads over the bills' details; why go to the trouble of corporatizing the postal services if privatization was just around the corner?[57] The postmasters and their LDP allies reacted

---

53. *Asahi shinbun*, June 7, 2001.

54. The Roundtable's official English name was "Advisory Council to Consider the Modalities of the Three Postal Businesses." A brief description of the roundtable's mandate and membership list can be accessed at: http://www.kantei.go.jp/foreign/policy/yusei/index_e.html (last accessed July 20, 2011).

55. Iijima, *Koizumi kantei hiroku*, 226; *Japan Times*, June 5, 2001; Asahi *shinbun*, November 12, 2001.

56. *Japan Times*, May 1, 2001.

57. *Asahi shinbun*, September 25 and November 9, 2001.

by moving into high alert, viewing what should have been the culmination of Hashimoto's fairly moderate reform blueprint as a surreptitious step toward more sweeping change. Koizumi tried to calm his skittish opponents by telling them that while he hoped to explore the future of the postal services, he was not about to hoist his privatization ideas on the policy process.[58]

But Koizumi's subsequent words and actions sent a much different message. He announced, for instance, that the current round of reform would be conducted as a battle over "whether the LDP will crush the Koizumi cabinet or the Koizumi cabinet will crush the LDP." And in November, as fallout from the Kōso Kenji scandal drew the public's attention to the postmasters' illegal electoral activities, the roundtable released a statement on Japan Post that urged the wholesale abolition of the commissioned post office system and an end to Japan Post's ownership of—or investment in—the small, private firms that serviced the postal network (the postal family enterprises).[59] It appeared that Koizumi and his advisors were angling to unravel the postal regime before privatization had even reached the official government agenda.

Koizumi's impatience to proceed with privatization made corporatization and the liberalization of mail far more controversial than they might otherwise have been. In December, large, bipartisan networks of anxious Diet members were established in both chambers of the Diet to advocate the preservation of the postal network and universal service.[60] Zentoku publicly opposed the privatization option as an affront to universal service and demanded the "preservation of state management of the postal public corporation" (*yūsei kōsha no kokuei iji*),[61] months before the public corporation had even been established. Never ones to enthuse over Hashimoto's corporatization plan, the postmasters were now defending it as the lesser of two evils.[62] All the while, the postmasters

---

58. *Asahi Newspaper*, August 28, 2002; Iijima, *Koizumi kantei hiroku*, 226–27.

59. *Nihon keizai shinbun*, November 15, 2001.

60. *Asahi shinbun*, December 6 and 12, 2001.

61. *Asahi shinbun*, November 12 and 21, 2001.

62. The business community was highly critical of corporatization. In late 2001, the Keizai dōyūkai (Association of Corporate Executives) issued a report arguing that the proposed Japan Post would be difficult to manage and unable to make sound investment decisions. It also warned of a major blow to taxpayers should the public corpora-

opposed mail liberalization on the grounds that it would drive many small post offices into bankruptcy—something their LDP allies also hoped to avoid, since it would weaken the postmasters' vote-gathering functions.

Koizumi's reaction to this cacophony of opposition was true to character. In a move reminiscent of his 1997 threat to resign his cabinet position if his minimum demands for postal reform were not adopted, in 2002 he threatened to dissolve the cabinet if the LDP did not endorse his reform bills. Cornered, the LDP's Executive Council agreed on April 23 to submit the bills to the Diet, even though it had not given the bills' contents the party's formal stamp of approval. It was, Koizumi's private secretary later wrote, "a moment that opened a hole in the LDP's decision-making apparatus,"[63] namely, in the informal system of preliminary review (*jizen shinsa*) that enabled the party to check the powers of both the bureaucracy and the prime minister.

The conflict over mail liberalization then moved into the Diet, where party heavyweights like Nonaka Hiromu, Aoki Mikio (chairman of the LDP's Upper House caucus), and Asō Tarō (chairman of the PARC) resolved to secure the sorts of compromises that would make reform more palatable to the postal regime.[64] From the start, the deliberations were mired in conflict. Koizumi wanted private sector firms to participate in the growing, highly lucrative, but heretofore lightly regulated "direct mail" sector, which he broadly defined to include all noncorrespondence.[65] The postal tribe, by contrast, wanted the law to subsume direct mail under the category of postal mail, thereby subjecting it to strict government regulation.[66] By effectively curtailing private-sector deliveries of direct mail, the provision would guarantee Japan Post's control over a veritable cash cow; this, in turn, would shield post

---

tion ultimately fail. The postal services, the organization concluded, should be divided into separate, service-specific corporations (*Asahi shinbun*, September 25, 2001).

63. Iijima, *Koizumi kantei hiroku*, 228.

64. *Asahi shinbun*, May 17, 2002; *Kyodo News*, May 18, 2002.

65. The volume of direct mail had been increasing in recent years as that of letters (including postcards) declined. By 2002, direct mail amounted to 25 percent of the total market for mail (*Japan Times*, July 4, 2002).

66. Since the early Meiji period, postal mail was legally designated a government monopoly. Violators of the law were technically subject to arrest.

offices from financial decline and help preserve the vote-gathering functions of the postmasters. But Koizumi refused to capitulate. Repeating his threat to dissolve the Lower House if the bills were not passed on his terms, Koizumi incurred the wrath of his party colleagues, including former Prime Minister Hashimoto, who complained that he was defying policymaking custom.[67] Undeterred, Koizumi went on to proclaim that liberalizing mail would constitute a milestone on the road to privatization,[68] a statement that many condemned as an unnecessary provocation of the postmasters and their allies. Even the DPJ's Matsuzawa Shigefumi, Koizumi's former ally on postal privatization, questioned the wisdom of the remarks.[69]

As his opponents lambasted him in the Diet for trying to introduce "American-style" business techniques to the mail service,[70] Koizumi's uncompromising stance grew more and more untenable. Recognizing that he lacked the political wherewithal to defeat the "forces of resistance" (*teikō seiryoku*) in the face of plummeting public approval ratings, which had dropped to just 43 percent in June 2003,[71] Koizumi pulled a surprise about-face and announced that he would entertain compromises so long as they did not curtail private participation in the mail sector.[72] The ploy worked. The Lower House passed a series of amended bills on July 9 and the Upper House followed suit on July 24,[73] just one week before the Diet session was to end. But the price of "victory" was a series of concessions to the postal regime that further weakened Koizumi's reputation for decisive leadership. Contrary to the roundtable's recommendations, Japan Post would be permitted to invest in private, postal family enterprises.[74] A requirement that Japan Post deposit a portion of its income into the national treasury was watered down so that

---

67. *Nikkei Weekly*, June 10, 2002.

68. *Asahi shinbun*, June 1, 2002.

69. Iijima, *Koizumi kantei hiroku*, 229; *Nikkei Weekly*, June 27, 2002.

70. Sōmu iinkai meeting transcript, no. 20, 154th session, June 4, 2002. http://kokkai.ndl.go.jp/SENTAKU/syugiin/154/0094/main.html (last accessed July 25, 2011).

71. *The Nikkei Weekly*, June 10 and June 27, 2002; *Japan Times*, July 5, 2002.

72. *Japan Times*, July 2, 2002.

73. The DPJ opposed the bills as an impediment to effective competition (*Japan Times*, July 4, 2002).

74. *Japan Times*, July 2, 2002.

the mail service could keep postage rates low.[75] And a pledge was inserted into the bills to maintain the postal network at its current levels following the establishment of Japan Post.

More controversially, although the legislation theoretically opened the door for private operators to deliver most kinds of mail, including letters and postcards, it made it all but impossible for those operators to secure the necessary licenses. The mail service was divided into special and ordinary services, both of which were subject to government licensing procedures. For special (that is, express and other courier) services, firms had to confine their business to predefined urban markets and guarantee delivery within three hours. To secure a license to deliver items within the ordinary service, participants had to agree to service the entire national market at uniform rates (universal service), operate six days per week, and guarantee delivery to anywhere in the country within two days. More problematically, new entrants had to erect 100,000 mailboxes each nationwide—a very costly and unnecessary requirement for parcel delivery firms like Yamato that serviced their customers either door-to-door or at local retail shops. These regulations were in part designed to prevent private firms from crowding profitable urban markets to the neglect of rural communities, which Japan Post would be forced to service at a loss. Needless to say, they made the national market highly unattractive to the private sector. Although several motorcycle and other courier companies entered local special service markets after 2003,[76] not a single private firm applied for a license to enter the market for ordinary service in the two years following Japan Post's establishment.[77] The president of Yamato Transport, Japan's leading parcel delivery firm, angrily announced even before the bills were passed that his firm was abandoning its plans to seek entry into the mail sector: "We cannot expect fair competition in a sector where the Ministry of Internal Affairs and Communications and the new postal service public corporation form a united front as the referee and the principal player."[78]

———

75. *Japan Times*, July 25, 2002.

76. Motorcycle courier services (*baiku bin*, or "bike mail") had existed for several years in many cities to transport certain kinds of documents between companies (*Asahi Newspaper*, July 5, 2002).

77. Kinoshita, "The Economics of Japan's Postal Services Privatization," 2.

78. *Asahi Newspaper*, June 13, 2002.

Behind that united front was a postal regime determined to slow Koizumi's march toward privatization. The regime failed, however, to secure an important condition penned by members of the LDP's postal tribe: a moratorium on privatization discussions in the first four years following Japan Post's establishment.[79] Koizumi flatly rejected the provision. Led by Aoki Mikio, LDP leaders eventually agreed to abandon it.[80] No more enamored of the prime minister's tactics than anyone else in the party, Aoki feared the electoral repercussions of the prime minister's retaliatory tactics should the moratorium be approved. Aoki's concession only incensed members of the postal tribe. Arai Hiroyuki, one of the clause's primary architects, resigned his position as chairman of PARC's posts committee in protest, claiming that he was taking responsibility for the party's concessions to Koizumi.[81]

Although Arai's resignation made it look as if the forces of resistance had been defeated, Koizumi's 2002 postal reform record—like Hashimoto's in 1998—was in fact quite mixed. On the positive side of the ledger, the legislation marked the first time since 1873, when Maejima Hisoka removed the feudal courier services (*hikyaku*) as competitors in the mail sector, that private firms were officially authorized to independently collect and deliver mail.[82] This accomplishment can be attributed to three factors: Koizumi's defiance of important LDP policymaking traditions; his eventual willingness to compromise with his opponents; and the postal regime's realization that some degree of cooperation with Koizumi would bestow benefits on conservative politicians at election time by preserving the prime minister's reformist image.

The 2002 legislation also fleshed out the Hashimoto government's guidelines for the corporatization of the postal services. Although confined largely to the administrative structure of the services, these changes can be viewed as "first-order reform" insofar as they altered the balance of power between the state and the market within the postal sector. With the benefit of hindsight, we also know that corporatization had

---

79. Iijima, *Koizumi kantei hiroku*, 229.

80. *Asahi Newspaper*, July 4, 2002.

81. *Asahi Newspaper*, July 5, 2002.

82. Recall that private firms had long been contracted to collect and deliver the mail *on behalf of* the government mail service.

unintended consequences of enormous political significance; as later sections illustrate, by driving a wedge between pro- and anti-market postal officials, corporatization weakened the cohesiveness of the postal regime and contributed to Koizumi's momentum on the road to postal privatization.

On other counts, Koizumi was far less successful in 2002. Competition in the mail service had been introduced in name only; what was intended to be a first-order reform—one that would transform the economic and institutional foundations of the mail service beyond the stipulations of corporatization—did little more than tinker with the status quo. Moreover, Koizumi had failed to "crush the LDP" or decisively weaken the political power of vested interests within the postal sector. His leadership credentials now in doubt, the prime minister's reform agenda was still beholden to politics as usual. It would be many more months before rifts within the postal regime and untapped institutional opportunities would enable Koizumi to break out of that mold.

ASSESSING JAPAN POST

On April 1, 2003, Japan Post (Nihon yūsei) was officially launched with Ikuta Masaharu, the former president of Mitsui O.S.K. Lines, at the helm.[83] The aim of corporatization was to achieve greater levels of profitability—particularly in the flailing mail service—by introducing private sector management and accounting principles to the postal services. Koizumi and others reasoned that if profitability were achieved in the mail sector through the introduction of new products and services, resistance to more radical reform would dissipate.[84] It was a tall order, and Koizumi pinned his hopes on Ikuta—a hard working, "market-oriented restructurer" (*shijō genrishugi no risutoraya*)[85]—to deliver.

Japan Post's establishment marked a sea change in the administrative institutions of the postal services. The special account for postal services that had been manipulated for so many years to advance the MIC's interests was abolished. And whereas legislation was once required to intro-

---

83. Japan Post was legally designated a *kokuei kōsha*, which translates as "government public corporation."

84. *Asahi Newspaper*, August 28, 2001 and April 3, 2003.

85. Yamawaki, *Yūsei kōbō*, 24.

duce new products and services, all that was needed now was the approval of the Minister of Internal Affairs and Communications. Ikuta's innovations added to the corporation's newfound flexibility. He injected greater transparency into the services, established high-level committees to carry out horizontal coordination among the postal services, issued two-year action plans to reduce costs and improve the productivity of postal employees, and reversed the old bottom-up decision-making process within the postal system by empowering high-level leaders— himself included.[86] And amidst a flurry of media attention, he borrowed from the Toyota production model to rationalize work at "collection and delivery" (*shūhai*) post offices (both ordinary and commissioned) by streamlining functions, improving technology and worker training programs, eliminating waste, and the like.[87] Starting with the large Koshigaya post office in Saitama prefecture, by 2005 the "Japan Post System" had expanded to incorporate 1,000 post offices around the country. By the end of their first year under the new system, the post offices had increased the productivity of their mail operations by 10.2 percent.[88] Even the postmasters admitted that the reforms had improved both the efficiency of operations and employee attitudes.[89]

Ikuta also accelerated the transformation of the local post office into a multi-functional facility that served the interests of its customers. For years, the post offices had strived to expand its range of services. In 2001, the government passed a law which authorized local governments to commission local post offices to perform simple government functions.[90] The arrangement was particularly welcome in remote areas where local governments were in the throes of financial cutbacks and/ or administrative amalgamations. From 2003, the mail service extended its delivery hours and a slew of new services were introduced, from per-

---

86. Ibid., 22, 25–26.
87. *Asahi Newspaper*, April 3, 2003.
88. Japan Post, *Annual Report: Postal Services in Japan: 2006*, 6.
89. "Akushon puran no genba kara," 10. Over time, some postal employees began to complain about increased workloads and heightened pressure to perform.
90. Ministry of Public Management, Home Affairs, Posts and Telecommunications, *2004 White Paper: Information and Communications in Japan*, 68. These functions include providing copies of residence cards and selling bus passes to the public, as well as co-operating with the localities to prevent disasters.

sonalized postage stamps to various life insurance products. The post offices collaborated with private banks to share ATM services, and several were permitted to open flower and small convenience shops in their facilities.[91] Most conspicuously, Japan Post contracted with Lawson convenience stores to administer Yu-Pack, its parcel delivery service. Yu-Pack had always struggled to keep up with private providers like Yamato; in 2002, it occupied a mere 5.7 percent of the total parcel delivery market.[92] Ikuta correctly reasoned that reforming and expanding Yu-Pack in partnership with Lawson would help Japan Post compensate for declining revenues in the mail delivery service.[93] Ikuta made significant progress toward fulfilling that objective, thanks largely to Yu-Pack's competitive prices and reliance on Lawson's vast distribution network; in fiscal 2005, the ratio of income from letter post to that from parcel post was 4:1, compared with 9:1 for FY 2003.[94] By the end of FY 2007, Yu-Pack's total market share had increased to 8.4 percent.[95]

Among some of Ikuta's other reforms were steps to rationalize Japan Post's relationship with private "postal family enterprises." Within a year of its establishment, Japan Post liberalized the bidding process for subcontractors and introduced stricter price monitoring of affiliated firms. In time, Ikuta claimed, 30 to 40 percent of all bids were coming from firms outside of the postal regime.[96] The financial results were immediate: the price for new employee uniforms dropped more than 50 percent by 2004 and fees for servicing the network's infrastructure were declining.[97] Ikuta also made changes to the postal savings system, including the introduction of "investment trusts," Japan's answer to mutual funds, and the installation of a new computer system to help curb individual depositors from exceeding the 10-million-yen combined limit on postal savings accounts. Launched in March 2004, the system blocked depositors who had reached their limit from making postal savings deposits at ATMs.[98]

---

91. *Japan Times*, February 19, 2004.
92. Japan Post Group, *Annual Report: 2009*, 83.
93. Yamawaki, *Yūsei kōbō*, 25.
94. Japan Post, *Annual Report: Postal Services in Japan: 2006*, 6.
95. Japan Post Group, *Annual Report: 2009*, 83.
96. Inose, *Kessen*, 62–64.
97. *Japan Times*, April 2, 2004.
98. Inose, *Kessen*, 66–67.

These and related changes had the desired effect: by the first anniversary of Japan Post's establishment, Ikuta had transformed the mail service's operating deficit into a respectable surplus. By the end of fiscal 2005, its third year of operations, the corporation posted an overall net income of 1.933 trillion yen, a significant increase over the 1.238 trillion yen recorded for the previous year.[99] For the postal regime, this was evidence enough that further reform was unnecessary. Koizumi and his allies, the banking sector, the pro-banking media, the private transport firms and, most significantly, many Japan Post employees, countered that too many problems remained within the new system to stop the postal reform process at corporatization. To build their case for privatization, they pointed to a number of alleged problems.

First, there were serious inconsistencies within the public corporation that were impossible to sustain over the long haul. As Koizumi and Matsuzawa wrote in 1999, it was paradoxical to accord public servant status to the employees of a "public corporation"; with their innate sense of entitlement and job security, these employees would forever function as a brake on the corporation's long-term institutional flexibility and profitability.[100] "Japan Post currently has 400,000 employees,"[101] Koizumi pointed out in 2004, "but I doubt the postal services are something that only civil servants can do."[102] Labor made up as much as 60 percent of Japan Post's total costs by the early 2000s; if full-time employees were to lose their public servant status, their numbers could be cut significantly.

Second, the pro-privatization camp was quick to accuse Japan Post of undercutting the private sector. New participants in the mail service faced numerous restrictions and were required to pay taxes, unlike Japan Post, which was tax exempt.[103] That tax-exempt status also allowed Yu-Pack to charge lower rates than private competitors like Yamato, whose share of the parcel delivery market at convenience stores was now in decline. This, complained the president of Yamato, represented an unfair

---

99. Japan Post, *Annual Report: Postal Services in Japan: 2006*, 6.

100. Yūsei min'eika kenyūkai, "Min'eika de yūsei jigyō wa kō kawaru," 30–31.

101. Japan Post had about 260,000 full-time and 120,000 part-time employees around the time of its establishment.

102. *Asahi Newspaper*, October 13, 2004.

103. *Asahi Newspaper*, April 3, 2003.

advantage; when given the choice, of course consumers would choose the postal system's cheaper service![104] The commercial banks, for their own part, complained that the postal savings system did not have to pay either taxes or deposit insurance. And private insurers, which had suffered during the 1980s after the postal insurance system raised its rates of return, were angry that Japan Post did not have to contribute to the industry's policyholder protection fund, which was established in 1998.[105] Both banks and insurers also regarded Japan Post's introduction of new financial products as unfair intrusions onto their turf.

Third, the size of Japan Post's financial services was still untenably large. With 230 trillion yen by 2005, postal savings deposits equaled the combined total of Japan's four largest banks (Mizuho, Mitsui Sumitomo, Tokyo Mitsubishi, and UFJ). And at 120 trillion yen, the postal insurance system exceeded the combined totals of its four largest competitors.[106] Meanwhile, the public was becoming more aware of problems within the postal financial services as a result of Japan Post's new disclosure rules. For instance, a report issued under Ikuta's watch in July 2005 revealed that 1.98 million depositors were exceeding the 10-million-yen ceiling on total postal savings deposits, a feat made possible by opening accounts under the maiden names of married women or the names of dead people.[107] Since Ikuta's new computer monitoring system was not resolving the problem, critics demanded that the postal savings system be subjected to the same regulations that governed private-sector banks.[108]

Fourth, critics were still troubled by the relationship between the post office's financial services and the FILP. Although the automatic transfer of postal funds into the FILP had been officially terminated as of January 2001, Japan Post continued to invest the bulk of its funds in FILP bonds and FILP agency bonds. By the time Japan Post was launched,

---

104. Inose, *Kessen*, 128. Yamato eventually severed its contract with the Lawson chain.

105. As they struggled to keep up with the postal insurance system, several private insurance firms experienced significant drops in profitability, and six went bankrupt (*The Economist*, March 27, 2003).

106. Inose, *Kessen* 16.

107. *Asahi shinbun*, September 1, 2005.

108. Inose, *Kessen*, 20.

only 1 percent of postal savings deposits and 4 percent of postal insurance proceeds were being invested in the stock market.[109] Furthermore, substantial portions of postal investments were being channeled through the FILP system into debt-ridden semi-government corporations that were depriving the private sector of new development opportunities. In short, although Japan Post had scored some remarkable successes during its first year, it did virtually nothing to solve the related problems of the FILP and Japan's bloated market for government bonds, which, in Koizumi's mind, were the ultimate targets of financial reform.[110]

Ironically, Ikuta's efforts to enhance the transparency of postal operations were attracting new adherents to radical reform by illuminating Japan Post's weaknesses as well as accomplishments. The experiences of Sonoda Hiroyuki, a senior LDP Lower House Diet member, are a telling case in point. A one-time opponent of postal privatization, Sonoda's careful analysis of Japan Post convinced him of the need for further change. "Mr. Ikuta's four-year plan for transforming the postal services may have scored some successes," he recalled in 2006, "but it did not go far enough. As Japan Post outran its usefulness, there was no other option but to break up and privatize the postal services." In October 2004, Sonoda moved to the front lines of the privatization movement by accepting the chairmanship of PARC's special subcommittee on postal reform.[111]

---

109. *Japan Times*, May 13, 2003.

110. Some analysts continued to worry that postal privatization would precipitate a major public financial crisis by drying up postal system investments in government bonds. For this reason, they opposed reforms that might incentivize the postal financial firms to shift their funds toward the stock market. Others correctly assumed that the risk-averse postal services would reduce investments in government bonds only gradually after privatization, thus avoiding a major financial crisis. For more on the debate over the evolving relationship between the postal financial services and the government bond market, see Keiichiro Kobayashi, "The Points of Contention Surrounding Postal Services Reform."

111. Interview, Sonoda Hiroyuki, LDP Lower House Diet member, Tokyo, July 14, 2006.

PREPARING FOR FURTHER REFORM

No sooner did the ink dry on the 2002 reform legislation than Tanaka Naoki, the chairman of the Roundtable on Postal Services Reform, presented Koizumi with a series of options for the future of the postal system that included the outright abolition of the postal savings and insurance services.[112] Given how heavily the postal network's survival depended on proceeds from the two financial services, the proposal sent shivers through the postal regime. All but silent on the issue, Koizumi opted to put privatization on the back burner until it was clear that Japan Post could effectively compete with private-sector rivals.[113]

A year later, Koizumi was sufficiently convinced of Japan Post's viability to take the next step. On June 23, he bluntly informed Ikuta Masaharu in front of a gathering of leading businessmen and bureaucrats that Ikuta was not only Japan Post's first president; he would also be its last. To Takenaka Heizō, who attended the event, this was a not-so-cryptic message that Koizumi wished to begin privatizing the postal system after the termination of Japan Post's first intermediate plan, in spring 2007.[114]

Three months later, on September 20, Koizumi won his second LDP presidential race, earning 399 votes to Kamei Shizuka's 139.[115] Since Kamei's sympathies lay with the postal regime at this time, the gap between the two candidates could be read as a major victory for the privatization camp. But the contrast between the two candidates was not as straightforward as it seemed, for it was clear that more and more LDP lawmakers were supporting Koizumi's presidency despite their dislike of postal privatization. Even Aoki Mikio, who as leader of the LDP's Upper House caucus controlled the flow of government electoral subsidies to his colleagues in the chamber, and many other members of the 100-member-strong Hashimoto faction—the postal regime's traditional

---

112. *Asahi Newspaper*, August 28, 2002; Iijima, *Koizumi kantei hiroku*, 229–30. For a detailed analysis of the Roundtable's proposals, see Keiichiro Kobayashi, "The Points of Contention Surrounding Postal Services Reform."

113. *Asahi Newspaper*, August 29, 2002.

114. Takenaka, *Kōzō kaikaku no shinjitsu*, 143.

115. Koizumi earned 194 Diet-member votes and 205 local votes. Kamei won 66 Diet-member votes and 73 local votes. The other two contenders in the race were Fujii Takao (65 votes) and Kōmura Masahiko (54 votes). *Japan Times*, September 21, 2003.

stronghold—were throwing their lot behind the prime minister as their best hope for an LDP victory in the upcoming 2003 Lower House election. Koizumi's electoral allure was proving very useful in overcoming opposition to his liberal economic principles.

Buoyed by the results of the presidential election, Koizumi shuffled his cabinet on September 22 and named it the "Reform Promotion Cabinet" (*kaikaku suishin naikaku*).[116] Four days later, in his speech to the opening session of the Diet, he announced his intention to begin privatizing the postal services on April 1, 2007. That same day, he instructed the CEFP, the government's "engine of reform" (*kaikaku no enjin*),[117] to take charge of the privatization process under the leadership of Takenaka Heizō, Minister of State for Economic and Fiscal Policy. Koizumi had dramatically bypassed the MIC as the nucleus of the postal policymaking process, thus diminishing the postal regime's ability to sway the course of events.

The exchange relationship between LDP politicians and the postmasters, for its own part, was under siege. Shortly before the 2003 presidential election, the Hashimoto faction's Nonaka Hiromu abruptly resigned his Diet seat—in part because of Aoki's support for Koizumi as LDP president.[118] Nonaka's departure symbolized a growing rift among the postmasters' LDP allies, particularly in what was once the Tanaka faction; more and more faction members seemed to have fallen under the influence of Koizumi's electoral charms. A year later, after failing to report a large political donation from the Japan Dental Association, Hashimoto resigned his position as faction head and announced that he would not run in the next Lower House election. Tanaka Kakuei's posthumous grip on the postal regime was clearly on the wane.

But the postal regime was by no means dead. The postmasters and postal workers had mobilized en masse to oppose Koizumi, and they still enjoyed the support of influential politicians in the LDP and the DPJ, respectively. As the privatization movement picked up steam, moreover, postal employees attracted a legion of sympathizers, many of them

---

116. Iijima, *Koizumi kantei hiroku*, 231–32.

117. *AERA*, April 17, 2007.

118. *Japan Times*, September 10, 2003; Estévez-Abe, "Japan's Shift Toward a Westminster System," 649.

LDP politicians from outside of the postal tribe. Kamei Shizuka was a representative case in point. Never known as a close ally of the postmasters, by late 2004 Kamei had established himself as one of the anti-privatization camp's most vocal and persuasive spokespersons. The presence of Kamei and others like him—both within and outside of the LDP—broadened the anti-privatization movement beyond the long-standing networks of the postal regime. And the purpose of that movement was simple: to prevent Koizumi from doing mischief to the postal network and its constituent services.

Koizumi's allies looked much different. An eclectic collection of intellectuals, businessmen, politicians, and pro-business media representatives, the privatization camp paled next to the postal regime in terms of its organizational cohesion. Indeed, one would be hard-pressed to find evidence that these different groups networked with one another to lobby on behalf of Koizumi's goals. Also noteworthy was the lukewarm presence of the commercial banks—the institutions most likely to benefit from the privatization of the massive postal savings system. While the banking associations were all in favor of shrinking the postal savings system, they doubted that Koizumi's privatization plan would achieve that goal. Others in the pro-privatization camp also supported postal privatization in principle but publicly argued over the details of Koizumi's blueprint. Ideologically as well as organizationally, Koizumi's friends were a far more diffuse group than the "forces of resistance."

Stage II: Koizumi's Postal Privatization Legislation

By the summer of 2004, Prime Minister Koizumi had acquired a decidedly mixed record on structural reform. On the one hand, he and Takenaka had done much to resolve the non-performing loan crisis in the commercial banking system. The government was also in the midst of abolishing, reorganizing, or privatizing dozens of special corporations (*tokushu hōjin*),[119] a major component of Koizumi's efforts to reform the "exit" (*deguchi*) side of the FILP system. In addition to significantly low-

---

119. Targeted corporations included the Housing Loan Corporation, the New Tokyo International Airport Public Corporation, and the Japan National Oil Corporation. Thirty-nine of these were reorganized as incorporated administrative agencies rather than privatized (Cargill and Sakamoto, *Japan Since 1980*, 219).

ering FILP expenditures, the restructuring of special corporations reduced government involvement in the economy and the number of
amakudari posts available to retiring bureaucrats. (Since it did not affect
vast swaths of vested interests, the restructuring proved much less politically contentious than postal privatization.[120]) On the other hand,
the 2002 postal reform legislation had accomplished little, Koizumi's
attempt to privatize the controversial public highway corporations was
mired in stalemate, and plans to reform the pension system had stalled.
Koizumi's performance was rewarded with public approval ratings of
less than 50 percent and yielded a loss of one seat for the LDP and a
gain of 12 seats for the DPJ in the July 2004 Upper House election. Although Koizumi could take solace in the fact that Takenaka had won
more votes than any other candidate in the election, two-and-a-half
times the number captured by Hasegawa Kensei, the postmasters' candidate,[121] he interpreted the election returns as a message to step up the
pace of reform.

It is perhaps no accident that the summer of 2004 also witnessed a
sea change in Koizumi's approach to policymaking. In a 1996 interview,
Koizumi had commented on the absurdity of delegating administrative
reform to bureaucrats. "In administrative reform," he said, "the official
is the patient, not the doctor. A patient cannot wield a scalpel and operate on himself! Even if the bureaucrat is knowledgeable about administrative reform, the most he can manage is to swallow some sweet-
tasting medicine."[122] But it seems that Koizumi had lost sight of this
wisdom during the first three years of his administration. In keeping
with a long precedent in Japan for depending on the bureaucracy to reform itself, entrusting postal reform to the MIC in 2002 had allowed
the usual phalanx of anti-reform interests to deprive that process of any
concrete value. Koizumi's attempts to privatize the Japan Highway
Public Corporation (Nihon dōrō kōdan; JH)—a goal that was integrally
linked to long-term FILP reform—met a similar fate.[123] For years, the

---

120. Ibid., 219–20.

121. Takenaka won 720,000 votes, Hasegawa 280,000 (*Asahi shinbun*, July 12, 2004).

122. *Shūkan Tōyō keizai*, September 7, 1996.

123. For a more detailed analysis of JH reform, see Uchiyama, *Koizumi and Japanese Politics*, 44–47.

JH's balance books had been in disarray as it spent massive sums collected from unpopular tolls on new road construction. Koizumi's objectives were to privatize the corporation and reduce its costs, eliminate tolls, and cap future road construction.[124] But given that Koizumi had depended on the Ministry of Land and Transportation (MLT)—a ministry that was highly susceptible to the pressures of the construction industry and other vested interests—the resulting legislation fell far short of his objectives.[125] Although the JH was soon divided into three separate firms that were subject to competitive market forces, the government retained its ownership of some roads, the MLT claimed control over CEO appointments to the privatized firms,[126] the tolls continued, inefficient "family enterprises" connected to the public corporations were preserved,[127] and the pace of new road construction slowed only marginally.

The flip side of bureaucratic control over the reform process was Koizumi's failure to exercise decisive leadership when it mattered the most. In the case of postal reform, he removed himself from the final stages of the 2002 decision-making process and allowed a series of numbing compromises to be inserted into the bills. In the JH case, Koizumi refused to openly back the chairman of the relevant advisory committee during squabbles over the details of reform that eventually led to emasculating compromises.[128] Although it would appear in both instances that Koizumi had "lost interest in reform,"[129] he was, to be fair, between a rock and a hard place. His most powerful opponents were highly placed in the LDP policy tribes, and for as long as he relied on the ministries to hammer out the details of reform, he could expect those tribes to bring pressure to bear on the legislative process. If he pushed back too hard, the reform processes would have stalled before the bills had even been drafted. Better to stand back and allow his op-

---

124. Kakumoto, *Mittsu no min'eika*, 19.

125. Itō, "Kantei shudōkei seisaku kettei to Jimintō," 31.

126. This measure may make it hard for the privatized firms to resist building unprofitable new roads demanded by politicians (Cargill and Sakamoto, *Japan Since 1980*, 219).

127. Ibid.

128. Mishima, "Grading Japanese Prime Minister Koizumi's Revolution," 742–43.

129. Ibid.

ponents to "debone" (*honenuki suru*) the legislation, since weak reform laws were better than no laws at all for a prime minister whose political legitimacy rested on the promise of change.

Entrusting ultimate authority over the second stage of the postal reform process to the eleven-member CEFP helped Koizumi exercise hands-on leadership and to out-maneuver his opponents. Lodged in the Cabinet Office and led by and answerable to the prime minister,[130] the CEFP consisted of the cabinet's leading economic ministers and several high-profile individuals from the private sector.[131] By pulling cabinet ministers out of their bureaucratic bailiwicks, making them directly accountable to the prime minister, and publicizing council minutes on its official website within days of each meeting, the council was theoretically positioned to prioritize Koizumi's liberal economic principles, minimize the ability of special interests to sway the proceedings through bureaucratic channels, and prevent individual council members from pushing their private agendas. During the Mori administration, the council had failed to live up to its potential, meeting only seven times and accomplishing very little.[132] Some scholars chalked this up to the bureaucracy's organizational ethos, which prevented bureaucrats from interacting flexibly and effectively with one another across ministerial lines.[133] But it is likely that old-fashioned interest group pressures were also to blame. As Takenaka himself was only too aware, even the supra-ministerial CEFP was susceptible to interest group and bureaucratic machinations.

Takenaka took several steps to ensure that the CEFP would follow Koizumi's lead on postal privatization without succumbing to the influences of vested interests. First, he selected private-sector council mem-

---

130. In the case of postal privatization, Takenaka presided over CEFP deliberations in Koizumi's stead.

131. Under Koizumi, the council consisted of the prime minister, the governor of the Bank of Japan; the chief cabinet secretary; the Minister of Finance; the Minister of Economy, Trade, and Industry; the Minister of Internal Affairs and Communications; the Minister of Economic and Fiscal Policy; and four private sector representatives (Iijima, *Koizumi kantei hiroku*, 20).

132. Katō, "Reforming the Japanese Bureaucracy"; Takenaka, *Kōzō kaikaku no shinjitsu*, 245. Koizumi's private secretary estimates that the council met 187 times during Koizumi's tenure (Iijima, *Koizumi kantei hiroku*, 20).

133. Katō, "Reforming the Japanese Bureaucracy," 35.

bers who supported his and Koizumi's views on privatization, excluding media, labor, and citizen group representatives.[134] The ultimate aim was to organize the CEFP to function like the Council of Economic Advisors in the United States,[135] as a panel of professionals who would provide expert advice to the prime minister on important economic issues.

Second, Takenaka and his aides drew up a list of five basic principles that were to guide CEFP discussions on postal privatization, which began in the fall of 2003.[136] Contrary to custom, in which "guiding principles" were subject to negotiation at various stages of the decision-making process, Takenaka presented his principles as inviolable and extracted a pledge from council members to adhere to them throughout the proceedings. Briefly stated, the principles were essentially requirements that postal privatization: 1) invigorate (*kassei*) society and the economy; 2) be consistent with past financial reforms; 3) enhance the convenience of postal customers; 4) make use of the human and infrastructural resources of the postal system; and 5) preserve the employment of the greatest possible number of employees within the system.[137] Significantly, the fourth and fifth principles acknowledged the concerns of the anti-privatization camp about the possible adverse effects of privatization on the postal network and its employees. The concessions did not, however, prevent council discussions from sinking into conflict.

Third, recognizing early on in the deliberations that the CEFP lacked the necessary expertise to proceed quickly and effectively on postal privatization, Takenaka established the "Takenaka Team" or "guerrilla unit" (*gerira butai*).[138] This was an informal working group of pro-reform bureaucrats, Takenaka aides, and economic and financial experts that was in charge of drawing up the plans for postal privatization. The team's very existence downgraded the CEFP into a venue for authorizing, rather than originating, those plans. It was the Takenaka Team that laid out the government's basic position on postal privatization, including the commitments to break up the postal system into independent,

---

134. Noble, "Front Door, Back Door," 113.
135. Yamawaki, *Yūsei kōbō*, 140.
136. Takenaka, *Kōzō kaikaku no shinjitsu*, 152.
137. Ibid., 149–51.
138. Takenaka had also established a "Takenaka Team" to grapple with the non-performing loan problem (ibid., 154).

service-specific firms; remove government guarantees of postal savings deposits and life insurance policies; subject the services to the same regulations that governed relevant private sector competitors; and establish a level playing field between the services and the private sector.[139]

Fourth, in a private meeting in January 2004, Takenaka and Koizumi resolved to establish the Postal Privatization Preparation Office (Yūsei min'eika junbishitsu; PPPO) within the Cabinet Secretariat. By serving as the CEFP's secretariat on postal privatization, the PPPO, with the Takenaka Team at its core, symbolized the fact that the Kantei had wrested full control of the privatization process from the MIC.[140] Consisting of nearly 100 market-oriented academics and officials from throughout the bureaucracy,[141] the PPPO was divided into a small office in charge of hammering out basic features of the privatization plan and a much larger unit for fleshing out the plan's details.[142] In September 2004, the PPPO produced the Postal Privatization Basic Plan (Yūsei min'eika kihon hōshin) and later drafted the corresponding legislation.[143]

Koizumi was a huge proponent of the PPPO, choosing several of its key members himself. On April 26, he arrived at the PPPO's offices in Kasumigaseki to attend its opening ceremonies, hung a wooden signboard on the wall that he had spontaneously calligraphed, and after greeting the new employees assembled before him, reminded them that they were there to serve the Japanese people.[144] The event was widely reported by the press, and the accompanying photograph of Koizumi, Takenaka, and a PPPO official standing next to the freshly painted signboard sent a clear message to the public that the prime minister was ultimately in charge of the postal privatization process.[145]

139. Ibid., 156–57.
140. Ibid., 157–58.
141. Yamawaki, *Yūsei kōbō*, 122–23.
142. Ibid., 244–45.
143. Takenaka, *Kōzō kaikaku no shinjitsu*, 122.
144. Ibid., 160; Iijima, *Koizumi kantei hiroku*, 241.
145. Takenaka, *Kōzō kaikaku no shinjitsu*, 156.

Fig. 6.1   Takenaka Heizō (left), Koizumi Jun'ichirō (center), and another official (right) at the Postal Privatization Preparation Office, April 2004. Koizumi's presence signified that the prime minister was ultimately in charge of the reform process. Used by permission of Mainichi/Aflo.

In the past, legislating postal reform followed a predictable script. Given the level of politicization within the postal sector, the broad parameters of non-routine postal policies would be set by the LDP or the prime minister. After an advisory committee issued its recommendations, postal bureaucrats would flesh out a series of bills that would then wind their way into the LDP's PARC, where members of the postal tribe (*yūsei zoku*) would make changes via the process of preliminary review. Upon receiving the endorsement of the LDP's Executive Council, the bills would then be forwarded to the Cabinet for final approval. The problem was that the process was so riddled with veto points that reform bills were often watered down beyond recognition by the time they reached the Diet—if they even got that far. In theory, Koizumi's brand of prime ministerial leadership (*kantei shugi*), which centralized the postal privatization process in the CEFP and, more specifically, the PPPO, altered this script by depriving the regime of its customary veto points.[146]

146. For more on Koizumi's influence on policymaking veto points more generally, see Estévez-Abe, "Japan's Shift Toward a Westminster System."

To the politicians and bureaucrats of the postal regime, this was nothing short of heretical.

But in the end, Koizumi and Takenaka failed to completely insulate the policy process from debilitating interest group pressures. One participant in a liaison committee (*renrakukai*) established under the CEFP observed that council deliberations were frequently slowed by demands from the MIC, which feared a substantial loss of power through privatization and was only willing to tolerate a plan that "suited its convenience."[147] Takenaka himself revealed that several PPPO bureaucrats had defied orders by leaking information about the deliberations to members of the postal tribe.[148] More problematically, Japan Post President Ikuta Masaharu and posts minister Asō Tarō stalemated the proceedings by opposing the government's requirement that the postal services be broken up into three independent services;[149] top LDP leaders threatened to withhold the party's approval of the government plan if Asō's concerns were not adequately addressed.[150] All the while, council members wrangled over what the corporate structure of the privatized services should look like and questioned Koizumi's target date of April 1, 2007 for launching the reforms.[151] After several weeks of stalemate, Koizumi called Ikuta and Asō into a rare private meeting and forced them to back down. In marked contrast to his behavior during the JH deliberations, Koizumi was no longer prepared to sit back and let others determine the course of policymaking.

On September 7, 2004, the CEFP formally approved the Postal Privatization Basic Plan, the blueprint for subsequent legislation. Three days later, after key LDP leaders lined up behind the government, the cabinet followed suit—but not without a fight.[152] In a dramatic encore

---

147. Interview, name withheld on request, Tokyo, July 13, 2006.

148. Takenaka, *Kōzō kaikaku no shinjitsu*, 176.

149. Ikuta opposed the breakup of the postal services for fear of losing the synergies among the three services and hence damaging the survival of the postal network.

150. Although Asō's staunch position may have been motivated by a concern for the future of the postal tribe, at least one scholar argues that Asō was more worried about alienating the rest of the LDP than appearing as if he were speaking on behalf of the "forces of resistance" (Itō, "Kantei shudōkei seisaku kettei to Jimintō," 32).

151. Iijima, *Koizumi kantei hiroku*, 244–45.

152. Takenaka, *Kōzō kaikaku no shinjitsu*, 165–71.

of his 2002 exploits, Koizumi secured these approvals by threatening to dissolve the cabinet, or worse, the Diet. LDP lawmakers condemned the prime minister's privatization plan and strong-arming tactics, but few had the courage to stand in his way and risk an electoral backlash.

After securing LDP and cabinet approval of the Basic Plan, Koizumi once again shuffled his cabinet—now dubbed the "Cabinet to Carry Out Postal Privatization" (Yūsei min'eika jitsugen naikaku)—and named Takenaka as minister of state for postal privatization.[153] Later that fall, during a dinner with ten government and LDP leaders, Koizumi testily announced that he would not stray from the Basic Plan in the months ahead and ordered his uncomfortable colleagues to stay the course. It was, Takenaka later recalled, a "declaration of war" (*sensen fukoku*).[154]

REACTIONS TO THE POSTAL PRIVATIZATION BASIC PLAN

In terms of its sheer scope, Koizumi's privatization blueprint was unprecedented in the history of Japanese postal reform. Japan Post would be broken up into four companies, one each for mail collection and delivery, postal savings, postal insurance, and the post office network, plus a government holding company that would eventually divest its shares in the postal savings and insurance companies. The holding company would retain at least one-third of its shares in each of the mail and network firms. Transforming the postal system into discrete, service-specific firms had three professed objectives: 1) to prevent losses in one service from adversely affecting the performance of the other services (risk interception); 2) to clarify the administrative responsibilities (*keiei sekinin*) of each service; and 3) to incentivize each service to minimize costs and become more results-oriented (*gyōseki hyōka*).[155]

The Basic Plan also included measures to level the playing field between the postal services and their competitors. The postal savings and insurance firms would be subjected to the same laws and regulations as other private-sector firms. Government guarantees for savings accounts and insurance policies would be eliminated, although they would remain in place for accounts and policies established before the actual

153. Iijima, *Koizumi kantei hiroku*, 247–48.
154. Takenaka, *Kōzō kaikaku no shinjitsu*, 181–82.
155. Hashimoto Kenji, "Yūsei jigyō no bapponteki minaoshi ni mukete," 4.

privatization process began. Finally, the plan deprived the postmasters and postal workers of their status as public servants, thereby reducing the size of the national civil service by one third. These and other provisions were also designed to provide the services with stronger incentives to turn a profit while increasing the range of postal products available to consumers.

In addition to touting the virtues of "efficiencies through competition,"[156] the Basic Plan included language and measures to reassure skittish citizens about the fate of their beloved post offices: the government would protect the postal network; the postal savings firm would conduct itself as a "family bank"; and the postal network company would continue to provide social services to the elderly in local communities.

As the government prepared to translate the Basic Plan into legislation, Takenaka took to the road in a postal privatization "television caravan." Traveling to points throughout the country, Takenaka spoke to local dignitaries and appeared on 21 local television programs.[157] Given the public's ambivalence about privatization, the publicity campaign came not a moment too soon. Following the 1997 release of the Administrative Reform Council's interim report, a *Nihon keizai shinbun* survey revealed that only 36 percent of voters supported the privatization of postal savings, while 54 percent opposed it.[158] By contrast, an *Asahi shinbun* poll conducted shortly after the Basic Plan's 2004 release showed that public opinion was warming to the idea of privatization, with 45 percent of those surveyed supporting Koizumi's proposal and only 33 percent opposing it; the remaining respondents were undecided.[159] But what troubled the government was the extent of public disinterest in the issue. In a list of five pressing issues currently before the government, postal privatization ranked dead last, with only *2 percent* of Japanese viewing it as the "most important" issue before the govern-

---

156. Keiichiro Kobayashi, "The Points of Contention Surrounding Postal Services Reform."

157. Takenaka, *Kōzō kaikaku no shinjitsu*, 175.

158. Conducted by the *Nihon keizai shinbun* on September 7–8, 1997. Reported by JPOLL (Japanese Public Opinion Database) at http://roperweb.ropercenter.uconn.edu

159. Cited in *Asahi Newspaper*, September 29, 2004.

ment.[160] In a Jiji Press poll that was also conducted in fall 2004, 73 percent of respondents claimed they knew little to nothing about the Basic Plan, while 62.6 percent said that they wished the government would do more to explain privatization to the public.[161] Even as late as March 2005, a Kyodo News survey of 1,015 voters revealed that only 22.7 percent wanted to see postal privatization enacted that year; 53.9 percent preferred more extensive discussions before the legislative process proceeded.[162] These statistics suggest that more Japanese approved than disapproved of privatization, but few really understood or cared about it.

In addition to explaining postal privatization to ordinary citizens, Takenaka's television caravan revealed the extent of government efforts to strike a balance between its commitment to liberal-economic reform within the postal sector and appeasing the postal lobby. In meeting after meeting, Takenaka argued that it was "socialistic thinking" to assume that the state should monopolize the postal services, repeating Koizumi's mantra that the government must transfer as many functions as possible to the private sector as Japan strived to enhance its global economic competitiveness. In reaction to complaints that privatization was too much too soon, he pointed to successful postal privatization efforts in the Netherlands, Germany, and other countries.[163] Takenaka also tried to reassure jittery rural residents that the government was committed to protecting the postal network, universal mail service, and many of the *himawari* and other social functions performed by the postal system.[164] To prove his point, he announced amidst great fanfare that the government would guarantee at least one postal facility for each village and establish a large government-administered fund (Community Contribution Fund: *Chiiki/shakai kōken kikin*) to assist struggling post offices.

---

160. Pension and welfare problems ranked at the top (52 percent), followed by economic and employment issues (28 percent), diplomacy and defense (9 percent), and amending the constitution (5 percent).

161. Reported and analyzed in Sadamitsu, "Yūsei min'eika kihon hōshin kettei uke yoron chōsa."

162. Cited in *Japan Times*, March 7, 2005.

163. Takenaka, *Kōzō kaikaku no shinjitsu*, 21, 29.

164. Ibid., 60–63.

Meanwhile, books defending the postal status quo proliferated on retail bookshelves. "I love mail," wrote one author, a former salaryman. "I'm one of those people who is moved by the sight of the mail carrier delivering the mail at the same time every day." Why, he asked, did the services need to be privatized? Why was privatization being forced on the public? The author then invited readers to log on to a new website run by the "Association for Fans of the Post Office" (Yūbinkyoku fan no kai).[165]

In his own way, Japan Post President Ikuta Masaharu helped fuel the ideological fires between the pro- and anti-privatization camps. As a top representative of Keizai dōyūkai, in 2001 Ikuta had advocated the complete abolition of postal savings and insurance. As President of Japan Post, however, he surprised observers by supporting privatization in principle but calling for the application of universal service not only to mail collection and delivery, as the Basic Plan stipulated, but also to the privatized postal savings and insurance firms—an internationally unprecedented proposal that Koizumi and Takenaka categorically rejected. Critics interpreted Ikuta's shifting stance on postal reform as evidence that he was falling victim to the persuasive powers of the postal regime. But Ikuta retorted that he had simply acquired a deeper understanding of the postal system and its impact on society. After touring post offices around the country, Ikuta was worried about the future of rural villages of which he himself was a product. There might be compelling economic reasons to shut down indebted rural post offices, he argued, but these entities had important financial and social functions to perform. Guaranteeing universal service for all three postal services would help struggling post offices stay afloat and serve their communities. Ikuta also spoke out against reducing employment levels within the postal system—a move that was widely expected within a privatized postal system—even though he had just trimmed approximately 20,000 workers from Japan Post's payroll. The privatized companies, he reasoned, would need to maintain employment at current levels in order to continue providing quality service to the public.[166] Ikuta may have had

---

165. Nomura, *Asunaro mura no sangeki*, 3–4. See http://www.post-fan.jp for information about the fan club.

166. Yamawaki, *Yūsei kōbō*, 33–35, 37.

reasons of his own to advocate broad universal service and high employment within the postal system, but his disagreements with the Basic Plan lent added legitimacy to the anti-privatization camp's argument that postal privatization would be hard on rural Japanese society.

Business and financial interests were also sending mixed signals about postal privatization. On the one hand, Keidanren and Keizai dōyūkai endorsed Koizumi's Basic Plan as the best possible option under prevailing political circumstances.[167] The commercial banking sector, on the other hand, continued to voice misgivings. The Japan Bankers Association was disappointed that the plan did nothing to directly reduce the number and size of postal savings accounts or to curtail the system's involvement in new financial ventures in which its sheer size gave it an unfair advantage.[168] In a fit of irritation, Takenaka retorted that the commercial banks were equating privatization to the "coming of the black ships."[169]

The postal tribe had its own concerns. In addition to their fears about the future of the postal network and their long-term electoral prospects, many LDP politicians worried about how the Koizumi plan would affect the fabric of local society. For instance, Arai Hiroyuki, one of the postal regime's best known spokespersons, opposed a government proposal to allow privatized post offices to become convenience stores on the grounds that this would put unfair competitive pressure on small retailers. The post office, Arai argued, should stick to what it did best: function as a "financial and social safety net" in the community.[170] To Arai, the beauty of the post office was that it embodied a distinctly Japanese "public business model" that addressed both the needs of individual consumers and the well-being of society. Arai also dismissed as un-tested speculation the government's argument that private postal firms could guarantee universal service, reminding the government of its historical mission to compensate for market deficiencies and guarantee a civil minimum.[171] Like the postmasters and many of his LDP col-

---

167. Inose, *Kessen,* 101.

168. Japan Bankers Association, "Chairman's Comments on the 'Basic Policy on the Privatization of Japan Post,'" September 10, 2004.

169. Inose, *Kessen,* 39.

170. Ibid., 148 and 164.

171. Interview, Arai Hiroyuki, Tokyo, March 26, 2003.

leagues, Arai still saw a role for the *ōyake* (official)—the MIC bureaucrat or local postmaster who stood for economic stability, fairness, and the interests of the weak. The unfettered market, he concluded, was grossly overrated.[172]

Many LDP politicians also spoke out against the breakup of the postal system into its three component services. Having one employee provide all three services, Arai pointed out, was a convenient, cost-effective way to run a post office,[173] but breaking them up would require a division of labor among postal employees that was likely to inconvenience the public. Minister of Internal Affairs and Communications Asō Tarō agreed.[174] Asō had a poor relationship with Koizumi and was angered that the prime minister had not consulted him in spring 2004 before appointing Takenaka as minister of state for postal privatization.[175] In retaliation, Asō pulled no punches in his criticisms of the Basic Plan, calling frequently for the retention of the three services under one corporate roof.

Many others—some of them Koizumi's friends—grumbled about the Basic Plan in general and Koizumi's concessions to the postal regime in particular. Economists complained about the national scope of the proposed postal savings firm, calling for a breakup of the company into regional firms in order to create a truly level playing field with the commercial banks. Borrowing a page from the postal regime's playbook—and in a marked departure from Koizumi's original position—the government countered that breaking up postal savings would hurt post offices in underpopulated areas where the volume of savings was low.[176] The economist Matsubara Satoru, a frequent advisor to the Koizumi government, criticized Koizumi for failing to adequately explain how

---

172. Inose, *Kessen*, 159. Many ordinary Japanese who opposed privatization agreed with Arai. Postal privatization, one citizens group argued, would decrease the power of bureaucrats (*kan*), a traditional source of social stability, while empowering the people (*min*)—not ordinary people but rather wealthy and influential businesspeople who were motivated by market principles. The end result of all this would be a widening of Japan's already troubling socio-economic "gaps" (*kakusa*). Shirokawa, "Doko ga mondai," 13–14.

173. Inose, *Kessen*, 148.

174. Yamawaki, *Yūsei kōbō*, 136.

175. *Japan Times*, March 6, 2004.

176. Interview, Yoshino Naoyuki, Faculty of Economics, Keiō University, Tokyo, January 8, 2007.

the plan would financially invigorate the private sector, or how the privatized postal services would acquire the necessary skills to make sound investment decisions.[177] Others simply railed Koizumi for taking reform too far. The LDP's Katō Kōichi, for example, criticized the prime minister for his fixation on reform, likening him a to "city politician" who had "no affinity for the soil." Katō believed that Koizumi's flippant nature and fixation on postal privatization and governmental decentralization were alienating voters, particularly in rural areas.[178]

Curiously, the fate of the commissioned postmasters figured only marginally in the growing controversies over postal privatization. The Basic Plan, for instance, had virtually nothing to say about the commissioned post office system aside from designating the privatized post offices as branch offices (*shiten*) of the network corporation and stripping the postmasters of their status as public servants. Japan Post President Ikuta, for his own part, had long wanted to streamline the system and subject the postmasters to periodic transfer, but stopped short of calling for the abolition of the commissioned post offices.[179] Policymakers—along with the attentive public—were at odds over the issue of the postmasters' future; some believed that the postmasters would work harder and turn a profit if fully exposed to market forces,[180] and others worried that the postmasters' loss of bureaucratic status would jeopardize the privatization process by eroding the public's trust in the postal system. But with memories of Zentoku's interference in the Hashimoto postal reform process still fresh in their minds, it appears that policymakers had resolved to postpone judgment on this hot-button issue to a later date.[181]

FROM BLUEPRINT TO BILLS

Koizumi and Takenaka shrugged off their critics and forged ahead with the Basic Plan, in spring 2005 securing the cabinet's endorsement of a series of four postal privatization bills. That the process had progressed this far was nothing short of remarkable, given the history of postal re-

---

177. *Japan Times*, September 11, 2004.
178. *Asahi Newspaper*, September 9, 2004.
179. Yamawaki, *Yūsei kōbō*, 192.
180. Inose, *Kessen*, 105.
181. Yamawaki, *Yūsei kōbō*, 194.

form and the fact that only a handful of LDP lawmakers openly supported the Basic Plan.[182] How, then, did Koizumi and Takenaka manage to transform their vision for postal privatization into concrete legislation without succumbing to the "forces of resistance"?

Part of the explanation, we have observed, had to do with Koizumi's
and Takenaka's ability to take full advantage of new policymaking organs like CEFP and to supplement those organs with more ad hoc ones
like the PPPO. Together, these institutions enabled the pro-privatization
team to reduce the effects of debilitating bureaucratic turf battles and
pressures from interest groups and *zoku* politicians. Had the CEFP and
the PPPO not existed, it is doubtful that the Basic Plan would have ever
seen the legislative light of day.

Second, enhanced executive powers enabled Koizumi on at least one
occasion to fend off bureaucratic efforts to regain the upper hand on
postal privatization. After failing to significantly influence the Basic Plan,
Koizumi's opponents in the MIC teamed up with postal tribe politicians
in early 2005 to float an alternative set of bills. Backed by Minister Asō,
the bills provided for cross-shareholding among the postal firms and for
the postal savings and insurance companies to directly subsidize the mail
and network firms. By encouraging institutional and financial interdependence among the postal companies, the bills promised to do a better
job of preserving the postal network and thus shoring up the electoral
fortunes of conservative politicians who depended on the postmasters'
support. The Koizumi camp dismissed the rival bills as financially untenable; since postal savings deposits were projected to shrink over the
next decade or two, the postal firms would soon find themselves looking
to the government for subsidies. The Koizumi camp also claimed that
it would be difficult to apply banking supervision rules to the MIC's ver-
sion of the postal savings firm, and that the entire scheme would under-
mine the principles of a "normal" financial market.[183] Arguing that barriers between the postal financial companies and the government must

---

182. Takenaka estimated that only 10 percent or so of his LDP colleagues supported
postal privatization (Takenaka, *Kōzō kaikaku no shinjitsu*, 180). At least two LDP politicians
I spoke with in 2003 put the estimate closer to 30 percent, but observed that few supporters were willing to make their private views public.

183. Interview, Kinoshita Nobuyuki, Director General, PPPO, Tokyo, January 9, 2007.

be removed, rather than reinforced, the Koizumi camp refused to give the bills a second thought. Amidst protests from Asō and members of the postal tribe, Koizumi then ordered the demotion of the two bureaucrats who had spearheaded the renegade scheme.[184] The incident, which was dubbed a "Koizumi shock" within the LDP,[185] was a stunning illustration of executive power. It also marked an essential step toward weakening the MIC's opposition to the Basic Plan.

Third, the MIC's aborted attempt to influence the policy process obscured an important development within the ministry that also worked to Koizumi's advantage: a growing rift among bureaucrats over the virtues of postal privatization. After 2003, more and more Japan Post employees and MIC officials were concluding that the now corporatized postal services would require more freedom to compete if they were to achieve greater profitability and uphold the national postal network.[186] There was also evidence that some Japan Post employees were beginning to resent state controls over budgeting and salaries and that they and postal officials were viewing privatization as inevitable—so inevitable, in fact, that the two groups were meeting secretly to discuss their options.[187] While it appears that many officials were worried about breaking the services into discrete companies, it is clear that the MIC was no longer speaking with a unified voice on postal privatization. The tide was turning, and at the price of unity within the postal regime.

Fourth, the government's willingness to compromise strengthened its position vis-à-vis the anti-privatization camp. Although Koizumi refused to budge on the fundamental tenets of the Basic Plan, he and Takenaka were prepared to address key demands from the postal regime early in the policy process. Among those concessions were promises to maintain one postal facility for every village and to introduce a large government-run fund to support individual post offices (the Community Contribution Fund). Although both schemes would weaken the postal system's freedom to cut costs, they helped strengthen political support for the idea of postal privatization. Meanwhile, both Koizumi and Takenaka

---

184. Yamawaki, *Yūsei kōbō*, 64–65.
185. Takenaka, *Kōzō kaikaku no shinjitsu*, 182.
186. Interview, Kinoshita Nobuyuki, Director General, PPPO, Tokyo, January 9, 2007.
187. Yamawaki, *Yūsei kōbō*, 92.

took pains to consult with relevant ministers during the legislative drafting stage, which Takenaka and his "guerrilla unit" ultimately controlled, knowing full well that not doing so would only increase the likelihood of legislative failure.

In the final analysis, Koizumi's efforts did little to dilute complaints from his staunchest LDP critics that he was defying policymaking custom. In mid-October 2004, former Minister of Internal Affairs and Communications Katayama Toranosuke—a friend of the postmasters and no fan of postal privatization—called on the prime minister to consult more regularly with LDP leaders on privatization, suggesting that a failure to do so would be undemocratic.[188] That same month, former Prime Minister Mori Yoshirō predicted on a Sunday morning television talk show that Koizumi's antics would cost the LDP an election, had one been imminent.[189] And in a speech to the Upper House in January 2005, Aoki Mikio demanded that Koizumi adopt a "sincere, humble, and cooperative" position on postal privatization.[190] Not to be outdone, Katō Kōichi grumbled that Koizumi harbored an irrational penchant for quarrels.[191] Katō was right, in a sense. As the protests intensified, Koizumi portrayed himself and his allies as righteous samurai warriors struggling to destroy the stronghold of an opposing feudal lord. "We have only filled in the outer and inner moats," he observed with relish after the Cabinet approved the Basic Plan in fall 2004. "We now have to take on the inner sanctum [*honmaru*]. The battles of winter and summer also await us."[192] Koizumi was evidently enjoying himself as he struck at the heart of LDP resistance.

Again and again the LDP took up the gauntlet, doing everything it could to stall the advance of privatization short of ousting their popular leader from power. For example, the party established a PARC subcommittee on postal privatization that met eleven times before releasing, on December 21, 2004, a petition (*mōshiire*) for an amended privatization plan that made fuller use of the postal network, paid more heed to the

188. *Japan Times*, October 15, 2004.
189. *Japan Times*, October 18, 2004.
190. *Japan Times*, January 26, 2005.
191. Yamawaki, *Yūsei kōbō*, 63.
192. *Asahi Newspaper*, September 17, 2004.

people's convenience, and guaranteed the social functions performed by the postal services.[193] Meanwhile, the Postal Services Roundtable (Yūsei jigyō konwakai) expanded under the leadership first of Nonaka and then of former Lower House Speaker Watanuki Tamisuke; by spring 2005 it included more than 200 Diet members. Although other smaller, overlapping groups had formed as well, including a study group (*benkyōkai*) centered around the LDP's postal tribe known as "The High Road" (Ōdōkai),[194] the roundtable was widely viewed as the nucleus of LDP resistance to postal privatization.[195]

In reaction to the LDP's foot-dragging, Koizumi played his last and most potent card: the threat of a snap election. On April 26, the LDP and Kōmeitō finally capitulated. Fearing that Koizumi would make good on his threat, the Executive Council broke with party tradition and moved to approve the bills on the basis of a majority—rather than a consensus—vote. Kamei Shizuka, by now an avowed enemy of the prime minister, was so incensed by the Executive Council's capitulation to Koizumi's pressures that he vetoed the final vote.[196]

At the eleventh hour, Koizumi's enhanced executive powers and electoral acumen had convinced a reluctant LDP and cabinet to endorse his privatization bills. But Koizumi had by no means ended the conflict; he had simply postponed it. As Koizumi's private secretary later explained, LDP leaders let Koizumi have his way in spring 2005 knowing full well that the ruling and opposition parties would have ample opportunity to emasculate the bills on the Diet floor.[197] To wit, Arai Hiroyuki, now a member of the Upper House, urged his disgruntled LDP colleagues to vote their individual conscience on postal privatization.[198] Party discipline was breaking down.[199]

---

193. Iijima, *Koizumi kantei hiroku*, 250–51.

194. Ōshita, *Kamei Shizuka*, 53.

195. *Japan Times*, March 9, 2005.

196. Iijima, *Koizumi kantei hiroku*, 257.

197. Ibid.

198. *Asahi Newspaper*, September 17, 2004. Arai lost his seat in the 2003 Lower House election but was elected to the Upper House in July 2004.

199. For a theoretical analysis of the factors that drove individual LDP lawmakers to defy party discipline on the postal privatization vote, see Nemoto, Krauss, and Pekkanen, "Policy Dissension and Party Discipline."

THE DIET DELIBERATES

As the government prepared to submit its privatization bills to the Diet in spring 2005, the postmasters entered full-blown crisis mode. Reeling from Koizumi's 2002 legislation and sensing more trouble ahead, Zentoku officials urged rank-and-file members in 2003 to continue their ongoing fight against radical postal reform and protect their cherished postal institutions.[200] The postmasters thus launched a massive lobbying campaign that targeted politicians from all points on the political spectrum. In 2006, Sonoda Hiroyuki, the pro-privatization LDP Diet member who headed the party's subcommittee on postal privatization, recalled that the pressure was at times overwhelming.[201]

Although still a force to be reckoned with, the postmasters were feeling the gradual loss of LDP support as Koizumi's privatization crusade gained momentum. Zentoku's May 2, 2005, annual meeting in Osaka was a telling illustration of just how far the exchange relationship between the postmasters and the ruling party had deteriorated. Once attended by a raft of high-ranking LDP politicians, the meeting boasted only one noteworthy LDP representative—Hasegawa Kensei, the freshman Upper House Diet member and former MIC career bureaucrat. In his address to the group, Hasegawa portrayed Koizumi and Takenaka as enemies of the postmasters and vowed to help defeat the privatization bills.[202] In another revealing moment, the heads of Zentei and Zen'yūsei, the two main postal unions, apologized to the postmasters for the trouble they had caused during their postwar campaigns against the commissioned post office system.[203] Several weeks later, on July 4, the postmasters and union members held their first joint demonstration in Nagatachō, the day before the Lower House voted on the bills.[204]

---

200. Zenkoku tokutei yūbinkyokuchōkai, *50-nen no ayumi*, preface.

201. Interview, Sonoda Hiroyuki, LDP Lower House Diet member, Tokyo, July 14, 2006. A leading member of the postal tribe was kept waiting for more than 30 minutes in the reception area of Mr. Sonoda's office while I—a foreigner—conducted my interview. It was a revealing example of the postal regime's political decline during the Koizumi years.

202. Yamawaki, *Yūsei kōbō*, 134.

203. Ibid., 133–34.

204. Ibid.

As the bills moved into the Diet and the Koizumi camp prepared for a "protracted war" (*jikyūsen*),[205] the DPJ launched its own attack on the privatization plan. Given the DPJ's reformist stance and past collaboration with Koizumi on postal privatization, many observers had expected the party to try to one-up the government by proposing a more radical privatization plan. But the DPJ surprised everyone by failing to deliver until after the 2005 election, when opportunities to change the bills' contents had all but evaporated. In the interim, the party resorted to sabotage. In May 2005, the DPJ voted against establishing a special Lower House committee to deliberate on the bills and boycotted the chamber for twenty days. When the party finally returned to the chamber on June 3, it bombarded Takenaka with questions that had little bearing on the bills' contents, accused Takenaka and his team of scandalous behavior, and defied Diet custom by failing to submit its questions in advance of the sessions.[206]

The DPJ's failure to sway the direction of postal privatization was testament to Koizumi's and Takenaka's leadership skills. The two men had put the internally divided DPJ in a no-win situation. Supporting the government's privatization plan would have alienated Zentei's patrons and other elements of the party's left wing, and opposing it outright would have angered its reformist members and damaged its public image. Launching a carefully choreographed assault on the specifics of the bills, however, would have exposed the party's loss of initiative to Koizumi and Takenaka. DPJ President Okada Katsuya struggled in vain to strike a balance among the party's contending groups.[207] The ultimate irony is that while in the past the DPJ had been quick to attack the LDP for catering to interest groups, once Koizumi had seized the initiative on postal privatization, the DPJ was all but immobilized by special interests.[208]

After a staggering 109 hours of committee deliberations,[209] the Lower House submitted the bills to a vote on July 5 amidst jeers from the

---

205. Takenaka, *Kōzō kaikaku no shinjitsu*, 196.
206. *Asahi shinbun*, May 25, 2005; Takenaka, *Kōzō kaikaku no shinjitsu*, 200–212.
207. Yamawaki, *Yūsei kōbō*, 165.
208. Ibid., 161.
209. Takenaka, *Kōzō kaikaku no shinjitsu*, 216. Takenaka estimated that this matched the length of 1960 Lower House deliberations on the U.S.-Japan Mutual Security Treaty.

ruling and opposition parties and warnings from Koizumi that "opposition would be tantamount to a movement to overthrow the cabinet" (*hantai wa tōkaku undō da*).[210] The bills passed by a mere five-vote margin, with 37 LDP Diet members voting against them and 14 others either abstaining from or boycotting the vote.[211] Fifty-one out of 250 ruling party lawmakers had followed Arai Hiroyuki's entreaty to vote their individual consciences on postal privatization. The next day, Zentoku representatives visited many of their LDP friends to thank them for their support.[212]

A week later the bills reached the Upper House, where LDP opposition to postal privatization—and to Koizumi's leadership tactics—was even more pronounced. As in the Lower House, a special committee was established to deliberate on the bills. The DPJ's left wing initially stole the show by insisting that postal workers retain their status as public servants and accusing Koizumi and Takenaka of trying to remake Japan in America's (excessively) capitalist image.[213] While lawmakers wrangled, the postmasters descended en masse on Nagatachō. As Takenaka later recounted, their presence was redolent with meaning:

On Tuesday, July 27, upon returning to my Upper House Diet members' office for the first time in a while, I sensed a strange atmosphere surrounding the building. A tremendously large group of petitioners had flooded the place. They were commissioned postmasters from the localities, pressuring the Upper House Diet members from their regions to oppose the privatization bills. They'd come all the way to Tokyo to exert open [political] pressure [on the privatization process].

---

210. Ibid., 66. Koizumi was not the only one to issue tough warnings to LDP lawmakers in the summer of 2005. Legend has it that leaders of the LDP's anti-privatization faction cajoled members of the postal tribe and other LDP colleagues to sign a "blood oath" (*keppanjō*) to vote against privatization. In true samurai spirit, Watanuki Tamisuke informed his colleagues that those who violated the oath would "vomit blood and die, and then descend into hell." A small number of those who dared to defy the oath suffered no such divine retribution, but were unlucky enough to lose their seats in the September election (Ōshita, *Kamei Shizuka*, 54–55).

211. The final tally was 233 yes votes to 228 no votes. Among those who voted against the bills were two vice ministers and two parliamentary secretaries; Koizumi fired them all within hours of the vote (*Japan Times*, July 6, 2005).

212. Yamawaki, *Yūsei kōbō*, 135.

213. Takenaka, *Kōzō kaikaku no shinjitsu*, 219–20.

It goes without saying that the postmasters are public servants and that it is illegal for them to participate in political activities. But they had vacated their offices in order to engage in these activities. I thought to myself that this sort of disregard for appearances was a mark of the postal system—and of the postmasters' power. At the time of JNR privatization, did local stationmasters ever intrude on [*oshikakeru*] Diet members' buildings in the name of anti-privatization? I concluded that once postal privatization was carried out, a system of more responsible governance would have to be introduced.[214]

The postmasters' petition campaign had the desired effect: on August 8, after 80 hours of committee deliberations, the chamber rejected the bills by a vote of 125 to 108; 22 LDP lawmakers had opposed the bills and 8 more had abstained from or boycotted the vote. Even more so than their Lower House colleagues, Upper House LDP lawmakers had voted their consciences. The forces of resistance had scored a major and potentially decisive victory.

Stage III: The 2005 Election and Beyond

What happened next is now the stuff of political legend. Arguing that the Upper House vote constituted an untenable victory for powerful vested interests and the bloated civil service, Koizumi dissolved the Lower House on the evening of August 8 (the so-called *yūsei kaisan*; "postal dissolution") and called an election; the ballot was later scheduled for September 11, 2005. As symbolized by one of his campaign slogans, "Don't stop the reforms!" (*kaikaku o tomeru na!*), the election was to be fought as a referendum on postal privatization and the future of structural reform. If voters rejected postal privatization by voting against the LDP/ Kōmeitō coalition, Koizumi would step down as LDP president and prime minister.[215] Koizumi then proceeded to withhold the LDP's official endorsement of the 37 candidates who had voted against the bills— the postal "rebels" (*zōhansha*)—and recruit young, pro-privatization first-time candidates—the "assassins" (*shikaku*)—to run against them. By cleansing the LDP of anti-reformist elements and casting the election in clear policy terms, Koizumi had presented the country with a black-

---

214. Ibid., 221.
215. *Japan Times*, August 9, 2005.

and-white choice between change and stagnation.[216] It was a masterful manipulation of the voters, many of whom were still ambivalent about—if not downright confused by—postal privatization.[217]

Koizumi's adversaries in the LDP were appalled by his actions. Fearing defeat, most disapproved of his open defiance of LDP electoral practices and consensus-based norms.[218] "An attempt to pit an LDP member against another [in the same constituency]," remarked postal rebel Kobayashi Kōki, "reminds me of the Roman Empire forcing prisoners to fight against ferocious beasts simply for the emperor's pleasure."[219] (Kobayashi, it turns out, lost his seat to Environment Minister and former anchorwoman Koike Yuriko on September 11.) Clearly, the 2005 election was for many LDP politicians as much a battle over Koizumi's top-down leadership tactics as it was a referendum on postal privatization.[220]

In a bid to more effectively support "reformist" candidates in the election, a number of postal rebels banded together to form new political parties. Arai Hiroyuki and Kobayashi Kōki helped establish the New Party Japan (Shintō Nippon; NPJ) under the leadership of maverick Nagano Governor Tanaka Yasuo, himself an opponent of postal privatization. Kamei Shizuka joined forces with Watanuki Tamisuke,

---

216. Many of Koizumi's critics argued that his simplistic portrayal of the election as a vote for or against postal privatization and long-term reform obscured the reform issues that voters cared about most, like pensions (Shirokawa, "Doko ga mondai," 11).

217. For a quantitative analysis of the effects of Koizumi's leadership style, policy issues, and party manifestos on voting behavior in the 2005 election, see Ikeda Ken'ichi, "The Impact of the Postal Reform on Japanese Voters."

218. Traditionalists in the LDP complained not only about Koizumi's strong-arming tactics during the postal reform process, but also about his refusal to adhere to factional alignments, seniority rules, and other informal party rules as he made his cabinet and other appointments. For more on Koizumi's defiance of party custom, see Nemoto, Krauss, and Pekkanen, "Party Dissention and Party Discipline."

219. *Japan Times*, August 11, 2005.

220. Estévez-Abe, "Japan's Shift Toward a Westminster System," 638.

Kamei Hisaoki, and Hasegawa Kensei, among others,[221] to launch the People's New Party (Kokumin shintō; PNP).[222] In a not-so-veiled criticism of Koizumi's leadership tactics, the PNP vowed to "respect the voice of each party member."[223]

Koizumi's electoral gambit administered a coup de grâce to the electoral partnership between the LDP and the postmasters. In the lead-up to the 2004 Upper House election, a number of Taiju members had threatened to abandon the party in retaliation for Koizumi's reforms;[224] the fact that the postmasters managed to gather only 280,000 votes behind their favorite candidate suggests that several had delivered on that threat. The events of 2005 simply widened the scope of the postmasters' revolt. Although some postmasters opted to support LDP candidates on the assumption that Koizumi was nothing but a passing phenomenon,[225] Zentoku and Taiju officially abandoned the party during the campaign. (This did not, however, stop the postmasters from contacting virtually all LDP candidates at their local constituency offices, pressuring them to stand up to Koizumi and his privatization plans.[226]) Both associations vowed to back the rebels in constituencies where they were running as either independents or members of the PNP or NPJ. Where there were no rebels running, association chapters were given the freedom to back whomever they preferred. For the first time in their postwar history, the postmasters failed to speak with a unified voice in an election.

With the postmasters' backing, fifteen rebels—most of them in rural or semi-rural constituencies—were reelected,[227] including former Minister of Posts and Telecommunications Noda Seiko, Watanuki Tamisuke,

---

221. Former Minister of Economy, Trade, and Industry Hiranuma Takeo joined the party after successfully running as an independent in the 2005 election.

222. While the NPJ is widely perceived as having an urban bias in its policy preferences, the PNP is more representative of the countryside.

223. Ōshita, *Kamei Shizuka*, 31.

224. *Asahi Newspaper*, July 13, 2004.

225. It appears that many LDP officials also believed that "normalcy" would return to Japanese politics following Koizumi's departure. Interview, Arai Hiroyuki, Tokyo, March 26, 2003; Christensen, "An Analysis of the 2005 Japanese General Election," 502.

226. Interview, Sonoda Hiroyuki, LDP Lower House Diet member, Tokyo, July 14, 2006.

227. Christensen, "An Analysis of the 2005 Japanese General Election," 504.

Hiranuma Takeo,[228] and Kamei Shizuka.[229] In addition, two rebel incumbents (Kamei Hisaoki and Taki Makoto) who had lost their seats in single-member constituencies were returned to the Diet on the PR list—the so-called rebel zombies.[230] The rebels' respectable showing can be explained by a number of factors, not least of which was the zealous mobilization of the postmasters associations in support of their campaigns—a phenomenon that highlighted the continuing importance of clientelistic ties in non-urban constituencies.[231] Money was also a consideration. As Matthew Carlson explains, compared to Koizumi's fresh-blooded assassins, the incumbent rebels were advantaged by years of fundraising experience and the freedom to transfer stockpiled campaign funds out of the LDP even after they had lost the party's endorsement.[232]

At the end of the day, the LDP emerged from the September 11 election with a stunning 296 seats. The Kōmeitō added 31 seats to the coalition's majority, and the DPJ lost 64 seats. Thanks in no small part to Koizumi's skillful campaign tactics—dubbed "Koizumi Theater" (*Koizumi gekijō*) by his detractors, his control over the LDP's selection of candidates in single-member districts, and his manipulation of the party's PR list so that many of his (inexperienced and under-funded) assassins were all but guaranteed victory, the LDP had secured its largest win since the 1986 Lower House election.[233]

On October 11, the Lower House passed Koizumi's package of six postal privatization bills with 200 votes to spare. Of the rebels who had

---

228. Koizumi forced Hiranuma to resign his cabinet post in August 2005 after he refused to support postal privatization.

229. Noda met frequently with Zentoku throughout the campaign. She beat her opponent, a professional economist, by 15,800 votes in a single-member district in Gifu prefecture (Yamawaki, *Yūsei kōbō*, 177).

230. Carlson, "Japan's Postal Privatization Battle," 612.

231. I am grateful to Ethan Scheiner for pointing this out to me. For more on the history and significance of clientelistic ties in elections, see Scheiner, *Democracy Without Competition in Japan*.

232. Carlson, "Japan's Postal Privatization Battle," 611–14. Carlson also shows how Koizumi tightened LDP rules after the 2005 election so that candidates could no longer transfer funds from their party branches to alternative political organizations after losing the party's endorsement.

233. *Japan Times*, September 13, 2005. The LDP secured 300 seats in 1986.

been reelected on September 11, only a small handful, including Kamei Shizuka and Hiranuma Takeo, voted against the bills. The Upper House followed suit three days later with a 34-vote margin. The bills were passed unchanged save for one small point: to accommodate the delays caused by the election and allow for the reconfiguration of the postal system's computer network, the government agreed to postpone the start date for the privatization process from April to October 2007. Koizumi would tolerate no other amendments.

Conclusion

Koizumi may have overstated things a little by portraying postal privatization as the biggest reform since the Meiji Restoration,[234] but he had, by all accounts, accomplished a great deal. As the concluding chapter elaborates, the institutional and administrative structure of the postal system had been overturned and the power of the postal regime significantly reduced. Theoretically, private financial firms could look forward to a more level playing field in their respective markets. Prime ministerial leadership over the policymaking process had been strengthened, and to the detriment of bureaucratic influence. Last but not least, Koizumi had loosened the stranglehold of *zoku* politicians and special interests over the policy process and accelerated the decline of intra-LDP factions. From the vantage point of late 2005, it appeared that the Japanese political economy had been transformed.

Postal privatization was the result of innovative leadership exercised in a changing institutional, political, and ideological environment. Policymaking institutions launched in 2001 had given Koizumi and his allies the bureaucratic and political space to outmaneuver privatization's opponents. An accelerating decline—one that Koizumi helped fuel—in the exchange relationship between the LDP and the postmasters, combined with deepening divisions within the MIC, had diluted the postal regime's power and enhanced Koizumi's influence over the policy process. Koizumi's leverage was further strengthened by the growing legitimacy of comprehensive financial reform following many years of on-and-off recession and in anticipation of intensifying demographic pressures on

234. *Japan Times*, October 14, 2004.

public coffers. The postal system was the last, untouched frontier of financial reform, and proponents of the postal status quo found it more and more difficult to sidestep change.

Could postal privatization have succeeded had Koizumi not been at the helm? Probably not. As this chapter has illustrated, it was Koizumi's risk-taking leadership style that enabled changing institutional and political environments to yield significant results. To be sure, Japan has had a few innovative prime ministers in the past (Tanaka, Nakasone, and Hashimoto immediately come to mind), but none matched Koizumi in both their commitment to market-oriented reform and willingness to so dramatically defy the norms and taboos of the policymaking and electoral processes. But the era in which Koizumi governed is a telling illustration of the limits of leadership as the sole explanation for postal privatization's success. Had Koizumi been in power before the institutions created by the 1998 Basic Law for the Reform of Central Ministries and Agencies were introduced, it is unlikely that he would have been able to formulate a comprehensive postal privatization plan and translate it into concrete legislation. Had he governed before the 1994 reform of the Lower House electoral rules and the changes they imposed on LDP factions and presidential leadership, he would have faced much higher risks when he gambled the fate of his government on a snap election, manipulated the selection of LDP candidates, and conducted the 2005 election strictly on policy terms. In short, Koizumi's power depended as much on the institutional and political environment of the early 2000s as that environment depended on him to reach its full potential.[235]

The story of postal privatization involved more than institutional and political change; it also marked the latest stage in a long-term debate in postwar Japan between two contending visions of the political economy. At one level, as T. J. Pempel writes, the privatization story marked a division "between 'continuity' and 'change,' 'resistance' and 'reform,'" and "'pork' and 'productivity.'"[236] But the debates also touched on contend-

---

235. Or as Margarita Estévez-Abe put it from the perspective of the relationship between structure and agency: "Koizumi is as much a 'product' of *structural* changes in how politics is played as he is an agent of specific rule changes" ("Japan's Shift Toward a Westminster System, 633).

236. Pempel, "Learning to Lose is for Losers," 109.

ing sets of values—one old, the other new. While proponents of the postal status quo advocated the survival of an activist, paternalist government, reformers pressed for a smaller, more laissez-faire state. One side championed the virtues of financial and social security, equality, and community, and the other supported the principles of individualism, self-responsibility, and market competition. Both sides argued that their preferred vision for the postal system served the public interest, with the postal regime and its supporters defending the ability of government (or public) enterprise to serve the common good, and the Koizumi camp claiming that markets were perfectly capable of doing the job. As the privatization process unfolded and tensions rose, the two sides verbally abused one another. The postal regime, Koizumi and Takenaka cynically remarked, were out-dated defenders of socialistic thinking that had no place in a globalizing world, likening elements of the postal regime to the inner sanctum (*honmaru*) of the last remnants of feudal power.[237] Not to be outdone, regime representatives branded Koizumi a handmaiden of soulless, capitalist values. "The person who does not recognize in the post office the embodiment of Japanese culture," Arai Hiroyuki wrote in 2003, "cannot be a true Japanese."[238] Viewed in these terms, Koizumi's victory may not have been as epoch-making as the Meiji Restoration, but it certainly was the biggest single retreat since the 1980s administrative reform movement from the values and ideas of the Japanese developmental state. What remains to be assessed, however, is the actual scope and depth of that retreat.

---

237. Koizumi, "Foreword," 4.
238. Arai, *Yūbinkyoku o Amerika ni uriwatasuna*, 44.

CONCLUSION

The Revenge of the Postal Regime

Japan today, in the wake of Koizumi's theatrical politics, has lost many of the features that used to underpin Japanese society: the placid and graceful sense of unity, a sense of fellowship, and sympathy among citizens . . . . Instead we are faced with a society where . . . young people are preoccupied by the pursuit of wealth. It is also a society where corruption is widespread—from central government officials to prefectural governors. All of these developments stem from the shift toward a profit-oriented society modeled on the United States. Japanese should reacquaint themselves with a culture of shame, and learn to have a higher regard for morality and dignity. The administration should strive for a society that restores the spirit of *bushidō* . . . which involves self-sacrificing dedication to the public interest.

—Nakasone Yasuhiro

Former Prime Minister Nakasone's lament would seem to suggest that Koizumi Jun'ichirō had revolutionized Japan—but not for the better. By overemphasizing neoliberal economic principles, Nakasone suggested, Koizumi had struck at the heart of Japan's communal society, pushing the country toward a new cultural ethos that embraced the worst of American values. Others agreed. LDP Diet member and former Koizumi ally Katō Kōichi argued that by weakening the foundations of "human society" (*ningen shakai*), Koizumi's reform agenda had deprived ordinary Japanese of a defining social mission. "In the Meiji period," Katō observed, "Japan focused on developing its economy and military. After the war, our aim was catching up to Western economies. Now,

EPIGRAPH: Comments translated in *Daily Yomiuri*, January 7, 2007.

in our efforts to meet the challenges of globalization, we're losing our sense of purpose [*mokuhyō ishiki*]. This is our biggest problem today."[1]

The commissioned postmasters also bemoaned the loss of Japanese tradition and a sense of purpose following the October 2005 passage of Koizumi's postal reforms. With privatization, Maejima Hisoka's post office—a community focal point that to many Japanese represented a uniquely humanitarian way of life—faced possible bankruptcy, layoffs, and a decline in its social welfare functions. After decades of zealously shielding the commissioned post office system against threats from first left-leaning unions and then the neoliberal postal privatization movement, the postmasters braced themselves for the demise of the defining institutions of their profession.[2]

Whereas Koizumi's detractors marked the passing of better days, his proponents welcomed the political changes to come. One analyst proclaimed that Koizumi had orchestrated a veritable regime change, dealing the final blow to Tanaka Kakuei's brand of "interest distribution politics" (*reiki haibun seiji*) and ushering in a "2005 system" (*2005-nen taisei*) that prioritized decisive prime ministerial leadership. Koizumi's postal privatization process, he opined, was destined to produce a more prosperous and democratic future.[3]

With the benefit of hindsight, we know that neither the cultural doomsayers nor the political optimists had called Koizumi's reforms correctly. Yes, postal privatization marked a significant step toward a more market-oriented political economy. And yes, Koizumi had pulled the rug out from under a postal regime that had done so much in the past to stymie market-oriented reform. But Koizumi also granted a number of concessions to his political foes that preserved some of the basic values and institutions of the old state-run services. These concessions, moreover, have allowed the "forces of resistance" to partially regroup and threaten some of Koizumi's accomplishments. In short, Koizumi Jun'ichirō may have introduced some transformative changes to the postal services, but by no means did he erase Maejima's institu-

---

1. Katō Kōichi, lecture, Saitama University, July 13, 2006.

2. Interview, four commissioned postmasters, Kitakyūshū, July 10, 2006.

3. Yamawaki, *Yūsei kōbō*, 5, 8.

tional legacy and the vested interests that supported it. As a result, the future of the post office continues to remain uncertain.

Letting the Private Sector Do
What the Private Sector Can Do

The privatization legislation that was passed by the Diet in mid-October 2005 introduced major structural changes to the postal services. On October 1, 2007, Japan Post was dissolved and primary responsibility for postal operations divided among four joint-stock companies: Japan Post Service Co., Ltd., which administers the collection and delivery of mail; Japan Post Bank Co., Ltd.; Japan Post Insurance Co., Ltd.;[4] and Japan Post Network Co., Ltd., the entity that oversees the network of local post offices and to which many of the functions of the three other service companies are delegated.[5] All four firms fall under the jurisdiction of Japan Post Holdings Co., Ltd., a government-owned holding company. When the privatization process began in late 2007, the savings and insurance firms boasted combined financial assets of approximately 300 trillion yen—188 trillion in postal savings deposits and 113 trillion in insurance policy contracts.[6]

Japan Post Group's work force totaled just over 240,000 full-time employees,[7] making it the largest corporate work force in Japan.[8] In autumn 2007, the two main postal unions—the once militant Zentei, with approximately 136,000 members, and the more moderate Zen'yūsei, with 84,000—merged to form the Japan Post Group Union.[9] All postal employees, including the commissioned and ordinary postmasters, lost their status as public servants.

The 2005 legislation states that Japan Post Holdings must begin selling its shares in the service firms by 2011. For Japan Post Bank and

---

4. Postal savings accounts and insurance policies that predate privatization fall under the purview of a special fund (Dokuritsu gyōsei hōjin yūbin chokin/Kan'i seimei hoken kanri kikō) administered directly by the MIC.

5. In addition, Japan Post Network can offer products and services that are unconnected to mail and postal savings and insurance.

6. *Japan Times*, October 2, 2007.

7. Japan Post, *Annual Report: Postal Services in Japan: 2007.9*, 25–27.

8. Sakai, "The Privatization of Japan Post is Unstoppable," 1.

9. *Japan Times*, June 22, 2007.

Japan Post Insurance, the privatization process should be completed by 2017. Japan Post Holdings, however, will continue to exist beyond 2017 as a partially government-owned holding company. As part of the government's legal obligation to guarantee universal service in the collection and delivery of mail, the holding company will control one-third of the shares in each of the mail and network firms.

Several of the postal system's competitive advantages were abolished as of October 1, 2007, most conspicuously the explicit government guarantee of postal savings accounts and life insurance policies. Now, postal savings deposits of up to 10 million yen and interest on those deposits are covered by the deposit insurance system, just like deposits in other private-sector banks. (The government guarantee will remain intact for postal savings accounts and insurance policies that were established on or before September 30, 2007.) Second, the last vestiges of the system of tax exemptions for postal savings depositors (the *maruyū* system) were abolished. Third, the postal savings and insurance firms must now pay corporate, property, and other taxes, although many of these obligations are being phased in gradually.[10] Finally, the firms must abide by the same industry laws, regulations, and oversight procedures that govern their respective competitors in the private sphere.[11]

The government's supervisory role within the postal system has also changed. In accordance with the stipulations of the 2005 legislation, on November 10, 2005, the government established the Postal Privatization Promotion Headquarters (Yūsei min'eika suishin honbu) to serve as the primary coordinator of the privatization process during both the preparation (2005–2007) and transition (2007–2017) periods.[12] The organ is headed by the prime minister and consists of the Minister of Internal Affairs and Communications, the Minister of Finance, and the heads of

---

10. The privatization legislation stipulates, for instance, that the postal insurance and banking firms will be exempted during the transition period from paying license recordation taxes, real estate acquisition taxes, and automobile acquisition taxes for asset flows from Japan Post into the two privatized firms (Cohen, "Policy Challenges and the Privatization of Japan Post," 16).

11. These laws include the Banking Act, for postal savings, and the Business Insurance Act, for postal insurance.

12. Interview, Kinoshita Nobuyuki, Director General, Postal Privatization Promotion Office, Tokyo, January 9, 2007.

other key economic ministries. That same month, the Postal Privatization *Preparation* Office (Yūsei min'eika junbi shitsu) was reconstituted as the Postal Privatization *Promotion* Office (Yūsei min'eika suishin shitsu), placed under the jurisdiction of the Headquarters, and charged with the task of overseeing the day-to-day business of the privatization process. The PPPO also functions as the secretariat to the five-member Postal Privatization Committee (Yūsei min'eika iinkai), which was set up under the Headquarters in April 2006 to monitor the privatization process, provide advice to relevant ministries about licensing new entrants into the postal markets, make recommendations about the expansion of services, and so on. Headed by Tanaka Naoki, the former chairman of Koizumi's Roundtable on Postal Services Reform, the committee must provide the Headquarters with a critical assessment of the privatization process every three years. In contrast to the days when postal bureaucrats called the shots within the postal sector, these new organs have applied detailed transparency rules to their proceedings and policies.[13]

The once mighty postal bureaucracy emerged from the postal privatization process with its influence diminished and its morale low. Unlike the policy process surrounding the privatization of NTT, which was centered in the Ministry of Posts and Telecommunications and resulted in an expansion of the ministry's regulatory powers over the telecommunications sector,[14] the postal privatization process occurred outside of MIC corridors and dramatically reduced the ministry's powers over the postal services. Although the MIC continues to exercise regulatory and licensing authority over the mail and network firms,[15] as well as direct control over postal savings accounts and insurance policies that were established prior to privatization, its influence over the new postal savings and insurance services has been drastically reduced. Moreover, although the MIC was heavily involved after October 2005 in preparing

---

13. Committee minutes and other relevant information can be accessed through a government website: http://www.yuseimineika.go.jp (last accessed October 24, 2011).

14. See Vogel, *Freer Markets, More Rules.*

15. The MIC will continue to license new entrants into the mail delivery market. As of this writing, however, the government has not yet liberalized the many regulations relating to competition within the mail service that were established by legislation enacted in 2002 (see Chapter 6). It is still inordinately difficult, in other words, for firms other than Japan Post Service to deliver the mail.

the postal network for the changes to come and served as an advisor to other bureaucratic organs connected to the various postal services,[16] the ministry's influence was curtailed once primary authority over the transition and privatization processes was granted to new, supra-ministerial organs lodged in the Cabinet Office. In a telling illustration of the damage wrought by these changes to the ministry's esprit de corps, in the months preceding October 2007, the number of bureaucrats in the MIC's postal divisions declined as several sought transfer to the more innovative Japan Post Group.[17]

With the passage of Koizumi's postal privatization legislation, the *iriguchi* (entrance) to the FILP system theoretically narrowed. Now that the postal savings and insurance systems were to be dislodged from the state's control and exposed to freer market forces, many predicted that Japan Post Bank and Japan Post Insurance would seek more lucrative returns on their funds by investing more of them in private markets at home and abroad, rather than in conservative government bonds. To help cement the break between the postal financial services and the FILP, Koizumi and Takenaka reduced the number of government financial institutions that had once played a major role in administering FILP funds.[18] These developments, combined with the incremental changes to the FILP introduced since the Hashimoto administration, helped streamline FILP institutions, rationalize accounting procedures, enhance transparency, and reduce the size of the overall FILP budget and the portion of that budget devoted to public works projects.[19]

Ceteris paribus, postal privatization produced a number of institutional and market-oriented changes that advance the ideals of economic liberalism. As the postal financial services lose their formal government guarantees and experience the same regulatory controls that govern private-sector financial institutions, a more level playing field is created between the postal financial services and its competitors. This, Koizumi

---

16. Interview, Postal Administration Bureau officials, MIC, Tokyo, January 10, 2007.

17. Interview, MIC official, Philadelphia, February 8, 2007.

18. Starting in 2008, two financial institutions were privatized, one abolished, and the remaining five consolidated into one public corporation (Cargill and Sakamoto, *Japan Since 1980*, 217).

19. Noble, "Front Door, Back Door," 115. For more on the FILP reform process, see Park, *Spending Without Taxation*, especially Chapters 7 and 8.

and many economists believed, should be good for the country. As competition between the postal financial services and their private-sector competitors intensifies, the bloat in the postal savings and insurance systems should shrink as ordinary Japanese embrace new incentives to save and invest their income elsewhere. Meanwhile, enhanced competition within the private financial sector, combined with new motivations for the postal savings and insurance firms to pursue more profitable investment opportunities, should attract more foreign investment into the country,[20] contribute to stronger economic growth rates, and, over the long haul, expand government coffers.

Financially, it appears that the postal services performed fairly well during the first three-and-a-half years under Japan Post Group's wing. As Tables C.1 and C.2 illustrate, in FY 2008 and FY 2009 Japan Post Holdings, the financial firms, and the Group as a whole experienced noteworthy increases in their total net income and net assets. But these figures mask some troubling trends—even for the financial services. The postal savings system, for instance, is struggling with a long-term decline in its total volume of deposits. Peaking in late FY 1999 at 260 trillion yen, or one-third of total household savings, total deposits slipped to 191 trillion yen by FY 2006 and 176 trillion yen in FY 2009.[21] Although Japan Post Bank has managed to significantly reduce the rate of decline in recent years, as the population ages and the financial sector continues to diversify, it is highly unlikely that the service will experience another surge in deposits comparable to that of the 1990s. Consumer demand for postal life insurance policies has also been variable. Between FY 2001 and FY 2006, the number of new policies sold dropped from 5.19 million to just 2.38 million.[22] Japan Post Insurance has since managed to reverse this decline; over the three consecutive fiscal years ending March 31, 2010, the number of policies sold increased from approximately 1.8 million to 2 million. Meanwhile, the firm has experienced some positive trends in the sale of its individual annuities; between FY

---

20. *Japan Times*, March 29 and October 2, 2007.

21. Yoshino, "Yūbin chokin no shōrai to zaisei tōyūshi," 57; Japan Post Group, *Annual Report: 2010*, 47.

22. Japan Post, *Postal Services in 2006*, 13; Japan Post, *Postal Services in 2007*, 14.

Table C.1: Japan Post Group Net Income (in billions of yen)

Fiscal Year	JP Group	JP Holdings	JP Network	JP Service	JP Bank	JP Insurance
2007	277.2	42.5	4.6	69.4	152.1	7.6
2008	422.7	109.0	40.8	29.8	229.3	38.3
2009	450.2	145.3	32.9	47.4	296.7	70.1

SOURCE: Japan Post Group, *Annual Report: 2009*, 18; *Annual Report: 2010*, 10.

Table C.2: Japan Post Group Net Assets (in billions of yen)

Fiscal Year	JP Group	JP Holdings	JP Network	JP Service	JP Bank	JP Insurance
2007	8,311.4	8,046.5	204.6	269.4	8,076.8	904.2
2008	8,746.1	8,147.1	244.3	281.9	8,179.5	1,072.7
2009	9,625.9	8,265.3	267.1	226.9	8,839.5	1,169.3

SOURCE: Japan Post Group, *Annual Report: 2009*, 18; *Annual Report: 2010*, 10.

2008 and FY 2009, the number of policies sold increased from 243,000 to 455,000.[23] Given declining public confidence in the insurance sector more generally, however, we can expect future increases in the sale of insurance policies to be sluggish at best.

Given these downward trends in consumer demand for postal services, how can we explain the Japan Post Group's generally positive performance? The Group's fairly respectable returns on (very conservative) investments are certainly one contributing factor. Also important has been the services' newfound freedom to introduce a spate of innovative new products and services, including investment trusts. But some economists familiar with the inside workings of the services have observed that the most important determinant has been aggressive cost cutting.[24] Unfortunately, the positive effects of cost cutting cannot last forever; once reformers run out of things to cut, the services' income and assets indicators will more closely reflect the long-term decline in consumer demand for postal services.

—————

23. Japan Post Group, *Annual Report: 2009*, 81; Japan Post Group, *Annual Report: 2010*, 59.

24. Interview, Yoshino Naoyuki, Financial Services Agency, Tokyo, June 9, 2009.

Of particular concern to both Japan Post Group executives and government administrators has been the health of the mail service. Although Japan Post Service's Yu-Pack parcel delivery service initially did quite well, expanding from 2.53 million pieces in FY 2007 to 2.77 million in FY 2008, the numbers dropped to 2.64 million in FY 2009, a decline of 4.7 percent. Meanwhile, the proliferation of email, Internet, and mobile phone usage has sent demand for correspondence mail into a downward spiral. In FY 2008 and FY 2009, the total volume of domestic mail items (excluding parcels) handled by Japan Post Service dropped by 3.5 percent and 3.0 percent, respectively, over the previous years.[25] This trend will be almost impossible to reverse.

In sum, the postal system weathered the early stages of the privatization storm admirably well, but long-term demographic and economic trends strongly suggest that its future will be one of decline. Key actors both within and outside of the new postal firms are working hard to stave off that decline—but at the expense of the underlying principles of Koizumi's market-oriented postal reform plan.

Re-Embedding Maejima's Post Office

Japan's experience with postal privatization evokes Karl Polanyi's classic depiction of confrontation between the forces of change and continuity in the context of economic transformation. Markets of all kinds, Polanyi observed, are social as well as economic entities, and when they are forced to change in ways that upset the fabric of the societies in which they are embedded, societal interests will invariably protest.[26] Wolfgang Streeck and Kathleen Thelen take these observations a step further by arguing that radical economic reforms may very well spark institutional reactions that "re-embed the very same market relations that liberalization sets free from traditional social constraints."[27] As the reaction to Koizumi's postal privatization legislation reveals, the vehicles for reasserting traditional market relations are often the very political interests that stand to lose the most from reform.

----

25. Japan Post Group, *Annual Report: 2009*, 82; Japan Post Group, *Annual Report: 2010*, 36.

26. Polanyi, *The Great Transformation*.

27. Streeck and Thelen, "Introduction," 4.

We would be hard-pressed to think of economic institutions more deeply embedded in their constituent societies than Japan's state-run postal services. And this was a relationship forged by design. When Mae-jima Hisoka set out to modernize the post office during the early Meiji period, he was convinced that the mail and postal savings services had a social, as well as economic, mission to fulfill. Over the course of several generations, the services contributed not only to the expansion of national communications and military and economic growth but also to the development of local community cohesion, the public's identification with the state, and social welfare. In the process, the services came to represent and reinforce values that we now tend to associate with a bygone era: safety, financial security and predictability, equality, self-sacrifice for the sake of the common good, state paternalism, full employment and social stability, and the like. As we have seen, the postal regime and many ordinary Japanese opposed postal privatization as an ideological and institutional shift toward economic neoliberalism that struck at the very essence of Japanese identity and culture.

The postal regime's opposition to Koizumi's alleged excesses was at the heart of a series of compromises that were folded into the government's postal privatization blueprint between its release in September 2004 and the following summer. Some analysts praised these compromises as a necessary step toward building a viable political constituency behind the privatization scheme.[28] Others criticized Koizumi and Takenaka for "selling out" to disgruntled vested interests and questioned their commitment to establishing a level playing field between the postal services and their private competitors. Whatever the case may be, the compromises—together with steps taken by the Japan Post Group to prepare for a more competitive business environment—preserved many of the rules, norms, and organizational structures of the state-run postal services.

The fate of the mail service is a revealing case in point. Koizumi had at one time hoped to privatize mail, but eventually succumbed to LDP pressure to preserve government control of the system. The economic rationale behind his capitulation was a compelling one that motivates states the world over: since it may be too much to expect private (read

---

28. Yamawaki, *Yūsei kōbō*, 130.

profit-motivated) companies to service all communities equally, given the relatively high cost of mail delivery in sparsely populated areas, the government must step in to equalize service for all residents, regardless of where they reside. The political value added of the government's commitment to universal service in mail collection and delivery is particularly high in Japan, where the income gap between urban and rural areas has grown pronounced in recent decades and the ratio of elderly to younger citizens in rural areas has been increasing.[29] Since the elderly tend to rely more heavily on mail than younger citizens, depriving these regions of universal mail service would be widely interpreted as a governmental repudiation of the cherished principle of social equality. (To be sure, meeting the needs of graying rural residents also advanced the LDP's electoral interests, since the party's main base of support has historically been rooted in the countryside.)

The government made a number of other compromises to allay the postal regime's and the public's fears about the effects of privatization on the services. Starting in late 2004, for example, Takenaka promised the Japanese public that the government would guarantee the survival of at least one post office for every village.[30] The government also agreed to establish the Community Contribution Fund to support vulnerable post offices, an idea that was fleshed out by Takenaka's "guerrilla team" as a compromise response to demands from the LDP and the postmasters that universal service be formally applied to the postal financial systems.[31] Funded with a portion of the profits from the sale of shares in the postal insurance and postal savings companies between 2011 and September 30, 2017, the money will be used not only to help post offices provide basic services but also to finance social welfare programs.[32] Originally set at 1 trillion yen, the amount was doubled during the 2005 Diet deliberations. Needless to say, both the fund and Takenaka's guar-

---

29. Interview, Yoshino Naoyuki, Faculty of Economics, Keiō University, Tokyo, July 15, 2006.

30. Ibid., and interview, Okina Yuri, Japan Research Institute, Tokyo, July 13, 2006.

31. Takenaka, *Kōzō kaikaku no shinjitsu,* 188. The idea was that by propping up struggling post offices, rural residents would retain their access to the postal savings and insurance systems.

32. Proceeds from the sale of these shares will also be used to lower Japan's national debt (Porges and Leong, "The Privatization of Japan Post," 8).

antee had political, as well as economic and social, implications; by shielding small post offices from bankruptcy, these measures helped preserve the postal network's role as a provider of social services and an institutional vehicle for mobilizing the vote.

Members of Koizumi's privatization camp grudgingly accepted the need for compromise measures to provide de facto universal service in the postal financial systems and to guarantee the survival of the postal network—even at the expense of neoliberal efforts to reduce costs within the services. As one insider observed, Koizumi himself had concluded that privatization was more likely to succeed over the long haul if bankruptcies were kept to a minimum and employment levels within the services remained stable; only then could privatized firms expect to maintain worker morale, attract talented employees, and thus increase their profitability.[33] Political motivations were also at play; if safeguards were not installed to protect the long-term viability of the postal network, the chances for political sabotage as privatization unfolded would most certainly increase.

Far more controversial among postal privatization advocates was the decision to establish *national* postal savings and insurance firms. During the late 1990s, when Koizumi partnered with sympathetic opposition-party Diet members to formulate a model postal privatization plan, he took his cue from the privatization of NTT and JNR and called for the breakup of the national postal financial services into regional firms. To Koizumi, these measures would help guarantee fair competition between the postal firms and private banks, which were organized primarily at the regional and city levels, and between the postal insurance system and private providers, which had long been dwarfed by their state-run rival. But members of the postal regime promptly vetoed the plan. The postmasters and LDP Diet members from sparsely populated regions worried that region-specific postal savings firms in their areas would lack the financial wherewithal to do well in a competitive market. Maintaining a nation-wide firm, they argued, would permit heavily populated regions with relatively high volumes of deposits to cover for less advantaged regions. The 2005 postal legislation gave Japan Post Bank the right to re-

---

33. Interview, Yoshino Naoyuki, Faculty of Economics, Keiō University, Tokyo, July 15, 2006.

consider the national scope of the postal savings system between 2007 and 2017, but given the postal regime's opposition and Koizumi's departure from government in September 2006, the service faces few incentives to do so.[34] Not surprisingly, economists and private-sector banks have criticized Japan Post Bank's massive size for violating the principle of fair competition within the financial sphere.[35]

Also controversial was the Koizumi government's decision to allow Japan Post Holdings to buy back as much as one-third of its shares in the postal savings and insurance firms after 2017. The decision assuaged those who worried about the services' capacity to navigate market forces without government protection, but bankers and many media analysts opposed it for giving the postal financial services yet another political-economic advantage over their private-sector competitors.

The thorny issue of the postal system's competitive advantage is further underscored by measures introduced by the services themselves to enhance their long-term survival. As we observed in Chapter 6, declining consumer demand has long prompted the mail service to develop innovative new products and business partnerships. Yu-Pack, the mail firm's package delivery service and primary delivery vehicle for the "hometown packages" program, introduced special services a number of years ago for the transport of golf clubs, refrigerated goods, skiing equipment, and airport-bound luggage.[36] In 2006, Japan Post launched "Pospacket," a low-cost delivery service for small packages.[37] The mail service also concluded partnerships with several private-sector firms, including Lawson, which now offers Yu-Pack services at their convenience stores, and Nippon Express and ANA to develop international air cargo and ex-

---

34. Some of Takenaka's close associates believed that his ultimate wish was the wholesale disappearance of the postal savings and insurance systems. If this were indeed so, political pressure and the concomitant threat of debilitating sabotage during the transition and privatization periods forced him to abandon his wish. Interview, Japan Development Bank executive, Tokyo, January 11, 2007.

35. Privatization, observed the chairman of the Japan Bankers Association, should be about "right-sizing" a government entity that had ballooned in size under government protection, rather than venturing into new business areas (*Japan Times*, October 2, 2007).

36. Cohen, "Policy Challenges and the Privatization of Japan Post," 40.

37. Japan Post, *Annual Report: Postal Services in Japan: 2006*, 30.

press courier services. Yu-Pack and Pospacket have since expanded their market shares, thanks to the mail service's past tax-exemptions and its reduced tax burden since 2007. Since taxes will be levied only gradually on Japan Post Service (and on the two postal financial services),[38] we can expect the firm to continue innovating as it seeks to undercut its competitors.

Meanwhile, Japan Post Network introduced a new service to help homeowners improve their home security and plan for moves, launched an online shopping mall for Chinese-speaking residents, introduced a new printing service for greeting and business cards, and began serving as an intermediary for the sale of government bonds, automobile insurance, and other financial services offered by private-sector firms.[39] And the firm continues to perform local government functions, including documentation services, the sale of public transportation passes, and even the promotion of local tourism.

The postal system's financial services have taken steps of their own to enhance their competitiveness in the face of declining consumer demand. For instance, Japan Post Insurance began selling variable annuities, developed new life insurance policies targeted at corporate employees, and expanded its popular hospitalization riders on its insurance policies. Japan Post Bank has been even more active. In 2005, the firm ventured into new financial territory by selling "investment trusts."[40] The results were promising for the first few years: in FY 2008, for instance, the firm sold 1,010,339 trusts, a 67 percent increase over the previous year. In FY 2009, however, the number of trusts sold dropped precipitously to approximately 760,000.[41] Since the investment trusts were introduced while the postal services were still a public corporation,[42] the Japan Bankers Association condemned them as inherently unfair. The United States Trade Representative (USTR) even weighed

---

38. Yamawaki, *Yūsei kōbō*, 211–12.

39. Japan Post Group, *Annual Report: 2009*, 2–5, 28–54.

40. Japan Post Bank's investment trusts are diversified investment portfolios that include Japanese and foreign stocks, bonds, and real estate investment offerings.

41. Japan Post Group, *Annual Report: 2009*, 80; Japan Post Group, *Annual Report: 2010*, 28.

42. *Japan Times*, October 2, 2007; Sakai, "The Privatization of Japan Post is Unstoppable," 2.

in on the issue, writing at length in its 2006 recommendations to the Japanese government that a level playing field should be established between the postal savings system and its private sector competitors *before* Japan Post introduced new investment products.[43] (A former PPPO official counter-argued that only by diversifying its product offerings would Japan Post Bank develop into a "normal" private financial institution that could eventually be listed.[44])

Japan Post Bank continued to innovate after privatization officially began. In 2008 and 2009, the firm launched its own debit and credit cards,[45] started offering private-sector home loans (mortgages) at the local post office,[46] and began training some of its employees to serve as "certified financial planners."[47] In 2008, the two financial firms also made formal requests to the government to raise ceilings on the maximum value of ordinary savings accounts and insurance policies.[48] All told, friends of the post office have praised these and related innovations for helping the local post office fulfill its long-standing goal to become a "one-stop service center."

As the services scrambled to outdo their competitors in a more market-oriented setting, their relationships with postal family enterprises and special corporations emerged from Koizumi's postal privatization crusade only partially diminished. Granted, many noteworthy reforms have been introduced. Thanks to the introduction of more transparent and competitive procedures, for example, many subcontracting firms connected to the postal services now offer cheaper and more efficient

---

43. United States Trade Representative, *Annual Reform Recommendations*, 35.

44. Interview, Kinoshita Nobuyuki, Secretary General, General Executive Bureau, Financial Services Agency, Tokyo, June 2, 2009.

45. The Japan Post Bank offers Visa, MasterCard, and JCB credit cards.

46. As of this writing, Japan Post Bank is exploring the possibility of offering its own home loan products.

47. Interview, Yoshino Naoyuki, Financial Services Agency, Tokyo, June 9, 2009. After receiving training from a private service, certified financial planners must then take a government-sponsored examination.

48. Japan Post Bank made the request in anticipation of joining an online transaction network of private banks in 2011. The bank argued that postal savings customers would be inconvenienced if they were restricted from transferring or receiving more than 10,000 yen (*Japan Times*, March 31, 2008).

services.[49] Special corporations have also experienced some reforms, but many of their distinctive traits remain. The Postal Services Center, for instance, lost its control over the lucrative "hometown packages" service to Japan Post Network, but now provides "business support" to local post offices as a subsidiary of the network firm. The center is also expected to remain an *amakudari* destination for retiring postal bureaucrats and other individuals in the postal system, despite ongoing government efforts to abolish the practice.[50]

To prepare for the 2007 start of postal privatization, in October 2005 the three special corporations that offered social services to postal employees merged to form a single organization called Postal Welfare (Yūsei fukushi).[51] In addition to providing postal employees and their families with a variety of different services, Postal Welfare owns significant real estate assets: as of March 2006, it possessed a network of 1,520 high-rent post office buildings and approximately 180 employee dormitories, and its total assets were estimated at nearly 445 billion yen.[52] It, too, may be functioning as a destination for post-retirement postmasters, other employees within the Japan Post Group, and perhaps even bureaucrats involved in postal administration.

Meanwhile, the future of the Mielparque postal savings halls and particularly the postal insurance inns remains a source of controversy for the postal services. During the privatization deliberative process, Takenaka denounced the debt-ridden networks as tangential to the postal system's core business concerns and wanted them sold.[53] Although Japan Post tried to stave off radical reform by reducing costs within the two networks and closing several units, the 2005 privatization legislation ob-

---

49. Interview, Japan Post Holdings executive, Tokyo, July 6, 2010.

50. *Shūkan Daiyamondo*, December 2007, 43.

51. The three special corporations were the Postal Mutual Aid Society (Yūsei gojokai), the Postal Welfare Association (Yūsei fukushi kyōkai), and the Postal Benefits Association (Yūsei kōsaikai). They, like their successor, were all classified as *zaidan hōjin*. See Chapter 4 for an explanation of the history and functions of these organs.

52. *Asahi shinbun*, February 27, 2007.

53. Takenaka, *Kōzō kaikaku no shinjitsu*, 177. The postal insurance inns have recently run annual deficits of approximately four billion yen. The Mielparque and the inns are expected to become even more cost-ineffective as they lose their tax-exempt status (*Asahi shinbun*, January 31, 2009).

ligated the services to sell off or withdraw from the management of all Mielparque and inns by 2012.[54] In 2008, Japan Post Holdings transferred management of the Mielparque to a subsidiary of the Watake Wedding Corporation. But as a later section illustrates, its attempt to sell the inns has failed; as of this writing, they remain under the postal system's control with no prospective buyer in sight.

Finally, no analysis of the future of the postal system would be complete without a closer look at the FILP. As a result of the reforms since the 1990s, the size of the FILP shrunk dramatically from an all-time high of approximately 260 trillion yen in 1999 to 180 trillion yen in FY 2007.[55] That said—and despite Koizumi's strong opposition to the FILP's market-distorting characteristics—the fund still has broad support as an instrument of state policy. In keeping with postwar trends, the program's objectives have shifted in response to changing national priorities. Interestingly, industrial development appears to be on the rise as a FILP objective; after shrinking from 15.8 percent in 1995 to a recent low of 1.5 percent in 2005 and 2006, 8.3 percent of the FY 2009 FILP budget was dedicated to industrial and technological development. With the recent privatization of the Japan Housing Loan Corporation, the portion of FILP funds channeled into public housing dropped from 35.3 percent in the 1995 budget to a mere 4.3 percent in 2009. A growing portion of the budget has been earmarked for small-and medium-sized enterprises (from 15.3 percent in 1995 to 26.9 percent in 2009) and for the environment (from 16.4 in 1995 to 23.7 in 2006 and 18.4 in 2009). Although funds for education and social welfare—hospitals and child and elder care facilities—have consistently hovered at approximately 10 percent between 2005 and 2009 (the combined total was only 6 percent in 1995), the FILP continues to benefit disadvantaged regions via appropriations for road construction (from 7.7 percent in 1995 to 22.3 in 2007 and 15.7 in 2009) and smaller programs like "regional development" and agriculture/forestry/fisheries (both 3 percent or less since 2005).[56] It is also telling that approximately one-third of all FILP funds has been disbursed in the form of loans

54. Ibid.
55. Yoshino, "Yūbin chokin no shōrai to zaisei tōyūshi," 57.
56. Budget figures taken from the Ministry of Finance, *FILP Report: 2009*.

to cash-strapped municipal governments.[57] In short, in its pursuit of economically significant objectives, the FILP remains a policy tool for equalizing some of Japan's social and regional disparities.

Despite the postal system's theoretical independence from the FILP system since 2001, the savings and insurance firms still channel as much as 80 percent of their proceeds into the purchase of government bonds, including FILP and FILP agency bonds; the remainder is used to purchase domestic stocks and foreign stocks and bonds.[58] The postal system's continuing reliance on government bonds can be attributed to a number of factors, not least of which is the low interest rates offered by domestic financial markets. For as long as these rates remain low, the financial firms will face few incentives to invest their funds in riskier ventures. Some analysts attribute the system's financial conservatism to risk aversion, pure and simple,[59] or to the relative inexperience of its administrators.[60] Although the postal system's investment behavior may change as the Japan Post Group hires more and more executive-level employees from the private sector, for the time being, at least, Japan Post Group's cautious investment strategies—along with the financial firms' image as being "too big to fail"—may be propping up the post office's traditional reputation as the safest financial haven in town.

The foregoing illustrates that while Koizumi and Takenaka had hoped to reduce the financial size and influence of the postal services,

---

57. The remainder flows to their targets through special accounts, government-affiliated financial institutions, independent administrative institutions, and the like. Interview, MOF, Financial Bureau (FILP Division) official, Tokyo, January 9, 2008.

58. Yoshino, "Yūbin chokin no shōrai to zaisei tōyūshi," 60. Since the market no longer distinguishes between FILP and other government bonds, it is unclear exactly what percentage of postal savings and insurance proceeds are invested in the FILP.

59. On the eve of privatization, Japan Post's capital adequacy ratio for its savings and insurance systems was over 50 percent—far more than the approximately 10 percent for commercial banks. Economists interpret the ratio as a measure of an institution's risk tolerance (*The Economist*, September 27, 2007).

60. The word from inside the postal services was that many administrators were nervous about assuming complete control over the investment of postal savings deposits and insurance premiums. One government official who helped plan the transfer of investment authority to the services told me that on January 1, 2001, he received a New Year's card (*nengajō*) from a postal official that stated, sarcastically, "Happy New Year and thanks a lot."

Japan Post, its successors, and remnants of the postal regime sought to do precisely the opposite. As a result of political compromises between the pro- and anti-privatization camps, several key institutions of the old state-run postal system, including the government's position as the services' "behind-the-scenes patron" (*ushirodate*),[61] have been at least partially preserved. The services have used the competitive advantages that are emerging from these re-embedded institutions to develop new and innovative ways to postpone the onset of further decline. The implications of all this for the Japanese financial sector are profound. For as long as the government provides an implicit guarantee of the postal network and its services and the Japan Post Group continues to invest in the FILP, the postal financial services will remain artificially inflated and Koizumi's goal of reinvigorating the private financial sector will never be fully achieved. For analysts worried about the health of Japan's economic and financial system, this is a problem. For those who prioritize the postal system's social and political functions, however, the partial re-embedding of state-run postal institutions into a more market-oriented setting is a source of great relief.

The Postal Regime Regroups, 2005–2009

There is perhaps no more telling indicator of the persistence of old rules and practices within the new postal system than the survival of the commissioned postmasters and the partial regrouping of the postal regime.

On the heels of the September 2005 Lower House election, the postmasters' electoral unity was in shambles and their leverage over postal administrators much diminished. The postmasters were also very concerned about the impact of postal privatization on their way of life. In July 2006, nine months after Koizumi's bills had cleared the Diet, I traveled to Kitakyūshū for the first time in four years to discuss the effects of postal privatization with a few of my postmaster contacts. Sitting around a table at a local Chinese restaurant, the four postmasters were in a black mood, flummoxed by Koizumi's surprising successes and worried about the future of their post offices. Mr. Morimoto, an

---

61. Yamawaki, *Yūsei kōbō*, 212.

older postmaster who ran a tiny facility on a small island near the city, voiced the prevailing sentiments of the group:

I never dreamed we'd reach this point. It's not that I oppose privatization per se, it's just that I'm worried about what the 2005 legislation will do to our post office culture. Many of Japan's post offices were established during the Meiji period, and they still stand for a traditional way of life. I'm afraid of what's going to happen to those traditions when the privatization process starts and we'll have to think more about profit than the welfare of our neighborhoods. What will become of our sense of community as this process unfolds? I really am worried. . . .

Mr. Kitaoka, a recently retired third-generation postmaster, agreed. Shortly after our meeting in 2002, Mr. Kitaoka transferred his postmastership to a senior employee after none of his children expressed interest in the job. Privatization, he said, would only accelerate these generational fissures within the ranks of the postmasters and their descendents, and to the detriment of the post office as a traditional center of community life.[62]

To address these problems, the postmasters allied with sympathetic politicians in the LDP and the opposition parties to pressure the government into softening the effects of the privatization process on local post offices. Their first objective: defeat Japan Post's campaign to eliminate the defining institutions of the commissioned post office system.

In 2006, Japan Post President Ikuta Masaharu announced that in order to carry out a renewal (*isshin*) of the postal services, the commissioned post office system—as feudal an institution, he believed, as the old Tokugawa domains (*han*)—would have to be reformed.[63] While Ikuta acknowledged the postmasters' many contributions to their communities over the generations, he sought to update the system in conformity with freer markets and "social common sense" (*shakai jōshiki*). It appeared that not even the postmasters could escape postal reform "with no sanctuaries" (*seiiki naki*).[64]

Designed to prevent the inheritance of postmasterships, Ikuta's proposed changes included lowering the maximum retirement age of the

---

62. Interview, four commissioned postmasters, Kitakyūshū, July 10, 2006.
63. *Asahi shinbun*, December 22, 2006.
64. Ikuta, *Yūsei kaikaku no genten*, 342–43.

commissioned postmasters from 65 to 60,[65] subjecting the postmasters to periodic transfer, buying up more post office buildings (which, Ikuta declared, were public assets that should not be located in private homes),[66] and making it easier for ordinary employees to become post-masters. Ikuta also resolved to abolish Tokusuiren, the locally rooted, government-administered association of commissioned postmasters that served as a channel for communications between the postmasters and the MIC. Controlled by Japan Post Network Co., the association's replacement would be far more centralized, with units at the prefectural—but not local—level, and would consist of ordinary as well as commissioned postmasters. The new structure would leave the postmasters with virtually no say over the association's operations.[67] As far as the postmasters were concerned, this was a "declaration of war" (*sensen fukoku*).[68]

A few months later, Nishikawa Yoshifumi, who had just assumed control of the prototype of Japan Post Holdings Co., Ltd., publicized an alternative plan that he had hammered out in consultation with the postmasters: the commissioned postmasters would no longer be referred to as such, their official retirement age would be set at age 65,[69] and Tokusuiren would be officially abolished, but the postmasters would be given some control over local units in the equivalent of a successor organization.[70] The proposal carried the day, and with positive ramifications for the postmasters. Although Nishikawa's intervention is unlikely to reverse the decline of inheritance practices among the postmasters, the postmasters will still have at least some bottom-up influence over how the postal services are run. This in turn will help preserve the influence of Zentoku, the postmasters' voluntary organization which has long depended on the postmasters' close integration into the postal ad-

---

65. The changes would, of course, eliminate the informal practice of allowing commissioned postmasters to serve until the age of 68.

66. Ikuta, *Yūsei kaikaku no genten*, 344; *Japan Times*, January 19, 2006. Ikuta believed that if owned by the network company, the post offices would face more incentives to develop a wider range of services.

67. Interview, Postal Administration Bureau officials, MIC, Tokyo, January 10, 2007. The postmasters are now employees of the Japan Post Network Co., Ltd.

68. *Hokkaidō shinbun*, July 19, 2007.

69. Ibid.

70. *Shūkan Asahi*, December 29, 2006.

ministration as it seeks to influence the outcome of elections and policymaking in the postal sphere. When Nishikawa replaced Ikuta as Japan
Post president in April 2007 after the latter's abrupt resignation,[71] he
praised the revised plan for maximizing the usefulness of the distinctive
human resources of the old state-run system. "Our company and Zentoku are partners in fate [*unmei kyōdōtai*]," he observed. "If we don't acti-
vate the strengths of the postal network, not only the network company
but also [postal] banking will fail."[72]

There are at least two reasons for this partial retreat from the spirit
of Koizumi's reform agenda. First, since Koizumi's lengthy (500-plus
pages) postal privatization legislation made virtually no mention of the
commissioned postmasters' future aside from the stipulation that they,
like the postal workers, would lose their status as public servants, the
path was clear for the postmasters to leverage some concessions from
postal administrators *after* the laws were passed. (And leverage they
did.) Second, Ikuta's resignation as Japan Post president just six months
before the privatization process was to begin and his replacement by
the more pro-postmaster Nishikawa suggest that Prime Minister Abe
Shinzō's government was eager to appease the postmasters in the
months leading up to the much-dreaded 2007 Upper House election.[73]
Despite Koizumi's best intentions to smash the LDP's dependence on
vested interests, his vulnerable successor still looked to the postmasters
as a vehicle for mobilizing the vote.

Zentoku, meanwhile, has tried to adapt to the new political and economic environment by carrying out a series of small reforms. First, in
keeping with the abolition of formal distinctions among postmasters,

---

71. Nishikawa retained his post as president of Nihon Yūsei while serving as Japan
Post president.

72. *Shūkan Asahi*, December 29, 2006.

73. Some have speculated that Abe asked Ikuta to resign early in response to pressure from the postmasters, who felt that Nishikawa was more sympathetic to their interests. Others believed that Ikuta resigned in opposition to the LDP's readmission of
the eleven postal rebels, which signified a retreat by the Abe government on postal privatization. Still others speculated that the LDP had pressured Ikuta to leave his post
after receiving numerous complaints about him from the postmasters. Whatever the
case, privatization advocates worried that Ikuta's departure would weaken the privatization process. *Shūkan Asahi*, December 29, 2006; *Asahi shinbun*, March 16, 2007.

Zentoku opened its doors to ordinary postmasters, increasing its total membership to approximately 20,000.[74] Zentoku then changed its official name from the National Association of Commissioned Postmasters (Zenkoku tokutei yūbinkyokuchōkai) to the National Postmasters Association (Zenkoku yūbinkyokuchōkai).[75]

Second, now that the postmasters are no longer public servants whose political activities are constrained by law, Zentoku has become more transparent. The association's website,[76] which it launched during the early 2000s, includes statements about its political objectives, critiques of the privatization process, and pictures of and statements by the association's political party "advisors" (*komon*). The website even addresses some of the postmasters' pressing occupational challenges, such as the declining rate of private ownership of individual post offices. Although Zentoku has yet to divulge detailed information about the postmasters' electoral practices, it is clearly trying to garner support from a broader cross-section of the population by operating within the media mainstream.

The association has remained true to its tradition by pledging to promote the quality of postal services, contribute to the development of local (*chiiki*) society, and improve the working conditions of Zentoku members. The difference now is that its policy objectives are shaped by the reality—rather than the threat—of postal privatization. Concerned about the cumbersome division of labor among the employees of the four postal firms, for instance, the postmasters modified their earlier call for "state administered, unified services" to push for a merger of Japan Post Service and Japan Post Network. And in an effort to protect post offices in depopulated communities and serve as broad a swath of the population as possible, they are demanding the formal adoption of universal service by the postal savings and insurance systems.[77] The post-

---

74. By late 2007, about 70 percent of ordinary postmasters had joined Zentoku (*Shūkan Daiyamondo*, December 2007, 42).

75. *Daily Yomiuri*, January 7, 2007.

76. See http://www.zentoku.org (last accessed October 24, 2011).

77. According to Zentoku's estimates, approximately 80 percent of profits for small, rural post offices are from the savings and insurance services. A universal service requirement for these services, then, would help ensure the survival of Japan's most vulnerable post offices. Under the 2005 privatization legislation, the savings and insurance

masters are also intent on protecting their ownership of individual post offices as Japan Post Network prepares to purchase many of them.[78] Achieving these objectives would help the postmasters preserve their *chiensei*—their local social capital that has long been the currency of their social connectivity and vote-mobilizing appeal.

To be sure, the chances of the postmasters fulfilling these and related goals depend on the willingness of politicians to assist them. In the immediate aftermath of the 2005 election and the passage of postal privatization legislation, the postmasters looked to the LDP for help. As Mr. Morimoto explained in July 2006, "Zentoku may not be as strong as it once was, but we still think it has a mission to fulfill. It is now trying to remobilize the postmasters and is determined to pressure the LDP to soften the edges of privatization. There are still some sympathetic politicians in the party—they'll help us."[79]

Even though the LDP's legitimacy now depended on the successful implementation of Koizumi's privatization plan, Mr. Morimoto was correct to point out that Zentoku still had highly placed friends in the party. To cite the most salient example, in fall 2006, after assuming the party presidency and prime ministership, Abe Shinzō invited twelve postal rebels who had been elected as independents in 2005 to rejoin the party, providing they signed a pledge to uphold the provisions of the postal privatization legislation.[80] Eleven rebels complied and returned to the party fold,[81] attracting sharp criticisms from the mass media and

---

companies are not obligated to provide their services to all post offices (*Shūkan Daiyamondo*, December 2007, 43).

78. In April 2007, the services announced a plan to purchase approximately 1,450 post offices (*AERA*, April 28, 2007, 11). It is unlikely, however, that the network company will completely eliminate the private ownership of post offices given the many economic pressures confronting the system in the context of both declining consumer demand for postal services and the post-2008 economic environment.

79. Interview, Kitakyūshū, July 10, 2006.

80. It was Nakagawa Hidenao, the LDP secretary general, who insisted on the pledge as a condition of reentry. Many of the party's senior politicians, including Aoki Mikio, supported the rebels' reentry but opposed the pledge (*Japan Times*, November 23, 2006).

81. The twelfth rebel, Hiranuma Takeo, former Minister of Economy, Trade, and Industry, had voted against the privatization bills in October 2005 and refused to sign

reformist—particularly junior—party members.[82] LDP supporters of the initiative, including most of the party's prefectural chapters,[83] believed that readmitting the rebels would strengthen the party's electoral chances at a time when it could no longer rely on Koizumi's charismatic personality to attract the floating vote.[84]

But in the end, the LDP failed to completely repair the ruptures in its exchange relationship with the postmasters. Although in 2006–2007 the postmasters wanted smooth relations with the party so that their interests could be effectively represented in the privatization process,[85] many refused to forgive the LDP for its betrayal in 2005 and transferred their political loyalties to the PNP, the NPJ, and the DPJ. By this time, they considered the PNP's Kamei Shizuka and Kamei Hisaoki, both LDP veterans and former rebels, and Hasegawa Kensei, a former MPT bureaucrat who had served in the Diet only since 2004, their most sympathetic allies. During the 2007 Upper House election campaign, Zentoku refrained from telling its members which candidates they should support, giving its regional chapters the freedom to decide how best to instruct their members. Today, Zentoku's main party patron is the PNP, and the postmasters are among the party's core constituents in prefectures where the party has a strong presence.[86] In 2007, the postmasters were carrying out functions for both the PNP and the DPJ that they had once performed for the LDP: fundraising, recruiting new members into the party and the *kōenkai* of individual party members, and mobilizing the vote at election time.

---

the covenant; he was subsequently refused reentry into the party. The other eleven rebels had all voted in favor of privatization and signed the party pledge.

82. *Japan Times*, October 27, 2006.

83. Thirty of the 47 party chapters approved the initiative (*Japan Times*, November 7, 2006).

84. *Shūkan Asahi*, December 29, 2006.

85. The postmasters were intent on weakening the Japan Post Group's plans to start buying up commissioned post offices. Others—particularly retired postmasters—continued to back the LDP because they simply "couldn't forget [past] favors" (*on ga wasurerarenai*). *Asahi shinbun*, May 22, 2007; *Tokyo shinbun*, July 12, 2007.

86. For example, of the PNP's nearly 5,000 registered members in Okayama prefecture in 2007, approximately 500 had connections to the postal system. But the prefecture's postmasters were not monolithically behind the PNP; Taiju's regional association apparently supported the LDP. *Asahi shinbun*, May 22, 2007.

These developments had interesting implications for the postal regime. As earlier chapters illustrate, the regime began as a kind of iron triangle consisting of the postmasters, LDP politicians, and postal bureaucrats, with the exchange relationship between the postmasters and the conservative party serving as the triangle's center. As the exchange relationship weakened in response to changing economic, demographic, and political circumstances, the iron triangle morphed into a looser alliance of interests that included the postal unions, the DPJ, and an expanding network of private-sector firms and semi-public corporations that were connected to the postal system. In the wake of Koizumi's reforms, the electoral exchange relationship between the LDP and the postmasters is all but gone, the postal bureaucrats have lost much of their influence, and more political parties are vying for the postmasters' allegiance. And as later pages further illustrate, the postmasters themselves are now willing to ally with whichever party best serves their interests. The postal regime, in short, now lacks a strong, unifying center.

The Politics of Re-Nationalization

To what extent, then, should we expect this broader but weaker postal regime to unravel Koizumi's privatization plan? The regime's defeat of Japan Post's efforts to completely dismantle the commissioned post office system illustrates that in areas where the details of reform have yet to be finalized, the regime can soften the effects of privatization by bringing direct pressure to bear on postal executives and relevant government officials.[87] Enacting legislation that would reverse the basic pillars of Koizumi's privatization legislation, however, will be far more difficult. Success in this endeavor would require fundamental shifts in the institutional, interest group, and leadership environments that enabled Koizumi's privatization agenda to succeed. As the remainder of this chapter illustrates, several such shifts have already taken place, although the prospects for another wave of significant postal reform are

---

87. Pressure from the "forces of resistance" on the privatization process has been intense since October 2005. One high-ranking Cabinet Office official who helped oversee the process confessed to feeling "extremely stressed by the adverse wind from the political side." Private correspondence, July 13, 2008.

still tenuous. But before we progress, it is important to identify the issues that have triggered the recent upsurge in anti-reform sentiment.

PROBLEMS AT THE POST OFFICE

Recognizing the importance of the post office in the everyday lives of ordinary Japanese, post-2005 LDP governments repeatedly promised that privatization would *not* inconvenience the public. The government's public relations literature made this point very clear. In a pamphlet released in fall 2007, for example, readers were reassured that the village post office would be preserved as privatization unfolded. Accompanying the text was an illustration of a stooped but cheerful senior citizen as he opened the door of his rural home to a beaming postal carrier.[88]

Despite Japan Post Group's commitment to "creating a new normal" (*atarashii futsū o tsukuru*),[89] both the group and the government attracted intense public criticism as the post-2007 privatization process unfolded. As befits an institution that is obligated to turn a profit, the Japan Post Group introduced or charged higher user fees for many services. Japan Post Bank introduced stricter identification requirements to prevent customers from exceeding the legal limit on combined postal savings accounts. And in 2006, the government unveiled plans to convert 1,048 collection (*shūhai*) post offices (both ordinary and commissioned) into less costly non-collection (*mushūhai*) facilities, reduce the operating hours of some facilities, and shut down many ATMs.[90] Designed to reduce costs, these measures led to cutbacks in employee hours and sparked formal complaints from dozens of local governments. Even more troubling to ordinary Japanese has been the closure of hundreds of simple post offices (*kan'i yūbinkyoku*), particularly in small, rural areas.[91] To

---

88. Naikaku kanbō yūsei min'eika suishin shitsu, *Min'eika de dō naru no?* 5.

89. A Japan Post Group slogan since 2007, "Creating a new normal" highlights the Group's professed flexibility in responding to consumer needs and market opportunities. In addition to "normalcy," the term *futsū* signifies universal access to postal services and citizen trust in those services.

90. Between March 2005 and March 2008, the number of ATMs declined by 1,128 units (Muramoto, "Saihen sareyuku yūbinkyoku," 63).

91. In addition to the pressures of privatization, the drop in the number of simple post offices reflected the closure of many local agricultural cooperatives that were contracted to carry out postal functions. The postal system lost more than 10 percent of

honor its pledge to preserve one post office per village, the government began deploying "mobile post offices" (*poskuru*) to underserved communities in 2008. Residents complained, however, that *poskuru* do not measure up to post offices that have the geographic permanence to provide services above and beyond the sale of stamps, savings accounts, and insurance policies.

An informal survey of 18,253 postmasters conducted by Zentoku in early 2008 suggests that many post office customers were inconvenienced by glitches in the privatization process. Sixty percent of postmasters stated that the number of customers at their post offices had declined in the six months since privatization began. Asked what the public complained about most, "having to show identification," "rising user fees," and "waiting in line" topped the list of responses.[92] The post office queues, which were longest for savings and insurance services, were the result of new regulations that were imposed on the post offices from October 2007. Since it took time for the postal employees to master the new regulatory guidelines,[93] the once simple tasks of opening postal savings accounts and purchasing postal life insurance policies developed into complicated and time-consuming processes.[94] (Ironically, the postal services were far less encumbered by regulations when they were government-owned.)

The survey also uncovered increasing disaffection among the postmasters and their employees. When asked if they had ever considered resigning their positions, 76 percent of postmasters answered in the affirmative; 24.5 percent claimed that they wanted to quit immediately. Approximately 72 percent stated that employee morale had decreased since October 1, 2007, whereas only 2.1 percent said that it was on the rise; 25.3 percent reported no change.[95] Other surveys reveal similar

---

the total number of simple post offices after mid-2008; the network company has since made some progress in reversing this trend (Hashimoto, "Yūsei jigyō no bapponteki minaoshi ni mukete," 10–11).

92. http://www.zentoku.org/about/press/kaiken080509.html (last accessed June 25, 2008).

93. Postal employees apparently had thick manuals under their desks that they frequently consulted while concluding postal financial transactions.

94. "Urano Yoshimi ni tou min'eika no risō to genjitsu," 48.

95. http://www.zentoku.org/enquete/0804.html (last accessed June 24, 2008).

trends. Of 213 postal employees polled by *Shūkan Daiyamondo* in late 2007, 48.4 percent stated that working conditions had worsened as a result of the privatization process, and only 2.8 percent reported improvements. Of that same group, 9.4 percent said that privatization was a good thing, and 46.5 percent said it was bad; 44.1 percent expressed no opinion.[96]

Employee complaints tended to center on overwork and tougher performance targets. Zentoku's survey found that more than 70 percent of postmasters were working ten or more hours per day.[97] And in the *Daiyamondo* poll, 59.2 percent of postal employees responded that their sales quotas (*noruma*) had gotten much tougher over the previous few months, and only 3.3 said that they had lightened.[98] Of particular concern were sales targets for New Year's postcards (*nengajō*), one of the mail service's most important revenue sources. *Nengajō* sales had been in decline since 2004. In late 2007, as part of a broader plan to increase mail revenues that included reducing the number of seasonal part-time employees, Japan Post Service increased its sales quotas. The result was intense pressure on individual full-time employees to improve sales and an increase in the incidence of employee "self-destruction" (*jibaku*)— buying up large numbers of postcards and then selling them at reduced rates either directly to consumers or to pawn shops.[99] Although the Japan Post Group does not officially acknowledge the existence of *jibaku*, its incidence is likely to increase as the group introduces new services and confronts market incentives to turn larger profits. As a result of these trends, fewer and fewer employees regard working for the post office as an act of public service and a source of pride, and it appears that the caliber of applicants for vacant positions is in decline.[100]

One of the biggest problems to arise out the postal privatization process has been the division of labor among postal employees. Before October 2007, employees who worked inside the commissioned post office were usually generalists who did everything from selling postage

---

96. *Shūkan Daiyamondo*, December 22, 2007, 51.
97. http://www.zentoku/enquete/0804.html (last accessed June 25, 2008).
98. *Shūkan daiyamondo*, December 22, 2007, 51.
99. Ibid., 34. Each full-time employee was required to sell around 10,000 *nengajō*.
100. Interview, Yoshino Naoyuki, Financial Services Agency, Tokyo, June 9, 2009.

stamps to administering postal savings accounts. Now, employees must work for one of four companies and are required to specialize in the specific services of that company. Consequently, an idle employee of Japan Post Service technically cannot assist her busy colleague in Japan Post Bank, even though customer demand may warrant it.

Jurisdictional issues have also had an impact on the post office's ability to perform social services. Mail carriers, all of whom work for Japan Post Service, are no longer at liberty to pick up the savings deposits of elderly local residents while on their rounds.[101] Japan Post Bank employees, for their own part, worry that mail carriers who perform this service will be increasingly vulnerable to theft. In the past, the local post office operated like a "greenhouse" in which losses resulting from accidents or theft could be covered by the postmasters' discretionary funds (*watari-kirihi*). Now that those funds have been eliminated and each service must account more fully for its own gains and losses, more and more post offices are reluctant to offer such services.[102] Meanwhile, many post offices are struggling to perform *himawari* services for housebound elderly residents, and the struggle is likely to continue with long-term reductions in the number of mail carriers and mounting pressures to generate higher profits. Although the 2-trillion-yen Community Contribution Fund established by the 2005 legislation will ensure that *himawari* and other social services will not completely disappear, the realities and pressures of operating in a more market-oriented system have significantly weakened the postal network's ability to deliver.

QUESTIONING KOIZUMI'S HANDIWORK

The government was well aware of problems at the post office; in fact, the Postal Privatization Committee was anticipating some of them even before the privatization process had officially begun.[103] In time, though,

---

101. By April 2009, Japan Post Group had granted special authorization to mail carriers in 2,652 post offices to carry out home visits for the postal savings service. This number is expected to increase (*Yomiuri shinbun*, April 4, 2009).

102. Interview, former official involved in post-2005 postal administration, Tokyo, June 2, 2009.

103. Minutes, Meeting no. 17, November 29, 2006. http://www.yuseimineika.go.jp/iinkai/kaisai.html (last accessed January 15, 2008).

several of Koizumi's detractors, including Prime Minister Asō Tarō, had learned to make an issue of them. In early 2009, Asō stunned reformist LDP lawmakers by publicly admitting that he had supported Koizumi's postal privatization plan only because he was obligated to do so as Minister of Internal Affairs and Communications. Although Asō later qualified his remarks by explaining that he had eventually come around to the idea of privatization,[104] he requested an early review of the privatization process, including a "rethink" (*minaoshi*) of Japan Post Group's corporate structure.[105] The Postal Privatization Committee dutifully complied, reporting in March 2009 that while it was concerned about the future profitability of the postal services in general and the mail service in particular,[106] the privatization process was more or less on track.[107]

Prime Minister Asō's remarks came in the midst of a major controversy surrounding the postal insurance inns. In keeping with the stipulations of the 2005 privatization legislation, in December 2008 Japan Post Holdings arranged to sell all 70 of its remaining inns and 9 postal employee dormitories to the Orix Group, a Tokyo-based financial services firm, for 10.9 billion yen.[108] As part of the deal, Orix promised not to lay off any employees—a costly commitment that should have pleased the postal regime. But no sooner was the deal publicized than Minister of Internal Affairs and Communications Hatoyama Kunio forced the holding company to abandon it, arguing that the bidding process had been too opaque and the selling price too low. Hatoyama went on to accuse Miyauchi Yoshihiko, Orix's chairman and a close Koizumi associate, of a conflict of interest.[109]

What drove the controversy were conflicting standards for handling national assets. Hatoyama and his supporters upheld long-standing government practices by assessing the value of the inn network on the basis

---

104. *Japan Times*, February 10, 2009.
105. Koizumi, now an ordinary backbencher nearing retirement, reacted to all this with derisive laughter.
106. Hashimoto, "Yūsei jigyō no bapponteki minaoshi ni mukete," 10.
107. Irizawa, "Yūsei kanryō no shizukanaru fukken de yūsei min'eika ga honenuki e?" 47.
108. *Japan Times*, June 12, 2009.
109. *Asahi shinbun*, January 31, 2009; *Sankei shinbun*, April 8, 2009.

Fig. C.1   Tokyo Central Post Office, July 2010. The now dilapidated Tokyo landmark was at the center of a 2009 controversy between Japan Post Holdings and Hatoyama Kunio, Minister of Internal Affairs and Communications. Photograph by the author.

of its assets, including the physical structures and the land they stood on. Japan Post Holdings, by contrast, adopted the accounting standards now in place for large private firms by factoring employee salaries and other liabilities into the selling price. Postal tribe politicians and others with vested interests in the inns, including those who were loath to expose their financial mismanagement,[110] claimed that the holding company's downward reevaluation of the inns in the context of the ongoing economic downturn was nothing short of scandalous—a sell-out of precious national assets and an example of the kind of "dirty business" that was common on Wall Street.[111] Hatoyama's detractors, including Koizumi, retorted that the government had violated privatization principles by intervening in the affairs of Japan Post Holdings.

Undeterred, Hatoyama confronted the firm a second time over its plans to redevelop the Tokyo Central Post Office. Built in the art-deco style in 1931, the low-lying and now dilapidated building threatened to drain the network firm's coffers once the latter started paying property

110. Tanaka, "Naze yūsei min'eika o atomodori sasete wa naranai no ka," 91.

111. Interview, former official involved in post-2005 postal administration, June 2, 2009.

taxes. Japan Post Holdings hoped to rectify matters by erecting a large, revenue-generating office tower on the site. Hatoyama protested that the renovation would destroy an important cultural asset and insisted that a larger portion of the original building be preserved. Japan Post Holdings went back to the drawing board and revised its reconstruction plans.

The controversies surrounding the postal insurance inns and the Central Post Office cast Nishikawa's presidency of Japan Post Holdings in a negative light. Increasingly, the postmasters and other members of the postal regime portrayed Nishikawa as a profit-hungry businessman, rather than an advocate for the public good. Hatoyama wanted him sacked as president, and resigned his post in protest in June 2009 after Prime Minister Asō—mindful of his government's mandate to implement postal privatization—refused to comply.[112] Hatoyama's successor, Satō Tsutomu, dutifully approved Nishikawa's reappointment.[113] But doubts surrounding the future direction of postal privatization remained. Satō, for instance, continued to criticize the corporate structure of the postal services and the need for Japan Post Holdings to divest its shares in the two postal financial firms. "No one believes these stock offerings are appropriate," he complained.[114]

As Koizumi's shadow faded and the LDP waffled on privatization, the opposition parties aggressively took up the cause of postal reform. In the summer of 2007, the DPJ teamed up with the PNP to table a bill to postpone the official start of the privatization process, now only weeks away. The bill was eventually defeated in the Diet, but the two parties and the SDPJ proceeded to form an alliance in the Upper House and to press for a freeze on the divestiture of shares in Japan Post Holdings and the two financial firms so that the parties would have sufficient time to draw up a plan to amend Koizumi's privatization legislation. Al-

---

112. Asō could not dismiss Nishikawa without harming the LDP government's reputation, for as an executive with the Japan Post Group observed, "The denial of the Nishikawa regime is almost tantamount to the denial of privatization" (*Nikkei Weekly*, June 29, 2009).

113. Nishikawa voluntarily took a 30 percent salary cut to "discipline himself" over the inn network's sale, and agreed to submit to the government a plan for improving operations at Japan Post Holdings (*Japan Times*, June 24, 2009).

114. *Japan Times*, June 27, 2009.

though the opposition parties failed to slow the pace of privatization, their commitment to reform was enough to win over the hearts and minds of the postmasters.

Efforts to undo some of Koizumi's postal reforms were also resonating with public doubts about neoliberal economic values and the social ramifications of structural reform. Such doubts had been germinating even while Koizumi was still in power, as evidenced by public reactions to his 2006 remarks that society would "lose its vitality unless people are very careful not to get jealous of successful ones or drag them down." One out of two Japanese voters expressed discomfort with this philosophy, claiming that they would welcome a review of structural reforms to prevent a further widening of Japan's already troubling social and economic disparities.[115]

Meanwhile, ordinary citizens continued to show respect for the local postmaster and his employees. In late 2007, *Daiyamondo* partnered with a private research institute to ask approximately 10,000 adults around the country to rank local personalities in terms of their trustworthiness. The postmasters and postal workers ranked second, at 25.6 percent, surpassed only by local policemen (48.3 percent).[116]

If ordinary Japanese were questioning structural reform and its poster child, postal privatization, they were even more inclined to do so with the onset of the 2008 global financial crisis. In 2008–2009, more and more critics were speaking out against the evils of "market fundamentalism" (*shijō genri shugi*)—excessive adherence to free market values and made-in-America globalization. Nakasone Yasuhiro and other LDP conservatives had long questioned the neoliberal "excesses" of Koizumi's prime ministership. But it was DPJ President Hatoyama Yukio's August 26, 2009, *New York Times* article that brought the trend to a head:

In the fundamentalist pursuit of capitalism people are treated not as an end but as a means. Consequently, human dignity is lost. How can we put an end to market fundamentalism and financial capitalism, that are void of morals or moderation, in order to protect the finances and livelihoods of our citizens? . . . In these times we must return to the idea of fraternity . . . as a force for mod-

---

115. Kyodo News poll from 2006, cited in *Japan Times*, February 8, 2006.

116. The list also included educators/teachers (15.8 percent), public officials (9.2 percent), and politicians (1.1 percent). *Shūkan Daiyamondo*, December 22, 2007, 51.

erating the dangers inherent within freedom. Fraternity as I mean it can be described as a principle that aims to adjust to the excesses of the current globalized brand of capitalism and accommodate the local economic practices that have been fostered through our traditions.

Hatoyama concluded that the global economy was damaging traditional economic activities and local communities, and pressed for the expansion of a social safety net.[117]

The postal regime would have been hard-pressed to find a better spokesperson for its cherished ideals. Granted, regime representatives had long been inclined to push the anti-globalization gauntlet to extremes. In 2003, when postal privatization was still but a vision for Koizumi, LDP postal-tribe member Arai Hiroyuki published a book warning that privatization would invite an American takeover of the postal services and the imposition of American-style capitalist (read socially insensitive) values onto the system.[118] In a similar vein, the PNP's Jimi Shōzaburō, a one-time postal reformer who had served as Hashimoto's Minister of Posts and Telecommunications, opined in 2009 that postal privatization was part of a global march toward American-style capitalist supremacy that had begun with the collapse of the Berlin Wall. Crediting the post office for leading nineteenth-century Japan's march toward modernity, Jimi, along with many others, championed deficit spending as a means to preserve the postal network and its social functions.[119] The postmasters, for their own part, routinely demanded a freeze on the sale of Japan Post Holdings' shares in the postal savings and insurance firms in order to prevent "vulture" (read American) funds from buying up the network.[120] Extremist sentiments aside, the postmasters shared with Hatoyama and many others in the DPJ a deep-seated belief that Japanese society had much to lose by marching blindly down the road toward neoliberal economic practices.

The timing of the August 30, 2009 Lower House election in the wake of the global economic crisis provided the DPJ with a perfect op-

---

117. The article was an English translation of a piece that later appeared in the September 2009 issue of the Japanese journal, *Voice*.

118. Arai, *Yūbinkyoku o Amerika ni uriwatasuna.*

119. Jimi, "Hontō ni yūsei min'eika wa hitsuyō nano ka."

120. *Asahi shinbun,* August 24, 2009.

portunity to solidify its alliance with the PNP and the SDPJ, and with the postmasters. For months, top DPJ leaders had been promising the postmasters "a fundamental reform of postal privatization," something that the LDP could never legitimately do after the 2005 election. Thus, when the Lower House was dissolved on July 21, 2009, the postmasters and their spouses and retired colleagues mobilized en mass behind the DPJ and the PNP,[121] distributing fliers, participating in rallies, manning the phones at candidates' electoral headquarters, making speeches on street corners, and persuading the voters to rally behind the DPJ and the PNP. And they did so in full view of the media for the first time in their history. Although the postmasters failed to elect several of their favorite candidates, they had become an important cog in the DPJ voting machine.

THE DPJ COALITION GOVERNMENT
AND "UNPRIVATIZING" THE POST OFFICE

The DPJ's spectacular electoral victory in 2009 and its formation of a coalition government with the PNP and the SDPJ shifted the balance of power between the forces for and against postal privatization. Key to that shift were the decisions of two strategically placed individuals: Ozawa Ichirō and Kamei Shizuka.

In 2006, the DPJ's Ozawa had pushed his party to distance itself from the LDP's stance on postal privatization in a bid to woo special interests like the postmasters.[122] In 2007, it was Ozawa who took the lead in forming a parliamentary group with the PNP and the SDPJ in the Upper House—a move that would help compensate for the DPJ's lack of a majority in the chamber; in exchange, Ozawa pledged to back the PNP's efforts to unravel Koizumi's postal privatization legislation.[123] And it was Ozawa who met frequently with the postmasters and Japan Post Group

---

121. In January 2008, Taiju renamed itself the Postal Policy Study Troup (Yūsei seisaku kenkyūkai). Although there are no concrete statistics on the group's electoral strength, some media observers estimate that the group was mobilizing up to 10,000 votes in each PR district during the 2009 Lower House election (*Asahi Newspaper*, August 27, 2009).

122. *Japan Times,* April 15, 2010.

123. *Daily Yomiuri*, October 17, 2007.

Union representatives to secure the postal network's electoral support, encouraging both groups to mobilize the vote behind DPJ or PNP candidates in return for promises to represent their interests in the policy-making sphere.

In Kamei Shizuka, an avowed opponent of postal privatization and of the "laws of the jungle" that allegedly inform it,[124] Ozawa found a strategic partner. Like Ozawa, Kamei had never been a full-fledged member of the postal regime while serving under the LDP banner; nor had he actively solicited the postmasters' electoral support. What drove Kamei to embrace the anti-privatization cause was in part his intense hatred of Koizumi Jun'ichirō. In the 2001 race for the LDP presidency, the two men had cut a last-minute deal in which Kamei pledged to withdraw his candidacy if Koizumi would soften his stance on postal privatization and consult Kamei on important cabinet and party appointments. But Koizumi never lived up to his promise, leaving Kamei feeling used and humiliated.[125] Ever the astute politician, Kamei proceeded to take revenge on Koizumi by helping to lead the charge against postal privatization, a position that found plenty of support among other LDP politicians who opposed Koizumi's polarizing leadership style. Kamei's opposition to postal privatization was also fueled by his long-standing sympathies for the underdogs of Japan: small businesses that were losing out to Asian competition, rural communities, and the elderly. Kamei claimed that he felt personally responsible for the plight of these groups, believing that his ill-fated deal with Koizumi in 2001 had helped pave the way for the ascendance of the structural reform movement.[126]

Once in power, Ozawa saw to it that Kamei became Minister of State for both Financial Affairs and Postal Privatization. (Hasegawa Kensei, the postmasters' "interest representative Diet member," was appointed Parliamentary Secretary for the Ministry of Internal Affairs and Com-

---

124. In his website, Kamei bids farewell to "the laws of the jungle" (*jakuniku kyō-shoku*) brought on by market fundamentalism. http://www.kamei-shizuka.net (last accessed October 28, 2009).

125. "Kamei Shizuka," 134.

126. Ōshita, *Kamei Shizuka*, 5, 299; *Sandē Mainichi*, June 27, 2010. Kamei's sympathy for the common man is expressed by his signature song, *Okaasan* ("Mother"). Sung to a traditional Japanese melody, *Okaasan* celebrates a mother's solicitous regard for her children and can be interpreted as a metaphor for the state's relationship with its people.

munications, a position that allowed him to play a major role in the reform process.) In October 2009, at Kamei's insistence, Nishikawa Yoshifumi resigned his post as president of Japan Post Holdings, citing fundamental differences with the new government over how the Japan Post Group should be run.[127] Kamei promptly replaced Nishikawa with Saitō Jirō, an Ozawa associate and former Administrative Vice-Minister of Finance. Saitō's appointment—along with that of three other former bureaucrats to vice-presidential positions in Japan Post Holdings—was at odds with the new government's electoral pledge to reduce the power of Japanese bureaucrats.

In late 2009, the coalition government used its majority in the Diet to pass the freeze on the sale of government shares in Japan Post Holdings, and of Japan Post Holdings' shares in the postal savings and insurance firms. The LDP abstained from voting after the DPJ refused to debate the contents of the bill.[128] Kamei then proceeded to draw up a plan for overhauling Koizumi's privatization legislation. Included in the plan were measures to: 1) merge the mail service, network, and holding companies; 2) obligate the government to hold more than one-third of the shares of this new firm at all times and to maintain the postal network at current levels; 3) require the merged firm to hold more than one-third of the shares of each of the two financial firms; 4) obligate the financial firms to provide universal service in postal savings and insurance; 5) lift the ceiling on combined ordinary postal savings accounts from 10 million yen to 20 million yen per person; 6) increase the maximum payout on postal insurance policies from 13 million to 25 million yen; and 7) convert up to 100,000 part-time postal employees into regular, full-time employees.[129]

Widely regarded as an "overwhelming presence" in the cabinet,[130] Kamei disregarded the counsel of his colleagues and normal decision-making procedures as he charged ahead with his agenda. Kamei explained that his aim was to return the postal system to its "public ser-

127. *Japan Times*, October 29, 2009.

128. *Japan Times*, December 5, 2009.

129. Hashimoto, "Yūsei jigyō no bapponteki minaoshi ni mukete," 15–17; Interview, two Japan Post Holdings executives, Tokyo, July 9, 2010.

130. *Shūkan Tōyō keizai*, May 1–8, 2010.

vice roots," where it would function as a buffer for disadvantaged citizens against free market forces.[131] The time had come, he argued, to recalibrate the balance between *kan* and *min* in ways that closed the many social gaps that had emerged in the wake of structural reform and the expansion of private-sector freedoms. He argued that there was nothing "backward" about his ambitions; had not other countries also woken up to the virtues of "mixed economies" following the 2008 global financial crisis?[132] Takenaka Heizō begged to differ. From late 2009 he seized every opportunity to publicly poke holes in Kamei's proposals, arguing that the new government was violating capitalist and democratic principles in its attempt to "re-nationalize" the postal firms.[133]

Kamei's political agenda was well served by the anti-privatization bill that cleared the Lower House of the Diet in late spring 2010. The pledge to raise the ceilings on postal savings accounts and insurance payouts promised to increase the flow of funds into the postal services that could then be used to maintain the postal network, provide universal service in postal savings and insurance, and invest in small businesses and rural communities.[134] Hiring tens of thousands of new postal employees would boost rural employment levels. Last but not least, merging the network and service firms with Japan Post Holdings would solve many of the logistical problems caused by the division of labor amongst the service firms, provide the government with a conduit for forcing the financial firms to guarantee universal service, and serve as a buffer for the declining mail service and the vulnerable postal network. In sum, these measures would position the postal system to help solve

---

131. *Asahi shinbun*, August 29, 2009.

132. Ibid.

133. Among other things, Takenaka complained that Kamei's proposals would strengthen the state's control over the postal savings and insurance services, put unfair competitive pressures on private-sector firms, dampen incentives for postal family enterprises to reform, and expose the taxpayers to possible bailouts of non-performing postal firms. As such, he maintained, the proposals marked a return to big government and was an affront to the people's will as expressed in the 2005 Lower House election. See Takenaka, "Yūsei 'saikokuyūka' wa minshushugi no hitei."

134. Kamei clearly assumed that the Japanese would flock to the postal savings and insurance systems once those ceilings were raised. As of summer 2010, there was no indication that this would indeed be the case (interview, Yoshino Naoyuki, Faculty of Economics, Keiō University, Tokyo, July 3, 2010).

many of the social problems that Kamei believed were rooted in Koizumi's neoliberal reform agenda.

Kamei's ability to act quickly and decisively on postal reform was facilitated by the nature of his position. As the head of a tiny party that fully backed him on postal reform—and whose support was essential to the DPJ government's ability to pass legislation—Kamei was given free reign to forge ahead with his plans and to ignore the advice of his colleagues and the PPPO.[135] As a minister of state, moreover, he did not have to answer to a large cohort of bureaucrats who might slow his progress on postal reform or serve as a vehicle for interest group pressures. But Kamei's initial accomplishments also reflected Prime Minister Hatoyama's weak leadership skills. From the start, Hatoyama found himself on the defensive as Kamei prioritized his personal agenda and seized the initiative on postal reform. When Kamei announced to the public in March 2010 that the government had drawn up a postal reform plan, Hatoyama was caught completely off guard. The prime minister eventually opted to approve the plan,[136] figuring that to do otherwise would simply expose the divisions within his cabinet to the public. But the move was too little, too late; the public was now fully aware of those divisions and of Hatoyama's inability to resolve them.[137]

In June 2010, shortly after the postal reform bills had cleared the Lower House and it looked like the Upper House would soon follow suit, the Ozawa-Kamei alliance came crashing down—and with it, the chances that Kamei's postal reform would soon see the legislative light of day. Ozawa resigned as Secretary-General of the DPJ in the midst of a debilitating financial scandal just as Prime Minister Hatoyama was vacating the party presidency (and the prime ministership). A few days later, Kamei quit his cabinet posts after Hatoyama's successor, Kan Naoto, refused to extend the Diet session so that the Upper House

---

135. For example, Kamei ignored the protestations of Sengoku Yoshito, a powerful cabinet colleague who at one time had advocated for a *reduction* of the ceiling on postal savings accounts (*Mainichi Newspaper*, March 26, 2010).

136. *Japan Times*, March 31, 2010.

137. In an April 2010 public opinion poll, 44 percent of respondents—the largest category—agreed with the statement that Hatoyama lacked leadership (*Yomiuri shinbun*, April 5, 2010).

could deliberate on the postal reform bills before the summer 2010 Upper House election.[138] Kan and Kamei were on the same page insofar as they championed financial reforms that would benefit rural Japan, but Kan had other interests besides postal reform. In the DPJ's 2010 election manifesto, which promised to "revive a healthy Japan" (*genki na Nihon o fukkatsu saseru*), a brief pledge to prioritize the speedy passage of the postal reform bills ranked a mere eighth in a list of ten policy commitments. Postal reform had been relegated to the back burner.

Kamei's postal reform proposal may have been downgraded on the DPJ's official list of priorities, but it clearly played a small but significant role in the coalition parties' dismal showing in the 2010 election. A Kyodo News public opinion survey conducted in 2008 revealed that more than 60 percent of the population—and 46 percent of LDP supporters—favored a review of Koizumi's postal privatization plan.[139] But in a spring 2010 Kyodo poll, 51 percent of those surveyed opposed the Hatoyama government's reform blueprint, while only 39 percent backed it; support for Kamei's party, the PNP, stood at zero.[140] The PNP went on in July to lose all three seats that were up for election, reducing its presence in the chamber to just three seats. Hasegawa Kensei's performance during the election is also revealing. Running in the national PR district, Hasegawa won approximately 407,000 votes, a dramatic increase over the 280,000 votes he had received in 2004.[141] These numbers suggest that the postmasters associations had fulfilled their pledge to back their "interest representative Diet member."[142] But Hasegawa failed to secure his seat because of the PNP's low share—1.71 percent,

---

138. Kamei's successor in these positions is Jimi Shōzaburō, a former postal rebel and PNP colleague who is equally committed to unravelling Koizumi's postal privatization plan.

139. *The Japan Times,* March 18, 2009.

140. *Japan Times,* April 15, 2010.

141. Since 2001, the Upper House PR district has been an "open list" system, which means that voters can cast their vote for either the party or for an individual candidate on the list.

142. *Asahi shinbun,* June 17, 2010.

Fig. C.2 Kamei Shizuka, stumping for People's New Party candidates during the 2010 Upper House election campaign. Kamei was the main architect of the DPJ coalition government's 2010 postal reform bills. Photograph by the author.

as opposed to 2.2 percent in 2007—of the overall PR vote.[143] Japanese voters may have favored amendments to Koizumi's 2005 postal privatization legislation, but if the PNP's electoral performance is any indication, they were concluding that the coalition government had taken reform too far.

The DPJ coalition government's backtracking on postal privatization between August 2009 and June 2010 reveals that the confluence of institutional, interest group, and leadership factors had shifted since Koizumi left power in 2006. Institutionally, nothing had fundamentally changed. As Frances Rosenbluth and Michael Thies observe, the parties were still incentivized by electoral rules and an empowered prime minis-

143. *Daily Yomiuri*, July 13, 2010; "UH 2010: Proportional Representation," *Twisting Flowers*, July 13, 2010, http://twistingflowers.com/2010/07/13/uh2010-proportional-representation/ (last accessed July 17, 2011).

tership to speak to the "median voter" rather than organized special interests.[144] The problem was that none of the parties, not least the DPJ and the PNP, had learned how to adapt to these incentives. Wracked by internal divisions and over-reliant on Ozawa's machine-style political tactics, the DPJ confronted the growing uncertainties of elections by shedding its reformist mantle and catering to the likes of the postmasters. And as it did so it engaged in a Faustian bargain with the anti-reformist PNP that accorded the tiny party far more power than its representation in the Diet would warrant.

The DPJ's increasing openness to anti-reformist voices further empowered the "forces of resistance" vis-à-vis neoliberal reformers in the wake of the 2008 economic crisis. Against this backdrop, Koizumi's successors failed to uphold the tenets of the 2005 postal privatization legislation, creating a leadership vacuum in the postal sphere that well-positioned spokespersons for the anti-privatization camp were only too happy to fill.

In the end, the postal regime's gains in 2009 and early 2010 proved short lived. With the downfall of Kamei and Ozawa and the loss of the coalition government's majority in the July 2010 Upper House election, the regime's chances of passing Kamei's radical reform bills plummeted. But the regime's determination to unravel Koizumi's handiwork has by no means abated. For as long as the postmasters and their elected representatives operate in an environment of social, economic, and electoral uncertainty, the "forces of resistance" will remain a political force to be reckoned with.

Postscript

In the immediate aftermath of the devastating 9.0-magnitude earthquake, tsunami, and nuclear accident that struck the Tōhoku region on March 11, 2011, the postal system quietly introduced a series of relief measures that evoked memories of the state-run postal system's humanitarian efforts in the wake of the 1923 Great Kantō Earthquake and the Allied fire bombings and atomic blasts of 1945. Included among the measures were provisions for residents in stricken areas to make emergency with-

---

144. Rosenbluth and Thies, *Japan Transformed.*

drawals from their postal savings accounts of up to 200,000 yen; even those who had lost all documented proof of their accounts were eligible to make the withdrawals. Within six weeks of the disaster, Japan Post Bank had concluded nearly 20,000 transactions under the program.[145]

For the time being, the DPJ is too preoccupied with post-disaster recovery and its own internal problems to pay much attention to the post office or to Kamei's reform bills, which continue to languish in the Diet. But as the political dust begins to settle, the future of postal reform could very well figure in debates about the country's political, economic, and social future. On the one hand, it is quite possible that as the region struggles to rebuild its communities and industries, business interests and others who favor market-oriented reform will gain the upper hand and reposition the policy process on a more neoliberal path. On the other hand, the remarkable dignity and selfless community spirit demonstrated by the region's hardest hit residents may strengthen calls for a reinvigorated financial and social role for more traditional institutions like the local post office. That being the case, we may witness yet another wholesale rethink of Koizumi's privatization legislation.

It is too soon to predict how debates about the future of the postal system and the political economy more generally will be resolved. But one thing is certain: for as long as it is able to do so, the "people's post office" will continue to operate as one of Japan's last remaining sanctuaries of traditional values in a rapidly changing world.

---

145. Japan Post Group. Various press releases (from March 12, 2011). http://www. japanpost.jp/pressrelease/index2.html?company=&branch=00&sort=1&mn=press& detail=1 (last accessed October 24, 2011).

Reference Matter

Works Cited

Aketa, Hiroshi. "Issues in the Privatization of Postal Life Insurance: A Practical Proposal for Equal Footing." *NLI Research*, September 22, 2004.
   http://www.nli-research.co.jp/english/socioeconomics/2004/li040922.html

"Akushon puran no genba kara" (The action plan from the field). *Yūsei kenkyū*, no. 643 (April 2004): 10–11.

Allam, David R. *The Social and Economic Importance of Postal Reform in 1840*. London: Harry Hayes, 1976.

Amyx, Jennifer A. *Japan's Financial Crisis: Institutional Rigidity and Reluctant Change*. Princeton, NJ: Princeton University Press, 2004.

Amyx, Jennifer A., Harukata Takenaka, and A. Maria Toyoda. "The Politics of Postal Savings Reform in Japan." *Asian Perspective* 29, no. 1 (2005): 23–48.

Anderson, Stephen J. "The Political Economy of Japanese Saving: How Postal Savings and Public Pensions Support High Rates of Household Saving in Japan." *Journal of Japanese Studies* 16, no. 1 (Winter 1990): 61–92.

Arai Hiroyuki. *Yūbinkyoku o Amerika ni uriwatasu na: yūsei min'eika o nerau gurōbarizumu no wana* (Don't sell out the post office to America: the globalization trap of postal privatization). Tokyo: Asuka shinsha, 2003.

Austen, Brian. *English Provincial Posts, 1633–1840: A Study Based on Kent Examples*. London and Chichester: Phillmore & Co., Ltd., 1978.

Beale, Philip. *A History of the Post in England from the Romans to the Stuarts*. Aldershot, UK: Ashgate, 1998.

Beasley, W. G. *Japan Encounters the Barbarian: Japanese Travelers in America and Europe*. New Haven, CT: Yale University Press, 1995.

Bullock, Robert. "Nokyo: A Short Cultural History." *JPRI Working Paper*, no. 41 (December 1997).
   http://www.jpri.org/publications/workingpapers/wp41.html

Calder, Kent E. "Linking Welfare and the Developmental State: Postal Savings in Japan." *Journal of Japanese Studies* 16, no. 1 (Winter 1990): 31–59.

Campbell, John L. *Institutional Change and Globalization*. Princeton, NJ: Princeton University Press, 2004.

Campbell, Robert M. *The Politics of Postal Transformation: Modernizing Postal Systems in the Electronic and Global World*. Montreal, QC: McGill-Queen's University Press, 2002.

Cargill, Thomas F., and Takayuki Sakamoto. *Japan Since 1980*. Cambridge, UK: Cambridge University Press, 2008.

Cargill, Thomas F., and Naoyuki Yoshino. *Postal Savings and Fiscal Investment in Japan: The Postal Savings System and the FILP*. Oxford, UK: Oxford University Press, 2003.

Carlile, Lonny E. "The Politics of Administrative Reform." In *Is Japan Really Changing Its Ways? Regulatory Reform and the Japanese Economy*, ed. Lonny E. Carlile and Mark C. Tilton. Washington, DC: The Brookings Institution, 1998, 76–110.

Carlson, Matthew. "Japan's Postal Privatization Battle: The Continuing Reverberations for the Liberal Democratic Party of Rebels-Assassins Conflicts." *Asian Survey* 48, no. 4 (July–August 2008): 603–25.

Christensen, Ray. "An Analysis of the 2005 Japanese General Election: Will Koizumi's Political Reforms Endure?" *Asian Survey* 46, no. 4 (July–August 2006): 497–516.

Civil Communications Section of the Supreme Commander of the Allied Powers. *Report on Survey of Japanese Postal System*. RG 331, National Archives and Records Service, Box #3185, February 1949.

Clinton, Alan. *Post Office Workers: A Trade Union and Social History*. London: George Allen & Unwin, 1984.

Cohen, Robert B. "Policy Challenges and the Privatization of Japan Post." Washington, DC: Economic Strategy Institute, 2006.

Cullinan, Gerald. *The United States Postal Service*. New York, NY: Praeger, 1973.

Curtis, Gerald. "The 1974 Election Campaign: The Political Process." In *Japan at the Polls: the House of Councilors Election of 1974*, ed. Michael K. Blaker. Washington, DC: American Enterprise Institute for Public Policy Research, 1976, 45–80.

Daunton, M. J. *Royal Mail: The Post Office Since 1840*. London and Dover, NH: Athlone Press, 1985.

Doi, Takero, and Takeo Hoshi. "Paying for the FILP." In *Structural Impediments to Growth in Japan*, ed. Magnus Blomström, Jennifer Corbett, Fumio Hayashi, and Anil Kashyap. Chicago, IL: University of Chicago Press, 2003, 37–69.

Dore, Ronald. *Stock Market Capitalism: Welfare Capitalism: Japan and Germany Versus the Anglo-Saxons.* Oxford, UK: Oxford University Press, 2000.

Duus, Peter. *The Abacus and the Sword: The Japanese Penetration of Korea, 1895–1910.* Berkeley, CA: University of California Press, 1995.

Ellis, Kenneth. *The Post Office in the Eighteenth Century: A Study in Administrative History.* London: Oxford University Press, 1958.

Enō Masaki. *Jitsuroku: tokutei yūbinkyokuchōsan* (An authentic account: mister commissioned postmaster). Tokyo: Shinpūsha, 2006.

Ericson, Steven J. *The Sound of the Whistle: Railroads and the State in Meiji Japan.* Cambridge, MA: Council on East Asian Studies, Harvard University, 1996.

Estevéz-Abe, Margarita. "Japan's Shift Toward a Westminster System: A Structural Analysis of the 2005 Lower House Election and Its Aftermath." *Asian Survey* 46, no. 4 (July–August 2006): 632–51.

Feber, Katalin. "'Run the State Like a Business': The Origin of the Deposit Fund in Meiji Japan." *Japanese Studies* 22, no. 2 (2002): 131–51.

Fowler, Dorothy Ganfield. *The Cabinet Politician: The Postmasters General, 1829–1909.* New York: Columbia University Press, 1943.

Fukutake, Tadashi. *Japanese Rural Society.* Trans. Ronald P. Dore. Tokyo, New York: Oxford University Press, 1967.

Fuller, Wayne E. *The American Mail: Enlarger of the Common Life.* Chicago, IL: University of Chicago Press, 1972.

Garon, Sheldon. *Beyond Our Means: Why America Spends While the World Saves.* Princeton, NJ: Princeton University Press, 2011.

———. "Fashioning a Culture of Diligence and Thrift: Savings and Frugality Campaigns in Japan, 1900–1931." In *Japan's Competing Modernities: Issues in Culture and Democracy, 1900–1931,* ed. Sharon A. Minichiello. Honolulu, HI: University of Hawai'i Press, 1998, 312–34.

———. "'Luxury is the Enemy': Mobilizing Savings and Popularizing Thrift in Wartime Japan." *Journal of Japanese Studies* 26, no. 1 (Winter 2000): 41–78.

Gluck, Carol. *Japan's Modern Myths: Ideology in the Late Meiji Period.* Princeton, NJ: Princeton University Press, 1985.

Hall, Peter. *Governing the Economy: The Politics of State Intervention in Britain and France.* New York: Oxford University Press, 1986.

Hall, Peter, and David Soskice, eds. *Varieties of Capitalism: The Institutional Foundations of Comparative Advantage.* New York: Oxford University Press, 2001.

Hara Shirō and Yamaguchi Osamu. *Yūbin chokin: katsuryoku aru shakai e no kōken* (Postal savings: contributing to an energetic society). Tokyo: Gyōsei, 1982.

Hashimoto Gorō, Iida Masayuki, and Katō Shūjirō. *Zukai Nihon seiji no shōhyakka* (A handbook of Japanese politics). Tokyo: Ichigeisha, 2002.

Hashimoto Kenji. "Yūsei jigyō no bapponteki minaoshi ni mukete" (Toward a drastic reevaluation of the postal services). *Rippō to chōsa*, no. 305 (June 2010): 3–24.

Hatagawa Ichirō. "Tokutei yūbinkyoku wa ika ni arubeki ka" (How should the commissioned post offices be?). *Toki to hōrei*, no 27 (March 1958): 13–19.

Hayasaka Shigezō. *Seijika Tanaka Kakuei* (The politician Tanaka Kakuei). Tokyo: Chūō kōron, 1987.

Hida chiku tokutei yūbinkyokuchōkai kaishi hensan iinkai, ed. *Hida no tokutei yūbinkyoku shi* (History of Hida's commissioned post offices). Hida, Gifu: Hida chiku tokutei yūbinkyokuchōkai, 1996.

Hill, Rowland. *Post Office Reform: Its Importance and Practicability*. 3rd ed. London: Charles Knight and Co., 1837.

Hirschman, Albert O. *Exit, Voice, and Loyalty: Responses to Decline in Firms, Organizations, and States*. Cambridge, MA: Harvard University Press, 1970.

Hobsbawm, Eric, and Terence Ranger, eds. *The Invention of Tradition*. Cambridge, UK: Cambridge University Press, 1983.

Honma Shūichi. *Tokutei yūbinkyokuchō ni natta boku no rakudai nikki* (My diary as a failed commissioned postmaster). Tokyo: Shinpūsha, 2003.

Hoshino Kōji. *Sekai no yūsei kaikaku* (Postal reform in the world). Tokyo: Yū-kensha, 2004.

Hunter, Janet E. "A Study of the Career of Maejima Hisoka, 1935–1919." Ph.D diss., St. Antony's College, University of Oxford, 1976.

———. "Understanding the Economic History of Postal Services: Some Preliminary Observations from the Case of Meiji Japan." CIRJE Discussion Paper Series, CIRJE-F-344. Center for International Research on the Japanese Economy, University of Tokyo, 2005.

Iijima Isao. *Koizumi kantei hiroku* (Secret records of the Koizumi administration). Tokyo: Nihon keizai shinbunsha, 2006.

Ikeda Ken'ichi. "The Impact of the Postal Reform on Japanese Voters: Japanese National Election in 2005." Paper presented to the American Political Science Association Annual Meeting, Philadelphia, 2006.

Ikeda Minoru. *Yūbin'yasan ga naiteiru* (Mr. postmaster is crying). Tokyo: Gendai shokan, 1999.

Ikuta Masaharu. *Yūsei kaikaku no genten* (The origins of postal reform). Tokyo: Zaikai kenkyūjo, 2007.

Inoguchi Takashi. "Japan's Upper House Election of 29 July 2001." *Government & Opposition* 37, no. 1 (Winter 2002): 38–54.

Inoguchi Takashi and Iwai Tomoaki. *Zoku giin no kenkyū* (Research on policy tribes). Tokyo: Nihon keizai shinbunsha, 1987.

Inose Naoki. *Kessen: yūsei min'eika* (The decisive battle: postal privatization). Tokyo: PHP kenkyūjo, 2005.

Irizawa Shōji. "Yūsei kanryō no shizukanaru fukken de yūsei min'eika ga honenuki e?" (Is postal privatization heading for emasculation as a result of the quiet rehabilitation of postal bureaucrats?). *Keizaikai* (April 7, 2009): 46–48.

Itō Mitsutoshi. "Kantei shudōkei seisaku kettei to Jimintō" (Policymaking based on prime ministerial leadership and the LDP). *Leviathan* 38 (Spring 2006): 7–40.

Jansen, Marius B. *The Making of Modern Japan.* Cambridge, MA: The Belknap Press of Harvard University Press, 2000.

Japan Center for Economic Research. "Postal Privatization in Japan and the Future of Banks and Life Insurers." Financial Report No. 13. Tokyo: Japan Center for Economic Research, October 2005.

Japan Post. *Annual Report: Postal Services in Japan: 2006.* Tokyo: Japan Post, 2006.

———. *Annual Report: Postal Services in Japan: 2007.9.* Tokyo: Japan Post, 2007.

Japan Post Group. *Annual Report: 2008.* Tokyo: Japan Post, 2008.

———. *Annual Report: 2009.* Tokyo: Japan Post, 2009.

———. *Annual Report: 2010.* Tokyo, Japan Post, 2010.

Jimi Shōzaburō. "Hontō ni yūsei min'eika wa hitsuyō nano ka: Jimi Shozaburō" (Is postal privatization really necessary?: Jimi Shōzaburō). *Zaikaijin* (March 2009): 36–39.

Jin Ikkō. *Ōkura kanryō: chō erīto shūdan no jinmyaku to yabō* (Ministry of Finance officials: the connections and ambitions of the ultra-elite). 2nd ed. Tokyo: Kōdansha, 1992.

John, Richard R. *Spreading the News: The American Postal System from Franklin to Morse.* Cambridge, MA: Harvard University Press, 1995.

Johnson, Chalmers. *Japan's Public Policy Companies.* Washington, DC: American Enterprise Institute for Public Policy Research, 1978.

Joyce, Herbert. *The History of the Post Office: From its Establishment Down to 1836.* London: Richard Bentley & Son, 1893.

Kabashima, Ikuo, and Gill Steel. "The Koizumi Revolution." *PS: Political Science & Politics* 40, no. 1 (January 2007): 79–84.

Kakumoto Ryōhei. *Mittsu no min'eika: dōro kōdan kaikaku, yūsei kaikaku to JR* (Three privatizations: highway reform, postal reform, and the JR). Tokyo: Ryūtsū Keizai Daigaku shuppankai, 2005.

"Kamei Shizuka: watakushi ga 'yūsei min'eika' o bukkowasu" (Kamei Shizuka: I'm going to smash 'postal privatization'). *Bungei shunjū* (December 2009): 130–35.

Kamiko Takahito. *Zentei rōdō undōshi: sōkatsu to 80-nendai tenbō* (A history of the Zentei labor movement: overview and prospects for the 1980s). Tokyo: Tabata shoten, 1982.

Kano Kazuhiko. *Chiiki to kurashi o posuto ga tsunagu: yūbinkyoku ga fureai mansai* (The mailbox connects regions and lifestyles: the post office is full of personal interactions). Tokyo: Nihon nōritsu kyōkai manejimento sentā, 2001.

Kasza, Gregory. *One World of Welfare: Japan in Comparative Perspective*. Ithaca, NY: Cornell University Press, 2006.

Kato, Junko. "Reforming the Japanese Bureaucracy: Perceptions, Potential and Pitfalls." *Japanese Political Reform: Progress in Process*. Woodrow Wilson International Center for Scholars, Asia Program Special Report, no. 117 (January 2004): 34–37.

Katsumata Yasuo. *Tokutei yūbinkyoku konjaku monogatari* (A story of changing times for the commissioned post offices). Kanagawa: Kachitomokai, 1983.

Kinoshita, Nobuyuki. "The Economics of Japan's Postal Services Privatization." Center on Japanese Economy and Business, Columbia University. Working Paper No. 263, August 2008.

Kitagawa Ryūichi. "Zenkindaiteki na mono no saihensei: tokutei yūbinkyoku seido to rōdō kumiai undō" (Shaking up premodern things: the commissioned postal system and the labor union movement). *Rōdō mondai* (January 1963): 76–85.

Kobayashi, Keiichiro. "The Points of Contention Surrounding Postal Services Reform." Research Institute of Economy, Trade and Industry (April 20, 2004).
http://www.rieti.go.jp/en/columns/a01_0126.html

Kobayashi Masayoshi. *Minna no yūbin bunka shi: kindai Nihon o sodateta jōhō dentatsu shisutemu* (A history of mail culture for everyone: the information and communications system that raised modern Japan). Tokyo: Nijūni, 2002.

Koizumi Jun'ichirō. "Forward." In *Yūsei min'eika ron: Nihon saisei no daikaikaku!* (The postal privatization debate: the biggest reform for the rebirth of Japan!), ed. Koizumi Jun'ichirō and Matsuzawa Shigefumi. Tokyo: PHP kenkyūjo, 1999, 1–4.

Köllner, Patrick. "Upper House Elections in Japan and the Power of the 'Organized Vote.'" *Japanese Journal of Political Science* 3, no. 1 (2002): 113–37.

Kowaguchi Makoto. *Yūsei no Sekigahara* (The postal system's Sekigahara). Tokyo: Kubo shoten, 1998.

Krauss, Ellis S., and Robert Pekkanen. "Reforming the Liberal Democratic Party." In *Democratic Reform in Japan: Assessing the Impact*, ed. Sherry L. Martin and Gill Steel. Boulder, CO: Lynne Rienner, 2008, 11–37.

Kuwayama, Patricia Hagan. "Postal Banking in the United States and Japan: A Comparative Analysis." Center on Japanese Economy and Business, Columbia University. Working Paper No. 139, October 1997.

Kyūshū chihō tokutei yūbinkyokuchōkai. *Kyūshū tokutei yūbinkyokuchōkai shi* (A history of the Kyūshū commissioned postmasters association). Kumamoto: Kyūshū chihō tokutei yūbinkyokuchōkai, 2000.

Lin, Chao-Chi. "How Koizumi Won." In *Political Change in Japan: Electoral Behavior, Party Realignment, and the Koizumi Reforms*, ed. Steven R. Reed, Kenneth Mori McElwain, and Kay Shimizu. Palo Alto, CA: The Walter H. Shorenstein Asia-Pacific Research Center, Stanford University, 2009, 109–31.

Lincoln, Edward J. *Arthritic Japan: The Slow Pace of Economic Reform*. Washington, DC: Brookings Institution Press, 2001.

Machida Tetsu. *Nihon yūsei: tokihanatareta kyojin* (The Japanese postal system: an emancipated giant). Tokyo: Nihon keizai shinbunsha, 2005.

Maclachlan, Patricia L. *Consumer Politics in Postwar Japan: The Institutional Boundaries of Citizen Activism*. New York: Columbia University Press, 2001.

———. "Post Office Politics in Modern Japan: The Postmasters, Iron Triangles, and the Limits of Reform. *Journal of Japanese Studies* 30, no. 2 (Summer 2004): 281–313.

———. "Storming the Castle: The Battle for Postal Reform in Japan." *Social Science Japan Journal* 9, no. 1 (April 2006): 1–18.

———. "Two Steps Forward, One Step Back: Japanese Postal Privatization as a Window on Political and Policymaking Change. In *Political Change in Japan: Electoral Behavior, Party Realignment, and the Koizumi Reforms*, ed. Steven R. Reed, Kenneth Mori McElwain, and Kay Shimizu. Palo Alto, CA: Walter H. Shorenstein Asia-Pacific Research Center, Stanford University, 2009, 157–77.

Maejima Hisoka. *Maejima Hisoka yūbin sōgyōdan* (Maejima Hisoka conversations about the founding of mail). Hayama, Kanagawa: Maejima Hisoka denki kankōkai, 1956.

Maeno Kazuhisa. *21-seiki wa Yūseishō no jidai: mura no yūbinkyoku kara uchū eisei made* (The 21st century is the era of the Ministry of Posts and Telecommunications: from village post offices to space satellites). Tokyo: Bijinesusha, 1987.

———. *Yūseishō to iu yakusho* (That government office called the Ministry of Posts and Telecommunications). Tokyo: Suna shobō, 1993.

Matsubara Satoru. *Gendai no yūsei jigyō* (The contemporary postal services). Tokyo: Nihon hyōronsha, 1996.

———. *Yūsei min'eika de kō kawaru: kokuei shinwa ni wa, mō damasarenai* (Change will happen like this with postal privatization: we won't be hoodwinked any longer by the myth of state management). Tokyo: Kadokawa shoten, 2001.

———. "Yūsei min'eika 'Koizumi gen'an' to wa nani ka" (What is Koizumi's plan for postal privatization?). In *Yūsei min'eika: Koizumi gen'an* (Postal privatization: Koizumi's plan), ed. Mizuno Kiyoshi, Matsubara Satoru, Chūjō Ushio, and Matsuda Makoto. Tokyo: Shōgakukan, 2001, 13–54.

Matsuda Makoto. "Yūsei sanjigyō ni 'kisei' suru gaibu dantai, fuamirii kigyōgun" (Parasitic outside groups and family enterprises in the three postal services). In *Yūsei min'eika: Koizumi gen'an* (Postal privatization: Koizumi's plan), ed. Mizuno Kiyoshi, Matsubara Satoru, Chūjō Ushio, and Matsuda Makoto. Tokyo: Shōgakukan, 2001, 93–126.

Ministry of Finance. *FILP Report: 2007.* Tokyo: Ministry of Finance, Financial Bureau, 2007.

Ministry of Finance. *FILP Report: 2009.* Tokyo: Ministry of Finance, Financial Bureau, 2009.

Ministry of Finance. *FILP Plan (Proposal) for 2010.* Tokyo: Ministry of Finance, Financial Bureau, 2009.

Ministry of Internal Affairs and Communications. *Historical Statistics of Japan,* 2010.

Ministry of Public Management, Home Affairs, Posts and Telecommunications. *2004 White Paper: Information and Communications in Japan.* Tokyo: Ministry of Public Management, Home Affairs, Posts and Telecommunications, 2004.

Mishima, Ko. "The Changing Relationship Between Japan's LDP and the Bureaucracy: Hashimoto's Administrative Reform Effort and Its Politics." *Asian Survey* 38, no. 10 (October 1998): 968–85.

———. "Grading Japanese Prime Minister Koizumi's Revolution: Has the LDP's Policymaking Changed?" *Asian Survey* 47, no. 5 (September–October 2007): 727–48.

Mizuno Kiyoshi. *Doitsu posuto vs. Nihon yūsei kōsha* (Deutsche Post vs. Japan Post). Tokyo: Chūkei shuppan, 2002.

———. "Yūsei min'eika e no nagaki michinori" (Traveling the long road to postal privatization). In *Yūsei min'eika: Koizumi gen'an* (Postal privatization: Koizumi's plan), ed. Mizuno Kiyoshi, Matsubara Satoru, Chūjō Ushio, and Matsuda Makoto. Tokyo: Shōgakukan, 2001, 127–218.

Moriyama Kamon and Nihei Mitsugu. *GHQ to senryōka no yūsei* (The GHQ and the postal system under occupation). Tokyo: Yūkensha, 1995.

Mulgan, Aurelia George. *Japan's Failed Revolution: Koizumi and the Politics of Economic Reform.* Canberra: Asia Pacific Press, Asia Pacific School of Economics and Management, 2002.

———. *The Politics of Agriculture in Japan.* London: Routledge, 2000.

Muramoto Tsutomu. "Saihen sareyuku yūbinkyoku" (The reorganizing post office). *Toshi mondai* 99, no. 11 (November 2008): 62–69.

Nagao, Hampei. "Communications in Japan." In *Western Influences in Modern Japan: A Series of Papers on Cultural Relations*, ed. Nitobe Inazo et al. Chicago, IL: Chicago University Press, 1931, 342–59.

Naikaku kanbō yūsei min'eika suishin shitsu. *Min'eika de dō naru no? Watashitachi no yūbinkyoku* (What will happen with privatization? Our post offices). Tokyo: Naikaku kanbō yūsei min'eika suishin shitsu, 2006.

Najita Tetsuo. *Hara Kei in the Politics of Compromise, 1905–15.* Cambridge, MA: Harvard University Press, 1967.

Nemoto, Kuniaki, Ellis Krauss, and Robert Pekkanen. "Policy Dissension and Party Discipline: The July 2005 Vote on Postal Privatization in Japan." *British Journal of Political Science* 38, no. 3 (July 2008): 499–525.

Nikkei Business. *Daremo shiranai yūsei teikoku* (The postal system empire that no one knows about). Tokyo: Nikkei BP sha, 2002.

Niigata nippōsha. *Za Etsuzankai* (The Etsuzan Association). Niigata: Niigata nippō jigyōsha shuppanbu, 1973.

Noble, Gregory W. "Political Leadership and Economic Policy in the Koizumi Cabinet." *Social Science Japan Newsletter* 22 (December 2001): 24–28.

———. "Front Door, Back Door: The Reform of Postal Savings and Loans in Japan." *Japanese Economy* 33, no. 1 (Spring 2005): 107–23.

Nomura Masaki. *Asunaro mura no sangeki: yūsei min'eika no soboku na fuan* (Tomorrow's village tragedy: unadorned uncertainties about postal privatization). Tokyo: Yūkensha, 2005.

Norgren, Christiana A. E. *Abortion Before Birth Control: The Politics of Reproduction in Postwar Japan.* Princeton, NJ: Princeton University Press, 2001.

OECD. *Promoting Competition in Postal Services.* Paris: OECD, 1999.

Ogata, Shijuro. "Financial Markets in Japan." In *National Diversity and Global Capitalism*, ed. Suzanne Berger and Ronald Dore. Ithaca, NY: Cornell University Press, 1996, 171–78.

Ogawa Tsunendo and Takahashi Zenshichi. *Tokutei yūbinkyoku seido shi* (A history of the commissioned post office system). Tokyo: Shijinsha, 1983.

Okina, Yuri. "Japan's Financial System Since the Bursting of the Bubble: Present Status and Issues for the Future." Tokyo: Japan Research Institute, May 2002.

Olson, Mancur. *The Logic of Collective Action: Public Goods and the Theory of Groups.* Cambridge, MA: Harvard University Press, 1965. Revised edition 1971.

Ōmori Shunji. *Kyokuchōkai monogatari* (A story of the postmasters association). Osaka: Teishin shinpōsha, 1977.

Ōshita Eiji. *Kamei Shizuka: tenbaku o yuku* (Kamei Shizuka: flights of fancy). Tokyo: Tokuma shoten, 2010.

Otake, Hideo. "The Rise and Retreat of a Neoliberal Reform: Controversies over Land Use Policy." In *Political Dynamics in Contemporary Japan*, ed. Gary D. Allinson and Yasunori Sone. Ithaca, NY: Cornell University Press, 1993, 242–63.

Park, Gene. *Spending Without Taxation: FILP and the Politics of Public Finance in Japan*. Palo Alto, CA: Stanford University Press, 2011.

Patterson, Dennis. "Electoral Influence and Economic Policy: Political Origins of Financial Aid to Small Business in Japan." *Comparative Political Studies* 27, no. 3 (October 1994): 425–47.

Pempel, T. J. "Learning to Lose is for Losers: The Japanese LDP's Reform Struggle." In *Political Transitions in Dominant Party Systems: Learning to Lose*, ed. Edward Friedman and Joseph Wong. London: Routledge, 2008, 109–26.

———. *Regime Shift: Comparative Dynamics of the Japanese Political Economy*. Ithaca, NY: Cornell University Press, 1998.

Pierson, Paul. *Politics in Time: History, Institutions, and Social Analysis*. Princeton, NJ: Princeton University Press, 2004.

Pierson, Paul, and Theda Skocpol. "Historical Institutionalism in Contemporary Political Science." In *Political Science: State of the Discipline*, ed. Ira Katznelson and Helen V. Milner. New York: W. W. Norton; Washington, DC: American Political Science Association, 2002, 693–721.

Polanyi, Karl. *The Great Transformation: The Political and Economic Origins of Our Time*. Second edition. Boston, MA: Beacon Press, 2001.

Porges, Amelia, and Joy M. Leong. "The Privatization of Japan Post: Ensuring Both a Viable Post and a Level Playing Field." Paper presented to 13th Conference on Postal and Delivery Economics, Antwerp, June 1–4, 2005.

Post Office Circular, no. 505 (October 20, 1885).

The Postal History Society Bulletin, no. 7 (July 1938).

Priest, George L. "The History of the Postal Monopoly in the United States." *Journal of Law and Economics* 18, no. 1 (April 1975): 33–80.

Richardson, Bradley M. "Social Networks, Influence Communications, and the Vote." In *The Japanese Voter*, ed. Scott C. Flanagan, Shinsaku Kohei, Ichiro Miyake, Bradley M. Richardson, and Joji Watanuki. New Haven, CT: Yale University Press, 1991, 332–66.

Rōdō sōgi chōsakai, ed. *Teishin jigyō no sōgi to kumiai undō* (Communications services disputes and the union movement). Vol. 14 of *Sengo rōdō sōgi jittai chōsa* (Survey on the condition of postwar labor disputes). Tokyo: Chūō kōronsha, 1959.

Roeder, C. *Beginnings of the Manchester Post Office*. Manchester, UK: Richard Gill, 1905.

Rogers, Lindsay. *The Postal Power of Congress: A Study in Constitutional Expansion.* Baltimore, MD: Johns Hopkins Press, 1916.

Rosenbluth, Francis McCall. *Financial Politics in Contemporary Japan.* Ithaca, NY: Cornell University Press, 1989.

Rosenbluth, Francis McCall, and Michael F. Thies. *Japan Transformed: Political Change and Economic Restructuring.* Princeton, NJ: Princeton University Press, 2010.

Sadamitsu Jō. "Yūsei min'eika kihon hōshin kettei uke yoron chōsa" (Public opinion on the postal privatization basic plan). *Jiji Top Confidential* (November 12, 2004): 14–16.

Sakai, Yoshihiro. "The Privatization of Japan Post is Unstoppable." Washington, DC: Center for International and Strategic Studies. February 8, 2008.

Samuels, Richard J. "Leadership and Political Change in Japan: The Case of the Second Rinchō." *Journal of Japanese Studies* 29, no. 1 (Winter 2003): 1–31.

Schaede, Ulrike. *Cooperative Capitalism: Self-Regulation, Trade Associations, and the Antimonopoly Law in Japan.* Oxford, UK: Oxford University Press, 2000.

Scheiner, Ethan. *Democracy Without Competition in Japan: Opposition Failure in a One-Party Dominant State.* New York: Cambridge University Press, 2006.

Scher, Mark J. and Naoyuki Yoshino, eds. "Introduction: Overview and Summary of Policy Proposals for Postal Savings in Developing Countries." In *Small Savings Mobilization and Asian Economic Development: The Role of Postal Financial Services,*" ed. Mark J. Scher and Naoyuki Yoshino. Armonk, NY: M. E. Sharpe, 2004, 3–20.

———. "Policy Challenges and the Reform of Postal Savings in Japan." In *Small Savings Mobilization and Asian Economic Development: The Role of Postal Financial Services,*" ed. Mark J. Scher and Naoyuki Yoshino. Armonk, NY: M. E. Sharpe, 2004, 121–45.

———. *Small Savings Mobilization and Asian Economic Development: The Role of Postal Financial Services.* Armonk, NY: M. E. Sharpe, 2004.

Schwartz, Frank. "Of Fairy Cloaks and Familiar Talks: The Politics of Consultation." In *Political Dynamics in Contemporary Japan,* ed. Gary D. Allinson and Yasunori Sone. Ithaca, NY: Cornell University Press, 1993, 217–41.

Segawa Kōsuke. *Koizumi Jun'ichirō to tokutei yūbinkyokuchō no arasoi* (The battle between Koizumi Jun'ichirō and the commissioned postmasters). Tokyo: Yell Books, 2001.

Sherman, Roger. "Competition in Postal Service." In *Competition and Innovation in Postal Services,* ed. Michael A. Crew and Paul R. Kleindorfer. Norwell, MA: Kluwer Academic Publishers, 1991, 191–214.

Shinoda, Tomohito. *Koizumi Diplomacy: Japan's Kantei Approach to Foreign and Defense Affairs.* Seattle, WA: University of Washington Press, 2007.

Shirokawa Masumi. "Doko ga mondai: yūsei min'eika" (Where's the problem?: postal privatization). In *Doko ga mondai! Yūsei min'eika* (Where's the problem! Postal privatization), ed. Shimin no koe. Tokyo: Kinohanasha, 2006, 9–58.

Sippel, Patricia. "Abandoned Fields: Negotiating Taxes in the Bakufu Domain." *Monumenta Nipponica* 53, no. 2 (Summer 1998): 197–223.

Smith, Thomas C. "Peasant Time and Factory Time in Japan." *Past and Present* 111, no. 1 (May 1986): 165–97.

Smith, William. "The Colonial Post-Office." *The American Historical Review* 21, no. 2 (January 1916): 258–75.

Sōmushō. *Nihon tōkei nenkan* (Japan statistical yearbook). Various issues.

Steinmo, Sven, Kathleen Thelen, and Frank Longstreth, eds. *Structuring Politics: Historical Institutionalism in Comparative Analysis.* Cambridge, UK: Cambridge University Press, 1992.

Steslicke, William E. *Doctors in Politics: The Political Life of the Japan Medical Association.* New York: Praeger, 1973.

Streeck, Wolfgang, and Kathleen Thelen. "Introduction: Institutional Change in Advanced Political Economies." In *Beyond Continuity: Institutional Change in Advanced Political Economies*, ed. Wolfgang Streeck and Kathleen Thelen. Oxford, UK: Oxford University Press, 2005, 1–39.

Takenaka Heizō. *Kōzō kaikaku no shinjitsu: Takenaka Heizō daijin nikki* (The truth of structural reform: Takenaka Heizō's ministerial diary). Tokyo: Nihon keizai shinbunsha, 2006.

———. *Yūsei min'eika: chiisa na seifu e no shikinseki* (Postal privatization: the litmus test for a small government). Tokyo: PHP kenkyūjo, 2005.

———. "Yūsei 'saikokuyūka' wa minshushugi no hitei" (Renationalizing the postal services is a denial of democracy). *Ushio* (August 2010): 82–87.

Tanabe Akira. "Yūseishō ni nozomu" (Facing the ministry of posts and telecommunications). *Kōmuin* (March 1953): 68–74.

Tanaka Naoki. "Naze yūsei min'eika o atomodori sasete wa naranai no ka" (Why can't we allow a retrogression of postal privatization?). *Foresight* 20, no. 5 (May 2009): 90–92.

Teishin sōgō hakubutsukan, ed. *Kindai yūbin no akebono* (The dawn of contemporary mail). Tokyo: Daiichi hōki shuppan, 1990.

Thelen, Kathleen. *How Institutions Evolve: The Political Economy of Skills in Germany, Britain, the United States, and Japan.* Cambridge, UK: Cambridge University Press, 2004.

Tierney, John T. *The U.S. Postal Service: Status and Prospects of a Public Enterprise.* Dover, MA: Auburn House Publishing Company, 1988.

"Tōhoku tokutei yūbinkyoku chōkai de uraganezukuri ga hakkaku" (Disclosure of bribe-making at the Tōhoku commissioned postmasters association). *Tōhoku zaikai* (January–February, 2002): 8–10.

Tōkyō chihō tokutei yūbinkyokuchōkai shi henshū iinkai, ed. *Tōkyō chihō tokutei yūbinkyokuchōkai shi* (A history of the commissioned postmasters association of greater Tokyo). Tokyo: Tōkyō chihō tokutei yūbinkyokuchōkai, 1979.

Tsuboi Sakae. *Ippon no matchi: watakushi no jinsei henreki* (A single match: my itinerant life). Tokyo: Asahi shinbunsha, 1955.

Tsujinaka Yutaka. *Reiki shūdan* (Interest groups). Tokyo: Tōkyō Daigaku shuppankai, 1988.

Uchida Hoshimi. "The Spread of Timepieces in the Meiji Period." *Japan Review* 14 (2002): 173–92.

Uchiyama, Yū. *Koizumi and Japanese Politics: Reform Strategies and Leadership Style.* Trans. Carl Freire. Routledge/University of Tokyo Series 1. London: Routledge, 2010.

United States Trade Representative. *Annual Reform Recommendations from the Government of the United States to the Government of Japan Under the U.S.-Japan Regulatory Reform and Competition Policy Initiative.* December 5, 2007.

"Urano Yoshimi ni tou min'eika no risō to genjitsu" (Questioning Urano Yoshimi about the ideal and reality of privatization). *Keizai kai* (April 4, 2007): 48.

Ushiki Yukio. *Chihō meibōka no seichō* (The development of local "men of distinction"). Tokyo: Kashiwa shobō, 2000.

Vaporis, Constantine Nomikos. *Breaking Barriers: Travel and the State in Early Modern Japan.* Cambridge, MA: Council on East Asian Studies, Harvard University, 1994.

———. "Post Station and Assisting Villages: Corvée Labor and Peasant Contention." *Monumenta Nipponica* 41, no. 4 (Winter 1986): 377–414.

Vogel, Steven K. *Freer Markets, More Rules: Regulatory Reform in Advanced Industrial Countries.* Ithaca, NY: Cornell University Press, 1996.

Wada Yoshitaka. "Zenkoku tokutei yūbinkyokuchōkai" (The national commissioned postmasters association). *Foresight* (February 1997): 120–23.

Walthall, Anne. *Peasant Uprisings in Japan: A Critical Anthology of Peasant Histories.* Chicago, IL: University of Chicago Press, 1991.

Westney, D. Eleanor. *Imitation and Innovation: The Transfer of Western Organizational Patterns to Meiji Japan.* Cambridge, MA: Harvard University Press, 1987.

Wray, William D. *Mitsubishi and the N.Y.K., 1870–1914: Business Strategy in the Japanese Shipping Industry.* Cambridge, MA: Council on East Asian Studies, Harvard University, 1984.

Wright, Maurice. *Japan's Fiscal Crisis: The Ministry of Finance and the Politics of Public Spending, 1975–2000.* Oxford, UK : Oxford University Press, 2002.

Yamaguchi Osamu. *Maejima Hisoka.* Tokyo: Yoshikawa kōbunkan, 1990.

———. *Tokutei yūbinkyoku: zenkoku tokutei kyokuchōkai no ayumi* (The commissioned post offices: a history of the national commissioned postmasters association). Tokyo: Gyōsei, 1993.

Yamamoto Hiroshi. "Kindaika soku moraru ga gōgi" (Discussing the morals of modernization). *Seiji keizai* 13, no. 8 (January 1958): 45–57.

Yamamura, Akiyoshi. "Tokutei yūbinkyokuchōkai no shōtai" (The identity of the commissioned postmasters association). *Shokun* (January 1998): 88–98.

Yamawaki Takeshi. *Yūsei kōbō* (Postal system tug-of-war). Tokyo: Asahi shinbunsha, 2005.

Yoshida Makoto. "Yūseishō enkaku shōshi" (A short history of the Ministry of Posts and Telecommunications). *Seiji keizai* 13, no. 8 (January 1958): 74–82.

Yoshino Naoyuki. "Policy Challenges and the Reform of Postal Savings in Japan." In *Small Savings Mobilization and Asian Economic Development: The Role of Postal Financial Services,* ed. Mark J. Scher and Naoyuki Yoshino. Armonk, NY: M. E. Sharpe, 2004, 121–45.

———. "Yūbin chokin no shōrai to zaisei tōyūshi" (Postal savings' future and the FILP). *Toshi mondai* 99, no. 11 (November 2008): 56–61.

Yūsei daijin kanbō chōsaka. "Tokuteikyoku no enkaku" (History of the commissioned offices). *Tokuteikyoku seido chōsakai teishutsu shiryōshū* (A collection of documents presented to the commissioned post office system study group). Tokyo: Yūsei daijin kanbō chōsaka, 1958, 2–11.

Yūsei jigyō kenkyūkai. *Nihon no yūsei: Heisei 15-nen ban* (The Japanese postal system: 1993 yearbook). Tokyo: Yūkensha, 2004.

Yūsei min'eika kenyūkai. "Min'eika de yūsei jigyō wa kō kawaru" (The postal services will change like this through privatization). In *Yūsei min'eika ron: Nihon saisei no daikaikaku!* (The postal privatization debate: the biggest reform for the rebirth of Japan!), ed. Koizumi Jun'ichirō and Matsuzawa Shigefumi. Tokyo: PHP kenkyūjo, 1999, 29–38.

Yūseishō, ed. *Yūsei gyōsei tōkei nenpō* (Yearly statistics on postal service administration). Various editions.

———, ed. *Yūsei 100-nen no ayumi* (A history of the postal system's 100 years). Tokyo: Teishin kyōkai, 1971.

———, ed. *Yūsei 100-nen shi* (A 100-year history of the postal system). Tokyo: Teishin kyōkai, 1971.

Yūseishō yōin kunrenka. *Tokutei yūbinkyoku: shōshūdan katsudō jissen jireishū* (The commissioned post offices: a collection of cases on small group activities). Tokyo: Gyōsei, 1987.

Zenkoku tokutei yūbinkyoku kyokuchō dairikai. *Zenkoku tokutei yūbinkyoku kyokuchō dairikai 30-nen shi* (A 30-year history of the representative group of the national commissioned postmasters). Tokyo: Zenkoku tokutei yūbinkyoku kyokuchō dairikai, 1993.

Zenkoku tokutei yūbinkyokuchōkai. *Tokuteikyoku taikan* (A repository of the commissioned post offices). Vol. 1. Tokyo: Zenkoku tokutei yūbinkyoku-chōkai, 1950.

———. *Tokuteikyoku taikan* (A repository of the commissioned post offices). Vol. 2. Tokyo: Zenkoku tokutei yūbinkyokuchōkai, 1962.

———. *Tokuteikyoku taikan* (A repository of the commissioned post offices). Vol. 3. Tokyo: Zenkoku tokutei yūbinkyokuchōkai, 1971.

———. *Zentoku 50-nen no ayumi* (A 50-year history of Zentoku). Tokyo: Zenkoku tokutei yūbinkyokuchōkai, 2003.

Zenteishin rōdō kumiai Zentei shi hensan iinkai, ed. *Zentei rōdō undōshi* (A history of the Zentei labor movement). Vol 1. Tokyo: Zenteishin rōdō kumiai Zentei shi hensan iinkai, 1995.

Newspapers and News Magazines

AERA
Asahi Newspaper
Asahi shinbun
The Economist
Japan Close-Up
Japan Times
Kyodo News
Mainichi Daily News
Mainichi shinbun
New York Times
Nikkei Business
Nikkei Weekly
Sandē Mainichi
Sankei shinbun
Shūkan Asahi
Shūkan Daiyamondo
Shūkan Tōyō keizai
Wall Street Journal
Yomiuri Newspaper
Yomiuri shinbun

Index

Harvard East Asian Monographs
(*out-of-print)

Harvard East Asian Monographs

Harvard East Asian Monographs

Harvard East Asian Monographs